WineWise

WineWise

YOUR COMPLETE GUIDE TO UNDERSTANDING, SELECTING, AND ENJOYING WINE

Steven Kolpan, Brian Smith, and Michael Weiss

THE CULINARY INSTITUTE OF AMERICA

John Wiley and Sons

The Culinary Institute of America:
President	Dr. Tim Ryan '77
Vice President, Continuing Education	Mark Erickson '77
Director of Intellectual Property	Nathalie Fischer
Managing Editor	Kate McBride
Editorial Project Manager	Mary Donovan '83
Editorial Project Manager	Lisa Lahey '00
Production Assistant	Patrick Decker '05

Published by John Wiley & Sons, Inc., Hoboken, New Jersey
Published simultaneously in Canada

For general information on our other products and services or for technical support, please contact our Customer Care Department within the United States at (800) 762-2974, outside the United States at (317) 572-3993 or fax (317) 572-4002.

Wiley also publishes its books in a variety of electronic formats. Some content that appears in print may not be available in electronic books. For more information about Wiley products, visit our web site at www.wiley.com.

LIBRARY OF CONGRESS CATALOGING-IN-PUBLICATION DATA:
Kolpan, Steven.
  Winewise / Steven Kolpan, Brian Smith, and Michael Weiss, the Culinary Institute of America.
    p. cm.
  Includes index.
  ISBN 978-0-471-77064-0 (cloth)
  1. Wine and wine making--Popular works. I. Smith, Brian H. II. Weiss, Michael A. III. Culinary Institute of America. IV. Title.
  TP548.K5785 2008
  641.2'2--dc22
                        2007022432

Printed in China

10 9 8 7 6 5 4 3 2

Contents

chapter 1

Palate pleasure
enjoying wine

Recently, wine surpassed beer and spirits as the alcoholic beverage of choice for Americans who drink. More people are enjoying wine than ever before in their homes, at parties and other social events, or when dining out. Many wine drinkers want more information, both about the wines they enjoy drinking and about wines they haven't tried yet. We've written this book with exactly these folks—you, our readers—in mind. Information is power, and a heightened awareness about wines will make you a smarter wine consumer, a more wine-knowledgeable host or guest, and a wine-savvy restaurant customer. You will be WineWise!

This chapter concentrates on basic information that will help you to understand why wine comes in so many different styles and flavors, the different ways that people enjoy wine, why some wines cost more than others, and what the label on the bottle can tell you. Instead of a separate chapter on winemaking, we decided to weave winemaking comments into this and other chapters, concentrating on the effect of winemaking decisions on the style of the wine without spending too much time on technical details. Subsequent chapters will introduce you to some of our favorite wines from the prominent wine-producing areas of the world, help you to get a handle on pairing wine with food, and give you some insider tips on what you need to know to enjoy wine at home or in a restaurant. The final section of *WineWise* includes a buying guide for specific wines at various price points. Equipped with all this information, you will be ready to enjoy all that the glorious world of wine has to offer.

A question of style

WE'VE ALREADY SUGGESTED that there are three key opportunities to enjoy wine: at home, in some other social setting (such as a party), or in a restaurant. We could also add that there are three other fun/functional uses for wine:

- as an aperitif—a drink before dinner
- as a drink in a social group or intimate setting
- as an accompaniment to a meal

With just these considerations, it becomes easy to see that the style of any chosen wine will vary according to its purpose. For example, we appreciate a drink before dinner if it is light and simple, something that excites the appetite, as opposed to something that is full, heavy, and immediately satisfying; save that wine for dinner.

So wine is made in many different styles to meet our various needs. To begin with, there are three basic styles of wine:

- still—without bubbles
- sparkling—with bubbles
- fortified—with added alcohol

Winemaking

FERMENTATION

Strangely enough, the bubbles and the alcohol come from the same place—fermentation. The process of fermentation depends on the presence of yeasts. Some winemakers use yeasts that are naturally present on the skin of the grapes, while others add a specific type of purchased yeast that has been isolated in a laboratory. As soon as the yeasts meet the sugar in grape juice, they start converting that sugar into alcohol and carbon dioxide. If the carbon dioxide is allowed to drift off into the atmosphere, the wine will be still—without bubbles. If the carbon dioxide is retained, the wine will be sparkling (see page 3 for how this is done).

The level of alcohol in a wine depends on how much sugar was originally present in the grape juice and on how much of the sugar is converted. If all of the sugar is converted to alcohol, the wine will con-

tain approximately 13% to 14% alcohol (in other words, 13% to 14% of the liquid contents of the bottle is alcohol). The wine will also be described as "dry," meaning not sweet, without residual sugar. But not all wine regions are the same. Some have cool climates, others are warmer. In general, a cool-climate site will produce grapes with lower sugar levels and higher acidity, creating wines that will have lower alcohol (maybe 12% or 12.5%) and a distinctly crisp, clean feel, with a pleasantly sour taste in the mouth (think lemon or grapefruit). In contrast, warmer places produce grapes with higher sugars and lower acidity, leaving the possibility of higher alcohol and a softer, smoother sensation in the mouth (think a blackberry-flavored milk shake).

If the winemaker chooses to stop the yeasts from completing their work, there will be residual sugar left in the wine, creating anything from a lightly sweet taste to a very sweet one. Within our three basic styles (still, sparkling, and fortified), then, there are three subcategories of dryness/sweetness:

- dry—no or very little sweetness
- lightly sweet, sometimes called off-dry
- very sweet, dessert-like

COLOR

To keep the pattern of threes going, it is well known that wine comes in three main colors:

- white
- red
- rosé

We would have to add that there are many variations of color within those three, from very pale white to deep, inky purple.

Most people think that the color of the grapes determines the color of the wine, but this is not always true. What is true is that red wine can only be made from red grapes, since the red color is extracted from the grape skins during the winemaking process. Similarly, white grapes can only produce white wine. But since almost all grapes have clear (or "white") juice, it is possible to squeeze white juice out of red grapes to make white wine. This also means that the winemaker can control the rate of color extraction from red grapes to produce a wine with only a small amount of pink color—a rosé wine. Rosé can also be made by blending a lot of white wine with a little bit of red.

These are the basics of winemaking, at least for producing still wines. To visualize a matrix of possibilities that offers many permutations of wine style, from a pale white, lightly sweet still wine to a dry rosé sparkling wine to a deep purple, very sweet fortified wine, read on.

Different skin contact time will result in lighter or darker degrees of pigmentation, as shown by these rosé wines.

BUBBLES IN THE BOTTLE

The Champagne method, or *methode champenoise* (now also used by places other than Champagne), requires that grapes be harvested by variety and by individual plot, and that grapes from different plots of land be fermented separately. The Champagne producer often ends up with dozens of lots of wine. But those wines are all still, not sparkling. They need to be blended together (sometimes with older wines from other vintages) to fit the "house style," which is the same from one production year to the next. That house style is bottled along with a small amount of extra sugar and yeast inside each bottle, and the bottle is closed with a cap (like a beer cap). The bottles are laid down horizontally in the cellar and left to rest, during which time the yeasts and sugar create a second fermentation inside that bottle, which causes carbon dioxide to be trapped in the wine. When the consumer opens that very same bottle, the carbon dioxide makes the wine bubbly.

But the work is not over yet. The second fermentation in the bottle also means that there is yeast sediment left in each bottle that has to be removed, but not before the winemaker allows the wine to take on the yeast flavors and aromas. If the bottle is left for a long time with the yeast lees inside the bottle, the yeasts will eventually break down and create enzymes and amino acids that have the effect of producing a

What is that name?

Most wine labels include a name of the wine. Increasingly, for most consumers all around the globe, the most common name on the label is simply the grape variety. So, if Shiraz grapes were used to make the wine, Shiraz will be the name of the wine on the label. For many Europeans, there is a traditional practice of using a place name as the name of the wine, such as Chianti in Italy, or Bordeaux in France. When a European wine uses a place name, it means that by law and by tradition only certain grape types can be used to make the wine. Throughout our chapters on the wines of Europe, many of which use place-name labels, we will indicate which grape types are used in which places.

A typical varietal label showing Shiraz as the grape variety.

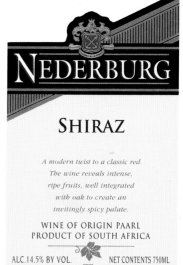

NEDERBURG

SHIRAZ

A modern twist to a classic red. The wine reveals intense, ripe fruits, well integrated with oak to create an invitingly spicy palate.

WINE OF ORIGIN PAARL
PRODUCT OF SOUTH AFRICA

ALC.14.5% BY VOL.   NET CONTENTS 750ML

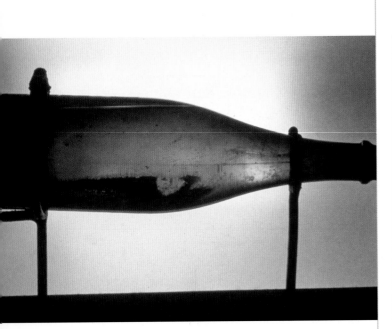

Yeast sediment collects on the lower side of the horizontal bottle after the second fermentation. Frederic Handengue; CIVC.

The explosive nature of disgorging by hand.

rich texture in the wine. That process takes at least one year. In the Champagne region, the minimum period for this is eighteen months, but many producers there leave their premium wines in this aging stage for up to five years.

To remove the yeast sediment from the bottle after aging, the bottles are agitated by hand or mechanically to drive the sediment into the neck of the bottle with the bottle inverted.

The inverted bottles then pass through a freezing solution that creates a plug of ice in the neck of the bottle. That plug contains all of the yeast sediment. When the bottle is turned upright, the cap is removed and the yeast pellet is expelled from the bottle. Immediately, more wine is added to replace the wine lost in the plug, and the winemaker may also take the opportunity to add a small amount of sugar solution (known as *dosage*) to adjust the final dryness/sweetness of the wine. Finally, a traditional sparkling wine cork is inserted.

THE SPIRIT IN THE BOTTLE

A wine is described as fortified when extra-high-proof spirit is added to the wine. If the spirit is added to the wine after the fermentation is complete, there will be no remaining sugar in the newly fortified wine, mak-

ing a finished product that is dry in taste, not sweet. Typical products of this type are the Fino and dry Oloroso Sherries of Spain (see page 229). To make a sweet fortified wine, the spirit is added very soon after the wine's fermentation has begun. The addition of the high-alcohol spirit halts the fermentation, leaving residual sugar in the wine. The Port wines of Portugal are a fine example (see page 241). Some sweet, fortified Sherries are also made by initially creating a dry Sherry, as above, and then adding concentrated, reduced grape juice as a sweetener. This is true of many Sherries labeled "Cream."

Body

With one more threesome, we can round out the basic vocabulary of wine. Depending on where the grapes are grown and what winemaking methods are used, the wine will be:

- light-bodied
- medium-bodied
- full-bodied, or heavy

This means that our impression of the "weight" of the wine in the mouth ranges from light (like lemonade) to medium (like orange juice) to full (like tomato juice). Light-bodied wines are usually associated with cool-climate areas and straightforward winemaking using stainless-steel vats and little or no aging (see page 6). To get to the full-bodied version, you need to put the wine through a rigorous body-building process, a sort of enhanced steroid program with oak aging and malolactic fermentation. We have further comments on these practices on page 7.

The price to pay

EVEN THE MOST CURSORY glance around a wine shop will reveal that a standard 750 ml (25.4 oz.) bottle of wine can carry a price as low as $5.99 or as high as $599. Is the second bottle really a hundred times better? We think the answer is a resounding NO! What makes the difference? What makes one bottle cost more than another?

The actual cost of producing a bottle of dry, still wine can be as little as 50 cents and rarely exceeds $20. So how do we get to $599? There are three main considerations in the pricing of wine:

- costs of production
- availability versus scarcity
- what the market will bear

Costs of production

All winemakers incur costs, but some incur higher costs than others. Those who have higher costs believe that they are producing a higher-quality wine. How does this work? Winemaking includes a series of decisions, and each one of those decisions will impact the style of the wine, the quality, and the price. Many of those decisions include incurring higher costs of materials and pursuing a more labor-intensive path. For every decision there are winemakers who defend the methodology, arguing that there is a discernible increase in quality. At the same time, there are winemakers who belittle these arguments and claim that their faster, less expensive, more mechanized methods result in wines that are just as good.

IN THE VINEYARD

These decisions go back to the very beginning of a vineyard and carry on through to the bottling and even the marketing of the wine. In California, the cost of vineyard land can run anywhere between $35,000 and $350,000 per acre, depending on whether it is already planted and whether it is deemed to be a premium and desirable site. For example, a flat, valley-floor strip of land with rich, fertile soils is cheaper and easier to plant and maintain than a rocky hillside plot with good exposure to the sun and protection from winds, but many people would claim that the hillside plot will produce better wine.

Vine density is an important consideration in producing wine. Planting a vineyard with wide spacing of 8 to 10 feet (2.42 to 3 meters) between the vines and between the rows makes for easier and more cost-effective mechanized maintenance and harvesting. But a spacing ratio of 3.3 feet by 3.3 feet (1 meter by 1 meter) will provide up to four times as many vines in the same amount of land and will demand a higher

A steep hillside vineyard is harder to work, necessitating more manual labor.

amount of intensive hand labor to maintain the vineyard. Though there may be more vines per acre, each plant is "programmed" by pruning to produce fewer grapes per vine. This requires more hand labor, which can be far more expensive than using machines in the vineyard.

And so it goes. Some vineyard owners pay a team of twenty pickers to go through the vineyard several times over a period of three or four weeks, hand-harvesting only those bunches that are visibly ripe into small plastic trays so that precious juice is not lost under the weight of too many bunches of grapes. Other producers swear that a mechanical harvester with a single operator can do just as good a job in twenty-four hours. The cost differential is enormous.

Tending the vineyard by hand, removing unwanted leaves and unripe bunches.

One of the highest costs in wine production comes in the form of strict selection of grape material before or at harvest time to ensure that only the finest fruit is made into wine. By going through the vineyard three to four weeks before harvesting and removing the weaker or poorer clusters of grapes, some producers maintain that they will produce better wine. What they are doing is lowering their yield, picking only the healthiest grapes, and harvesting perhaps 2 tons per acre (5 tons per hectare) rather than 5 tons per acre (12.5 tons per hectare).

After the grapes have been picked, some producers will pay workers to screen bunches of grapes, removing any unripe or moldy fruit as it moves along a conveyor belt prior to entering the winemaking process. Grapes that are afforded the extra-special care and attention described above will command higher prices. Napa Valley premium Cabernet Sauvignon grapes have been fetching as much as $4,800 per ton, Merlot as much as $3,400. Less highly regarded sites in California may command as little as $400 per ton for the same varietals.

Effect on Style. Wineries that produce a limited amount of wine in a labor-intensive process from premium land claim that they are producing a more hand-crafted wine that has more intense or more complex flavors that are characteristic of the place the grapes were grown, the *terroir*. Such wines cost more to make and will be priced accordingly.

COSTS AT THE WINERY

Most producers today use stainless-steel tanks for most if not all of their fermentation needs. But stainless-steel fermentation tanks are like coffeemakers—you can buy the basic model, or you can get the version with all the bells and whistles. The more expensive models provide the winemaker with greater control, especially temperature control, and temperature can make or break a successful fermentation. It can even dictate the style of the wine. A wine produced by a long, slow, cool fermentation will give the consumer a lot of fresh, forward fruit character, with a clean mouthfeel. But using that technology costs more, and the wines will be priced accordingly.

High-tech stainless-steel tanks keep everything under control in modern wineries.

There is still a place for barrel aging at many wineries.

Malolactic Fermentation. There are other choices as well. Most winemakers agree that consumers will enjoy certain wines more if the wine is put through a process called malolactic fermentation. This is particularly true of almost all red wines, some whites (such as Chardonnay) aged in barrels, and just a few sparkling and rosé wines. By introducing a friendly type of bacteria to the wine—a strain of lactobacillus, the active culture found in yogurt—the winemaker can convert a harsh form of acid (malic, the acid in green apples) into a softer one (lactic, the acid in milk), providing a richer, smoother feeling on the tongue. But all of this takes time and costs money.

Oak. Then there is the wood debate. For centuries, winemakers used wooden barrels to store wine, and that practice gradually evolved into purposely leaving wine in barrels to age. Current consumer preference favors a noticeable wood character in certain styles of wine, especially Chardonnay and most red wines. How that wood character is achieved is part of the cost equation. For a long time, the preferred type of wood for aging wine has been oak. Placing the wine in a brand-new oak barrel (as much as $950 for a barrel that holds 60 gallons [224 liters]) is far more expensive than leaving the wine in a stainless-steel tank that has been temporarily lined with rough-cut oak staves. The oak stave immersion method is in turn more expensive than stirring oak chips into the stainless-steel vat. Is there a difference? The purists tell us that the flavors and effects achieved from a real wooden barrel are far cleaner than the effect of oak chips. Certainly, a wine aged in a real oak barrel will cost more.

Barrel aging takes time, and that means that the wine is still at the winery, not on the wine store shelves or on a restaurant's wine list. Following barrel aging, some producers will insist on keeping the wine at the winery after bottling, allowing the wine to rest, giving the various characteristics of the wine a chance to marry and become a more harmonious whole. As we all know, time is money, and wines held back by the producer will cost more.

Oak: What the winemaker wants

The primary effect of an oak barrel on wine is to add to its flavor profile because the liquid helps to pull flavoring components from the barrel. The most obvious flavor is often described as vanilla, because the sap of oak contains vanillin.

Vanillin is found in the sap of European oaks, so that when wine is stored in oak barrels, the vanillin is leached from the oak staves into the wine. Whether it comes across to you as vanilla or butterscotch or caramel doesn't really matter—it all has the same effect of giving the wine that desired flavor and making the wine seem just a tiny bit sweet. It will also soften the texture of the wine, since the vanillin gives the impression of a smooth, syrupy consistency. In the case of white wines, that same consistency can be enhanced by leaving the wine on the lees—the spent yeast cells in the barrel (what the French call *sur lie*). As the yeast cells break down they release enzymes that contribute to a richer feel in the mouth.

If the wine stays in the barrel for too long, however, it may take on what we believe to be negative characteristics—too much wood flavor, which will overpower the wine's natural flavors, and too much tannin, a compound that masks the vanilla effect and leaves a drying sensation and bitter taste on the tongue. In recent years we have sampled far too many wines that taste mostly of wood. We would prefer to see winemakers use wood in the same way that a painter uses a frame. The job of the frame is to set off the picture, to enhance it. If the frame enters the picture, there is something wrong!

Clarification. As with almost all beverages today, we expect wines to be clear and free of haze. But fermentation is a messy process that creates all kinds of debris that can remain suspended in the wine. So the winemaker has to decide if the wine should be clarified or stabilized using additives or machinery, both of which speed up the clarification process. Or should the wine simply sit at the winery, allowing time and gravity to slowly achieve what humans and machinery can speed up? Critics of mechanical or chemical clarification charge that such processes strip the wine of its essential flavors and characteristics and that the wine will be better if left alone. Even though the machinery for clarification and stabilization is expensive, it is less expensive than keeping the wine at the winery. Anything that prevents the wine from reaching the consumer increases the cost.

Xtreme wines, xtreme costs

THERE ARE BIZARRE LENGTHS that some winemakers go to in order to produce something extraordinary. This is particularly true in the production of sweet and sparkling wines.

Oh so sweet

It is fairly easy to produce a simple, lightly sweet wine by stopping the fermentation before all of the sugars have been converted to alcohol. This leaves residual sugar in the wine, making the wine taste sweet. But to produce a very sweet, dessert-style wine, extreme steps are often taken. Grapes can be left to hang on the vine for an extended period of time until they dehydrate and become raisins, or until they are attacked by a specific type of mold, which also causes the grapes to dehydrate. As these grapes lose water, their sugar content is concentrated in smaller quantities of liquid, making them extremely sweet. The mold is

The beginning of botrytis on a ripe bunch of Riesling grapes.

Riesling grapes that have frozen on the vine and will be made into Eiswein (Icewine).

called *Botrytis cinerea* or "noble rot." It is considered a beneficial mold and is highly prized by producers of sweet wines—there is no carryover of moldy flavors to the wines. Because of the dehydration factor, these remarkably sweet wines are produced in very limited quantities, which in turn makes them very expensive, as much as $100 or more per half bottle.

As if the above were not extreme enough, winemakers in areas susceptible to freezing temperatures have taken matters one step further, allowing grapes to stay on the vine well past the regular picking date until they are frozen by the first very cold spell. The frozen grapes are harvested and pressed, producing minuscule quantities of very sweet juice, but leaving behind most of the grape's water content as ice. Once again, these measures result in very highly priced wines. The sweet Icewines produced along these lines will cost around $75 to $100 per half bottle.

Bubbling over

Many people still see sparkling wine as a luxury item, and much of that image is connected to price. The most expensive sparkling wines in the world continue to come from the Champagne region of France, commanding retail prices from about $35 to more than $250 per bottle. But there are reasons why Champagne and some other sparkling wines can be so expensive. As with any wine, very good wine comes from the highest-quality grapes, most often grown on premium vineyard sites—those grapes command high prices. But in the case of great sparkling wine, the winemaking process is very long and demands a very high level of skill (see pages 3–4).

The Champagne method takes time, skill, and labor. That's why some bottles of sparkling wine cost more than others. At the other end of the extreme is the relatively inexpensive method of trapping carbon dioxide gas in the original stainless-steel fermentation tank and then bottling the wine under pressure so as not to lose the gas. Using the tank method creates a very different style and quality of wine, with much bigger bubbles that fade more easily; this wine is sold at a much lower price point.

So why are some wines more expensive?

IT ALL COMES DOWN TO whether the wine-making methods tend more toward mass production or small batch nurturing. If the grapes are of a fashionable variety (such as Merlot), from a premium region (say, Napa), and from a prized plot of land (such as Three Palms Vineyard), the wine will be considerably more expensive than a Gamay wine from Macedonia.

And if the winemaker seeks to retain a level of individuality in the wine by keeping small batches separate, careful monitoring of the fermentation process, skillful blending, the use of wood, aging, or a combination of all or some of these approaches, those wines will also be higher-priced.

Availability versus scarcity

In any market, certain goods are in limited supply, and because they are rare but in demand, those goods can command high prices. In some instances output is artificially limited to keep prices high. In the case of wines, certain items are in short supply simply because it is impossible to produce any more.

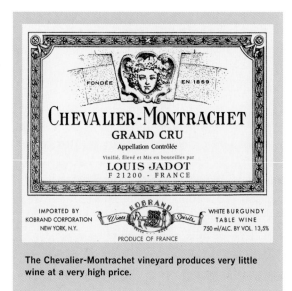

The Chevalier-Montrachet vineyard produces very little wine at a very high price.

For example, the 2.5-acre (1 hectare) vineyard of Les Caillerets in the village of Meursault in Burgundy, France, will produce only about 555 cases (6,660 bottles) of wine each year for the entire world market. For that reason alone it is in limited supply and will be priced accordingly.

Similarly, certain Champagnes from specific sites are available in very small quantities. Or some Champagnes are made in limited supply because they are aged for an extended period of time after the second fermentation in bottle and the producer does not want to commit a large segment of production to such long aging.

As we pointed out earlier, Icewines and botrytis-affected sweet wines are, by their very nature, limited and expensive. So it is the limited resources of grapes or juice that will create a limited product, but one that is in high demand and carries a high price.

What the market will bear

There are wines that are in relatively plentiful supply but are still high-priced. Those wines are not rare, but they have earned a reputation for being consistently very good. The best examples of these wines come from the Bordeaux region of France. The reputation for great wines from this region has been well established since the eighteenth century, so much so that modern wine collectors continue to be willing to spend large sums of money to acquire them. A case in point is the wine from Chateau Mouton Rothschild. The chateau produces around 34,000 cases of wine each year from an estate of 195 acres (79 hectares). That's a lot of wine, but the price per bottle on release is almost always well over $100. A well-earned reputation for consistently high quality can justify higher prices.

The same can be said for what have become known as boutique wines from producers all around the world, such as Screaming Eagle Cabernet Sauvignon from California, or Hill of Grace Shiraz from Australia. Although their annual production is fairly large, their reputation for quality means that they can charge a retail price of $200 to $500 per bottle for their wines (and considerably more on a restaurant wine list) and the market will bear it.

Brands versus *terroir* wines

Over the last two to three decades there has been a proliferation of branded wines in the marketplace. During the 1900s, place-named wines ruled the wine market, either from Europe or from New World producers who lazily "borrowed" a European place name,

such as Chablis or Champagne, to market their wines. But in the twenty-first century, New World winemakers have realized that their wines don't need the cachet of a European name to be successful, and the branding of wines is seen as a viable way of capturing and maintaining loyal fans.

The most successful brand to date in the United States has been the range of Australian wines offered under the [yellow tail]⅔ label, with their Shiraz currently the highest-selling red wine on the U.S. market. Other notable brands include Red Bicyclette from France and Ecco Domani from Italy (both brands are owned by Gallo Winery of California).

What do these brands offer? A surefire recipe for success—reliable quality, affordable prices, a consistent profile jam-packed with ripe, fruit-driven flavors, and smooth texture. There are no surprises in these wines, and that is exactly what millions of us want, all around the world. Such cookie-cutter wines are possible in a world where multinational corporations own vast tracts of vineyard land in sunny, flat areas where huge quantities of ripe grapes can be ensured every year.

In contrast, *terroir* wines originate from smaller plots of land in more challenging climates that create noticeable differences in the wines from year to year. They are

also more likely to include nonfruit aromas and flavors, such as wet rock or moist undergrowth, that are not appealing to everybody.

Is one "better" than the other? Is beer-battered deep-fried cod better than seared yellowfin tuna? No, they are different concepts, different approaches. Branded wines can be and usually are of very good quality. They have to be in such a competitive market. Without that quality they simply wouldn't survive. A branded wine should provide good quality at a good price, be fun to drink, and work well with your food. A *terroir*-driven wine should create a very different experience, perhaps a memorable one.

The importance of place

You may have noticed that we've made several references to the concept that where the grapes are grown is an important consideration in the quality of the wine. This concept is reflected in current labeling practices that include an indication of place on the label. In the wine world, the term *appellation* has come to mean a defined, named geographic area dedicated to growing grapes for wine production. Some appellations are considered to be premium areas for producing certain kinds of wines, and many places in the Old World (Europe) have become associated with one or more specific grape varieties.

How the appellation system works

ALL WINE-PRODUCING NATIONS of the world have appellation systems, and there are common characteristics to all of them. Appellations range from very small in area to very large. In many cases, smaller appellations can be found inside larger ones, just like those Russian dolls where the larger dolls have smaller dolls inside them. One general rule about the size of an appellation is that smaller appellations usually command higher prices for their wines. For the name of an appellation to be used on a wine label, most of the grapes must come from that region. Most nations have adopted legisla-

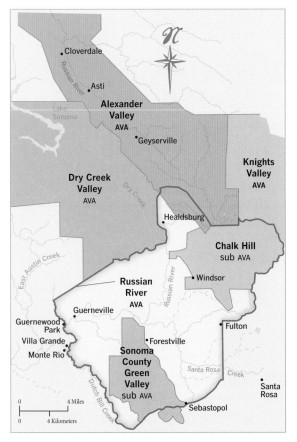

Smaller appellations such as Chalk Hill are clustered inside the Russian River Valley, which is in Sonoma County.

tion requiring that a minimum of 85% of all grapes used to make the wine must come from any place named on a label. Another common characteristic of appellation systems is that existing county or state names, such as Sonoma County or California, can be used as an indication of the origin of the grapes.

Two good examples of how the appellation system works can be found in the wine areas of Bordeaux and Sonoma.

The Bordeaux Appellations

1. You start with France, a national appellation.
2. Inside France is Bordeaux, a regional appellation.
3. Inside Bordeaux are several district appellations, one of which is Haut-Medoc.
4. Inside Haut-Medoc are six villages, each an appellation in its own right. They are St. Estephe, Pauillac, St. Julien, Margaux, Listrac, and Moulis.

5. If all the grapes used to make the wine came from vineyards within one of these villages, the label will include a phrase such as "*Appellation Pauillac Controlee.*"

The Sonoma Appellations

1. You start with California, a state appellation.
2. Inside California is North Coast, a regional appellation.
3. Inside North Coast is Sonoma County, a county appellation.
4. Inside Sonoma County is the Russian River Valley appellation.
5. Inside the Russian River Valley are two sub-appellations: one of them is Chalk Hill.
6. If more than 85% of the grapes used to make the wine came from vineyards in the Chalk Hill area, the label will include the name "Chalk Hill."

Associating place with grape

As mentioned before, some appellations in Europe become specifically associated with one or more grape varieties, both because certain areas have a long history of sticking with a particular grape variety or varieties, and also because the appellation laws in Europe often

Willamette Valley in Oregon has become famous for Pinot Noir.

require that a specific grape variety or varieties *must* be used to make the wine if the place name appears on the label. For example, white wine from the Burgundy region of France is made from Chardonnay only—the winemakers have no choice. Red wine from Burgundy in France is Pinot Noir. Case closed!

In contrast, New World wine areas (just about everywhere outside of Europe) have no laws that dictate what grape must be used in any appellation. Even so, some New World areas have become recognized as masters at producing wines from one particular grape—for example, Coonawarra in the state of South Australia is all about Cabernet Sauvignon, while the Willamette Valley in Oregon is Pinot Noir country.

There are also some other hints about grape variety that can be provided by the bottle shape. Historically, certain areas of Europe have used a specific bottle shape for their wines, and therefore those bottle shapes have become associated with certain grape types, so much so that New World producers often use the "traditional" bottle for the grape type they have used to make the wine.

Some of the bottle shapes are shown below with typical grape variety usage.

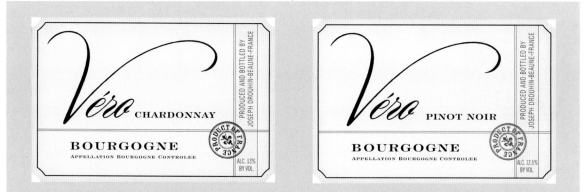

Joseph Drouhin's white and red Burgundy labels also identify the grape variety as Chardonnay and Pinot Noir, respectively.

Region	Bottle Shape	White Grapes	Red Grapes
Burgundy		Chardonnay	Pinot Noir
Bordeaux		Sauvignon Blanc, Semillon	Cabernet Sauvignon, Merlot
Rhône		Viognier	Syrah, Grenache
Germany		Riesling	
Chianti			Sangiovese

Closures

SINCE WE'RE TALKING ABOUT bottles and about enjoying wine, we think it's important to include some comments here on bottle closures. We are happy to report that we fully support the move by many producers to use screw caps to close the bottle instead of corks, and we strongly encourage consumers of all stripes to accept them. Screw caps are not a sign of inferior quality. In fact, in many ways, a screw cap could denote a wine of higher quality since the screw cap is impervious to any bacteria and provides an almost completely airtight closure. Corks have been notorious for becoming infected with bacteria or for not fitting properly and allowing air to seep into the bottle, both of which will spoil the wine.

This is not to say that we see a day when all wines will be stoppered with screw caps, but for those wines that are consumed within a year or two of production, we believe that screw caps are the way to go. Down with cork dorks! Send in the screw caps!

Choosing wine

ONE THING we want to emphasize up front is that most of the wines we buy for personal use are under $15 a bottle, in many cases under $10. How do we do that? By venturing off the beaten path to lesser-known wine areas and by experimenting with lesser-known grape types. If you know, for example, that you really like straightforward, fresh, fruity white wines to enjoy with grilled fish outdoors in the summertime, then we hope you will learn from this book that Albarino from Rias Baixas, Spain, and Moschofilero from Mantinia, Greece, fit that profile, and that you will try them.

Most of all, we believe that anyone can learn to taste wine and be his or her own critic. By following some of the simple steps below about tasting wine, and by trying some of our suggestions from the various regional chapters, you can create your own matrix of what it is you like, and why. We would encourage you to find a knowledgeable and reliable wine merchant or store clerk with whom you can discuss your preferences.

Our biggest word of warning is not to take as gospel everything that wine critics (including us) say about a wine. The practice of giving points (such as 86 out of 100 points, for example) to wines has gotten out of hand for several reasons. Most of those wines are tasted in the absence of food, and we believe very strongly that wine is food and is made to pair with other foods. We also believe that it is impossible to numerically quantify the pleasure that a wine can bring—there are far too many variables such as the climate, your disposition at the moment, the noise level, the company, and whether it's a banquet for two hundred at the White House or a picnic for two in front of the fire.

Given that most of the wines scored by critics are tasted without food, it is not surprising that the high scorers are full-bodied, in-your-face, aggressive, monster wines. This is often also true because so many wines are tasted in a row that it takes an extraordinary, even freakish wine to make the taster sit up and take notice. The most disheartening fact of high scores on wines is that wineries, stores, and restaurants use the scores as a sales tool; that means higher demand, which translates into higher prices for the wines. There has been some evidence in recent years that the influence of such critics is waning, and we encourage you not to rely on their reviews as the basis for your wine selections. Having said all that, we *want* to hear that you did not enjoy some of our wine suggestions and/or our wine-and-food pairings. Your objections will underscore our point that your palate is your own, and you should trust it. To get to that point, you need to taste, experiment, and enjoy.

Tasting and enjoying wine

WE ENCOURAGE YOU to develop the "mental habit" of tasting wine. Not that every sip of wine that enters your mouth has to be analyzed and commented on, but you will reap greater pleasure if you take a few minutes to objectively taste a wine before deciding whether you subjectively enjoy it. At the very least, you will get used to the idea that you can taste a wine in a restaurant and confidently accept it, or reject it if you feel it is not right.

All wine books will tell you that there are separate stages to tasting wine—look at it, smell it, taste it. That is true, but you will find the whole exercise easier once you understand that there are connections from one step to the next.

Appearance

We look at wine in the glass mostly to get an idea about the "strength" of the wine. A red or white wine that is relatively pale and translucent will probably be light in all of its characteristics—more delicate aroma, light flavor, an easy presence in the mouth. In contrast, a white wine that shows deeper gold hues or a red wine with deep purple, opaque notes will have a stronger, more assertive aroma and flavor and a tenacious, more powerful presence in the mouth. These are the essential differences between a light-bodied wine and a full-bodied one.

Aromas

In smelling a wine, there are three main aspects to consider: intensity of smell, simplicity versus complexity, and types of smell. Lighter, more delicate aromas usually follow from the visual conclusion that the wine is pale, and will help you to conclude that the wine is light-bodied. A more assertive, more powerful aroma will lead you in the direction of a fuller-bodied wine. You will also find that there is generally an associa-

tion between lighter wines, such Riesling or Gamay, and a simpler, more one-dimensional aroma, where fruit is the primary noticeable smell. In contrast, fuller-bodied wines such as Chardonnay or Cabernet Sauvignon are often accompanied by more complex aromas, where fruit is complemented by wood and mineral, earthy smells.

There are thousands of aromas that you might find in wines, but don't let that worry you. If you are new to this, the easiest way to proceed is to think of categories of smell, rather than specific smells. Is there a floral aroma? Or is it primarily fruit? Or are there vegetal or herbal notes? Those are great starting places, and from there you will find it is not hard to progress at your own speed to breaking those broad

The practice of recognizing aromas can be enhanced by adding fresh ingredients such as fruits or herbs to wine.

Riesling, Sauvignon Blanc	Chardonnay	Pinot Noir, Sangiovese	Merlot	Syrah, Cabernet Sauvignon
Green Fruits	**Yellow Fruits**	**Red Fruits**	**Purple Fruits**	**Black Fruits**
Green apple	Yellow plum	Red plum	Dark plum	Blackberry
Kiwi	Yellow tomato	Red berry	Dark cherry	Blackcurrant
Green pear	Lemon	Red cherry		Fig

categories into smaller ones *if you want to*. Remember, you don't have to. If you are the adventurous type, you might consider whether the floral aroma is light and fleeting or heady and perfumed—you can guess where those two different conclusions would lead you. Or you might distinguish between the smell of green, acidic fruits, such as limes, as compared to the rich ripeness of dark cherries and dark plums.

The spectrum chart on page 15 offers ideas about the "color" aromas that you might distinguish in wines, and suggests what grape varieties these are commonly associated with.

Most of all, aromas in wines should be pleasant; if you detect any unpleasantness when smelling a wine, do not hesitate to send it back in a restaurant or take it back to a wine store. The most objectionable of all smells in wine comes from wines that have been in contact with a tainted cork. Those wines are described as "corked" or "corky," and they smell of a dank, damp basement or wet, rotting cardboard. Once you come across it, you will never forget it, and you should store that smell away in your memory for future reference and action.

Taste

Much of the action of looking at and smelling wine is about impressions, pleasant or otherwise. It is when you place the wine in your mouth that you can make physical conclusions about the taste of the wine. We encourage you to recognize that anybody can taste, since we all have taste buds, and it will help you to remember that taste is a narrow concept. The Western world has traditionally accepted four tastes—sweet, sour, bitter, and salty—and tasting wine becomes much easier when you realize that only three of these are present in wine to any appreciable degree (wine is not really salty).

Sweet, sour, and bitter often show up in wine, singly or in combination, and are the result of components in the wine that came from the grapes. Sugars alert our sweetness-detecting taste buds, most of which are located on the tip of the tongue. The sweet effect is a light, fleeting, but pleasant sensation, simi-

lar to the initial impact of ice cream or a soda. Acids set the sour-sensing taste buds all a-tingle along the sides of the tongue and will also cause one set of salivary glands at the top of the cheeks to jump to attention. Many people appreciate this bracing sensation as it cleans and refreshes; it is exactly what is meant by "palate cleansing." Phenols, which are bitter compounds, have the greatest effect on the taste buds at the very back of the tongue, like the wickedly pleasant thrill of dark chocolate. The most common bitter component in wine is tannin, the same component found in black tea. It also has a drying, astringent effect on the tongue.

Indeed, many of our preferences in tastes can be predicted by the way we drink tea or coffee. If you add cream and sugar, you will probably prefer sweeter tastes and smoother textures in fresh, fruity wines. Espresso drinkers who take their coffee strong and black are more likely to appreciate bitter tastes and the drying effect found in powerful red wines. You can test this out for yourself by experimenting with sugar water, lemon juice, and strong tea to represent sweet, sour, and bitter. You can even see what happens when more than one taste is present by adding some of the lemon juice and then the sugar water to the tea.

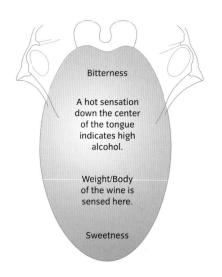

Where we sense the different aspects of wine on our tongue.

The tea will become less bitter with the addition of lemon and sugar and will take on the complexity of all three tastes, just as wine will.

We believe it is useful to recognize the presence or absence of sweet, sour, or bitter tastes. It is different from the highly complex world of attributing perceived "flavors" to wine, such as strawberry, apple, chocolate, or vanilla. Those have much to do with the aromas that were detected at the smelling stage. Initially concentrating on the three tastes is much more useful than pondering whether you detect apple or pear.

Determining the sweetness or lack of sweetness in a wine is very helpful in figuring out how you might use that wine with food (see page 278–303). An absence of sugar sweetness in wine means that all the sugars from the grapes have been converted to alcohol, and the wine is described as "dry" (see "Fermentation," page 2).

The level of acidity in the wine will impact our perception of what is called its "texture." Wines with high levels of acidity seem to be crisp or sharp, like biting into a Granny Smith apple, whereas wines with lower acidity appear to be softer and smoother, like milk. That perception of texture will also affect our use of the wine and what foods work well with it. Appreciable levels of bitterness in a wine can be an important factor in determining whether we actually like the wine, since the bitter taste is the last one noticed, at the back of the tongue, and stays with us longest.

Once you have mastered the three tastes, it is important to enjoy and savor what the wine offers, and even to see how the wine changes with time. You might even find it is fun to consider and describe the flavors of wines, launching into poetic and flowery descriptions. There's nothing wrong with that as long as you are sincere, and as long as you are enjoying the wine.

Glasses

OUR FINAL WORDS about enjoying wine have to do with glasses. We have used many different vessels in our wine careers and would never deny that circumstances may sometimes dictate that a simple tumbler is the appropriate glass (or even a jelly glass, if that's the only container available). But our experience tells us again and again that a good glass is often invaluable. Our recommendation is for a stemmed glass with a thin lip, as thin as the practical consideration of washing will allow. Try it—it makes a difference.

chapter 2

Great vines make great wines
major white grapes

Without grapes, there is no wine. Throughout the world, there are dozens, indeed hundreds, of white grapes used to make wine. Some of these grapes you've probably heard of—Chardonnay, Sauvignon Blanc, Riesling—but many of them—*Albarino, Cortese,* Semillon, and on and on—may not be so familiar.

We want to take you on a quick worldwide tour of the six major white grapes and their wines. Once you've familiarized yourself with these grapes, you'll begin to become *WineWise* about most of the white wines you're likely to encounter, buy, and enjoy.

In later chapters we'll mention some of the "minor" white grapes—fruits that make great wine but are closely identified with more specific wine regions and countries.

So get ready to learn a few things about some of the best-known white wine grapes in the world. It should come as no surprise to our readers that we'll begin with the grape that makes the wine drunk 'round the world . . . Chardonnay.

Chardonnay

Chardonnay: The profile

Chardonnay rules. The grape that growers, winemakers, and wine drinkers love, Chardonnay grows just about everywhere in the modern wine world. Unless forbidden by law to appear in the vineyards of a particular wine region of the Old World (such as in Bordeaux, France), Chardonnay vines show up in both cool and warm climates and in both the Northern and Southern Hemispheres. As much a brand—the accepted "vanilla" of wine—as it is a grape, Chardonnay defines whether a wine region has "arrived," whether it is part of the global club, and if it is to be taken seriously. Likewise, if we're at a party on planet Earth and have a glass of white wine, most of us assume that the wine is Chardonnay unless specified otherwise. The appeal of the familiar is strong, and Chardonnay has become our default white.

Many people believe that Chardonnay is "the grape that tastes like oak," and that's understandable because more often than not Chardonnay is fermented and/or aged in oak barrels, or exposed to oak chips. Unfortunately, some of the wines made from Chardonnay, including some expensive ones, are overoaked, which throws off the balance of flavors in the wines. These days, however, we taste far fewer wines that are reminiscent of lumber and far more that taste like fruit.

A well-made Chardonnay should contain flavors of apples and citrus and can be anywhere from light, crisp, and green/under-ripe when the grapes are

A varietal label. Chardonnay produced by the Benziger Family Winery, from fruit harvested in the Los Carneros district of California. (Courtesy of Kobrand Corporation)

grown in a cool climate to rich in tropical fruit notes such as pineapple and mango when the grapes come from warmer growing regions. When oak is added to the equation, the wine takes on both sweet vanilla and buttered toast flavors. Note that not all Chardonnay-based wines are oak-aged or oak-fermented, especially those from cooler climates, and some of these wines, redolent with refreshing acidity, are gaining in popularity, especially when paired with food.

Obviously, one of Chardonnay's charms is its wide range of styles. Another charm is that you can find drinkable Chardonnay for well under $10, extraordinary Chardonnay for well over $100, and a solid representation at every price in between those extremes. There is a style and price to please every potential Chardonnay consumer. No wonder it has become the most popular single varietal—white or red—in the world.

Grape growers and winemakers love working with Chardonnay for several reasons. First, the vine grows in varied climates and soils, and even though classic Chardonnay-based wines are made from cool-climate grapes, such as those that grow in Burgundy, France, or the Russian River Valley of California, acceptable wine is produced from grapes that grow in warm wine regions, too. Chardonnay grapes grow best in stony soil rich in calcium, but they will do just fine in far more fertile soils.

Chardonnay grapes. (© Ron Watts/Corbis)

Second, Chardonnay's yield in the vineyard—measured in tons per acre—is pretty flexible. As usual, the best wines begin with low-yielding vines, but quite drinkable Chardonnay can be produced from ripe grapes grown in relative abundance.

Third, Chardonnay grapes produce a base wine that is fairly neutral and needs the signature of the winemaker to create a style for the finished wine. Unlike other fine wines that are highly regarded for their raw materials (grapes) and noninterventionist winemaking techniques, successful Chardonnay needs the hand of the winemaker.

There are artisanal Chardonnay winemakers whose signature is unique and whose wines can be quite rare and expensive. More often, however, Chardonnay is the cash cow for a wine producer, and to meet consumer expectation, the signature of that producer becomes more of a rubber stamp than an autograph. While the best Chardonnay producers achieve balance and quality in their wines through a delicate touch and restraint, far too many Chardonnay producers pull out all the technical stops and end up with a manipulated wine geared to please the palates of a mass audience.

Sure, there has been some resistance to the universal acceptance of Chardonnay as the quintessential white wine, most notably the short-lived "ABC" (Anything But Chardonnay) fad that never became a real movement. Just protesting the ubiquitous Chardonnay by drinking other varietals puts the focus on its power in the marketplace and diminishes the attractive flavor profiles of other grapes. True, Riesling (see page 26) or Sauvignon Blanc (see page 24) may be the anti-Chardonnay, but each of these varietals has a lot more to offer as delicious white wine than as a protest drink.

We could go on and on about the glut of mediocre Chardonnay in the marketplace, but that would be too easy, too obvious. More important, dissing Chardonnay obscures the fact that this grape can—and does—produce some of the world's best white wines.

We should drink the wines we like and the wines we can afford. If, for example, you've found a $7 Chardonnay from Australia that you really enjoy, then that is a great wine for you to share with friends anytime at lunch or dinner. Expensive fine white Burgundy from France (by law, 100% Chardonnay, though the name of the grape does not appear on the label) is a special-occasion treat that will expose you to another world of Chardonnay. There is just so much Chardonnay available from so many different countries, in so many different styles, and at so many different price points. Let's take a look at some of the places that make delicious and distinctive Chardonnay.

France

Burgundy (see page 159) is considered the ancestral home of fine Old World Chardonnay. The thing to remember about Burgundy is that virtually all of its white wines with geographical names (the name of the place, not the grape, appears on the label) are 100% Chardonnay, and some of them—even the most affordable ones—can be delicious, even memorable. The three most important major subregions within Burgundy for fine Chardonnay are Chablis (see page 161), for crisp, green-fruit, high-acid, mineral-laden, often unoaked Chardonnay grown in a very cool climate and chalk/limestone soils; Cote de Beaune (see page 162), for rich, complex, balanced, oaked (but restrained) Chardonnay; and Macon (see page 163),

A "place-name" label. Puligny-Montrachet is a village in Burgundy, France, known for the high quality of its Chardonnay grapes. A white wine from Puligny-Montrachet is—by law—100% Chardonnay, even though the name of the grape does not appear on the label. (Courtesy of Kobrand Corporation)

which can produce warmer-climate, medium-bodied Chardonnays, some of them simple, several of them with pleasing mineral flavors and complexity.

Chardonnay is one of only three legal grapes in the Champagne region of France (see page 167) and the only white grape allowed in this famous sparkling wine. The only other grapes allowed in Champagne are Pinot Noir and Pinot Meunier, both red varietals. What Chardonnay does for Champagne is provide lightness and delicacy, as well as bracing acidity, especially because Champagne is the coldest grape-growing region in all of France.

Chardonnay grows in many other wine regions of France, particularly in southern France, where high yields in the vineyards most often result in drinkable, affordable, but not particularly memorable wines.

The United States and Canada

Chances are you've tasted several California Chardonnays (see Chapter 4), and some you've liked better than others. With about 100,000 acres (140,000 hectares) of Chardonnay planted, more than any other varietal, California grows this grape all over the state, from the coolest vineyard sites to the warmest. California has adopted the rich, oaky, vanilla style of Chardonnay as its signature, though there are some "leaner, greener" exceptions.

Wines whose labels read simply "California Chardonnay" can be produced from grapes grown anywhere in the state, and most often the source of the fruit in these wines is the warm Central Valley. These wines tend to be full-blown, rich, ripe, and oaky, with mature, ripe fruits in the background. Because the grapes are sourced in such warm conditions, these wines often lack the refreshing acidity that cool weather brings. You can easily buy a Chardonnay labeled "California" for under $10 in your wine shop or supermarket. When served chilled with broiled fish, roast chicken, or grilled vegetables, these wines will usually do their job: provide a suitable accompaniment to food.

If you are looking for Chardonnay of higher quality (at a higher price), wines produced from

Cakebread Cellars

NAPA VALLEY

Chardonnay

The Cakebread family makes wine in Napa Valley, California. Cakebread Chardonnay is one of the most popular wines served in upscale restaurants. (Courtesy of Kobrand Corporation)

grapes grown in the cooler growing regions of California can be good to exquisite. Prices start at about $14, but it is not uncommon to pay $35 or more for very fine Chardonnay from places such as Napa Valley, Carneros, Sonoma Coast, Russian River Valley, Edna Valley, Santa Maria Valley, and Santa Ynez.

New York State (see page 104) produces fine Chardonnay in the Finger Lakes, Hudson River Region, and Long Island, which feature cooler climates than the vast majority of California's cooler growing regions. Chardonnay from the Finger Lakes area does not rely on oak to define its style, as the ripe grapes maintain their refreshing fruit acids, and the finished wines can display a lovely balance of flavors. Chardonnay from cool-climate Long Island can also be impressive, the style a bit oakier than the Finger Lakes but with balance and zesty fruit. A small amount of very good, high-acid cool-climate Chardonnay is also produced in Hudson River Region vineyards and wineries.

In the Pacific Northwest, Washington State (see page 94) produces a wide variety of Chardonnay styles, but Washington concentrates on its red wines as flagships for the state. In Oregon (see page 99), some very good cool-weather Chardonnay is grown and produced, but Chardonnay takes a backseat to

Oregon's premier red varietal, Pinot Noir, and its premier white, Pinot Gris.

Chardonnay, from drinkable to extraordinarily good, is made in many states, from Texas to Rhode Island, Virginia to Michigan. In addition, Canada (see page 266) produces some fine Chardonnay wines, some of them from single vineyards. Canada's primary Chardonnay region is the Niagara Peninsula in Ontario; secondary is the Okanagan Valley in British Columbia.

The Southern Hemisphere

In South America, Argentina (see page 114) makes Chardonnay, but the wines that have reached the U.S. export market have so far not been impressive. They are inexpensive, drinkable, and mostly forgettable. Chile (see page 110), however, is beginning to show some promise in producing high-quality Chardonnay, especially from grapes grown in the cool-climate Casablanca region. These wines are inexpensive to moderately expensive and deliver delicious, ripe, balanced flavors without a preponderance of oak.

As with so many of the wines of South Africa (see page 132), Chardonnay is a mixed bag. Depending on the producer, the wines can be just drinkable or deep and complex. The best growers and winemakers in South Africa are making some lovely wines at affordable prices, and many are available in the U.S. export market.

New Zealand (see page 128) has made its reputation in the export market for its extraordinarily popular Sauvignon Blanc but actually grows almost as much Chardonnay. Chardonnay from the wine regions of Gisborne and Hawke's Bay, both located on the North Island of the country, are well known, with Gisborne Chardonnay featuring flavors akin to peaches and melon, while Hawke's Bay Chardonnay displays more citrus flavors—grapefruit and lime. Chardonnay produced from South Island fruit often comes from the Marlborough wine region, which produces juicy, tropical-fruit-driven wines with fresh, crisp flavors.

Australia (see page 120) produces rivers of Chardonnay, where the varietal is second only to Shiraz in acres planted. Much of Australia's Chardonnay is produced from grapes grown in the gigantic "Southeastern Australia" region, which takes in more than 90% of the vineyards in the entire country. Chardonnay labeled as "Southeastern Australia" should be inexpensive—usually under $10—and easily drinkable, featuring lots of tropical fruit flavors. These wines have more or less defined the "international style" of Chardonnay, and they are wildly successful in the marketplace.

In addition to mass-produced Chardonnay, Australia also produces some very elegant Chardonnay wines from smaller wine districts, such as the Limestone Coast, Clare Valley, Orange, and the Adelaide Hills.

The rest of the world

Chardonnay grows in just about any country that makes wine. Italy has grown Chardonnay successfully for decades, as has Spain. Portugal grows a little Chardonnay, and so do Germany, Austria, and Switzerland. Greece and Eastern Europe grow quite a bit of Chardonnay, and the new wine regions of China do, too. Chardonnay is everywhere.

Good, affordable Chardonnay is made both in Chile and Argentina.

Sauvignon Blanc

Sauvignon Blanc: The profile

Like the rest of the white varietals in the wine universe, Sauvignon Blanc lives in the shadow of Chardonnay. But Sauvignon Blanc seems poised to make its move as the next big white, or at least to claim the respect it has earned as a strong supporting player on the world wine stage.

Think "green." Sauvignon Blanc at its best exhibits its high acidity with flavors and aromas of green apples, green grapes, green herbs, and perhaps just a bit of green bell pepper. Lime, kiwi, green honeydew melon, and tropical fruits such as guava, papaya, and passion fruit make some Sauvignon Blanc–based wines, especially those from New Zealand and South Africa, smell and taste like a fruit salad in a glass, poured over calcium-rich stones.

The flavors of Sauvignon Blanc can shift in both subtle and dramatic ways, depending on where the grapes are grown. Let's survey the world of this "green" varietal.

France

Classic Old World Sauvignon Blanc, from the Loire Valley of France (see page 170), is chiefly represented

Sancerre is a village in the Loire Valley of France. A white wine labeled "Sancerre" must—according to French wine laws—be made from 100% Sauvignon Blanc grapes. (Courtesy of Kobrand Corporation)

by the wines Sancerre and Pouilly Fumé. These wines exhibit a high degree of minerality—chalk, limestone, and the brininess of the sea and seashells. The flavors and aromas of citrus fruits, especially lemon and grapefruit, are prominent in Loire Valley Sauvignon Blanc.

In Bordeaux, France (see page 151), Sauvignon Blanc is often blended with another grape, Semillon (see page 154), to produce a distinctive style of white wine. These wines tend to be medium- to full-bodied and more restrained in their acidity and fruit flavors. The classic versions of these Bordeaux blends come from the districts of Graves (see page 154). White wines from Bordeaux labeled as "Entre-Deux-Mers" (see page 154) or simply "Bordeaux" tend to be more about the straightforward, crisp flavors of Sauvignon Blanc and are meant for early drinking.

The United States: California

In California, where Sauvignon Blanc is the second most important white varietal—Chardonnay, of course, is first—you may find Sauvignon Blanc labeled as "Fumé Blanc." In the late 1960s, Robert Mondavi coined this name for a style of Sauvignon Blanc that is usually richer and fuller than a wine

Sauvignon Blanc grapes. (© Bryan Peterson/Corbis)

St. Supéry is a well-known and respected wine producer.

labeled "Sauvignon Blanc." Some people prefer the more "sophisticated" Fumé Blanc style, while others much prefer the "wild" style of Sauvignon Blanc, and some wine drinkers enjoy both styles, depending on the food they are pairing with the wine.

Sauvignon Blanc from the North Coast of California—Napa, Sonoma, and Mendocino counties—is the antithesis of the Chardonnay produced in the same region. Rather than the rich, oaky, vanilla flavors of Chardonnay that can overwhelm simpler foods, the refreshing, straightforward fruity flavors of Sauvignon Blanc are just the thing for fish—from ceviche to grilled tuna with tomatillo salsa—or a fresh goat cheese, tapas-style appetizers, or a chilled gazpacho. California Sauvignon Blanc has emerged as a food-friendly wine, gaining more space on restaurant wine lists and more adherents among American consumers.

New Zealand

For years, and until quite recently, classic Sauvignon Blanc was defined by the wines of the Loire Valley of France, such as Sancerre. The name of the grape—Sauvignon Blanc—has never appeared on the labels of these wines. In an increasingly varietal-conscious world, these wines have begun to lose their status as classic Sauvignon Blanc, and there are many wines and wine-producing nations ready to take their place, chief among them New Zealand.

New Zealand Sauvignon Blanc has, especially for many younger wine drinkers, become the classic expression of this varietal. Full of tart lime and tropical aromas and flavors, with grace notes of minerals, grass, and herbs, New Zealand Sauvignon Blanc is pure pleasure, an uncomplicated and fun wine—not a wine to exercise wine expertise on, but a wine to enjoy with a myriad of tasty dishes. A great accompaniment to spicy foods, especially Asian and Latin American flavors, this wine is like a squeeze of fresh lime juice, awakening and brightening flavors throughout the meal. Once you start to enjoy New Zealand Sauvignon Blanc, it can quickly become a favorite.

The best examples of this popular white are sourced from grapes grown in the vineyards of the Marlborough region, located at the northern tip of New Zealand's South Island. The wines are affordable, with many priced under $10, and some of the best available for between $15 and $20.

New Zealand Sauvignon Blanc is consumer-friendly in another way, too. Almost all of the New Zealand wines you will find in the U.S. market feature screw caps, not corks, as closures, making New Zealand Sauvignon Blanc a perfect wine for the dinner table or the picnic basket.

New Zealand Sauvignon Blanc, with its distinct style, is often described as a "fruit salad in a glass."

South Africa

South Africa's best white wine is its Sauvignon Blanc. When sourced from low-yielding vineyards in the cooler regions, the wines can be incomparable. With thirst-quenching acidity, a healthy dose of minerality, and green, tropical fruits in the mix, the wines are more fruit-driven than the wines of the Loire Valley, but a bit more restrained in their exuberance and slightly fuller-bodied than the wines of New Zealand.

Other countries

Australia produces a wide range of Sauvignon Blanc wines, from simple summer sippers to more complex wines with rich, jammy fruit balanced by a vein of mouthwatering acidity. With Australian Sauvignon Blanc you usually get what you pay for, and it is easy to find wines for under $10, but even the most expensive and best wines are under $20.

Chile produces some delightful Sauvignon Blanc, very much in the California style, but with a bit more forward fruit on the palate, especially from grapes grown in the cool Casablanca region, and the relatively new Leyda region. Sauvignon Blanc from Casablanca tends to be a bargain-priced gem.

Although perhaps a bit hard to find, Sauvignon Blanc from the Friuli–Venezia Giulia region of Italy is worth the search. Often just labeled as "Sauvignon," these can be some of the most elegant examples of Sauvignon Blanc produced anywhere in the world, with a grassy background and subtle fruit acids that refresh the palate.

Sauvignon Blanc: Other styles

As we noted earlier, in Bordeaux, France, Sauvignon Blanc is often blended with Semillon to produce an elegant dry white. However, the blend is also responsible for one of the most famous sweet wines in the world, Sauternes (see page 155). Sauternes is based on a heavy percentage (most often 75% to 95%) of botrytis-affected Semillon, with just a bit of Sauvignon Blanc for its refreshing acidity.

Sauvignon Blanc can also make a sweet wine on its own when produced from **late harvest** grapes. Late Harvest Sauvignon Blanc is a fairly rare wine, but several New World winemakers continue to produce this style.

Riesling
Riesling: The profile

While Chardonnay may get all the glory, many wine lovers believe that Riesling is the finest grape and makes the greatest wine—red or white—in the world. For the uninitiated, Riesling is perhaps the most misunderstood varietal, because so many people still believe that Riesling wines must be sweet. This is just not true. The truth is that Riesling can produce extraordinary wines in every style, from bone-dry to incredibly sweet.

Depending on where Riesling is grown, the flavor profile of the varietal can be as varied as its many vineyard sites. High acid is a hallmark of Riesling, with citrus—lemon, lime, grapefruit—and peach and pear flavors. On the nose and on the palate Riesling is rich with minerals, from slate to quartz, and even the smell (though not the flavor) of gasoline or diesel fuel. It is impossible to make a general statement about Riesling's flavor profile, as there are so many styles of Riesling in the bottle, and those styles change

Riesling grapes. (© Bryan Peterson/Corbis)

from vineyard to vineyard, region to region, and country to country.

For Riesling to achieve its full potential as one of the world's great varietals, it needs cold weather. Riesling is also extremely sensitive to the soil types of vineyard sites, absorbing the suggestion of mineral flavors. When the climate and soil are right, Riesling is perhaps the most *terroir*-expressive of all white varietals.

The vein of acidity that runs through fine Riesling will emphasize the green fruit flavors in the drier styles and cut the unctuous sweetness of the syrupy type. In all styles, the magic of great Riesling is that it is mouthwatering and refreshing because of the acidity that defines the varietal. While most Riesling wines, especially drier versions, are drunk young to celebrate their fresh, green flavors, the high level of acidity that refreshes these young wines also helps to preserve the wine; it is not uncommon to drink Rieslings that are more than ten years old.

With food, dry to semidry Rieslings can become "superhero" wines. Riesling is a perfect match with grilled fish accompanied by fruit salsas, fruit soups, or spicy Chinese, Thai, or Vietnamese food. Most of us love a rich dish, such as duck confit, with a medium- to full-bodied red, but try the confit with an exquisite dry to semidry Riesling, and the contrast of the fatty duck with the acid of the Riesling will create a perfect marriage on the palate: a luscious fruit glaze that will make the dish—and the wine—come alive. Great Riesling truly is magic with food.

We can't stress enough that fine Riesling is a product of its environment: climate and soil define the character of the varietal. Sure, you can grow Riesling in a warm climate, but it will taste flabby and flat. Grow it in rich, fertile soils, and you lose the minerality that Riesling lovers crave in their favorite wine. Luckily, there are still plenty of sites that are ideal for growing great Riesling, and wonderful wines from around the world—most of them with varietal labels—are currently available at reasonable prices.

While Chardonnay still rules the marketplace, Riesling is making a run (along with Sauvignon Blanc) for a distinguished second or third place in the hearts and minds of wine consumers. Let's explore the Riesling world.

Germany

In Germany (see page 250), Riesling is the most important varietal, the grape by which overall German wine quality is judged.

One of the classic growing regions for Riesling in Germany is the Mosel (formerly Mosel-Saar-Ruwer), named for the Mosel River. The Mosel features dramatically steep vineyards on south-facing slopes covered in slate stones, within a cold climate moderated by the warming effect of the sun's rays off the rivers. Mosel Rieslings are very high in acid, with citrus and green fruit flavors, and tend to be light- to medium-bodied. Traditionally, these wines are bottled in green-tinted flutes (the elegant, elongated 750 ml [25.4 oz.] bottle), reflecting their "green" style.

The other classic Riesling regions in Germany are located near or within the confines of the Rhine River Valley and are represented by the Rheingau, Rheinhessen, and Pfalz zones. Of the three regions, the Rheingau is best known for the quality of its Riesling wines, with Pfalz Riesling a close second. The three Rhine regions are considerably warmer than the Mosel and so produce wines that are richer, riper, fuller-bodied, and somewhat lower in acidity. Traditionally, wines from these regions are bottled in brown-tinted flutes, reflecting the warmer, earthier, richer style of the Rhine.

Until recently, Germany has had a tough time in the U.S. market with Riesling, even though the wines

German wine labels can be difficult to decipher, but German Riesling is easy to love. JJ Prüm is an established, quality-driven producer.

can be extraordinary. German wines are gaining serious traction in the United States, as wine consumers "discover" Riesling—in all its forms—as an extraordinary accompaniment to food, from appetizers through dessert.

France

Alsace (see page 146), which borders Germany, is home to a particularly French style of Riesling—full-bodied, dry, and higher in alcohol than most German Rieslings. Alsace Riesling enjoys cool enough weather to ramp up acidity in the grapes, but also many days of sunshine along the eastern side of the Vosges Mountains, so the grapes ripen fully. Alsace Riesling at its best can age well for years in the bottle, while the simpler wines are enjoyable in their youth—within two to five years of vintage. Riesling from Alsace is a wonderful match with flavorful fish dishes, but also with semisoft cheeses or white meats such as poultry or smoked pork.

Because of the German historical and cultural influence in this part of France, Alsace wines are labeled with the name of the varietal, making them accessible to the U.S. market. Alsace wines are bottled in the same elongated "flute" bottles as German wines.

There are sweet versions of Riesling produced in Alsace. Look for the label terms "*Vendange Tardive*" (late harvest, which can be anywhere from semisweet to quite sweet) or "*Selection de Grains Nobles*" (botrytis-affected, which produces lusciously sweet

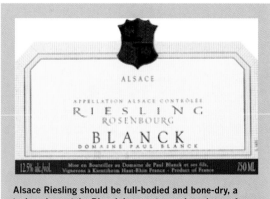

Alsace Riesling should be full-bodied and bone-dry, a truly unique style. Blanck is an esteemed producer of Alsace wines.

wines). As with the best Rieslings of Germany, Alsace wines, even when produced in a sweet style, feature a serious vein of acidity that refreshes the palate.

Austria

Close by the banks of the Danube River, Austria grows Riesling grapes that translate into some very elegant wines. One of the best wine regions in Austria for Riesling is Wachau, west of Vienna, which owes its cooling breezes to the Danube, and where the vineyards are planted on steep slopes.

Austria produces Riesling in as many styles and quality levels as Germany, but in the export market it has earned a reputation mostly for its bone-dry Riesling wines. In the U.S. market, Austrian Riesling can be hard to find and expensive—$25 and up—especially "Smaragd," the highest-quality wines from the Wachau region. These are fruit- and mineral-driven wines that, like the best wines of Germany and Alsace, can pair with hearty, rich foods, and are certainly ageworthy.

The United States and Canada

With the exception of high-quality Riesling made by a literal handful of artisanal winemakers in cooler pockets of the state, if California wineries stopped producing Riesling tomorrow, nobody would notice. The Golden State is just too warm to produce fine Riesling wines on anywhere approaching a commercial basis, especially when the coolest regions are wed to the far more profitable Chardonnay.

So if California is not big on Riesling, where else in the United States is Riesling a star? Travel cross-country and arrive at Riesling central: the Finger Lakes region of New York State (see page 104). Here, you will find a tiny production of ultra-fine Riesling wines, made from grapes grown on the stony banks of Cayuga, Keuka, and Seneca lakes. The climate is cold and snowy, with just enough sunshine and reflected warmth from the rivers to produce high-acid, "green" wines—from truly dry to very sweet—that are similar

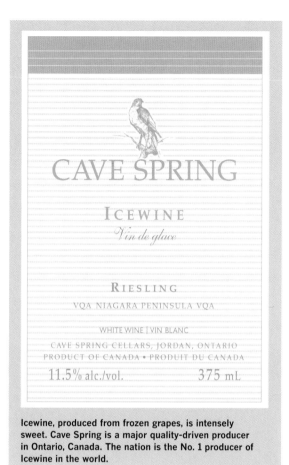

Icewine, produced from frozen grapes, is intensely sweet. Cave Spring is a major quality-driven producer in Ontario, Canada. The nation is the No. 1 producer of Icewine in the world.

ling grapes grown on the Niagara Peninsula of Ontario and in the Okanagan Valley of British Columbia.

Australia

While Germany produces the world's greatest Riesling wines in the widest variety of styles, it is Australia that is interpreting the varietal for the New World audience. Most Australian Riesling is produced for early consumption and immediate enjoyment, with a select few able to improve over time in the bottle.

Crisp and refreshing, Riesling from Australia tends to be lighter on the palate, with lime, ripe peaches, and tropical fruits in the background. Many of the wines have a bit of spice—nutmeg and ginger—that balances the luscious fruit flavors.

Australia's Rieslings are accessible, food-friendly, and priced to sell. Australian producers are, for the most part, making and marketing wines that will work with a simple grilled fish or the spicy flavors of Thailand, Cambodia, or Vietnam. The wines are good values, with some bottles priced less than $10, most in the low 'teens, and very few priced more than $20.

to the style of Germany's Mosel. Finger Lakes Rieslings, which sell for about $12 and up, represent good value for great wines.

A minuscule amount of fresh, crisp, fruit-driven Riesling is produced in the state of Idaho, from vineyards planted along the Snake River, and it is very good. Washington State (see page 94) produces a lot of Riesling, but many of the vines are planted in areas that are quite warm. The wines are mostly semidry to semisweet and often lack both the inspiring acidity and minerality of classic Riesling. The wines are fine as picnic wines with simple foods and are usually priced as easy-to-sip bargains. Some Washington producers see Riesling as an achievable challenge and are working hard to produce better wines.

Canada, with its cold climate, produces some lovely Riesling wines in several styles, from bone-dry to sweet to its specialty, Icewine, especially from Ries-

New York State's Finger Lakes region produces some extraordinary Riesling in several styles, from dry to sweet. Konstantin Frank was a pioneering winemaker and passionate advocate for quality wines from the Finger Lakes.

Gewurztraminer

Gewurztraminer: The profile

In the world of fine white wine, there is life beyond Chardonnay. If you want that life to include vibrant spices, honeysuckle and rose petal scents, and the unmistakable aroma of lychees, then you may want to give Gewurztraminer a try (say it five times fast: guh-VERTZ-tra-meener).

Gewurztraminer is not for the faint-hearted white-wine drinker, one who looks for subtlety and nuance in every sip. No, Gewurztraminer—both the grape and the wine—is anything but subtle, with its sexy, seductive, perfumed aromatics and its allspice, clove, and cardamom flavors. Fine Gewurztraminer is wine for the sensualist who revels in the wine's voluptuous full body and its fruit-and-spice exoticism.

The best Gewurztraminer vineyard sites are located in cool-weather regions and rely on low yields in those vineyards to amplify the natural appealing gifts that nature has bestowed upon the Gewurztraminer grape. If grape yields in the vineyard are too high, the finished wine will lack the perfume and power that Gewurztraminer lovers crave. With all the caveats inherent in growing the best examples of Gewurztraminer, it is no wonder that there is no wine region in the world where it is the most-planted varietal. Gewurztraminer is not a cash cow, like Chardonnay. The good Gewurztraminer grower must be committed to the varietal and treat it carefully, even lovingly.

Gewurztraminer grapes. (© Ron Watts/Corbis)

Hogue produces an affordable off-dry Gewurztraminer in the Columbia Valley of Washington State.

Classic Old World Gewurztraminer is a dry wine, with forward flavors of heady fruit and spice, intermingled and in balance. Alsace, France, is considered the definitive growing region for this style of Gewurztraminer.

New World Gewurztraminer is made in several different styles. It is hard to find wine as dry as the Gewurztraminer produced in Alsace, though a few producers try their best to produce a classic style. Most Gewurztraminer produced in the New World lacks the depth of minerality and spice of the Alsace style, but these fruitier versions can be quite attractive.

Let's take a quick peek at the world of Gewurztraminer—the grape and the wine.

France

If you've already read the section on Riesling in this chapter, then you might be familiar with Alsace (see page 146). Alsace is home to the classic Gewurztraminer: full-bodied, intensely aromatic, and most often dry (although we've noticed a consumer-driven trend toward sweetness among some producers). Alsace has the ideal growing conditions for pale pink Gewurztraminer grape: cool weather and lots of sunshine.

Great Alsace Gewurztraminer can age well for years. The simpler wines can be enjoyed in their youth, which means about three to five years after the vintage date. Like so many white wines from Alsace, Gewurztraminer behaves kind of like "a "red wine in drag," meaning that while it creates a great match with more complex, richer fish dishes, in addition it works beautifully not just with white meats—poultry and pork—but also with unusual pairings for a white wine, such as duck and game. Alsace Gewurztraminer is an ideal choice for smoked fish, smoked white meats, and charcuterie, as well as semisoft and moderately aged cheeses.

Gewurztraminer, much like its Alsatian partner, Riesling, sports a varietal label, making it an easy choice for American wine consumers. As is the usual practice in Alsace, Gewurztraminer is bottled in elongated "flute" bottles.

There are sweet versions of Gewurztraminer produced in Alsace. Label terms to look for are "*Vendange Tardive*" (late harvest, which can be anywhere from semidry to quite sweet) or "*Selection de Grains Nobles*" (botrytis-affected, which produces lusciously sweet wines). These wines will, like all of the best wines from Alsace, age well.

Germany

Alsace used to be part of Germany before it was part of France, and Alsace was where the Germans specialized in Gewurztraminer. Today, Gewurztraminer grows mostly in the *anbaugebiete* (wine regions) of Pfalz and Baden. Pfalz Gewurztraminer is rarely as dramatic a wine as its Alsatian counterpart; it is fruitier but less spicy. Baden, which is separated from Alsace by the Rhine River, produces some very elegant, full-bodied Gewurztraminer wines.

Austria

Here the grape is more likely to be called Traminer, and the wines tend to be less "*gewurz*" (spicy), except perhaps in the wine region of Steiermark, where the wines are both floral and full of spice. Other wine regions produce mostly sweet versions.

Italy

The Alto Adige region (officially a bilingual area, with Italian and German spoken, it was formerly part of Austria) is the birthplace of this grape. Here it is called Traminer Aromatico (Italian) or Gewurztraminer (German). Most of it grows around the town of Tramin, and the wines tend to be medium-bodied, floral but not very spicy in the nose and on the palate. We rarely see Gewurztraminer from Italy in the U.S. market.

The United States and Canada

In 1986, there were about 4,000 acres (1,600 hectares) of Gewurztraminer in the United States, but today there are fewer than 2,000 acres (800 hectares) under vine. The reason? Gewurztraminer, which needs a cool climate, is expensive to grow and labor-intensive to cultivate, and it almost never brings nearly as much

Sutter Home Winery in California makes a value-driven, consumer-friendly, semisweet version of Gewurztraminer that is just great with spicy foods.

money per ton of grapes as cool-climate Chardonnay (or even Sauvignon Blanc). In California, Gewurztraminer is planted in the cooler parts of Mendocino, the Russian River Valley, and Monterey. The wines are mostly off-dry, with a few truly dry wines, especially from the Anderson Valley in Mendocino. The Finger Lakes and Long Island wine regions of New York State produce a very small amount of fine Gewurztraminer, as do Washington State and Oregon.

Canada does not specialize in Gewurztraminer, at least so far, but there are several good examples planted and produced in the Okanagan Valley of British Columbia, including a small selection of some very exciting Icewines.

Pinot Grigio/ Pinot Gris

Pinot Grigio/Pinot Gris: The profile

Currently, Pinot Grigio is the single most popular imported varietal-labeled wine in the United States. Sometimes we wonder why. Great Pinot Grigio is produced in several different countries, but rarely. Most often and unfortunately, Pinot Grigio is just a decent quaff that quenches the thirst and doesn't offend food.

Pinot Grigio/Pinot Gris grapes. (Tracey Kusiewicz/Foodie Photography/Jupiterimages)

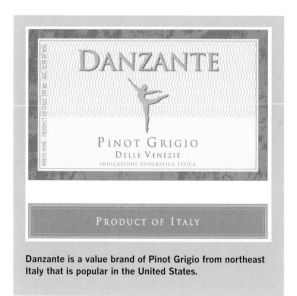

Danzante is a value brand of Pinot Grigio from northeast Italy that is popular in the United States.

Maybe that's what most of us want—a wine that is drinkable and inoffensive, a wine that does not challenge us. The popularity of Pinot Grigio is the engine that feeds its mass acceptance, making it an inclusive wine, one that everyone can agree on and enjoy.

Pinot Grigio, most closely identified with Italy, is not really an Italian grape. The grape is Pinot Gris (the "gray" Pinot), found most prominently in Alsace, France. In the vineyard, it is hard to tell if the grape is Pinot Gris or Pinot Noir until after color-changing *veraison,* as the leaves and grape shapes are identical. Pinot Gris is a variant of the Pinot Noir grape (as is Pinot Blanc).

At its best, Pinot Gris should be a full-bodied white wine, exhibiting spice, honey, honeysuckle, and nuttiness on the nose and tropical flavors on the palate, with just a touch of minerality. To achieve such concentration of flavor, fine Pinot Gris relies on low yields in the vineyard.

While Pinot Gris will always have its small number of admirers, it was not until the introduction of the label "Pinot Grigio" that this grape found its place in the sun and on so many dining tables around the world, but especially in the United States.

Maybe we just like saying "Pinot Grigio," a lovely phrase, almost sensual, but now nearly devoid of meaning. When we order Pinot Grigio in a restaurant or buy it in a shop, unless we have a favorite that we stick with, there's no telling what the wine will taste like. Fine Pinot Grigio is dry, but jam-packed with tropical fruits—mango, papaya, and pineapple, with a long, complex, rich finish. We've sampled bargain Pinot Grigio that tastes watery; moderate-priced Pinot Grigio that tastes like wine, sometimes pretty good food-friendly wine, but shows no truly distinctive varietal character; expensive Pinot Grigio that evokes the grape but has no sense of place (no *terroir*); and overpriced Pinot Grigio that was . . . well, overpriced and not terribly interesting.

Due to its popularity, you can easily find varietal-labeled Pinot Grigio just about anywhere. So, what countries and regions produce some of the best examples of this wine?

France

We think Pinot Gris from Alsace defines the wine made from this varietal, but if you like a lighter, more neutral style of Pinot Gris/Pinot Grigio, Alsace Pinot Gris is not for you. However, if you enjoy a full-bodied, assertive white wine without a lot of oak overtones that can pair beautifully with roast chicken or duck as well as grilled tuna or vegetarian lasagna, then you should try this classic wine from the Old World.

Italy

Of course, most wine drinkers look to Italy for high-quality Pinot Grigio, even though the grape is indeed a French interloper. There are several quality producers in northeast Italy, particularly in the bilingual (Italian/German) province of Alto Adige, which borders Austria, that make clean, Alpine-crisp wines. In the Friuli Venezia-Giulia province of Italy, which borders Slovenia (part of the former Yugoslavia), Pinot Grigio tends to be richer and fuller-bodied. You can expect to pay from $12 to $45 for these wines at retail.

The United States

The most important "Cal-Italian" white grape in the Golden State, California produces quite a bit of Pinot Grigio (and a bit of wine labeled "Pinot Gris"). Quality ranges from drinkable to excellent, and prices range from inexpensive to too expensive. Go with a producer whose reputation you trust, or ask a knowledgeable retailer or sommelier for a suggestion.

If we choose to drink Pinot Grigio from the United States, our first choice would be a wine from Oregon, where it is most often labeled "Pinot Gris." At

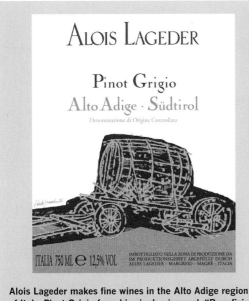

Alois Lageder makes fine wines in the Alto Adige region of Italy. Pinot Grigio from his single vineyard, "Benefizium Porer," is one of the best produced anywhere.

Oregon has embraced Pinot Gris as its No. 1 white grape, eclipsing Chardonnay. The wines can be complex and delicious with a wide variety of foods. King Estate is a large producer of high-quality Oregon wines.

their best, the wines are luscious and full-bodied, with mineral and fruit-driven flavors that create a great marriage with a wide range of foods. Pinot Gris may not be as hip a label choice as Pinot Grigio (even though they mean the same thing in different languages), but when you taste a fine Oregon Pinot Gris with your dinner, you'll be glad you defied what's popular with your friends in favor of what's happening on your palate.

Australia and New Zealand

One surefire way to confirm that this grape has "arrived" as one of the world's most popular varietals is to note that Pinot Grigio is one of the varietals in the spectacularly successful Australian wine brand, [yellow tail]® (more than 7 million cases of wine sold in each year in the United States). But it is not only price-driven brands such as [yellow tail]® that produce Pinot Grigio in the land down under. Artisanal wine producers in both Australia and New Zealand are focusing on Pinot Grigio as a quality varietal, and the wines are beginning to appear in the American market.

The appeal of Pinot Grigio is undeniable, perhaps based on its promise of comfort and reliability. Pinot Grigio—a varietal for the rest of us.

Viognier

Viognier: The profile

Just when we were comfortable pronouncing Chardonnay as our white wine of choice, along comes Viognier (vee-own-YAY) to make life difficult. Sure, it's inconvenient to learn the name of yet another French varietal, but pronouncing and tasting Viognier will be worth the effort.

Viognier is a white grape most closely identified with the northern Rhone Valley of France (see page 174), where it defines the Condrieu appellation, as well as the second-smallest appellation in all of France, Chateau Grillet. Both Condrieu and Chateau Grillet are quite expensive.

Now Viognier has come to the New World, and with a celebratory vengeance. Plantings of Viognier

Viognier grapes. (Diana Healey/Jupiterimages)

total more than 2,000 acres (800 hectares) in California, and the grape is being grown across the United States.

To thrive, the Viognier grape needs a warm climate; acidity in the finished wine is normally not very high. The best Viognier wines are not oak and alcohol bombs, but subtle wines with several layers of aroma and flavor. A rich wine, Viognier never forgets who brought it to the party: its grapes, not its barrels. You can pair Viognier with the same foods as Chardonnay, but chances are Viognier will give the food a chance to shine, while the Chardonnay might absorb the character of the dish in its own enforced complexity.

Grilled swordfish with peach salsa is a dream dish for Viognier, as are garlic-studded roast chicken and veal schnitzel. We have enjoyed Viognier as our Thanksgiving white wine. Pork roast with apples and pears finds a complementary "sauce" in Viognier.

Viognier is on a roll, appearing with increasing regularity on wine lists and on the shelves of wine retailers. Finding good Viognier is no longer the challenge it once was; you just have to choose the style, region, and producers you like.

France

If you are fortunate enough to taste a Condrieu or the even rarer Chateau Grillet, both produced from Viognier grown in the northern Rhone Valley, by all means do so. These are wines of wondrous depth and structure, with a sensuous, almost lanolin-like oiliness that coats the palate. It is not all that unusual to drink

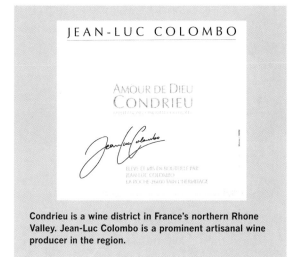

Condrieu is a wine district in France's northern Rhone Valley. Jean-Luc Colombo is a prominent artisanal wine producer in the region.

wines are produced from grapes grown in Washington, Texas, and Virginia, as well as California. These wines sell for between $10 and $25.

We might find the odd bottle of Australian, South African, or New Zealand Viognier, but these are rarities in the American import market. We're more likely to find a blended wine, comprising Viognier, Marsanne, and Rousanne, especially if the wine is produced in Australia.

Viognier can be a good wine for good value or it can be a very expensive wine, but it can be so much more. When you find the right wine with the right food, Viognier can be a wine of dreams, a wine of memories.

these whites at four to seven years old, but they are especially wonderful to drink when young and fresh.

French *vin de pays* producers are making lots of varietal-labeled Viognier in the Pays d'Oc region (see pages 144–145). These wines are good entry-level Viognier, relatively inexpensive whites for the thirsty masses.

The United States and the New World

New World Viognier is all about luscious fruit and an appealing, sexy viscosity, a palpable silky texture.

Some of the best American Viogniers have a wondrous perfumed apricot and peach nose and a background of tropical fruit flavors. Good Viognier

California wine producers are making quite a bit of Viognier, some of it very good. Toasted Head is known for the bear on the label and its good value.

chapter 3

Great vines make great wines
major red grapes

Red grapes not only make red wines but also white and rosé wines; still or sparkling. Sounds like magic. But red grapes are all about skin: show a lot of skin and you produce a red wine; a little bit of skin and you get rosé; no skin yields a white.

In the wide world of wine, there are hundreds of different red grapes that produce hundreds of different wines. We're going to start with the basics: six major red grapes that account for so many wines. These grapes often fly solo as the star of a wine (consider Pinot Noir), but sometimes they work and play well together in delicious blended wines (Cabernet Sauvignon/Merlot or Syrah/Grenache blends).

We'll start our survey of the major red grapes with the worldwide ruler of reds, Cabernet Sauvignon . . .

Cabernet Sauvignon

Cabernet Sauvignon: The profile

It seems that Cabernet Sauvignon is everywhere, and that perception is not far from wrong. Almost any recognized wine region that is moderately warm to hot grows Cabernet Sauvignon, and wine drinkers can't seem to get enough of this varietal. Why is it that this grape has captured the hearts, minds, and palates of millions of wine consumers and is now grown on hundreds of thousands of vineyard acres?

For one thing, Cab is always Cab. Wherever you grow it, the varietal makes a wine that is recognizable, true to its varietal character. With vibrant aromas of black cherries, black currants, black plums, black olives, and eucalyptus in a young wine, and hints of cedar and cigar box bouquets as it ages, Cabernet Sauvignon produces reliable, even predictable, full-bodied, in-your-face red wine, with high degrees of both tannins and acidity. Yes, there are differences between New World and Old World Cab, but once you get hooked on this grape, the similarities outshine the differences.

The popularity of Cabernet Sauvignon is both its strength and its weakness. Without the commanding presence of this varietal there simply would not be a successful wine industry and culture in Bordeaux, France, or the Napa Valley of California, or the Maipo

Cabernet Sauvignon grapes. (ImageSource/Jupiterimages)

Valley of Chile. Cab has put these regions on the world's wine map. But the tremendous popularity of Cabernet Sauvignon has also diminished the important traditional varietals of countries such as Italy and Spain, among others. If there are any grape types that can be accused of "wine imperialism," then the first suspects are Cabernet Sauvignon for red wines and Chardonnay for whites.

Why is Cabernet Sauvignon so successful in the vineyards of so many wine regions and so popular with wine consumers, from the neophyte to the auction-quality collector? For grape growers, Cab is a slam dunk; it grows in almost every wine-producing country of the world and adapts well to a wide variety of climates and soils. The grape has a thick skin and is resistant to many of the plant viruses and diseases that plague less hardy varietals.

Cabernet Sauvignon loves oak, especially the assertive spicy vanilla flavors of new oak barrels. The *barriques* used to age Cab are most often 60 gallons (224 liters) and if all of the barrels are new, the result can be a dramatic, over-the-top, overtly alcoholic, but smooth, sweet black cherry–like wine. Some of the best Cab wines use a regimen of new and used barrels to tone down the oak flavors in the finished wine, but the producers of these wines often do so at their peril. Why? Because many of the most influential wine writers and critics who assign numerical scores (such as 92—or, heaven forbid, 82—out of a possible 100 points) seem incapable of evaluating wines that are not loaded up with the overwhelming flavors of new oak.

Sometimes the wine critics get it right when it comes to Cab, but just as often we wonder, "What were they thinking?" when they assign a high score to a wine that tastes like a vanilla-flavored two-by-four. These wines, though they may garner a cult following of well-heeled consumers willing to pay high prices, will not highlight and enhance the flavors and textures of a rare steak or leg of lamb, especially when compared to a Cab (or perhaps another full-bodied red) that exhibits more restraint.

Yet another reason for Cabernet Sauvignon's worldwide success is its ability to work and play well with other grapes. Not all varietals are nearly as sociable. For example, if you want to produce a fine wine made from Pinot Noir or Chardonnay, don't blend with other wines made from different varietals. Conversely, an "anchor wine" made from Cabernet Sauvignon blended with, say, 15% to 25% Merlot and/or Cabernet Franc is a classic mix that started in Bordeaux and made its way around the world. For instance, many esteemed Napa Valley Cabs contain between 5% and 25% Merlot and/or Cabernet Franc.

Cabernet Sauvignon's ability to hook up with other attractive wines takes the creative handcuffs off the winemaker, who can create his or her own style of Cab partially based on the chosen blend. And winemakers are not limited to the classic Bordeaux blending model. In Tuscany, Italy, literally hundreds of "Super Tuscan" wines (see page 194) are based on blends of Cabernet Sauvignon and Sangiovese, the most important traditional grape of the region. In several wine regions of Spain (see pages 214–231), blends of Cab and Tempranillo-based wines are increasingly common. Australia (see page 120) is well known for making a wide range of Cabernet Sauvignon/Shiraz blended wines. The list goes on, but you get the drift.

Because Cabernet Sauvignon is so flexible, there are as many styles of wine as there are winemakers. However, even though the wines vary stylistically, the basic truth is this: Cab is one of the easiest wines to identify, as it exhibits loads of varietal character, whether it is priced at $10 or at $200. So why pay the big money for something that is supposedly special? Well, the best wines made primarily from the Cabernet Sauvignon grape display a sense of place, not just varietal character. What you are paying for is the address of the wine, not necessarily the grape that appears on the label. In Bordeaux, you are paying big bucks for the character of the soil and the heralded history of the estate (the chateau) on which the grape is grown. In the New World, a "California" Cab should taste decidedly different from a "Napa Valley" Cab, which should taste different from a "Rutherford" Cab (Rutherford is a town within the Napa Valley), and a "single-vineyard Rutherford" Cab should taste even more special than a wine made from grapes grown on more than one Rutherford vineyard or vineyard block. At each heightened level of perceived quality the price goes up, and the difference between the

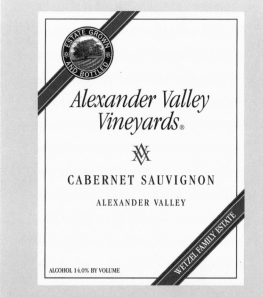

Three generations of the Wetzel family have been making fine wine at their Alexander Valley Vineyards estate, including this delicious—and reasonably priced—Cabernet Sauvignon.

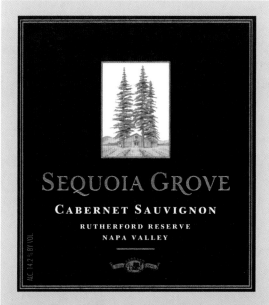

Sequoia Grove's Reserve Napa Valley Cabernet Sauvignon is produced from grapes grown only in Rutherford, a small town with a big reputation for Cab. (Courtesy of Kobrand Corporation)

"California" Cab and the Rutherford single-vineyard Cab could easily be more than $100.

Whatever style and price point you are comfortable with, most Cab is not for the faint-hearted when it comes to pairing with food. Maybe the world's admiration for this varietal is an expression of postindustrial wealth, because Cabernet Sauvignon does not allow us to eat low on the food chain. Rare red meat is what Cab is all about; just look at the wine list in any good steakhouse worth its salt and pepper. Hard cheese such as Parmigiano Reggiano, full of fat and with just an edge of sweetness, is also a great match for this wine. Try it with a delicate fish dish and you will be suffering through your meal, unless you like the metallic taste that the clash of harsh tannins and omega-3 fatty acids can bring.

Unlike the healthy skepticism tempered with genuine interest in other white wines that sometimes greets Chardonnay, Cab is still the king of reds, at least in the marketplace. Merlot, Pinot Noir, and lately Syrah (all three varietals are discussed later in this chapter) have their boosters and adherents, but the preeminent position of Cabernet Sauvignon remains unchallenged. Maybe it's the same reason that some people prefer hard rock to folk music, or love wall-sized aggressive abstract paintings and loathe small quiet landscape watercolors. Some people make football their religion; others love only women's tennis. Cab is bold and brawny and powerful, and its dark, brooding color and complex nature make a statement that appeals to those of us looking for a definition of what a "big red wine" should be. Certainly, there is more to life than Cabernet Sauvignon; however, in every kingdom there are many loyal subjects, but only one king. Cab rules.

France

The "Left Bank" of Bordeaux (see pages 156–158) is the quintessential classic region for both Cabernet Sauvignon vineyards and some world-famous wines, most often judicious blends of Cabernet Sauvignon, Merlot, and Cabernet Franc, with grace notes sometimes provided by Malbec and Petit Verdot. Outside of Bordeaux, southwest France grows a lot of Cabernet

Chateau Cordeillan-Bages is a well-known property in Bordeaux, France, located in the Village of Pauillac. The wine is made primarily from Cabernet Sauvignon grapes.

Sauvignon grapes and produces quite a bit of pretty good wine dominated by the varietal. The Mediterranean provinces of Languedoc and Roussillon (see page 179) in south-central France are awash in high-yielding Cabernet Sauvignon vineyards, where a huge volume of drinkable, varietal-labeled Cab from the Vin de Pays d'Oc appellation is produced.

Italy

Cabernet Sauvignon has been planted sporadically in the vineyards of Italy for hundreds of years, but today the varietal is planted in the majority of Italy's twenty provinces. Cabernet Sauvignon is sometimes produced as a single-varietal wine or as a Cabernet/Merlot blend, but more often it is blended with wines made from indigenous varietals.

The most heralded blend is Cabernet Sauvignon and Sangiovese, made famous by the much sought-after and often expensive Super Tuscans. Sangiovese is the backbone of virtually all the traditional wines of Tuscany—Chianti and Brunello di Montalcino, for example—and Cabernet Sauvignon turns out to be a successful partner in many of the region's non-traditional blended wines. Some of these wines are featured prominently on the wine lists of great restaurants and in upscale retail outlets. Some of the most famous examples in which Cabernet Sauvignon dominates the blend include Solaia, Sassicaia, Ornellaia, Excelsus, and Tinscvil.

In Veneto, Lombardy, and Emilia-Romagna it is easy to find Cab-based wines, often blended with Merlot and Cabernet Franc. Some interesting, delicious wines are now being produced in southern Italy and on the island of Sardinia, where Cabernet Sauvignon is often blended with indigenous varietals.

Spain

Cabernet Sauvignon is making its presence known in Spain, often blended with Tempranillo in the wine regions Ribera del Duero and Rioja, among others. In the Penedes region, anchored by Barcelona, the historic and cultural influence of France is expressed in the choice of grapes to make wine, and Cabernet Sauvignon is one of the most important red grapes of the region. It is not uncommon to find varietal Cabernet Sauvignon or a Cabernet Sauvignon/Merlot blend produced in Penedes, but it is just as common to find a Tempranillo/Cabernet Sauvignon blend from this region. Also, the small but prestigious region of Priorato produces Cab-based wines as either single-varietal wines or blended with the indigenous varietals Cariñena (Carignan) and/or Garnacha (Grenache).

The rest of the Old World

Cabernet Sauvignon grows in just about every wine-producing nation of the Old World, including Portugal, Greece, Bulgaria, Hungary, Romania, and even the warmer parts of Switzerland, Austria, and Germany. Cab is the most important red varietal in the wines of Israel and high-quality wines from Lebanon, especially the esteemed Chateau Musar.

The United States: California

Cabernet Sauvignon is the most widely planted red wine grape in the vineyards of California (Zinfandel is second; see page 55). So much of the Golden State provides a near-perfect match of climate and varietal that Cab has become a no-brainer to grow in the best "artisanal" single vineyards of the Napa Valley, the "industrial" vineyards of the Central Valley, and every peak and valley in between these extremes. These expensive artisanal wines may be produced from vineyards yielding less than 2 tons per acre (5 tons per hectare), while the utilitarian, value-driven industrial wines are produced from vines as big as small trees, yielding close to 15 tons per acre (37.5 tons per hectare). Whichever Cab you choose, and at whatever price point, it still tastes like California Cab, capturing sunshine in a bottle and showing off a jammy, sweet attack of voluptuous black fruit with a dry finish.

If you trade up from the under-$10 Cab to a $30-plus-plus-plus Cab, what you get is an ageworthy wine with deeper concentration of flavor, more subtlety and complexity on the palate and in the nose, and that sense of place (a single vineyard in Sonoma County's Alexander Valley, for example) that some wine consumers are willing to pay for, again and again.

As in Bordeaux, varietal-labeled Cabernet Sauvignon from California will often contain a healthy dose of Merlot and Cabernet Franc in the finished blend,

Rubicon Estate in Rutherford is owned by film director Francis Ford Coppola, and produces a fine Napa Valley "Cask Cabernet," complete with a hand-applied wood label.

allowing the individual wine producer to tweak the wine to meet his or her own standards of balance and quality, or just as often to anticipate taste preferences of the American wine consumer.

No one will argue that Cabernet Sauvignon has defined California's red wine industry, just as Chardonnay has defined white wine. The public has embraced California Cab, from the shelves of supermarkets to the wine lists of the world's most expensive restaurants.

The rest of North America

Cabernet Sauvignon maintains a serious presence in the warmer parts of Washington State's Columbia Valley, such as the Red Mountain and Yakima Valley regions. Although Merlot is the most planted red varietal in this mostly cool-climate state, Cabernet Sauvignon's ability to tough it out in cold weather allows producers to make some attractive wines.

In Oregon, there are about 600 acres (240 hectares) of Cab planted mostly in the Rogue Valley and Umpqua Valley, but Oregon Cabernet Sauvignon lives in the shadow thrown by the state's premier red varietal, Pinot Noir.

New York State's Long Island wine regions grow and produce some lovely Cabernet Sauvignon, but in such small amounts that they rarely leave the New York Metro area. New Mexico, Texas, and Virginia are among other small Cab-producing states.

Canada, because of its cold temperatures, produces a lot more Cabernet Franc than Cabernet Sauvignon, but Mexico can produce some drinkable Cabernet Sauvignon, even some very good ones, especially on the Baja peninsula.

South America: Chile and Argentina

Without Cabernet Sauvignon there probably would be no Chilean wine industry. Chile produces a lot of Cab for the export market, and in the 1990s it developed a reputation for true-to-varietal-type wines at bargain prices. You can still buy Chilean Cab produced from mostly high-yielding vineyards for under $10, but you can also find *terroir*-driven, single-vineyard wines from the Maipo, Colchagua, Aconcagua, and Curico wine regions with high prices to match their pedigree.

In Argentina, there is some varietal Cabernet Sauvignon produced, but Cab is most often reserved for blending with the nation's premier red wine, Malbec. At their best, these wines can exhibit assertive aromatics and complex flavors that make for some ageworthy wines with attractive prices.

Australia and New Zealand

Shiraz (Australia's name for the Syrah grape) is the showstopper in the vineyards of Australia and enjoys both critical and popular acclaim in the bottle. But Australia produces a lot of full-bodied, jammy Cabernet Sauvignon, too, and just as with Shiraz, it does so at every conceivable price point—from under $10 to over $100, and every price in between these extremes. Cabernet Sauvignon/Shiraz blends are also quite popular and can be delicious.

Wines labeled "Southeastern Australia" are value-driven, consumer-friendly wines, while Cab exhibiting the appellation "South Australia" is likely to kick it up a notch when it comes to quality and

Almaviva is consistently one of the finest—and most expensive—Cabernet Sauvignon wines from Chile's Maipo Valley.

price. The best Australian Cabernet Sauvignon originates in the vineyards of the Coonawarra region, followed closely by wines produced from grapes grown in McLaren Vale, Margaret River, or Clare Valley.

New Zealand produces some lovely Cabs as well as Cabernet Sauvignon/Merlot blends from vineyards in the Hawke's Bay region, located on the southern tip of the nation's North Island.

South Africa

A small number of wine producers in the Stellenbosch region of South Africa make some very fine Cabernet Sauvignon, sometimes blended with Merlot.

Merlot
Merlot: The profile

"Cabernet Sauvignon on Prozac" is one of the best definitions we've heard for most of the Merlot-based wines produced in the world today. Merlot is too often turned into a wine that has no rough edges and poses little or no challenge either to the drinker's palate or to his or her food. The Merlot grape is a fabulous blender with Cabernet Sauvignon, but with few notable exceptions—particularly wines produced from grapes grown in the vineyards of Bordeaux's

Merlot grapes. (Ben Fink/Jupiterimages)

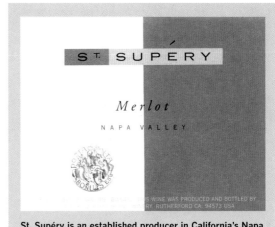

St. Supéry is an established producer in California's Napa Valley; the winery produces excellent Merlot.

Pomerol and St-Emilion districts—this varietal does not often make a compelling wine when left on its own in a bottle.

Merlot is wildly successful around the world, pleasing wine consumers in the Old World, but especially in the New World, and specifically in the United States. Merlot is the ultimate feel-good red, making wines that feature aromas and flavors of ripe, sweet chocolate-covered black cherries tinged with oaky vanilla overtones, complete with a silky, sexy, voluptuous texture. Most wines made from Merlot are predictable fun and don't require a lot of thought and analysis to enjoy; they're more of a one-night stand than a long-term relationship.

Stories of our friends and family members who "don't like red wines" but "*love* Merlot" abound, and with good reason. Most Merlot is completely accessible, from its juicy, rich, sweet flavors and its low levels of tannin and acid to its wide range of price points. While consumer-driven Merlot may not be the greatest match with many foods, it does work well with some and is usually at least inoffensive to others. Most Merlot is a modern miracle of marketing in that it is made with the consumer in mind, and the styles of the finished wines made from this grape fit the parameters of market research and prognostication.

Until the 1980s, Merlot was viewed as a blender, often used to soften the tannins and acids of Cabernet Sauvignon. When Merlot started to become more

A Merlot vineyard in the Pomerol region of Bordeaux, France, where Classic Old-World Merlot-based wines are produced. (Photo courtesy of Pomerol.org)

popular as a stand-alone varietal, the Napa Valley legend Robert Mondavi refused to produce a Merlot because he didn't think it made a very complete wine; he thought of it as kind of "hollow." What we think he meant is that Merlot doesn't often transform into a wine that is well balanced; it lacks what is sometimes called a good "middle palate," the weight and presence of the wine after its initial attack on the tongue and in the mouth. Classic wines display a fine middle palate, almost like a dotted line across the middle of your tongue. Except in rare cases, Merlot doesn't behave like this.

And yet there is great, fabulous, even otherworldly Merlot produced from relatively thin-skinned grapes grown in the cold clay and iron-rich soils of Pomerol and the sand/limestone/gravel soils of St. Emilion, both located on the "right bank" of Bordeaux (see pages 158–159). What is interesting about these wines is that they go against the grain of modern Merlot. They are not "Pow! In your face!" jammy-fruit and big-alcohol bombs, but are much lighter, more delicate, better balanced, and made to grace our dining tables, especially when we might be enjoying lamb, beef, or cheeses. Ironically, these wines tend to age much longer than the bigger, brawnier Merlot that many of us have come to know and enjoy.

For the "Merlot Majority," aging is hardly an issue, as we drink most Merlot within a few years of its vintage date. If we stop on the way home at the wine shop or supermarket and pick up a couple of bottles of two-to-three-year-old varietal-labeled Merlot from California or Washington State or Chile or wherever, we'll probably be happily drinking that puppy within the week. In a restaurant, we are likely to order a Merlot that makes us comfortable and content—one we've tasted before and enjoyed. Even if we're trying a New World Merlot we've never had before, it's unlikely that our first consideration is its age. No, aging Merlot—unless it is a great wine from a great estate—not only is unnecessary, but in most cases it's a bad idea. Unlike Cabernet Sauvignon, the grape with which it is so closely aligned in wine consciousness, Merlot usually lacks the tannins, acids, and overall structure that lead a wine to seriously improve with time.

Because Merlot is so popular, it is planted in almost all of the wine regions of the world except for the absolute coldest places. From Switzerland to Slovenia, from New Zealand to New York, from Austria to Australia, from Argentina to Italy, from South America to South Africa, Merlot is grown just about everywhere. Here are some of the countries and regions you're likely to encounter on the Merlot map.

A Sonoma gem. Matanzas Creek has long been recognized as one of the finest Merlot producers in the United States.

France

Merlot is the most planted grape in the Bordeaux region of France (see pages 151–159), and as the world clamors for soft, easy-to-drink reds, its varietal star is ascending here. While it plays a supporting role in the wines from the "Left Bank" of Bordeaux (including the Haut-Médoc and Graves regions), it is the star of the show on the "Right Bank" (Pomerol and St-Emilion) and in the satellite appellations that produce accessible, less-expensive Bordeaux wines.

Merlot is the third most frequently planted red grape in all of France, and its popularity is growing every year. It is grown throughout Provence and the southwest, and in the southern province of Languedoc, among many others. It may be used as the main grape or as a blender in these regions, and many *vins de pays* (see page 144)—inexpensive French wines with varietal labels—are 100% Merlot.

Italy

Merlot is huge in Italy (see pages 180–213), with plantings growing exponentially over the last decade or so. The northeastern regions mostly produce wines of no great distinction from vineyards with high yields, but they are easy to drink and affordable.

In the vineyards of Tuscany, Merlot has become an important grape for producing dozens of wines (see pages 189–193). Sometimes Cabernet Sauvignon is blended with Merlot, or with Merlot and Sangiovese, to create the very popular—and oftentimes very expensive—"Super Tuscans."

The rest of Europe

Merlot is planted in the warmer vineyard sites of Austria, Hungary, Romania, Bulgaria, and Moldova. In these countries the wines produced from the Merlot grape or from Merlot/Cabernet Sauvignon blends are drinkable and affordable. But it is in Switzerland's Italian-speaking Ticino region where Merlot positively dominates, producing some predictable quaffs and a few glorious wines.

The United States: California

The wines produced from the Merlot grape in California are much like the stereotypical images of Californians themselves: laid-back and mellow. The Golden State produces wines that are fruit-forward with sweet dark berry flavors, and most often low in acids and tannins. Styles range from light and fruity to massive and complex, but the wines are almost always silky, satiny, and smooth on the palate.

A lot of Merlot is planted in the very warm Central Valley. These wines are simple, easy-to-drink good values that taste like Merlot and work well with a burger, a sandwich, or a slice of pizza; they are not meant to knock your socks, or even one sock, off.

Merlot with more character is derived from the vineyards of California's cooler North Coast wine districts, especially Napa, Sonoma, and Mendocino counties. These wines are darker in color and more concentrated in flavor, and feature ripe-to-overripe fruit flavors in an often full-bodied, even massive high-alcohol wine. Some of these wines, especially those from the Napa Valley, can be very expensive and hard to find. In Sonoma County, the vineyards and

A fun label for a serious wine. L'Ecole No. 41, a moderately small producer, makes one of Washington's top Merlot wines from its estate in the Walla Walla wine region.

wineries of Sonoma Valley, Alexander Valley, and Dry Creek Valley also produce some fine Merlot wines.

Other states

Washington State has developed quite a reputation for the quality of its Merlot wines, both on the small-producer "boutique" level and the grand scale. Growers in the Columbia Valley and Walla Walla districts have to work hard to make sure all is right in the vineyard and have to pray for winters that are not too frigid. Washington State Merlot is second only to Chardonnay in total acres planted, and Merlot is the most important red grape in the entire Pacific Northwest wine industry.

South America: Chile

Merlot is affordable and tastes good to most wine consumers, and when you're paying about $10 at retail for a bottle of wine, those are usually the criteria for meeting customer expectations.

Australia and New Zealand

Although plantings of Merlot are increasing every year in Australia, it is a grape that has yet to really catch on as the basis for varietal-labeled wines (only 4% to 5% of its vineyards are planted with Merlot). Add to this the tradition of blending Shiraz—not Merlot—with Cabernet Sauvignon, and Australia has a bit of a learning curve to get over when it comes to producing Merlot on a large scale. Most of Australia is quite warm—ideal for Cabernet Sauvignon, but not cool enough for Merlot.

New Zealand is cooler than Australia, and the southern tip of the North Island may be an ideal climate to grow Merlot. Indeed, Merlot is New Zealand's third most frequently planted grape (Chardonnay and Sauvignon Blanc are first and second, respectively, making Merlot the most-planted red grape in the nation).

Merlot is not yet a major varietal wine in Australia, but its popularity is growing. This bottling from Stonehaven is fruity, medium-bodied, and attractively priced.

Pinot Noir
Pinot Noir: The profile

Pinot Noir is a very finicky grape that defies definition when it comes to style and expectation in the finished wine. Pinot Noir celebrates both its sense of place and the cult of the individual: where it is grown and who is growing it play significant roles in determining the character of the finished wine.

Growing Pinot Noir is not for everybody. Indeed, people who happily grow Chardonnay, Cabernet Sauvignon, and other less tricky varietals are often petrified by the idea of growing Pinot Noir. It isn't so much that these growers are incapable of doing a good job in the vineyards and the winery; it's that everybody has his or her own opinion on what a "good job" is when it comes to judging wines made from this grape.

More a cliché than a statement of certifiable fact is that the best wines made from Pinot Noir should mimic wines from Burgundy, France, where the grape has been cultivated for at least six hundred years and

Pinot Noir grapes. (©Jack K. Clark/Corbis)

rosé than true red wines; others are ponderous, heavy, and overtly alcoholic. Not to evade the question, but it is difficult to describe the ideal Pinot Noir because there are so many different styles available in the marketplace. So likeability becomes a question of very personal taste. In describing the ideal Pinot Noir, we're reminded of a quote by Supreme Court Justice Potter Stewart who in 1964 was asked to define obscenity: "I know it when I see it." This quote by one of the Supremes can be easily adapted to describing the ideal Pinot Noir: "I know it when I taste it."

Still, we want to be helpful to our readers, so when it comes to flavor, let's consider the broad strokes of Pinot Noir. If we can agree that with Pinot Noir you usually get what you pay for—an axiom that is perhaps truer for this varietal than for any other—then we can report some general observations. Bargain-priced Pinot Noir made for early drinking can be charming in its simplicity, tasting of strawberries and, to a lesser extent, cranberries and red raspberries. As you move up the quality ladder, the wines take on more complexity, with a mix of spiced strawberries and black cherries, as well as noticeably higher acidity on the palate. The most complex examples of fine Pinot Noir will demonstrate aromas and tastes of both red and black fruits, but in an earthbound, funky wrap of mushroom, leather, charred wood, smoke, and moist

possibly more than sixteen hundred. Pinot Noir is celebrated in Burgundy and is by law the only red grape allowed to be grown on its best vineyard sites. The beauty of great red Burgundy wine is also precisely the problem with Pinot Noir: each one tastes different. Each wine might taste wonderful, even seductive, but each seduces differently; one plays off its youthful energy and exuberance to choreograph a lusty dance of desirability, while another relies on its experience and voluptuous maturity to lure us into a garden of delights. When it comes to red Burgundy, one size does not fit all, and to define good Pinot Noir based on the "Burgundy model" is tired and meaningless.

Yet good Pinot Noir is the most food-friendly red wine on the planet. Balanced, with subtle fruits, bracing acidity, and moderate tannins, it is a wine that will pair with a myriad of foods, except for the most intense and the absolute lightest. This is a wine that is comfortable with grilled fish, pasta, roasted vegetables, most red meat dishes, game, poultry, and cheeses. Pinot Noir pairs with sashimi, with Thai, Cambodian, Vietnamese, and Chinese dishes; with many classic Middle Eastern foods, and on and on and on . . .

Of course, the wine world abounds with a lot of Pinot Noir that, if not really bad, certainly needs work. Some are way too light, more like unbalanced

Bouchaine is the oldest continuously operating winery in Carneros, a wine region that traverses both Napa and Sonoma counties and is known for its cool-climate Pinot Noir and Chardonnay.

soil. These wines can age from five to ten years and even longer, and are usually rare and expensive.

Pinot Noir is a thin-skinned grape that traditionally grows best in cool climates, such as Burgundy and Champagne in France, parts of Germany, Austria, and northeastern Italy. The Willamette Valley of Oregon and the coolest vineyard sites of Australia and New Zealand show great promise. The cooler growing areas of California—Carneros, Russian River, Anderson Valley—are also part of the mix.

Cool weather allows Pinot Noir to develop attractively high levels of acidity, although it can make ideal ripening difficult. Because the grape is light-colored and thin-skinned, tannins are usually soft and subtle. When all of the elements of nature collide successfully, Pinot Noir vineyards can provide the raw material for glorious medium-bodied wines. But these elements strike a delicate balance, and when things go wrong in the vineyard, the result can just as easily be wines that are unpleasant, sometimes with green, unripe flavors, sometimes with flavors of cooked and stewed fruits, overripe and foul.

There is no real consensus about what kind of soil is best for growing Pinot Noir, but most growers agree to disagree over soils rich in either limestone or clay. What almost all growers do agree on is that the soil must be well drained and not overly fertile, to keep yields low.

Winemakers have been known to add some Syrah (discussed next in this chapter) or other deeply colored wine to ramp up the color and body of Pinot Noir, but the best wines express their individual *terroir*—their sense of place—without the addition of other wines or the use of technological manipulation. In fact, Pinot Noir is probably the most *terroir*-driven of all red wines (it's Riesling for whites); certainly the Burgundians think so.

Burgundy's best vineyard sites (see page 160) are officially rated and government-certified as *premier cru* (first growth) and the even grander *grand cru* (great growth). The wines produced from these vineyards can be moderately to wildly expensive, and many are produced in such small amounts that most of us will never get to taste them even if we could afford them.

Since fine Pinot Noir is so site-dependent, it's time for us to take a quick look at some of the places that grow and produce some of the best examples of this wine.

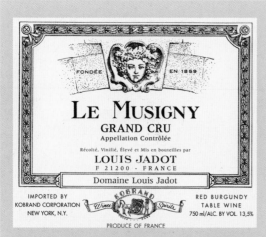

A very expensive wine from Burgundy, France, made from 100% Pinot Noir grapes. Le Musigny is a *grand cru* vineyard in the village of Chambolle-Musigny and is one of the finest Pinot Noir sites in the world. (Courtesy of Kobrand Corporation)

Dutton Estate produces extraordinary single-vineyard, site-specific Pinot Noir in the very cool Russian River Valley in Sonoma County, California. Dutton Estate wines are produced in small quantities and are quite expensive; they are worth every penny.

New Zealand is making a name for itself with cool-climate Pinot Noir. Grove Mill makes a very good wine in the Marlborough region.

France: Burgundy and Champagne

In Burgundy, the only red grape planted in the northern subregions of Cote de Nuits and Cote de Beaune (collectively known as Cote d'Or) is Pinot Noir (see pages 164–166). Here, *terroir* carries the day, as wines produced from a small vineyard, or a small part of a larger vineyard, will taste noticeably different from a vineyard site less than a thousand feet down the road.

There is also a lot of drinkable Pinot Noir from Burgundy that is more affordable than the most prized reds from the Cote d'Or, produced a bit further south in the Cote Chalonnaise subregion (see page 166).

In the Champagne region (see page 167), Pinot Noir is one of only three grapes; the other two are the red Pinot Meunier and the white Chardonnay. These are the only legal grapes in Champagne, and most Champagnes are made from a blend of wines made from varying percentages of these grapes. Champagne is the coldest wine region in all of France, and Pinot Noir ripens just enough to produce a wine that is high in acidity, which meshes beautifully with bubbles to refresh our palates. Since most Champagne is a white sparkling wine, there is very little skin contact—the skin is where all the color is—when Pinot Noir grapes are fermented.

The rest of Europe

Pinot Noir also grows in Germany (see page 250), where it is known as Spatburgunder, and in Austria (see page 260), where the grape is often called Blauer Burgunder. In Italy (see pages 180–211), where it is sometimes called Pinot Nero, the varietal is grown in Lombardy, where it is an essential constituent of the excellent sparkler Franciacorta. Pinot Noir is also widely planted in the Alto Adige region, where it produces fine still wine.

The United States: California and Oregon

California (see page 67) had to navigate a massive learning curve to succeed with Pinot Noir, and even today great California Pinot Noir is a rarity, though a sublime one. The coolest regions—Carneros, which is a shared appellation between Napa and Sonoma counties; the Russian River Valley in Sonoma; the Anderson Valley in Mendocino; the Santa Maria Valley in Santa Barbara; Santa Ynez in San Luis Obispo; and Mount Harlan in San Benito—are some of the premier growing regions for Pinot Noir.

The knock against California's Pinot Noir has been that the wines lack balance and are too jammy, too alcoholic, too "big," too Cabernet-like. California winemakers still produce some of these big bruisers, but more and more we are tasting Pinot Noir that is made with a gentle touch, with restraint.

Oregon (see page 99) is at the same latitude as Burgundy, and it has developed a well-earned reputation for its Pinot Noir. In particular, the Willamette Valley is one of the greatest places in the entire New World for growing this grape. The best of these wines are delicate but substantive and beautifully balanced. The overwhelming majority of Oregon Pinot Noir winemakers are artisans, producing small amounts of very fine wines. Prices run the gamut from bargains to very expensive, and quality runs from good basic varietal character to very special and rare, true to vineyard *terroir* and vintage conditions.

The Southern Hemisphere: Chile, New Zealand, Australia

Pinot Noir seems to have a bright future in the Southern Hemisphere. Chile's coastal Casablanca Valley (see page 112), which is best known for nurturing Chardonnay and Sauvignon Blanc, also provides a good home for Pinot Noir, producing very appealing wines that strike a balance between delicacy and juicy ripeness.

Down under, Pinot Noir looks like an upcoming star in New Zealand (see page 128). In the Martinborough region, on the southern tip of its North Island, and in Central Otago, on the southern tip of its South Island, cool-climate New Zealand is producing some very exciting and delicious Pinot Noir.

Australia (see page 120) produces a handful of good Pinot Noir wines, but it is still a newcomer here, with the Yarra Valley, located on the outskirts of Melbourne in the state of Victoria, showing real promise. Only about 2% of vineyard plantings in Australia are Pinot Noir, and much of the fruit is utilized quite successfully as part of the blend for *méthode champenoise* sparkling wines.

Syrah/Shiraz
Syrah/Shiraz: The profile

Syrah and Shiraz are actually the same grape, but with different names. "Syrah" is the Old World (European) name for the grape, while "Shiraz" is definitely a New World moniker, closely identified with, but not limited to, Australia.

There is more Syrah planted in France than anywhere else on earth (about 100,000 acres [40,000 hectares]), and Australia plants at least 70,000 acres (28,000 hectares) of Shiraz, securing second place. The United States and Argentina—both "Syrah" or "Shiraz" occur on wine labels from these countries—are in a virtual tie for third place, with about 12,000 acres (4,800 hectares) planted in each country. The

Syrah/Shiraz grapes. (©Lance Nelson/Corbis)

popularity of Syrah/Shiraz is growing, and plantings are increasing dramatically worldwide.

In Europe, the classic growing region for Syrah is the northern Rhone Valley of France (see page 174). The most famous Syrah vineyards in the world reside in the Hermitage, Cote-Rotie, St-Joseph, Cornas, and Crozes-Hermitage appellations, all of which give their names to heralded wines. This region is one of the coolest place in the world for growing Syrah, but its heat-retaining slopes, composed of granite soils, help to make ripening of the grape possible.

In the New World, the terms "Shiraz" and "Australia" (see page 120) have become synonymous. Original vine cuttings for Shiraz were brought from the Hermitage district of the Rhone Valley to Australia in the nineteenth century, and vineyards are located in various parts of the states of South Australia and New South Wales, with fewer plantings in the cooler states of Victoria and Western Australia. Overall, Australia's vineyards are the warmest sites in the world for growing Shiraz.

There are so many different styles of Syrah/Shiraz wines in the market that it is difficult to make any broad generalizations about its flavor and food-friendliness. The wine can be fashioned as a light-to-medium-bodied easy sipper that loves to accompany a burger and fries eaten at the beach, or as a massive

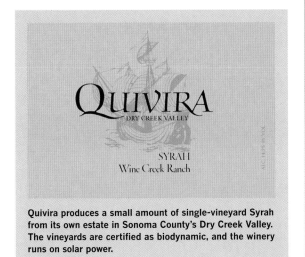

Quivira produces a small amount of single-vineyard Syrah from its own estate in Sonoma County's Dry Creek Valley. The vineyards are certified as biodynamic, and the winery runs on solar power.

in-your-face bruiser that needs braised short ribs and creamy mashed potatoes, preferably enjoyed in front of a fireplace during a snowstorm. In between these two extremes is a full gamut of Syrah/Shiraz styles, from sunny simplicity to extraordinarily earthy elegance.

Add to the multiple personalities of Syrah/Shiraz the fact that it is an excellent blending grape with a wide variety of both red and white varietals, and you might be forgiven for thinking that Syrah/Shiraz is just about the ideal wine grape. Actually, there may be no reason for forgiveness, as grape growers, winemakers, and wine consumers have embraced this varietal with wild enthusiasm. Syrah/Shiraz, perhaps to the exclusion of all other candidates, is slated to join the Chardonnay/Cabernet Sauvignon pantheon, creating a wine lover's trinity of taste.

Note: "Petite Sirah" is not Syrah and is not supposed to be Shiraz (though some people have their doubts). Petite Sirah is actually Durif, a grape whose ancestral home is the southern Rhone Valley. Petite Sirah wines, which are almost always big, bold, brawny, and brooding, can be very good, but they also can be over the top in terms of their alcoholic punch. There are some terrific, balanced Petite Sirah wines made in California, where the grape has a long history.

France: The Rhone Valley and Languedoc-Roussillon

As we mentioned earlier, the northern Rhone Valley defines classic Old World Syrah. The steep slopes, rich in granite soil, provide just enough sunshine and warmth for full ripening, but not too much. At their best, the Rhone wines made from Syrah are redolent of black fruits, feature complex earthy aromas, have a lovely tannin/acid balance, and offer a kick of cracked black pepper in the nose and in the mouth. Depending on what district the grapes are grown in, the wines can be lighter or darker in color, medium or full in body, with flavors that span from jammy to roasted fruits. Prices are all over the place, starting at around $15 for Crozes-Hermitage and approaching $75 and up for great single-vineyard Cote-Rotie and Hermitage wines. Rhone Valley wines are still a little bit of a secret in the U.S. market, and good value at all price points is the rule.

The Languedoc-Roussillon area, the "Midi" of the south of France, actually has twice as many Syrah vines planted as the Rhone Valley. Here an endless stream of drinkable and affordable varietal-labeled Syrah and Syrah blends are produced from very warm vineyard sites under the large Vin de Pays d'Oc appellation name.

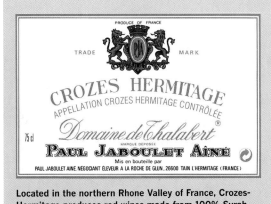

Located in the northern Rhone Valley of France, Crozes-Hermitage produces red wines made from 100% Syrah grapes; these can represent solid value for the consumer. Jaboulet is an established, multigeneration wine producer in the Rhone Valley.

The rest of Europe

We find small patches of Syrah planted all over Italy, where there are some producers making 100% Syrah wines, but many are blended with Italian varietals, especially Sangiovese in Tuscany and Nero d'Avola in Sicily. Several of these Italian wines are sold in the United States. Syrah is planted in the Valais region of Switzerland, and Swiss Syrah can be very tasty, but it is virtually invisible in the U.S. market.

The United States: California and Washington State

In the United States, we grow the grape and make the wine under either name, Syrah or Shiraz. California (see page 67) has been planting Syrah/Shiraz in earnest since the 1970s with the advent of the "Rhone Rangers," a group of producers who planted several varietals known to flourish in the Rhone Valley, Syrah chief among them. After a slow start in terms of consumer acceptance, California Syrah/Shiraz is now much sought after by wine lovers.

Syrah has become an important wine in Washington State and has garnered much attention. Hogue is a major wine producer in the Columbia Valley; the wines are good values.

Shiraz defines the Australian wine industry and is grown in many parts of the country. Reynolds makes this wine from grapes grown in the cool Orange wine district of New South Wales. The wine is a great value.

The label of Sin Zin, produced by Alexander Valley Vineyards, captures the hedonistic pleasure of California Zinfandel.

Today, Syrah/Shiraz is being planted in California's best wine-growing regions; the challenge is to find vineyard sites that are not too warm so that the finished wine is not a high-alcohol, full-bodied heady fruit soup. The best California Syrah/Shiraz wines, made from vineyards located in the cooler coastal regions of the Golden State, can be excellent, and tend to follow the Rhone model of Syrah. Wines of restrained, earthy power, they are great with hearty foods.

Washington State (see page 94) has gotten religion when it comes to Syrah/Shiraz, which is poised to replace Merlot as its most planted red grape. Here, Syrah/Shiraz thrives in the cooler climes of the Columbia Valley, the Walla Walla area, and especially the Yakima Valley. The best wines are deceptively soft and supple, with ripe, even sweet fruit flavors, but with balanced tannins and acidity; wines that are enjoyable now or ten years from now.

Australia

It's as simple as this: without Shiraz, there is no modern Australian wine industry. Australia (see page 120) has been growing Shiraz since the early 1800s, and for most of that time it was considered to be a reliable but undistinguished varietal; the future was all about Cabernet Sauvignon. Ha!

Starting in about 1990, Shiraz came out of its shell, and it came out big-time. With an international marketing push and with some very good wines that fit in perfectly with the New World wine drinker's shift from delicate wines to "Pow! Right in the kisser!" wines, people began to fall in love with Shiraz. In addition, you can buy varietal-labeled Shiraz from "Oz" for prices starting at about five bucks per bottle, as well as at every other price point imaginable; whatever the price, the wine is perceived as a very good value. Plus Shiraz fits the new, less formal bistro-style approach to dining that is permeating New World cultures. Take all these together, and it's clear that Australian Shiraz is the right wine at the right time. The Aussies even produce sparkling Shiraz for those of us who are bubbleheads.

Australian Shiraz continues its meteoric success in the international market and has spurred interest in the Syrah/Shiraz category in general.

Zinfandel
Zinfandel: The profile

When you listen to the 1970s Joni Mitchell song "California" or the Eagles' "Hotel California," do so with a glass of Zinfandel close by. Zinfandel is, if not by fact then at least by legend, California's own wine grape, and California is home to ZAP: Zinfandel Advocates and Producers, a not-for-profit group located in Rough and Ready, California, and solely dedicated to spreading the gospel about Zinfandel through its Zinposium series and its annual ZAP Festival—kind of like Burning Man, but most people keep their clothes on.

Zinfandel grapes. (©Jack K. Clark/Corbis)

So what if Zinfandel and the Italian grape Primitivo have the same DNA? Think of it as California's gift to Italy, even though nobody knows for sure where the grape originated. For a while it was thought to be Croatia, but no one is ever going to convince a wine-stained California Zin lover that the Left Coast is anything less than the spiritual home of its beloved varietal. And no one can deny that whatever the grape's patrimony, it was California that put Zinfandel on the map and a sumptuous wine in the glass.

We need to set the record straight: Zinfandel is a red grape, actually close to black in color. The reason we bring this up is that many of the un-Zinitiated think only of White Zinfandel, which is a pale pink wine, really a semidry to semisweet light-bodied rosé "cocktail" wine (under $10 and great with spicy pan-Asian flavors), pressed from Zinfandel grapes but with minimal skin contact (the skin is where all the color is).

The beauty of the real thing, however—deep, dark, rich, earthy red Zinfandel wine—begins in the warmer vineyard sites of California. Zin loves heat, and this is one of the few varietals that can actually benefit from a bit of overripening. The best climate combination for Zinfandel is a summer filled with really hot days (from 90°F/32°C and up) and pretty cool nights [a drop to 40° to 50°F(4.5° to 10°C)], enabling the grower to preserve both high degrees of ripeness and sufficient acidity in the grapes. California has at least 50,000 acres (20,000 hectares) of Zinfandel vines planted, and the best vineyards fit this ideal climate profile to a T (or in this case, to a Z).

The other wonderful thing about Zinfandel planted in California is that there are a lot of "old vines." Old-vine Zinfandel, made from grape vines planted in poorer soils and dry-farmed (no drip irrigation), often organically grown, with naturally lower yields, makes for wines of compelling complexity and depth. Sometimes the term "old vines" or "old vine" will appear on a label, but you should know there is no legal meaning for the term.

If you go to the ZAP Web site (www.zinfandel.org), you can jump to the Zinfandel Aroma Wheel, which is intriguing because it contains just about every smell known to wine and then some, and allows you to offer up new ones. It is true that, depending on the style of the finished wine, Zin can exhibit a wide variety of aromas: red fruits in a light wine, dried black fruits in a full-bodied version, a hint of black pepper in a young Zinfandel, dark chocolate

Joel Peterson, founder of Ravenswood, makes a wide variety of Zinfandel wines from select California vineyards and at several different price points.

Since 1969, Paul Draper of Ridge Vineyards has made some of the most elegant California Zinfandels from grapes grown on prized sites in Napa and Sonoma counties, the Santa Cruz Mountains, and Paso Robles.

in a mature, Port-style Zin. Confusing? Maybe a little. Basically, what you want to look for in any good glass of Zinfandel is the assertive aromas of fruits—red raspberries, cranberries, strawberries in the lightest versions, black cherries, black plums, even raisins and black figs in the brooding, big Zins. A pleasant smattering of herbs provides some grace notes, as do oak-barrel-inspired spice and vanilla.

Lighter Zins, which in reality are usually at least medium-bodied, are great wines for burgers, pizza, pasta, and roasted or grilled veggies. The big, earthy wines, which, when they are balanced and aged for about five years, are truly Zen Zins, are wonderful with hearty dishes, roasted or braised, as well as beef or pork barbecue. Leg of lamb and a hearty old-vine Zinfandel is such a sensual match, it's practically Zinful.

A good word about the price of Zinfandel wines: you can spend a lot of money on single-vineyard old vine, dry-farmed, organically grown Zin from a boutique winery, or you can spend five or six bucks in the supermarket or wine shop on a bottle by a mass-market producer. We have found that with very few exceptions Zin = pleasure no matter the price. There are no other varietals that spring to mind that provide such a democratic and egalitarian wine experience. Maybe the reason that Zinfandel has become a cult wine in California and elsewhere is that it cuts through all the nonsense of class-based wine snobbery and delivers that pleasure, that fun, at a price that everyone who drinks wine can afford. Don't be afraid to try a Zinfandel that sells for under $10 (and there are many of them); it may just become your favorite "house" wine.

Philosophically, Zinfandel and its place in the world have been summed up beautifully by Joel Peterson, the founder of California's Ravenswood winery, and one of the original ZAP members. When Joel created Ravenswood's tag line, he said a glassful about what Zin should—and should not—be. Taking its place among the greatest statements of all time, right next to $E = mc^2$, "Cogito, ergo sum," and "The check is in the mail," is the definitive Zinfandel proclamation: "No Wimpy Wines." When it comes to Zin, that says it all.

While Zinfandel grapes grow in several states, it is California that defines Zinfandel for Americans. Internationally, Italy is by far the most important producer of Zinfandel, but under its Italian name, Primitivo. Australia, Chile, Mexico, and South Africa also produce a small amount of Zin. We applaud the growing of this grape everywhere that it will make good wine, but in our hearts we know that when we want the real thing, we'll be livin' it up at the Hotel California.

Zinfandel in California

Zinfandel is the second most frequently planted red grape in California (Cabernet Sauvignon is first), and depending on where it is planted and when it was planted, results in the grapes and finished wines can be dramatically different.

Sonoma County grows a lot of Zinfandel, and producers here make some excellent wines, especially in the Dry Creek Valley wine district. Warm days and cool nights give Dry Creek Zin a perfect platform to excel. The slightly warmer Alexander Valley is also a fine place to grow the grape. Sonoma is home to several single-vineyard Zinfandel wines, which display their sense of place with delicious dignity.

The Napa Valley can produce some extraordinary Zinfandel, but here Zin lives in the shadow of Cabernet Sauvignon. Old-vine Zinfandel from the Redwood Valley of Mendocino County vineyards make some of the state's best wines. Paso Robles has some old vines, too, and has made quite a reputation for itself with artisanal Zinfandel from its boulder-strewn soils. In Santa Cruz, Paul Draper of Ridge Vineyards continues to make what many consider to be the finest Zinfandel wines ever produced in the history of the world; these wines really are singular and remarkable.

The Sierra Foothills wine region is synonymous with Zinfandel; more than 80% of the vineyards there are dedicated to the grape. There is quite a bit of old-vine Zin here, and the wines from both small and larger producers can be earthy, complex, and memorable.

In the very warm San Joaquin Valley, quite a bit of Zinfandel is grown, and a lot of it ends up in bargain-brand Zins; some is used for blending into other varietal-labeled wines. But the Lodi area, where the breezes from the Delta cool things off, produces some good, small-producer Zin, some of it from old vines.

Italy

In Italy (see pages 180–211) the grape is called Primitivo, and the wine world didn't take notice of it until 1994, when researchers at the University of California at Davis proved that Primitivo and Zinfandel have the same DNA. Since the DNA discovery, the southern province of Puglia has begun to specialize in Primitivo; most of these wines are quite satisfying and, in the true spirit of Zin, quite affordable.

Grenache

Grenache: The profile

Just a few (hundred) words about Grenache (Garnacha in Spanish). Grenache is the most widely planted red grape in the world, with most of those grapes growing in Spain (at least 225,000 acres [90,000 hectares]) and France (about 125,000 acres [50,000 hectares]). There is quite a bit planted in Italy (where it is sometimes known as Cannonau), and substantial amounts are found in Australia and California.

Although Grenache is beginning to develop a fine reputation both as a varietal and as a friendly

CHÂTEAUNEUF DU PAPE

Les Cèdres

PAUL JABOULET AÎNÉ

TAIN L'HERMITAGE - FRANCE

Chateauneuf-du-Pape, a justifiably famous wine from the southern Rhone Valley of France, can legally be made from as many as thirteen different grapes, but the blend is anchored by Grenache.

partner in blended wines, it hasn't always enjoyed its place in the sun. Grenache thrives on hot weather and can achieve very high degrees of sugar in its grape juice (which means it can achieve very high degrees of alcohol as a wine), and it has often been used to give some alcoholic "oomph" to weaker wines. Until recently, the only place that Grenache has received anything close to a full measure of respect is in the southern Rhone Valley, where it is often the anchor of the famous blended wine Chateauneuf-du-Pape (see page 174), among others. But lately things have been looking up for Grenache.

Some very good varietal-label Grenache and blends are being produced from grapes grown in Australia and in California. In Spain (see page 214), where this grape has always been taken for granted as a workhorse, old-vine Garnacha is producing magnificent wines in the Priorat region, even as it continues to be an important constituent in the red wines of Rioja, but subservient to the more esteemed Tempranillo grape. In the Navarra region, Garnacha makes some of the loveliest dry rosé wines in the world, just as Grenache does in the Tavel region of the southern Rhone Valley. On the Italian island of Sardinia, Cannonau can produce some delicious, earthy red wines.

Grenache was born to blend with Syrah and another red Rhone resident, Mourvedre. (It is not uncommon to see New World wines labeled as "GSM," which the cognoscenti recognize as a blend of Grenache, Syrah, and Mourvedre.) This blend is also the base for much fine Old World Chateauneuf-du-Pape. These blended wines, whether they are produced in the Old World or the New, can be exciting and soul-satisfying, perfect winter warmers with stews and roasts.

Grenache grapes. (Photo courtesy of Kobrand Corporation)

chapter 4

Living in the USA
California

There is probably no better time in history to be an American wine drinker. So many wines from so many wine regions, both established and off the beaten path, are available that it truly is an embarrassment of riches. How to choose from all of the gems that line the shelves of wine shops and supermarkets and jump off the pages of wine lists?

When it comes to wine, Americans, no matter their political leanings, seem to be of one mind, one heart, one palate. We love our country's wines, and we vote with our wallets and purses for wines produced in the United States. American wine consumers are a patriotic bunch: mostly, we "drink American," while enthusiastically dabbling with foreign wines from all over the planet.

Many of us have become *"locavores"* when it comes to enjoying food and wine, and that's great because all 50 states produce wines for an increasing audience of Americans. Still, there is only one 800-pound gorilla in America's wine cellar that cannot be ignored, and that commanding presence is California . . . .

The new American wine culture

BY THE TIME YOU READ THIS PAGE, the United States will be well on its way to becoming the world's number one wine-consuming nation, a position it is predicted to hold before the year 2010. This rise in consumption represents a true sea change for a country and culture that in the past has been far more identified with beer and spirits. There are some compelling reasons why the United States has risen to the top when it comes to wine consumption, including the following facts:

- There are now more than 5,000 wineries in the United States, and every state, including Alaska and Hawaii, takes part in that total. Twenty-five years ago, there were about 1,500 wineries; thirty years ago there were only about 250. Forty of the fifty states have commercial vineyards; the others buy grapes or juice from other states. And wine has become big business in the United States. The wine industry contributes more than $60 billion to the U.S. economy and provides close to 600,000 jobs.

- As Americans, we seem to love our own wines, but not just the wines of California. Nationwide,

The Wine World with a California Attitude

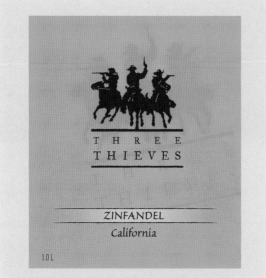

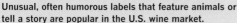

Unusual, often humorous labels that feature animals or tell a story are popular in the U.S. wine market.

Hells Canyon Winery in Idaho makes award-winning wine, including this delicious Cabernet Sauvignon Reserve.

we consume about 70% domestic wines. This patriotic percentage would probably be even higher, but the price-attractive wines of Australia, New Zealand, Argentina, and Chile are also quite popular here, accounting for about 15% of the total U.S. wine market.

- Wine is perceived as, and has been scientifically proven by physicians and researchers around the world to be, a healthy beverage when consumed with food and in moderation. In the minds of many Americans, wine has become a nearly guilt-free pleasure.

- Americans love to dine out in restaurants, and wine is an important part of that dining experience. Traditionally, "wine destination" restaurants are perceived as white-tablecloth venues where prices can be extravagant, but that perception is as dated as an over-the-hill bottle of Merlot. Dining and wine have become a lot more egalitarian, a lot more accessible. Starting in 2004, Olive Garden, the well-known kind-of-Italian restaurant chain, put together a chain-wide wine list of just thirty-eight wines, but with thirty-three of the wines available by the glass, all of them available to taste for free.

The result: Olive Garden gives away 35,000 cases of wine per year but sells 1 million cases per year, making the chain the No. 1 restaurant venue for wine sales in the entire country. In doing so, Olive Garden (and other wine-savvy restaurateurs and chains) has turned the idea of a "wine destination" restaurant on its ear. Clearly, wine has become a part of eating out, whether it's to grab a pizza or burger, a bowl of pasta and a salad, or an elaborate and formal multicourse dinner.

- Over the last decade there has been an increase of 35% to 40% in the total wine-drinking population of the United States, driven not only by people traditionally considered to be the American wine drinkers—male, white, middle- or upper-class, middle-aged or older—but also more by women, who now account for close to 65% of the wine purchased in the United States, and by younger wine drinkers. People in their twenties and early thirties love to try a wide variety of wines, especially what the industry calls "adventure brands," wines with curious and humorous names—Smashed Grapes, Smoking Loon, Plungerhead, 3 Blind Moose, Fat Bastard, Mad Housewife, Screw Kappa Napa, and, of

This sign, located on Highway 29 in the Napa Valley, is a symbolic gateway to the world of California wine.

course, Cat's Pee on a Gooseberry Bush are just eight examples among hundreds of such brands. These wines are tasty and fun and are also attractively priced, usually less than $12 per bottle (although a bottle of the elegant Used Automobile Parts is 50 bucks!).

- Per capita wine consumption has been dropping precipitously in France, Italy, Spain, and Portugal, nations that have been closely identified with wine as their national beverage of choice.

- Exports of French wine to the United States have suffered incremental losses in the past several years, while exports of Italian and Spanish wines have more than held their own in the United States. Portugal has begun to make some inroads in our market, but overall, with the exception of the fortified wine Port, Portugal is a minor player here.

- Exports of American wines have grown exponentially and now stand at more than $1 billion per year. About 60% of this wine is sold to the countries that make up the European Union (EU), even though the European wine industry is heavily subsidized by government and very tough taxes and tariffs are placed on American wines imported to EU member nations. In addition, Canada, Japan, and Mexico, the top three non-EU export markets, account for more than $225 million, or more than 20% of total wine exports.

- Ironically, our own per capita wine consumption still is quite low, even when compared to the sliding European per capita figures (an average of about 13 gallons [49 liters] per capita in Italy, France, and Spain, but only a little more than 2 gallons [7.5 liters per capita] in the United States). However, the combined population of Italy, France, and Spain is about 160 million; the population of the United States is about 300 million. While we appear to have a growing and dedicated core of wine drinkers, less than 15% of American wine drinkers consume more than 45% of total wine consumed in our country. What this means is that we have a lot of room to grow in both our per capita and total consumption, and since 1996 we have seen steady annual growth in one or both of these metrics.

The United States is developing a measurable and largely home-grown wine culture, and it doesn't just stop at increased wine consumption. The Napa Valley, for example, is the hottest tourist destination in California (Disneyland is second; think about it), but it may also surprise you to know that more than 750,000 people per year visit the vineyards and wineries of Virginia, and the spectacular Biltmore Estate, located in Asheville, North Carolina, is the most-visited winery in the United States. Wineries and vineyards have become tourist destinations, and wine has become a prominent symbol of a sophisticated, relaxed, and enjoyable American lifestyle, both at home and in restaurants. We see wine in our movies (remember *Sideways*?), our literature (and not just in wine books), our colleges (wine courses are immensely popular on campuses throughout the nation), and of course, television (note the rise of the Food Network and its various wine-conscious offspring). Wine software (some good, some not so good) abounds, and Web sites dedicated to wine (again, quality can be very high or very low) are literally innumerable.

There is no doubt that this is wine's moment to shine in America, and it is also the perfect moment for you to become WineWise. This is the best time to be an educated wine consumer because the bounty of quality wines available in the American marketplace has never been greater or more affordable.

The language of the label

THE UNITED STATES is a great place to start to learn about and enjoy wines, because American wine labels are pretty easy to understand. Knowing what's on the label is critical to knowing what's in the bottle (or box), and once you get the hang of it, reading and decoding wine labels will become second nature, providing an essential first step to becoming an informed wine consumer. So let's jump into the deep end of the wine pool right now and immerse ourselves in learning all about American wine labels.

The AVA system

Every major wine-producing country has a system for naming places where grapes grow to make wine. Some of these places are famous (Napa Valley in the United States, Bordeaux in France, and Chianti in Italy are all good examples), but many more are not so well known. These place names, famous or obscure, appear on wine labels and always represent where the grapes for the wine are grown.

Why is this important? Well, the reason some people are willing to pay a lot of money for certain wines has a little bit to do with what grape type the wine is made from, but a lot to do with where those grapes are grown. The "address" of the wine is what separates a world-class white Burgundy from just another French Chardonnay (Chardonnay is the premier white grape for the Burgundy region in France) or a great Napa Valley Cabernet Sauvignon from just another California Cab. Sure, wine drinkers love certain grape varietals, but connoisseurs and wine geeks can make a fetish out of where those grapes are grown.

We're not recommending that you obsess about where the grapes for a particular wine are grown, but the vineyard site—the place from which the finished wine emerges—has a lot to do with the quality of that wine. Certainly, there are artisan winemakers in both famous and not-so-famous wine regions that pour their heart and soul into their wine, and you can taste that passion in the finished product. So much of what the French call *terroir*—the unique qualities that the soil and climate grant to particular vineyards in specific regions—is tied up with the integrity and passion of the grape growers and winemakers of those regions. There are also producers in those same regions that make pretty good to very good wine and trade on the fame of those places. Of course, sometimes the reputation can be blown out of proportion, and it's definitely true that lousy wine can be produced from grapes grown in a famous region.

The reputation of a named wine-growing region—an appellation—is also very important to the commercial success of the wines produced from the vineyards in that region. So, making sure that place name is displayed prominently on the wine label becomes a very important factor in the selling and

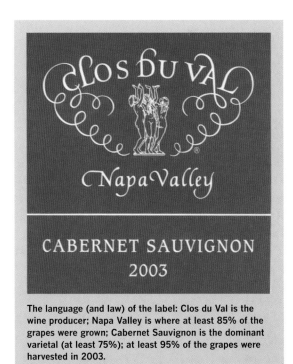

The language (and law) of the label: Clos du Val is the wine producer; Napa Valley is where at least 85% of the grapes were grown; Cabernet Sauvignon is the dominant varietal (at least 75%); at least 95% of the grapes were harvested in 2003.

marketing of that wine. Just having the words "Napa Valley" on a bottle of expensive Cabernet Sauvignon is an immense advantage to the financial health of any Napa Valley–based wine producer.

You should note that in the United States sometimes these named places can be very small districts, with as little as 60 acres/24 hectares in the entire district (the appellation "Cole Ranch" in Mendocino County), or humongous regions, encompassing parts of several states (the appellation "Lake Erie" takes in parts of New York, Pennsylvania, and Ohio).

Every country has a different name for its system of naming wine-growing regions, as you'll see when you read about the wines of each of these nations. In the United States, each of these place names is officially and legally registered as part of a system called American Viticultural Areas, or AVAs. Currently, there are more than 190 distinct AVAs in the United States, about 120 of them in wine-behemoth California (better than 90% of the wine made in the United States originates in California vineyards). When the name of an AVA appears on a wine label, it means that at least 85% of the grapes used in that wine have been grown in that named AVA. So if a wine is labeled as a 2003 Clos du Val Napa Valley Cabernet Sauvignon (see label on page 63; Clos du Val is, in this case, the name of the wine producer), it means that, by federal law, at least 85% of the fruit used in that wine had to be grown in the Napa Valley AVA. The other 15% can be grown anywhere.

If a county name appears on a label ("Sonoma County," for example), 75% of the grapes must have been grown in that county. Wines with a "California" appellation on their labels (which must be made from grapes sourced only from vineyards in California), as well as many wines with county appellations, are normally quite drinkable and quite affordable (about $5 to $20).

The grape name

Let's continue decoding the same label—the 2003 Clos du Val Napa Valley Cabernet Sauvignon. We already know that at least 85% of the grapes that make the wine had to grow in vineyards located within the

An example of an estate-bottled, single-vineyard wine label, from Sebastopol Vineyards' Dutton Ranch in California's Russian River Valley.

Napa Valley AVA, but what percentage of the wine had to be made from Cabernet Sauvignon grapes? By federal law, the wine must contain at least 75% Cab. The other 25% can be any grapes. So if a wine is labeled with a grape name—a varietal label—the wine must be made from at least 75% of that named varietal.

The vintage

Same label again: the 2003 Clos du Val Napa Valley Cabernet Sauvignon. What we know so far is that the wine must be made from at least 85% Napa Valley grapes and at least 75% Cabernet Sauvignon. What is the minimum percentage of the grapes that had to be harvested in 2003 to make it to the label? The answer is 95%. Up to 5% of the finished wine can be made from grapes from an earlier or (in the case of aging wines before release) later vintage—the year in which the grapes are harvested. This 5% of wiggle room gives the winemaker the chance to tweak the wine, adjusting for subtle nuances in color, aroma, or flavor.

Not all wine producers will make their wines using legal minimums of place, grape, and vintage. There are wines that do take to blending (Cabernet Sauvignon and Merlot, for example, are classic blenders), and there are wines that do not (such as Chardonnay and Pinot Noir). Sometimes adding 17% Merlot to a wine labeled "Cabernet Sauvignon" is a good thing, but adding 20% of much cheaper Chenin Blanc to a wine labeled "Chardonnay" is just a way to save money and make a mediocre wine. Quality-minded producers will, for example, produce a 2007 Napa Valley Chardonnay from 100% Chardonnay grapes grown in the Napa Valley and will probably use 100% of the grapes harvested in 2006 unless they feel strongly that tweaking the vintage with some older or younger wine might improve the finished product.

Also, remember that label laws are *federal minimums* by which all states and producers must abide. Producers in a few states, such as Oregon (see page 99) and Washington State (see page 94), have chosen to exceed the legal minimums for minimum AVA percentage and/or minimum grape percentage, to call attention to the quality and enhance the marketing of their wines.

Other label terms you might find

Here are some other words and phrases you might find on some wines produced in the United States, and their meanings.

Reserve: About as close to consumer fraud as you can get, this term has almost no legal meaning in this country. "Reserve" can appear on the label of any vintage-dated varietal-labeled wine produced in the United States, including the cheapest wines churned out in mass quantities by any wine producer. This is an outrage that really needs to be addressed, especially to benefit the small group of producers who continue to use the term ethically. A wine that's produced from grapes grown in the best vineyards, that is aged longer in the best oak casks, or has some other special

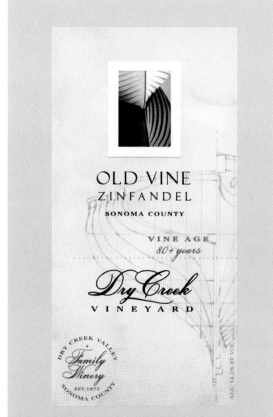

Although there is no legal definition of "old vine," the wines, especially old-vine Zinfandel, can be excellent. Vines more than eighty years old, as mentioned on this label, really are "old."

A dramatic proprietary label. Élu from St. Supéry Winery in the Napa Valley is a relatively expensive red wine anchored by Cabernet Sauvignon.

attributes really qualifies as a "reserve" wine. Until a code of conduct for the use of the term is adopted, we think "reserve" should be banished as a legal term for wines produced in the United States.

Estate-bottled: "Estate-bottled" is a beautiful and increasingly rare thing, a label phrase with real meaning. What it means is that the producer of the wine (the "estate") has grown the grapes or closely supervised the growing of the grapes, produced the wine, and bottled the wine. The producer has not bought any grapes or juice to make the wine. If the name of an AVA (Russian River Valley, for example) appears on a label along with "estate-bottled," as it almost inevitably does, that means that 100% of the grape growing, winemaking, and bottling were undertaken in that named AVA.

Single-vineyard: If "single vineyard" appears on a label (for example, "Dutton Ranch," a vineyard located within the Russian River Valley AVA), then 95% of the grapes had to have been harvested from that specific vineyard.

Grown, produced, and bottled: A similar outward sign of quality as "estate-bottled," but with a bit more flexibility for the producer. Grapes are grown, wine is made, and bottling is done by the producer, but without the geographical and percentage limits imposed by "estate-bottled." A wine that is "grown, produced, and bottled" by a Sonoma Valley winemaker can, for example, still source 15% of its grapes outside the Sonoma Valley, as long as that producer grew those grapes.

Produced and bottled: This usually means that the producer purchased at least some of the grapes for the wine but made the finished wine and bottled it. Buying grapes is not necessarily a bad thing, and if you buy from famous and highly regarded vineyards (such as Dutton Ranch, mentioned above), you will have to wait in line, sometimes for years, to buy those grapes and pay a serious premium when you do. This significantly raises the price of the wine in the bottle. Of course, there are also producers who buy grapes on the spot market, paying the lowest price possible for grapes or grape juice, and then make and bottle the wine. These wines should be (but aren't always) inexpensive.

Bottled or cellared: These terms could mean anything. The producer may have bought finished wines, maybe blended them for consistency and price advantage, and then bottled or boxed them. We usually avoid these wines, but if we find one or two that work for large gatherings, we never pay more than five or six bucks per bottle, and neither should you.

Old vines: There is no legal definition for "old vines." If you see this term on a label, the producer wants you to think that the wine in the bottle is somehow special—more complex and elegant, or more rustic and earthy. You see the term "old vine" or "old vines" on several California Zinfandels, and indeed, some of these wines are made from the fruit of vines that are more than seventy or eighty years old. But you are just as likely to find this unrestricted phrase on a bottle of Merlot made from vines that are maybe twenty or twenty-five years old. Again, the reputation of the producer means a lot when it comes to "old vines," which may or may not be really "old."

Unfiltered: This means that the wine has not been filtered, or at most has been minimally filtered, before bottling; there is no serious legal standard for "unfiltered." Quite a few winemakers believe that unfiltered wines are better expressions of the finished wine. The idea is that by not stripping the wine of subtle shades of color, desirable aromas, and better flavor, the wine is more of an artisanal product, more "honest." We have found that some unfiltered wines hold true to this ideal, and to filter them would be a mistake. We have also found unfiltered wines that have so little character to begin with that filtering would make them even less interesting. Unfiltered wines are usually red, because most consumers will not readily accept a cloudy white wine, especially one without a stellar reputation.

A note about generic and proprietary labels

Now you know how to read a vintage-dated, AVA-named, varietal label, and that should help you to understand the label terminology of more than 90% of the wines produced and sold in the United States.

The rest of the wine labels you might run into will fall into two categories: generic labels—a fast-fading, formerly popular category of cheap, manipulated wines often sold in large glass jugs or big boxes named for famous wine regions of the world (Chablis, Burgundy, etc.) but made from grapes grown in high-yielding, hot-weather vineyards of California. As they make a hasty retreat from the marketplace, the only reason to know about these wines at all is to know enough not to buy them.

But there is another, small category of wines that you will encounter, those with proprietary labels, that you'll want to know about and possibly taste (especially if somebody else is paying). These wines do not sport varietal labels; they display "fantasy" labels, and are named for real or imagined people, mythological places, or a favorite symbol, phrase, or word chosen by the producer of the wine. Opus One, Insignia, Rubicon, Meritage, Tribute, Rubaiyat, Magnificat, Tapestry, Hommage, Cain Five, Mythology, and Elu (see label on page 65) are but several of many American reds with proprietary labels. Conundrum, Blancaneaux, and Eroica are just three of the smaller category of whites. These wines can be quite expensive, especially the reds (most are in the $60 to $150 range at retail, far more on wine lists), which are mostly Cabernet Sauvignon–based blends. The whites certainly aren't inexpensive, either (most retail in the $25 to $50 range).

You'll find other terms and phrases on a wine label, but they're pretty self-explanatory: alcohol percentage ("13.5% alcohol by volume," for example), how much wine is in the bottle or box (a standard bottle is filled with 750 milliliters of wine, the equivalent of about 25.4 ounces; boxes tend to house the equivalent of four bottles—100 ounces [3 liters], and the winery address. Note that the winery address may or may not be located in the same AVA as the vineyards; that's not a problem. Unless the wine is estate-bottled, it is perfectly legal to grow the grapes in one place and produce the wine in another place. Remember, the AVA is all about where the grapes are grown, not necessarily where the finished wine is produced.

So now that we've reviewed the basics of American wine labels, let's move on to the state where most American wine hails from, California.

California: The Garden of Eden?

I N 1937, Woody Guthrie, one of America's original singer-songwriters, the (early) Bob Dylan of his day, penned a song about California entitled "(If You Ain't Got the) Do Re Mi." Guthrie wrote:

> California is a garden of Eden, a paradise to
>   live in or see;
> But believe it or not, you won't find it so hot
> If you ain't got the do re mi.

Why do we trot out an old folk song lyric to discuss modern California wines? California is the nation's largest wine producer, and when you see those lush vineyards growing throughout most of the state, you could mistake it for paradise. But it is also true that in California you often get what you pay for, and unless you're willing to part with a big wad of cash—the "do re mi" Woody Guthrie sings about—you just won't get a chance to taste the best that California has to offer.

Far Niente is a highly regarded multigeneration wine producer in California's Napa Valley. The wines are quality-driven and expensive, even by Napa Valley standards.

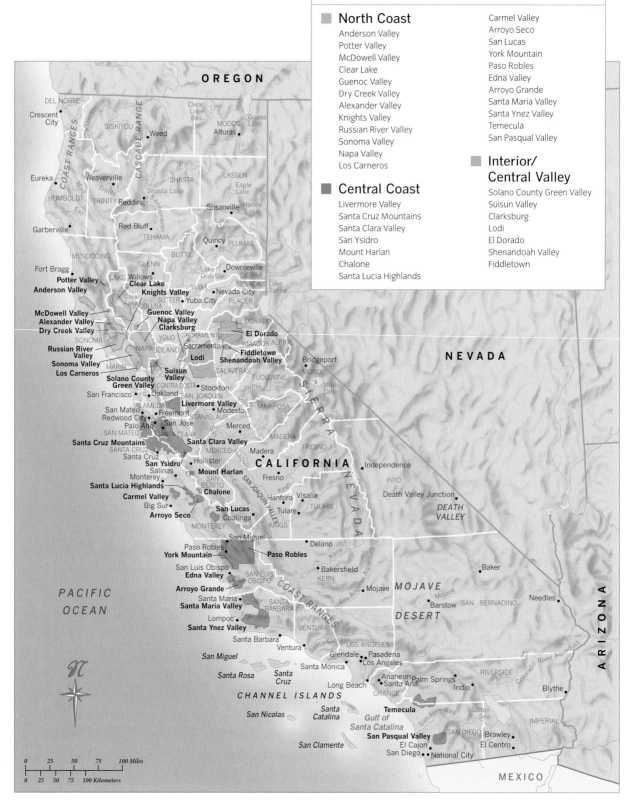

California

North Coast

Anderson Valley
Potter Valley
McDowell Valley
Clear Lake
Guenoc Valley
Dry Creek Valley
Alexander Valley
Knights Valley
Russian River Valley
Sonoma Valley
Napa Valley
Los Carneros

Central Coast

Livermore Valley
Santa Cruz Mountains
Santa Clara Valley
San Ysidro
Mount Harlan
Chalone
Santa Lucia Highlands

Carmel Valley
Arroyo Seco
San Lucas
York Mountain
Paso Robles
Edna Valley
Arroyo Grande
Santa Maria Valley
Santa Ynez Valley
Temecula
San Pasqual Valley

Interior/ Central Valley

Solano County Green Valley
Suisun Valley
Clarksburg
Lodi
El Dorado
Shenandoah Valley
Fiddletown

Wine regions of California.

We're not saying that California doesn't provide some great bargains—or at least good wines at fair prices—but you really have to become WineWise to find these wines. And that means finding producers who consistently maintain a high ratio of quality to price and recognizing the "second labels" of wineries that are best known for expensive or "cult" wines but which pay their bills by producing reliable, affordable wines.

In a way, California has done its job of marketing wines produced in "a garden of Eden" almost too well. To make our point, here's our California wine quiz. Don't worry, there are just two questions:

Question 1: What's the first place you think of when you think of California wines?

We're guessing that most of our readers answered "Napa Valley." (Please take your pulse and lie down for a moment if you didn't.)

Question 2: What percentage of all California wines is produced in the Napa Valley?

a. 75%

b. 50%

c. 30%

d. Less than 5%

Choice (d) is the correct—and, for most people, surprising—answer. Napa, and to a lesser extent Sonoma, seems to have captured the public imagination when it comes to California wines, but both counties together (and Sonoma is twice is large as Napa, with a lot more acres of vineyards) account for less than 15% of the Golden State's wine production. Many of us think that California's best wines *must* come from Napa or Sonoma, but this is wrong, too. While Napa and Sonoma do produce great wines, there are many other places in California—some you've never heard of—that also make impressive wines.

So, where do we find California's best wines (and best bargains)? Let's take a look at some of the things we need to know to make our search successful and fun.

Life beyond Chardonnay (and Merlot and Cab)

CALIFORNIA MADE its initial reputation for fine wines based on two red grapes and just one white grape, all three of which are grown in the Napa Valley and in Sonoma. The reds are Cabernet Sauvignon and Merlot; the white is Chardonnay. And while it's true that you can find great wines from California by sticking with these three grape types, you will insulate yourself, pay way too much money for wine, and never really experience all that California has to offer the *WineWise* reader.

Believe us: there is life beyond Cabernet, Merlot, and Chardonnay. California produces some excellent whites: Sauvignon Blanc (sometimes labeled as "Fumé Blanc," Gewurztraminer, and Viognier come to mind. There are also some extraordinary reds: Zinfandel, Pinot Noir, and Syrah (sometimes called Shiraz here), among others. Vineyards are often sited in regions and districts that may not be household AVAs in your house, but they are in ours.

As is true with wines from all over the world, the reputation of the producer is most often the No. 1 consideration in choosing a wine from California (or from anywhere else). Some California producers make only wines that are rare and expensive—the "cult" wines that get so much of the attention and the hype in the American wine press. Other producers make high-quality wines that we can enjoy as a daily, integral part of meals. A growing number of California producers make both a small number of flagship wines, which are expensive and hard to find, and wines that are more accessible and affordable, perfect for everyday drinking and enjoying with food.

In the following pages, we're going to introduce you to a gazetteer of California wines, both inordinately expensive and extraordinarily value-driven. Guess which ones excite us more. By now, we hope you realize that while we admire and respect the singular wines that we may taste two or three times during the course of our lives, we absolutely love turning our *WineWise* readers on to good wines that they can afford and enjoy, made by passionate people who want to provide that affordable, enjoyable experience.

WineWise
California AVAs

North Coast AVA

The North Coast AVA, which includes Napa, Sonoma, Mendocino, Lake, Marin, and Solano counties, is an appellation of convenience, but one that suggests quality. If a producer makes a wine from 50% Sonoma County grapes, 20% Mendocino County grapes, and 30% Lake County grapes, the AVA on the label will be "North Coast." Or if a wine is made from 70% Lake County grapes and 30% Napa County grapes, the AVA on that label will also read "North Coast." You get the picture: a wine made from any combination of grapes sourced from these counties is rewarded with the North Coast AVA. The North Coast AVA provides assurance to the consumer that the wine is made from grapes grown in what are perceived to be marquee wine-growing areas, and "North Coast" on the label allows the producer to charge a bit more for the wine.

NAPA COUNTY

The best-known Napa County AVA is Napa Valley. Smaller sub-AVAs of the Napa Valley AVA that you might find on the label include Atlas Peak, Chiles Valley, Diamond Mountain, Howell Mountain, Carneros (shared with Sonoma), Mount Veeder, Oak Knoll District, Oakville, Rutherford, Saint Helena, Spring Mountain District, Stags Leap District, Wild Horse Valley, and Yountville.

Less than a hundred miles north of San Francisco, the Napa Valley AVA includes almost all of Napa County and has a total of fourteen sub-AVAs within it, a number that is sure to increase in the coming years. Each producer in the sub-AVAs is entitled to use either its own AVA name on the label ("Mount Veeder," for example), or the general—and famous—AVA "Napa Valley."

There are about 225,000 acres/90,000 hectares contained within the Napa Valley AVA, and vineyards cover about 48,000 acres (19,500 hectares) of that area. This is the most expensive agricultural land in

Which AVA sells the wine?

The North Coast has become a popular AVA associated with high quality by consumers, so sometimes a wine made from 100% Lake County fruit will bear the name "North Coast" instead of the "Lake County" appellation. The reason a producer may choose to label a wine this way involves nothing more than consumer acceptance. "North Coast" is an AVA that resonates with quality-conscious consumers, but "Lake County" may not. Throughout California (and other parts of the world), producers will often opt to label their wines with a larger AVA that has gained the trust of the consumer, even when that producer could label that same wine with a smaller, more specific AVA. This is all perfectly legal. After all, if you grow 100% of your Cabernet Sauvignon grapes in the Chiles Valley, which is a sub-AVA of the larger Napa Valley AVA, which AVA will you print on your label? Well, if you want to sell your wine at a premium price, "Napa Valley" will be your AVA of choice, at least until "Chiles Valley" becomes a household name in homes of wine lovers and on restaurant wine lists.

On the other hand, if a smaller AVA has attained fame and widespread consumer acceptance, the producer will definitely choose to use that smaller AVA. For example, the Napa Valley sub-AVAs of Stags Leap District and Rutherford, both of which have a worldwide reputation for great Cabernet Sauvignon, are far more likely to label their wines with "Stags Leap District" or "Rutherford" than with "Napa Valley." But don't be surprised if the famous Napa Valley is mentioned in the text of the market-driven "back label" of these wines, just to make sure that the producers have covered all the bases.

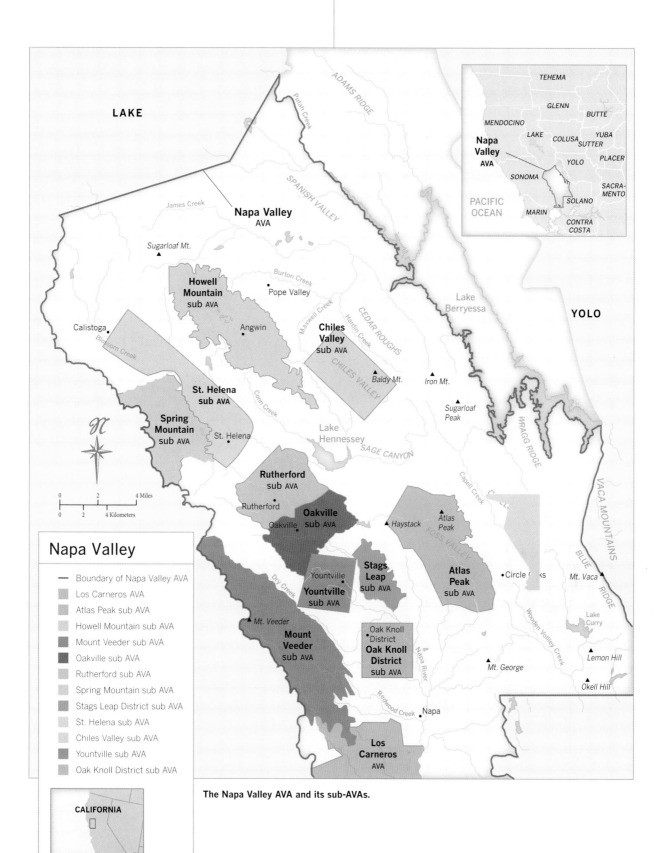

The Napa Valley AVA and its sub-AVAs.

A North Coast AVA wine, produced by the Benziger Family, from fruit grown in any combination of Napa, Sonoma, Mendocino, or Lake counties. This is a really good Sauvignon Blanc at a really fair price—usually under $15—and should be easy to find. (Courtesy of Kobrand Corporation.)

the United States, with current prices ranging from about $125,000 to $350,000 per acre, depending on location. There are more than 300 wineries within the Napa Valley AVA, even though the total AVA area is only thirty miles long and five miles wide. Nestled between the Mayacamas Mountains to the west and the Vaca Mountains to the east, the Napa Valley, which is shaped like a bowl, benefits from the cool breezes and the moist fog that roll in from San Pablo Bay early in the morning, followed by warm sunshine that pervades the region for several hours per day, and finished by cool evenings. Temperatures can fluctuate up to 20° throughout the different sub-AVAs, creating appealing microclimates for particular grape varietals.

Speaking of varietals, although there is fine Zinfandel, Merlot, Cabernet Franc, Syrah, Chardonnay, and Sauvignon Blanc produced in the Napa Valley, there is one grape that rules here: Cabernet Sauvignon. Napa Cabs must be included in any list of the world's great wines, which at their best are luscious and fruit-driven, but also complex; accessible when young, but also ageworthy; full-bodied "sunshine in a bottle," but with a delicate balance of blackberry and black currant fruit, alcohol, tannin, and acidity.

The Napa Valley is also home to some world-famous Cabernet blends, which feature proprietary labels (see page 67). The original idea for producing these wines was to make a fine wine in the tradi-

tion and spirit of Bordeaux, France (see page 151). In Bordeaux, many wines are anchored by Cab, but they are almost always blended with Merlot and Cabernet Franc, among other grapes. The Napa versions, most of which could legally be labeled as Cabernet Sauvignon because they contain more than 75% of that grape, are also often blended with a bit of Merlot and Cabernet Franc. Some of these wines, which are made in relatively small quantities and can sell for far more than $100 per bottle at retail, have become quite famous and find homes on some of the best restaurant wine lists in the United States and beyond.

Although producers in the Napa Valley are not the only folks making these American "Bordeaux blends"—this wine style is produced throughout California and several other states—the concept of these wines originated here, and the Napa Valley proprietary Cab blends continue to define the category. By the way, you may sometimes hear this entire category of reds referred to as "Meritage" wines.

Cabernet Sauvignon and Cabernet blends are closely identified with the Napa Valley AVA, and Napa Valley wine producers get to charge a premium for their address. In the recent past, Napa Valley Merlot was extremely popular, second only to Cab, but consumer desire for Merlot, especially expensive Merlot, has waned considerably over the last several years (the "*Sideways* effect"). There are a handful of producers in the Napa Valley known for their Merlot—Duckhorn "Three Palms Vineyard," which sells at retail for just under $100, the justifiably famous Beringer "Ban-

An estate-bottled Cabernet Sauvignon produced from the fruit of a single vineyard (Dollarhide) in the Napa Valley.

Famous Cabernet Blends of the Napa Valley

Some of the most famous proprietary-labeled Cabernet Sauvignon blends in the Napa Valley include the following (sometimes expensive) wines, listed in alphabetical order. The name of the wine is followed by the name of its producer.

Anthology Conn Creek

Cain Five/Cain Concept/Cain Cuvée Cain

Cardinale Kendall-Jackson

Claret Atlas Peak Vineyards

Claret/Diamond Mountain District Red Ramey

Dominus/Napanook Dominus Estate

Double T Red Trefethen

Elu St. Supéry

Generations Charles Krug

Hommage Clos Pegase

Howell Mountain Red Duckhorn (actually more Merlot than Cabernet)

Insignia Joseph Phelps

J. Daniel Cuvée Lail Vineyards

King of the Gypsies Behrens & Hitchcock

Magnificat Franciscan Oakville Estate

Opus One Robert Mondavi Winery and Baron Philippe de Rothschild partnership

The Oracle Miner Family Vineyards

Oroppas St. Clement

Persistence Reynolds Family Winery

The Poet/M. Coz/CE2V Cosentino

Quintessa Agustin Huneeus

Rubaiyat Cakebread Cellars

Rubicon Rubicon Estate

Tapestry Reserve BV (Beaulieu Vineyard)

Terzetto Volker Eisele Family Estate

Trifecta Beaucanon Estate

Trilogy Flora Springs

croft Ranch Howell Mountain" Merlot, which sells for about $80, and the hard-to-find Lewis Cellars Merlot (about 100 cases produced each vintage), which is usually found only on selected wine lists at close to $200, are probably among the most prized. Chappellet is a fine and time-tested Merlot producer. As a category, however, Napa Valley Merlot is currently in a nosedive in the annual varietal beauty pageant.

Zinfandel is a grape that grows nicely in parts of the Napa Valley and can create a memorable wine. The same is true of Sauvignon Blanc and, to a lesser extent, Chardonnay, which does well in the cool-weather Carneros sub-AVA (see page 75). Still, it is Cabernet Sauvignon that brought the wine producers of the Napa Valley to the party, and they don't appear to be leaving the festivities with anyone else.

Napa Valley Favorites. When it comes to the wines of the Napa Valley, money talks. If you have dollars to burn, you're feeling flush, or you want to celebrate, then navigating the Napa Valley is pretty easy: pay big money, get big wine. It is difficult to find really great values—very good wines at very fair prices—among wines that carry the Napa Valley AVA on their labels. Difficult, but not impossible if you're WineWise.

We find that if you focus on some of the old, established names in the Napa Valley, those families and companies that owned their vineyard land and wineries before the modern "gold rush" in the Valley, you just might get some very good wines at very good prices. As we have said before and will say again in these pages, the reputation of the producer is really important in making wine-buying decisions. There are producers making wines that sell for extravagant prices, and their wines are worth it because drinking that wine is a singular, if expensive, experience. If that producer creates a wine that is more consumer-friendly in terms of its price, we'll bet you the price of the bottle that the "bargain" wine will be good, too. Then there are those rare producers—rare especially in the Napa Valley—who pride themselves on making wines that are high in quality but moderate in price.

The following wineries are some of our favorite Napa Valley producers. Please note that some of these producers make second-tier wines with the "California" appellation on the label, but we have included in this list only those wineries that display the Napa Valley AVA on their labels. Most bargains in the Napa Valley are defined as wines under $25, which elsewhere in the world might be considered moderately expensive.

Producers whose wines are mostly expensive but worth it include Acacia, Amusant, Araujo Estate, Artesa, David Arthur, Azalea Springs, BV (Beaulieu Vineyard), Benessere, Beringer, Burgess, Cafaro, Cain, Cakebread, Cardinale, Caymus, Ceja, Chanticleer, Chappellet, Chateau Montelena, Clos du Val, Clos Pegase, Corison, Cosentino, Robert Craig, Cuvaison, Diamond Creek, Domaine Carneros, Domaine Chandon, Dominus Estate, Downing Family, Duckhorn, Dunn, Dyer, Ehlers, El Molino, Etude, Far Niente, Fife, Flora Springs, Robert Foley, Forman, Franciscan, Franus, Freemark Abbey, Frog's Leap, Girard, Grgich Hills, Groth, Hagafen, Hall, Havens, Heitz, The Hess Collection, Jade Mountain, Jarvis, Kuleto Estate, La Jota, Lail, Lamborn, Larkmead, Lewis, Liparita, Livingston-Moffett, Lokoya, Mayacamas, Merryvale, Miner Family, Robert Mondavi Winery, Mumm Cuvee Napa, Newton, Nickel & Nickel, Patz & Hall, Peju Province, Joseph Phelps, Pine Ridge, Plumpjack, Pride Mountain, Provenance, Quintessa, Kent Rasmussen, Rubicon Estate, Rudd, Schramsberg, Selene, Sequoia Grove, Shafer, Signorello, Silver Oak, Robert Sinskey, Sky, Smith-Madrone, Spottswoode, Stag's Leap Wine Cellars, Stags' Leap Winery, Steltzner, Storybook Mountain, Swanson, Philip Togni, Trefethen, Truchard, Turley, Turnbull, Vineyard 7 & 8, Volker Eisele Estate, Voss, Whitehall Lane, York Creek, and ZD Winery, among many others.

Napa Valley producers who offer (relative) bargains include Atlas Peak* (an asterisk indicates wines that are widely available), Beaucanon, Blockheadia,* Buehler, Conn Creek, Joel Gott,* Green and Red,* William Hill,* Honig,* Charles Krug,* Luna,* Markham,* Louis M. Martini,* Nichelini, Raymond,* Rombauer,* Round Hill,* screw kappa napa (skn),* Gustavo Thrace, and Trinchero Family.*

Some WineWise Napa Valley Sub-AVAs.
Currently, the Napa Valley AVA contains fourteen sub-AVAs within it. We're going to take a look at some of the majors and some of their best-known producers. Read on to find out more about:

- Carneros, an AVA that is shared with Sonoma County, and is best known for Pinot Noir, Chardonnay, and sparkling wines

- Oakville, Rutherford, and Stags Leap, three notable AVAs located on Napa's valley floor, each known primarily for extraordinary Cabernet Sauvignon wines and Cabernet-based "Bordeaux blends"

- Howell Mountain AVA, Diamond Mountain District AVA, Spring Mountain District AVA, Mount Veeder AVA, and Atlas Peak AVA, the five "mountain" AVAs within the Napa Valley, all of which are known primarily for great Cab but also produce small amounts of white wines.

Opus One—a partnership started by Robert Mondavi and Baron Philippe de Rothschild—has been seen as the flagship for the "Bordeaux blends" of the Napa Valley since its first vintage in 1979.

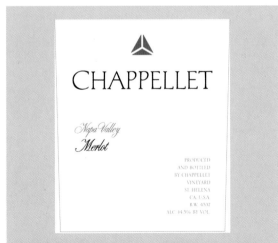

The Napa Valley can produce very good Merlot, and the Chappellet family's winery consistently produces some of the best Merlot in Napa.

Vineyards in Carneros.

THE "COOL" REGION: CARNEROS AVA. Officially named "Los Carneros," this area is actually an AVA that is shared by both Napa and Sonoma counties, as it borders the north coast of San Pablo Bay. Carneros is also the coolest sub-AVA within the larger Napa Valley AVA, featuring early afternoon fog and cool air. Because of its cool climate, Carneros is the ideal site to plant Chardonnay and Pinot Noir, two varietals that thrive in cool weather, developing crisp acidity in both the fruit and finished wine. Fine varietal-labeled still wines are made from these grapes, but so are delicious sparkling wines that often use a blend of Pinot Noir and Chardonnay as base wines.

Carneros producers who make wines that are expensive and worth it include Acacia, Artesa, Ben-essere, Beringer, Bouchaine, Cakebread, Ceja, Cline, Clos du Val, Clos Pegase, B.R. Cohn, Cuvaison, Etude, Franus, Frog's Leap, Havens, Paul Hobbs, Jacuzzi, Kistler, Landmark, Patz and Hall, Joseph Phelps, Kent Rasmussen, Schug, Shafer, Robert Sinskey, Robert Stemmler, St. Francis, Truchard, Voss, and ZD.

Producers of (relative) bargains include Ben-ziger,* (an asterisk indicates wines that are widely available), BV (Beaulieu Vineyard),* Buena Vista,* Carneros Creek,* Charles Krug,* Rombauer,* Saints-bury "Garnet" Pinot Noir,* Steele/Shooting Star,* Tria, and Valley of the Moon.*

In the "beautiful bubbles" category, Domaine Carneros, Domaine Chandon, and Gloria Ferrer offer some pretty good values for some very good *methode champenoise* wines.

THE "VALLEY FLOOR": OAKVILLE AVA, RUTHERFORD AVA, AND STAGS LEAP DISTRICT AVA. We've grouped these three famous sub-AVAs of the Napa Valley AVA together for two reasons. First, they are located close by each other in the central Napa Valley. Driving on Highway 29, the main drag in the Napa Valley, you'll encounter the towns of Rutherford and Oakville right next to each other, with Rutherford sited north of Oakville. Take a turn to the right off Highway 29 when you're in Oakville and you'll end up on the

A note about producers

You may notice that throughout this chapter, several California wine producers are listed more than once. That's not a mistake. The same producer can make wines from vineyards all over California, and it is not unusual for that to happen.

So don't get confused if you see the same producer's name several times and in several different AVAs, or the wines listed as both relative bargains and expensive. That is the way the California wine industry works: the same producer can create expensive Cabernet Sauvignon from the Napa Valley AVA and Sonoma County's Alexander Valley AVA, as well as a very good $12 Cabernet Sauvignon that just reads "California" on the label.

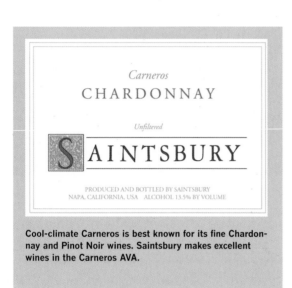

Cool-climate Carneros is best known for its fine Chardonnay and Pinot Noir wines. Saintsbury makes excellent wines in the Carneros AVA.

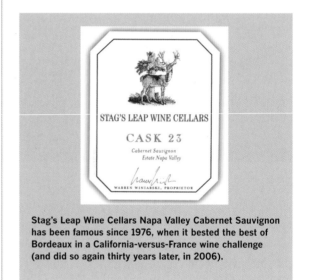

Stag's Leap Wine Cellars Napa Valley Cabernet Sauvignon has been famous since 1976, when it bested the best of Bordeaux in a California-versus-France wine challenge (and did so again thirty years later, in 2006).

Silverado Trail and in the Stags Leap District AVA. Together, these three Napa Valley sub-AVAs account for about 13,000 acres/5,200 hectares of some of the most expensive agricultural real estate in the world, dedicated largely to Cabernet Sauvignon vineyards. Cab made from the grapes grown in these three AVAs is full-bodied, rich, complex, and ageworthy; the best wines age gracefully and can be quite expensive.

Stags Leap is the smallest AVA of the three, only two square miles/five square kilometers, half of it (1,500 acres/600 hectares) planted to vines. Wines produced from Stags Leap fruit are powerful, with firm tannins. This description applies not only to the much-heralded Stags Leap Cabs but also to the Merlot and Petite Sirah wines produced here. The AVA is home to some of the best-known California "cult" Cabs, especially Shafer Hillside Select and three wines from Stag's Leap Wine Cellars: "Fay Vineyards," "Cask 23," and "S.L.V."

The Oakville AVA has about 5,000 acres/2,000 hectares of vineyards, with the vines planted mostly on the valley floor. Oakville Cabernet Sauvignon at its best is scented with fragrant fresh herbs, especially mint and sage. Coffee and tobacco also come through in the nose of the wine. Balance is achieved on the palate by the taste of black currants and sweet cherries, coupled with a slight astringency provided by tannins. Oakville is home to many heralded wines, none more famous than Opus One, produced in partnership by Robert Mondavi and Baron Philippe Rothschild, one of the first proprietary-labeled "Bordeaux blends."

Newer "cult" Cabs from Oakville include Dalla Valle, Harlan Estate, and Screaming Eagle, all of which are hard to obtain and seriously overpriced when you do find them ($500 at retail for Screaming Eagle, and even more on a wine list? Please!).

The Rutherford AVA is about 7,000 acres/2,340 hectares, most of it Cabernet Sauvignon. At harvest, Cabernet Sauvignon planted in the Rutherford AVA is worth about $30 million; that's just the grapes, not the finished wine. There are about thirty wineries in Rutherford, and at least twenty-six of them produce Cabernet Sauvignon wines. Rutherford Cab features dramatic tannins that often turn into a decadent sundae of bitter chocolate and black fruits—plums and cherries—on the palate. Herbs, especially mint, are prominent in the nose of Rutherford Cab. Since 1880, when Inglenook was founded by Finnish sea captain Gustave Niebaum, Cabernet Sauvignon has defined Rutherford (the original Inglenook is now known as the Rubicon Estate and is owned by cinema *auteur* Francis Ford Coppola). This mono-grape identity was further cemented, starting in the early 1900s by BV (Beaulieu Vineyard). Tiny amounts of Merlot, Cabernet Franc, and Zinfandel are also planted in the Rutherford AVA.

If there are any bargains to be found in Stags Leap, Oakville, or Rutherford, we don't know what they are. These wines are going to be expensive to wildly expensive and should be saved for special dinners on special occasions. Here are some well-known producers.

Stags Leap District AVA: Chimney Rock, Cliff Lede, Clos du Val, Ilsley, Pine Ridge, Regusci, Shafer, Silverado, Robert Sinskey, Stag's Leap Wine Cellars, Stags' Leap Winery, and Steltzner.

Oakville AVA: Cardinale Estate, Cosentino, Dalla Valle, Downing Family, Far Niente, Franciscan, Girard, Groth, Harlan Estate, Miner, Oakville Ranch, Opus One, Pahlmeyer, Plumpjack, Rudd, Screaming Eagle, Silver Oak, Swanson, and Turnbull.

Vineyards in the Stags Leap District.

Rutherford AVA: David Arthur, Beaucanon, BV (Beaulieu Vineyard), Cakebread, Caymus, Conn Creek, Frog's Leap, Grgich Hills, Kathryn Hall, Honig, Livingston-Moffett, Peju Province, Quintessa, Round Hill, Rubicon Estate, Sequoia Grove, Staglin Family, St. Supéry, Sullivan, Villa Mt. Eden, Voss, Whitehall Lane, and ZD.

THE MAGNIFICENT MOUNTAINS: HOWELL MOUNTAIN AVA, DIAMOND MOUNTAIN DISTRICT AVA, SPRING MOUNTAIN DISTRICT AVA, MOUNT VEEDER AVA, AND ATLAS PEAK AVA. We've grouped these five sub-AVAs of the Napa Valley together because the grapes from mountain vineyards express a very different *terroir* than do valley floor vineyards. These five AVAs share high-altitude rocky terrain, soils that don't retain a lot of water, and roots that go deep. You end up tasting a wine with some real complexity and structure and a kind of "wild" mountain character that's almost unpredictable from vintage to vintage. Again, these five mountain AVAs are focused on Cabernet Sauvignon, with a smattering of Cabernet Franc and Zinfandel, and just a bit of Chardonnay and Riesling.

Rubicon is the flagship wine of Francis Ford Coppola's Rubicon Estate in the Rutherford AVA in the Napa Valley. Rubicon is one of the expensive, highly regarded "Bordeaux blends," dominated by Cabernet Sauvignon.

At more than 2,000 feet/610 meters above sea level, the Howell Mountain AVA escapes the fog that envelops the floor of the Napa Valley, but because of its elevation, this Napa sub-AVA enjoys moderately warm to relatively cool weather even when the sun is shining. Howell Mountain, with only 600 acres/240 hectares of vineyard planted, is known for two varietals: Cabernet Sauvignon and Zinfandel. Randy Dunn made this AVA famous with his Dunn Howell Mountain Cabernet Sauvignon. Another much sought-after wine is Beringer Howell Mountain Bancroft Ranch Merlot. Storybook Mountain Vineyards makes some of our favorite Zinfandels here.

The Diamond Mountain District AVA covers a rugged 5,000 acres/2,000 hectares along the Mayacamas mountain range in the northeastern Napa Valley. Diamond Mountain Cab is powerful stuff meant for aging, with an almost chewy texture and assertive tannins. Small artisanal producers have been the rule on Diamond Mountain ever since 1972, when Al Brounstein, the founder of Diamond Creek Vineyards, first produced three single-vineyard Cabs ("Red Rock Terrace," "Gravelly Meadow," and "Volcanic Hill").

The Spring Mountain District AVA, with altitudes as high as 2,600 feet/790 meters, is above the fog line of the Napa Valley but gets cool afternoons and warm evenings. Now famous for its Cabernet Sauvignon, Spring Mountain first received attention for its Riesling and Chardonnay wines, and a few producers, including Stony Hill and Smith-Madrone, still specialize in elegant whites. Hand-picked mountainside vineyards are small, as is total wine production. Cain Vineyard and Winery produces its "Cain Five" from Spring Mountain fruit and was the first California winery to produce a wine using all five of the classic Bordeaux red varietals: Cabernet Sauvignon, Merlot, Cabernet Franc, Malbec, and Petit Verdot.

The Mount Veeder AVA is placed atop the highest peak—2,700 feet/825 meters—of the Mayacamas Mountains. With slopes as steep as 30 degrees, vineyards are difficult to plant and harvest, but that same angle allows for great sun exposure and soil drainage. The finished wines, most of them Cabernet Sauvignon, are distinctively spicy and feature unbridled flavors of wild berries and chewy tannins—wines to last the test of time.

Spring Mountain Vineyard.

The Atlas Peak AVA is sited high above the stone foothills of Stags Leap and across the valley floor from Mount Veeder. Facing west, the vineyards love the direct sunlight afforded them, as well as the cool breezes that envelop the area in the afternoon. The most famous producer here is Atlas Peak Vineyards, founded by Piero Antinori, perhaps the most famous wine producer in Tuscany, Italy. Storybook Mountain produces a robust Zinfandel here, and this Napa sub-AVA shows a lot of promise with that varietal.

There are almost no bargains to be found in wines labeled with any of these mountainous Napa Valley sub-AVAs, but there are some very fine wines made by these producers if you've got the do re mi—and, in several cases, the patience to find them.

Howell Mountain AVA: Beringer, Robert Craig, Dunn, Robert Foley, Forman, La Jota, Lail, Lamborn Family, Lokoya, and Storybook Mountain.

Diamond Mountain District AVA: Azalea Springs, Diamond Creek, Dyer, J-Davies/Schramsberg, Lokoya, Reverie, Stonegate, and Von Strasser.

Spring Mountain District: Behrens & Hitchcock, Beringer, Cain, Fife, Robert Keenan, Newton, Pride Mountain, Smith-Madrone, St. Clement, Stony Hill, Philip

Togni, Vineyard 7 & 8, and York Creek.

Mount Veeder AVA: Chateau Potelle, Robert Craig, Franus, The Hess Collection, Jade Mountain, Mayacamas, Mount Veeder Winery, and Sky Vineyards.

Atlas Peak AVA: Ardente, Atlas Peak Vineyards, Elan, Pahlmeyer, Storybook Mountain, and William Hill.

SONOMA COUNTY

The best-known AVAs in Sonoma County include Sonoma Valley, Russian River Valley, Alexander Valley, Dry Creek Valley, and Carneros (shared with Napa). Other WineWise AVAs you might find on the label are Bennett Valley, Chalk Hill, Green Valley, Knights Valley, Northern Sonoma, Rockpile, Sonoma Coast, and Sonoma Mountain.

Sonoma County is twice as large as its neighbor Napa County and has more acres of vines planted than any other single coastal county in California—about 50,000 acres (20,000 hectares). Sonoma is not nearly as showy as Napa, with far fewer millionaire industrialists turned wine producers and a lot more multigenerational grape growers and winemakers. The Sonoma culture of tradition and longevity shows in its best wines, produced at more than 200 resident wineries.

Atlas Peak in the Napa Valley.

If you pushed us against a wall and asked, "Okay, who makes better wines overall, Napa or Sonoma?" we'd have to say it's Sonoma hands down, with the exception of Cabernet Sauvignon (which in Sonoma can still be very good to excellent). Unlike the Napa Valley, which is Cab-centric, Sonoma County makes very fine wines from a wide variety of varietals, including excellent examples of Pinot Noir, Merlot, Chardonnay, Sauvignon Blanc, and even Gewurztraminer. The quality of the wines can be stellar, and although prices can be quite high and are getting higher, it is still relatively easy to find good values in delicious Sonoma wines if you're WineWise.

Unlike the all-encompassing and more commercially driven appellation "Napa Valley," it is quite common to see "Sonoma County" on these wines. If you want to sell a bottle in Napa, "Napa County" won't do it, "Napa Valley" will. Not so in Sonoma. You should never shy away from wines with the "Sonoma County" label, which indicates that most of the grapes were picked in the county. Remember, it's a big county with lots and lots of vineyards, so when you purchase the wine of a trusted Sonoma County producer, you're going to get good quality, often at a good price.

Following are some of the best buys in "Sonoma County"–labeled wines. Note that most of these producers also produce wines from more specific AVAs

St. Francis is one of the benchmark wineries of Sonoma County, known for its high quality. (Courtesy of Kobrand Corporation)

within Sonoma County (for example, Alexander Valley, Russian River Valley, etc.); those wines are almost sure to be more expensive than those labeled "Sonoma County." Prices for wines by these producers are especially appealing among the white varietals, with plenty of good-value reds, too.

Sonoma County Favorites. Good producers at good prices are Belvedere, Benziger Family, Blackstone, Chateau St. Jean, Chateau Souverain, Clos du Bois, Domaine St. George, Gallo Family Vineyards, J. Garcia (for Deadheads and others), Grand Archer,

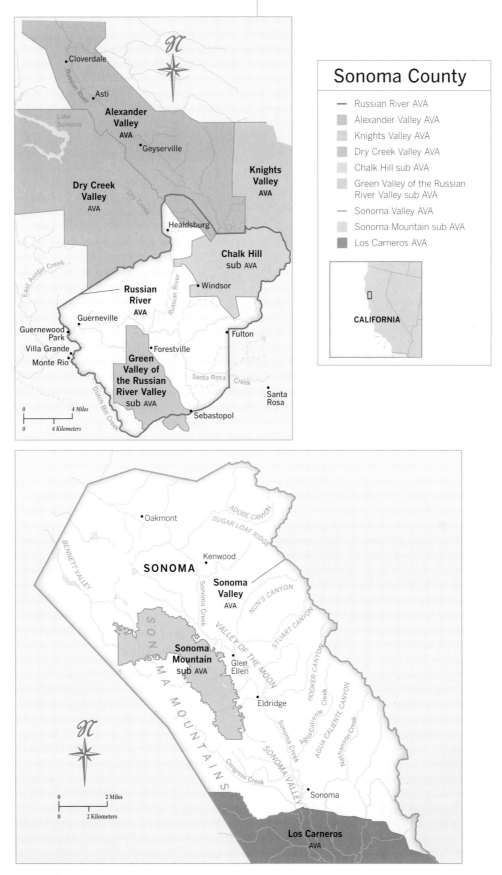

Sonoma County.

Kenwood, Marietta, Murphy-Goode, Rancho Zabaco, Ravenswood, Sebastiani, Seghesio, Simi, St. Francis, Rodney Strong, Taft Street, and Valley of the Moon.

Relatively expensive but still a bargain for the quality of its wines is Matanzas Creek Winery. This winery also lists one of Sonoma County's newest AVAs, Bennett Valley, on some of its labels.

Some WineWise Sonoma County AVAs. Sonoma County contains thirteen AVAs. One of these is the Carneros AVA, which is shared with Napa and which we've already talked about (page 75). Of the remaining AVAs, four are actually sub-AVAs. Also, unlike in Napa, where Cabernet Sauvignon rules, some specific AVAs in Sonoma County have come to be identified with specific varietals. Let's take a look at some of the key AVAs of Sonoma, the grapes they're known for, and some of the best-known producers in each AVA.

SONOMA VALLEY AVA (SUB-AVA: SONOMA MOUNTAIN). The Sonoma Valley AVA is justifiably famous as one of the most important places in the history of the northern California wine industry. A large AVA (161 square miles/417 square kilometers), its weather patterns are so varied that no single varietal dominates. It is easy to find good wines made from Chardonnay, Sauvignon Blanc, Pinot Noir, Merlot, Zinfandel, and Cabernet Sauvignon. The Sonoma Mountain AVA is a sub-AVA of Sonoma Valley. Wine quality is high in the Sonoma Valley AVAs and bargains are hard to come by, but there are some worth exploring.

Sonoma Valley vineyard.

Iron Horse, owned by the Sterling family, produces some of the best estate-bottled, vintage-dated sparkling wines made in California, as well as very fine estate Pinot Noir and Chardonnay, all in the very cool Green Valley, a sub-AVA of the larger Russian River Valley.

Some of the best-known producers in the Sonoma Valley AVA are Biale, Carmenet/Moon Mountain, B. R. Cohn, Gundlach Bundschu, Hanzell, Haywood, Robert Hunter, Kistler, Kunde Estate, Louis M. Martini Monte Rosso Vineyard, Ravenswood, Sebastiani, Smothers/Remick Ridge, St. Francis, and Joseph Swan; there are many others.

Wine producers in the Sonoma Mountain sub-AVA include Benziger Family Estate, Kenwood's Jack London Ranch, and Laurel Glen.

RUSSIAN RIVER VALLEY AVA (SUB-AVAS: CHALK HILL AND GREEN VALLEY). With more than 9,000 acres/3,600 hectares of planted vineyards, the Russian River Valley contains close to 20% of the total plantings in Sonoma County. The southern section of the AVA borders the banks of the Russian River and the western section is close to the Pacific Ocean, creating a cool and damp climate, perfect for growing both Chardonnay and Pinot Noir. Many wine lovers believe that this AVA produces the best, *terroir*-driven wines made from these two varietals, and we would agree. Especially where Pinot Noir is concerned, California has had a hard time taming this finicky grape and finessing a delicate finished wine, but Russian River Pinot Noir has gained the respect of the wine world. These wines can be intense, rich, and concentrated, while still delicate and balanced.

In the warmer areas of this AVA, Zinfandel, Gewurztraminer, Sauvignon Blanc, and even a bit of Merlot and Cabernet Sauvignon flourish.

Iron Horse, the best-known producer in the Green Valley AVA, produces wonderful estate-bottled Chardonnay and Pinot Noir, but it has made its name on several different signature blends of vintage-dated, estate-bottled *methode champenoise* sparkling wines.

Russian River Valley wines are uniformly expensive, but their quality often justifies the high price tags. Some of the best-known producers are:

Russian River Valley AVA: Battaglini, Davis Bynum, La Crema, Merry Edwards, Gary Farrell, Foppiano, Frei Brothers, Fritz, Gallo, Hartford Court, Paul Hobbs, Hop Kiln, J Vineyards, Kistler, Martinelli, Martini and Prati, Martin Ray, Rochioli, Rutz, Sauvignon Republic, Sonoma-Cutrer, Joseph Swan, Taft Street, Topolos, and Williams Selyem.

Chalk Hill sub-AVA: Chalk Hill Winery, Chateau Felice, and Rodney Strong.

Green Valley sub-AVA: Dutton Estate/ Sebastopol Vineyards, Dutton-Goldfield, GoldridgePinot, Hartford Court, Iron Horse, Orogeny, Tandem, and Marimar Torres.

ALEXANDER VALLEY AVA AND KNIGHTS VALLEY AVA. The Mendocino County line is the northernmost boundary of Sonoma's Alexander Valley AVA, and its eastern boundary is the Knights Valley AVA. Alexander Valley is a large AVA, with nearly 12,000 acres/4,800 hectares of vineyards, starring Cabernet Sauvignon and Chardonnay, with Merlot and Zinfandel playing important supporting roles. There are both small and large wine producers in the Alexander Valley. When you see this AVA printed on a wine label, it is an outward sign of quality, a wine worth considering. Although Alexander Valley has its share of expensive wines, relative bargains can still be found, even among estate-bottled wines.

There are only three wineries in the Knights Valley AVA, and only two use the AVA on their labels: Peter Michael and Anakota. Both producers specialize in single-vineyard wines, and the wines are wildly expensive. However, the behemoth winery Beringer owns about 540 acres (218 hectares) in Knights Valley and produces an extraordinary Cabernet Sauvignon, as well as Alluvium, a red Bordeaux blend, and a white blend, Alluvium Blanc. The Beringer wines are sometimes a bit hard to find, but the reds sell for about $35, Alluvium Blanc for about $20. Not bad when your neighbor, Sir Peter Michael, has a waiting list of people ready to pay hundreds of dollars per bottle for his single-vineyard Chardonnays and his "Les Pavots" red Bordeaux blend.

Some of the best-known producers in the Alexander Valley AVA include Chateau St. Jean, Francis Ford Coppola Presents, deLorimier, Ferrari-Carano, Herzog (kosher), Geyser Peak, Lancaster Estate, Peter Michael, Ridge, Rodney Strong, Sebastiani, Silver Oak, Simi, Stonestreet, Stuhlmuller, T-bar-T, Trentadue, and Robert Young Estate. Relative bargains in Alexander Valley wines include Alexander Valley Vineyards (including estate-bottled selections), Clos du Bois, Frei Brothers, Murphy-Goode, and Windsor.

Benziger "Tribute" is a red blend from the Sonoma Mountain AVA, made from grapes grown in certified biodynamic vineyards. Biodynamics is a sustainable farming practice that the Benziger family has adopted for its best wines, with excellent results in both the vineyard and the bottle. (Courtesy of Kobrand Corporation)

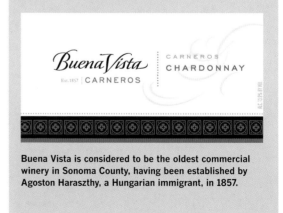

Buena Vista is considered to be the oldest commercial winery in Sonoma County, having been established by Agoston Haraszthy, a Hungarian immigrant, in 1857.

The Dry Creek Valley AVA specializes in Zinfandel. This is the label of a fine single-vineyard Zin produced by Dry Creek Vineyards, a quality-driven producer.

The Alexander Valley AVA in Sonoma County. Alexander Valley Vineyards is a leading producer.

DRY CREEK VALLEY. The wines of the Dry Creek Valley AVA sum up the contradictions in the modern California winemaking industry. With dozens of small family-owned vineyards and wineries making fine wines here, the largest landholder and producer in all of Sonoma County—Gallo—is also located in Dry Creek. Healdsburg, the formerly quiet town that anchors Dry Creek, has become increasingly expensive and exclusive as the fortunes of the local wine industry have grown. This AVA has made its reputation on Zinfandel and is considered to be perhaps the finest region for the grape in all of California. Sauvignon Blanc is the stellar white grape here. There are increasing plantings of Syrah and Cabernet Sauvignon in Dry Creek vineyards. Dry Creek Zin is something special and is highly recommended. There are both good values and very expensive boutique wines produced here, but you can't go too far wrong with Dry Creek Zinfandel, no matter the price.

Some of the best-known producers in the Dry Creek AVA include David Coffaro, Dry Creek Vineyard, Gary Farrell, Ferrari-Carano, Foppiano* (the asterisk indicates a good value), Frick,* Fritz, Gallo Family Vineyards/Gallo Sonoma Estate,* Handley,* Manzanita Creek, Martin Family, Mia's Playground,* Nalle, Pedroncelli,* Pezzi-King, Preston, Quivira, A. Rafanelli, Rancho Zabaco,* Ridge Lytton Springs, Seghesio, Simi, and Tria.*

MENDOCINO COUNTY

Although grapes are the second-most-productive cash crop in Mendocino County (marijuana has long held the No. 1 spot), Mendocino's wines are second to none. Home to many old-vine, dry-farmed organic vineyards, Mendocino produces wines that have a lot of soul, a lot of history. Among reds, Zinfandel is the star in the all-encompassing Mendocino AVA and the Redwood Valley AVA, but some very fine Cabernet Sauvignon is produced in those AVAs, along with Syrah and other red grapes that are originally native to the Rhone Valley of France—Grenache, Mourvedre, Carignan, Petite Sirah. Good examples of Sauvignon Blanc are also produced in Mendocino County, and in the cool-weather Anderson Valley AVA, great Pinot Noir, Chardonnay, Riesling, and Gewurztraminer reign. Also in this AVA you'll find Roederer Estate, among the best *methode champenoise* sparkling wine producers in the country.

Organic farming has long been a trademark of this region, as championed by the Lolonis family (producer of the fun and inexpensive Ladybug wines, along with many more serious wines), Fetzer, Frey, and many other growers and producers in Mendocino.

Many of the red wines of Mendocino have great depth of flavor, allowing you to "taste the soil," meaning that the wines have a rustic edge that other wines lack. Mendocino reds are not wimpy. Chardonnay can exhibit great delicacy, the Sauvignon Blanc is lime-juice lovely, the Riesling crisp and complex, the Gewurztraminer spicy and dry. Sparkling wines from the Anderson Valley are some of the best made anywhere in the New World: thirst-quenching and refreshing, but also complex and very food-friendly.

It is amazing to us that the wines of Mendocino still live in the shadow of Napa and Sonoma, but maybe that's a good thing. If the secret were out, Mendocino wines might not continue to be among the best values in fine California wines, and that would be a shame for *WineWise* readers (and authors). We think that just about any Mendocino wine is worth tasting, many of them several times.

The best-known AVAs in Mendocino County include Mendocino, Anderson Valley, Redwood Valley, and McDowell Valley. Following are some of the best-known producers working in each AVA.

Mendocino County appellation or Mendocino AVA: Blockheadia, Bonterra, Brutocao, Copain, Dunnewood, Eaglepoint Ranch, Fetzer, Hidden Cellars, Parducci, and Sean Thackrey.

Anderson Valley AVA: La Crema, Edmeades, Goldeneye, Greenwood Ridge, Handley* (an asterisk indicates a producer of

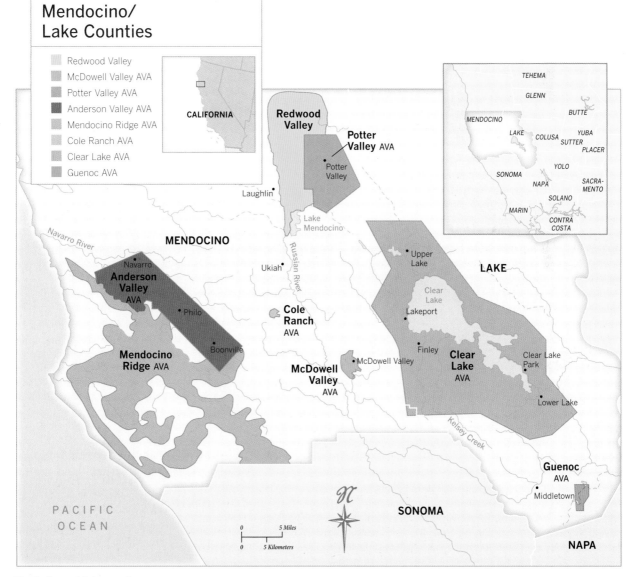

Mendocino and Lake counties.

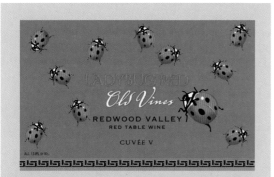

The Lolonis family has been growing grapes and making wine in Mendocino's Redwood Valley for three generations; their grapes are grown organically. Lolonis produces wonderful varietal wines, especially Zinfandel, but has become best known for their Ladybug Red and Ladybug White wines, which are delicious and affordable.

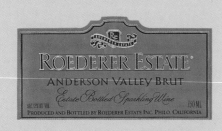

French-owned Roederer Estate makes very fine sparkling wines in the cool-climate Anderson Valley of Mendocino County.

sparkling wine), Husch, Lazy Creek, Littorai, Londer, Navarro, Roederer Estate,* and Scharffenberger.*

Redwood Valley AVA: Fife, Frey, Gabrielli, Graziano, Lolonis, and Steele.

McDowell Valley AVA: McDowell Valley Vineyards.

LAKE COUNTY

The best-known AVAs in Lake County are Clear Lake, Guenoc Valley, and High Valley.

Clear Lake, the largest body of fresh water in California, is located north of Napa and Sonoma and east of Mendocino. The cool Clear Lake AVA, where all but 500 acres of Lake County's 3,800 acres/1,540 hectares of grapes are planted, is known primarily for the quality of its Sauvignon Blanc. Clear Lake is also the source for fine Cabernet Sauvignon, Cabernet Franc, Merlot, Zinfandel, and Sangiovese.

The biggest player here is Kendall-Jackson Winery more likely to use "California" on their attractively priced entry-level wines), with smaller producers making artisanal wines in the Clear Lake AVA; there are single-winery operations in the Guenoc Valley AVA and the High Valley AVA. While the Clear Lake AVA or the Lake County appellation appears on more bottles of wine, the region is still a feeder of grapes for moderately priced wines that are more likely to carry "North Coast" on their labels. There are some very good bargains to be had from this region. Following are some of the best-known producers.

Clear Lake AVA or Lake County appellation: Ployez, Shooting Star, and Wildhurst. All of these producers' wines are extraordinary values.

Guenoc Valley AVA: Guenoc Winery produces mostly expensive estate-bottled and single-vineyard wines.

High Valley AVA: Brassfield Estate produces fine wines at about $15 to $25.

Central Coast

The Central Coast AVA encompasses Alameda, Contra Costa, Monterey, San Benito, San Francisco, San Luis Obispo, San Mateo, Santa Barbara, Santa Clara, and Santa Cruz counties. Other WineWise AVAs you might find on the label include Arroyo Seco, Edna Valley, Livermore Valley, Monterey, Mount Harlan, Paso Robles, San Francisco Bay, Santa Cruz Mountains, Santa Lucia Highlands, Santa Maria Valley, Santa Ynez Valley (encompassing the Sta. Rita Hills sub-AVA).

The Central Coast AVA is a huge appellation, with almost 100,000 acres/40,000 hectares of planted vineyards. With both small and large producers producing both artisanal and industrial wines, it is impossible to make a generalization about this unwieldy AVA.

What we can say is that what is unofficially known as the "North Central Coast" is centered around the AVAs contained in Monterey County, with smaller but important producers in the Santa Cruz Mountains AVA (San Mateo, Santa Clara, and San Cruz counties) and Livermore Valley AVA (Alameda County), home to Wente Vineyards, the first commercial producer of Chardonnay in California.

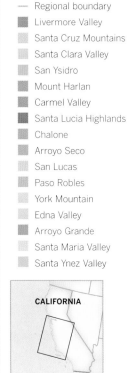

Central Coast

- — Regional boundary
- Livermore Valley
- Santa Cruz Mountains
- Santa Clara Valley
- San Ysidro
- Mount Harlan
- Carmel Valley
- Santa Lucia Highlands
- Chalone
- Arroyo Seco
- San Lucas
- Paso Robles
- York Mountain
- Edna Valley
- Arroyo Grande
- Santa Maria Valley
- Santa Ynez Valley

CALIFORNIA

California's interior and Central Valley.

Monterey County vineyards supply producers of "fighting varietals"—the name given to varietal-label wines that sell in the $7 to $12 range and "fight" for shelf space in supermarkets and retail shops. Wines made from Monterey grapes are often blended with wines made from other parts of the state, and so most often the appellation that appears on the label of these relatively inexpensive but quite drinkable wines is "California."

The Monterey AVA is one of those county-wide-and-beyond AVAs, but some smaller AVAs in this part of the North Central Coast have developed a reputation for great wines, mostly whites, with a smattering of extraordinary Pinot Noir, too. The Arroyo Seco AVA is known for Chardonnay, Riesling, and

Gewurztraminer; the Chalone AVA for Chardonnay, Pinot Blanc, and Pinot Noir; the Santa Lucia Highlands AVA for high-elevation Chardonnay and Pinot Noir as well as Cabernet Sauvignon and Merlot grown closer to the Salinas Valley floor; and Mount Harlan for single-vineyard Pinot Noir (especially the Jensen, Mills, Selleck, and Reed vineyards).

What can be considered the "South Central Coast" comprises the counties of Santa Barbara and San Luis Obispo and has made a reputation for itself not only with the film *Sideways* but also with very fine Pinot Noir and Chardonnay produced from grapes grown in the Santa Maria Valley AVA and Santa Ynez Valley AVA in Santa Barbara County, and the Edna Valley and Arroyo Grande AVAs in San Luis Obispo

Wildhurst makes very good wines that express the soils and climate of Lake County at affordable prices.

Josh Jensen's Calera Wine Company produces extraordinary wines from single vineyards on California's Central Coast and in the Mount Harlan AVA.

County. Also in San Luis Obispo you will find the Paso Robles AVA, which still lives in the shadow of Napa and Sonoma, even though it produces wonderful examples of Zinfandel and Cabernet Sauvignon, as well as Syrah, Grenache, Petite Sirah, and several other varietals native to the Rhone Valley of France. The reds of Paso Robles are unique, especially those from vineyards planted on the west side of Highway 101 (rocky, dry soils), and are often great values.

Here are some of the region's best-known producers.

Central Coast AVA, Monterey AVA, Santa Barbara County, San Luis Obispo County: Antelope, Au Bon Climat, Beckmen, Bernardus, Bonny Doon, Byron, Calera, Callaway, Chalone, Edna Valley Vineyard, Fetzer Five Rivers, Foley, Hitching Post, Jekel, Los Olivos, Meridian, Millbrook, Mirassou, Robert Mondavi Private Selection, Morgan, Fess Parker, Qupé, Scheid, Talbott, Ivan Tamas Estates, and Wente.

Arroyo Grande, Edna Valley, Santa Maria, Santa Ynez, Santa Lucia Highlands, Santa Cruz Mountains, Sta. Rita Hills, and Mount Harlan AVAs: Andrew Murray, Au Bon Climat, Babcock, Bargetto, Byron, Cambria, Cottonwood Canyon, David Bruce, Fiddlehead, Firestone, Thomas Fogarty, Foxen, Gainey, Jaffurs, Justin, Kynsi, Lane Tanner, Mer Soleil, Morgan,

Ojai, Rancho Sisquoc, Sanford, Santa Cruz Mountain Winery, Saucelito Canyon, Smith and Hook, Steele, Talley, Testarossa, Whitcraft, and Zaca Mesa.

Paso Robles AVA: Adelaida, L'Aventure, Castoro, Dunning, Eberle, Edmunds St. John, EOS Estate, Justin, J. Lohr, Peachy Canyon, Rabbit Ridge, Ridge, Roudon-Smith, Tablas Creek, Talley, Turley, Martin Weyrich, Wild Horse, and York Mountain.

SIERRA FOOTHILLS AVA AND CALIFORNIA'S INTERIOR

Sierra Foothills. The Sierra Foothills AVA covers seven counties (Amador, El Dorado, Mariposa, Nevada, Placer, Tuolumne, and Yuba) and includes more than a hundred wineries and close to 5,000 acres/2,000 hectares of planted vineyards. Soon after the California gold rush, this area became the mother lode for California wine production, but by the time Prohibition hit in 1919, the region's wine industry was little more than a memory. It was revived in the 1970s because of the availability of relatively inexpensive land. The growing conditions are excellent for Zinfandel above all, but also for Cabernet Sauvignon, Merlot, Syrah, and Petite Sirah, as well as some red "Cal-Italians," Sangiovese and Barbera. Whites that do well in the region include Chardonnay and Sauvignon Blanc.

The Amador County appellation is just as likely to appear on a wine produced from this region, especially if it is Zinfandel. There are still hundreds of acres of pre-Prohibition vines planted in the area, and Amador County or Sierra Foothills Zin is almost always a soulful treat at an affordable price. Many of the wines can be found for under $10, and it is rare to break the $20 barrier unless the wines are sourced from heralded single vineyards (translation: worth the $20-plus price tag).

We highly recommend wines from this region of California for their quality, their earthiness, and their value. Still largely undiscovered—almost 90% of the grapes grown here are sold to producers outside the region—these gems are high on our lists of great and affordable wines.

In the Sierra Foothills AVA, Amador County, and Calaveras County, some of the best-known producers are Amador Foothill, Black Sheep, Boeger, Chatom, Easton, Karly, Lava Cap, Madrona, Montevina, Renaissance, Renwood, Sierra Vista, Silver Fox, Sobon Estate, St. Amant, Stevenot, Sutter Ridge, and Z-52.

California's Central Valley. Most often referred to in oversimplified wine-speak as the San Joaquin Valley, this region is best known as *the* source for inexpensive "fighting varietals" and the increasingly shrinking generic-label category ("Chablis," "Burgundy," "Champagne," etc.). Most often, wines from this region, which grows grapes for close to 70% of the wines produced in the state, will receive the "California" appellation on the label. Two notable exceptions that have become increasingly popular and

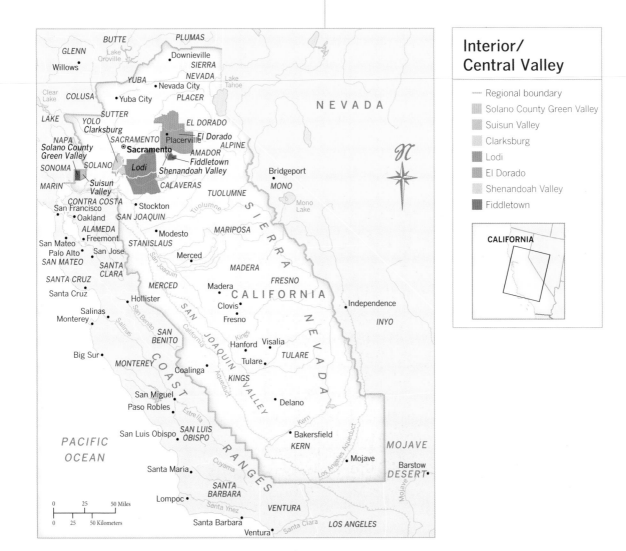

California's interior and Central Valley.

The Sierra Foothills, where gold was first discovered during California's gold rush, is the ancestral home of the state's wine industry, with some very good wines from some very old vines.

Amador County is home to some of the oldest Zinfandel vines in California, and several producers make earthy, brawny Zins. Montevina, owned by the Trinchero family, makes a prime example of the style.

sought-after in the last ten years are the Clarksburg AVA and the Lodi AVA.

Clarksburg, with 9,000 acres/3,600 hectares under vine, is known for excellent Chenin Blanc and Petite Sirah. Clarksburg is home to Bogle, a sixth-generation producer that farms more than 1,200 acres (485 hectares) and is famous for quality wines at very fair prices.

Lodi, in the northernmost part of the San Joaquin Valley, benefits from the breezes of cool air provided by the Sacramento River delta. Over the last ten years, Lodi has become a sought-after AVA, especially for Zinfandel. Famous Zin producers such as Ravenswood, Turley, and Joel Gott produce wines proudly bearing the Lodi AVA on the label. Today, it is easy to find single-vineyard Zinfandel from the Lodi AVA. Prices for these wines are still reasonable, but they are quickly increasing. If you're a *WineWise* reader who loves great Zin and great value, check these wines out now, before the prices go crazy. Here are some of the best-known producers.

Clarksburg AVA: Bogle, Dancing Coyote, Dry Creek, Ehrhardt, Herzog (kosher), and Tantalus.

Lodi AVA: Bogle, Borra, Delicato/Gnarly Head, E², Fenestra, Joel Gott, Harmony Wynelands, Herzog (kosher), Jessie's Grove, J. Lohr, Pepperwood Grove/Sebastiani, Ravenswood, Talus, Van Ruiten Family, and Woodbridge/Robert Mondavi.

"California" wines

Wines, whether in bottles, or boxes, that simply have the word "California" on their label are usually inexpensive wines produced on a moderately large to frighteningly humongous level. The grapes are planted and harvested throughout the state, and wines with the "California" appellation are usually produced using purchased grapes. There are easily hundreds of brands, and sometimes multiple brands might be owned by the same producer (Gallo, the single largest family-owned winery and the second-largest wine producer in the world, owns dozens of separate wine brands—Turning Leaf, Gossamer Bay, Dancing Bull, Indigo Hills, Carlo Rossi, and many others—all bearing the "California" appellation).

Wine geeks and wine snobs (for whom there is a special place in hell) often dismiss "California" wines as somehow beneath them, not worth drinking. Much like someone who declares a book or film obscene without reading the book or screening the film, these people show their own ignorance. Admittedly, we are not talking about the world's greatest wines here, but "California" wines serve several useful purposes. They are good entry-level wines for folks who are just getting into wine. They are affordable. And most of the time they are true to their varietal type, so if you have little experience with, say, Sauvignon Blanc or Merlot and you want to find out about them without making a heavy financial commitment, these are good wines for you to enjoy.

As the California wine industry has expanded, an interesting phenomenon has occurred. Quite a few well-known producers in Napa and Sonoma have started second-label wines with "California" labels. Robert Mondavi, the Napa Valley legend, was among the first to do this, establishing the budget-friendly Woodbridge line of California varietal wines. Sometimes the wines are marketed under their own names, and sometimes they create a fantasy brand. We think that this is a good subcategory for the WineWise consumer. Napa or Sonoma wineries that have established a reputation for quality in their home bases cannot risk putting out an inferior "California" wine, even at a much lower price point. If they do, the bad word of mouth will come back to bite them. These wines, which define the "fighting varietal" category, start at under $5 and rarely exceed $15. So don't make the bonehead move that the truly uninformed wine consumer makes in passing by one of these "California" appellation wines because it's "too cheap." That would not be WineWise.

Obviously, we can't—nor would we want to—list all the "California" wine brands, so we'll limit ourselves to producers we trust. But if you see a "California" wine for seven or eight bucks and something about it calls to you (usually it's a pretty label; that's okay, we've all fallen for those), pick it up, and enjoy it. These days, chances are the wine will be better than you expected.

Of the "California" appellation wines, some of the most reliable producers (some of which offer very good bargains) include Amberhill, Antelope Valley, Arrow Creek, Barefoot Cellars, Benziger, Beringer, Blackstone, Bogle, Bonny Doon, BV Coastal Estates, Camelot, Callaway Coastal, Canyon Road, Carmenet, Cline, Francis Coppola Presents, Corbett Canyon, Dancing Bull Zinfandel, Delicato, Dog House, Dunnewood, Echelon, Estancia, La Famiglia, Fetzer, Folie a Deux, Foppiano, Forest Glen, ForestVille, Daniel Gehrs, Joel Gott, Herzog, Hess Select, Husch, Ironstone, Jewel Collection, Kendall-Jackson, Kenwood, Korbel (sparkling), J. Lohr, Marietta Cellars, Meridian, Mirassou, Le Mistral, Pepi, Pepperwood Grove, R. H. Phillips/Toasted Head, Quady, Rabbit Ridge, Ravenswood Vintners Blend, Round Hill, Smoking Loon, Sutter Home, Talus, 3 Blind Moose, Turning Leaf, Vendange, Wine Block, and Woodbridge/Robert Mondavi.

Talus is a fairly large wine producer in Lodi, California. The Lodi AVA has become an important wine region, especially for red wines.

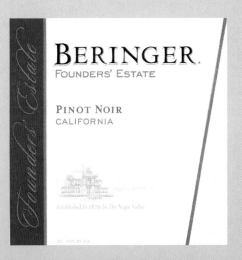

Beringer is a famous name in Napa Valley, but like so many other well-known and respected producers, it also produces a wide variety of "California" wines. About 75% of the state's wines bear the simple "California" appellation, meaning that the grapes are sourced throughout the state.

Coppola Bianco, a budget-priced, easy-drinking "California" Pinot Grigio.

chapter 5

Living in the USA
Washington, Oregon, New York

You could challenge yourself to taste every single wine produced in California and never repeat yourself for the rest of your life. While it might be fun, you'd be missing out on some of the best wines produced in the United States—the wines of Washington State, Oregon, and New York State.

Life without Merlot and Syrah from Washington, Pinot Noir and Pinot Gris from Oregon, or Riesling and Cabernet Sauvignon from New York is not much of a life for an American wine drinker. These three states have emerged from California's shadow to establish their own identities, their own signatures, their own wines.

Let's take a tour of the most important wine regions in Washington, Oregon, and New York. Hopefully, our wine-stained prose will get you to try some of these wines or to confirm your appreciation for wines from these states; we can almost guarantee that once you've tried them, you'll love them. We'll start our excursion in the nation's second-largest wine-producing state, Washington . . .

Washington

IF YOU THINK that only California makes good American wine, you are missing a whole lot. Stylistically, Washington State wines lie somewhere between the exuberant fruitiness of California or Australia and the sometimes too reserved, sometimes just plain underripe nature of French wines. In other words, Washington State offers the best of both worlds—ripeness and the subtle intrigue of nuanced flavor. Washington State and its wine producers certainly have a good thing going: the history of vineyard development is astounding, and the potential for future expansion is mind-boggling. Even though the

rate of growth has slowed from a new winery opening every eleven days in 2000 to every fifteen days today, that rate is still unheard of in other parts of the world. As for future growth, imagine this: the current area of planted vineyards in the entire state is a little more than 30,000 acres (12,000 hectares)—but the available area that could be planted in the Columbia Valley, Washington's largest AVA, is 11 *million* acres (4.5 million hectares).

What does Washington have to support its claim that it is and will be an important producer of premium-quality wines? First and foremost, it has a climate that is conducive to optimal ripening of a number of different grape varieties. Second, it has established an academic/scientific/practical backing for the wine industry in the form of two- and four-year degree programs in viticulture and enology (that's grape growing and winemaking for the rest of us) at Washington State University to help satisfy the industry's ever-growing need for trained personnel. Third, the Washington Wine Commission is an industry-financed organization that promotes and protects the quality image of Washington wines by creating labeling standards that go beyond the federal government's requirements.

Before we get into the various AVAs and their attributes, let's look at Washington's special labeling provisions and their impact, the major grape varieties used, and the climatic advantages that the state's vineyards enjoy.

Washington's label language

As a mature consumer, wise in the ways of the marketing world, you are probably aware that there is much hyperbole in product labeling. And as a *WineWise* reader, we hope you have learned that, in some respects, wine labels are no different. The Washington Wine Commission created the Washington Wine Quality Alliance to address some of those inconsistencies and to provide consumers with a greater assurance of wine quality. Unfortunately, the provisions adopted by the Alliance need be followed only by the Alliance's member wineries, and not all of the state's

The sweeping expanse of Columbia Valley vineyards.

wineries are members. However, it is a pretty safe bet that most if not all of the state's producers agree with the labeling standards and follow them.

PLACE NAMES

If a place name is used on a Washington wine label, 100% of the grapes must come from that place, as compared to 85% under the federal standard. This applies to any place name. Obviously that includes all of the AVAs within the state, but it also applies to other foreign place names that are still used by American producers of generic-label wines. By this standard, then, the use of terms such as "Chablis" and "Champagne" is not permitted.

RESERVE

The Wine Alliance has taken a similarly hard line on the use of the word "Reserve" on labels, and once again we applaud them. In Washington, the term "Reserve" may be applied to a maximum of 10% of total production, which may not exceed 3,000 thousand cases, and the wine labeled as "Reserve" must be demonstrably higher in quality. This is certainly a step in the right direction. We hope the future will see other vague terms defined, such as "old vines." What about it, Washington?

GRAPE TYPE

Were you hoping that Washington's wine laws require 100% of whatever grape is named on the label? Well, that is not the case, and for very good reasons. In terms of tons harvested in 2005, Merlot and Cabernet Sauvignon racked up an impressive 38,000 tons, from a total red grape harvest of 52,000 tons. And if two red grapes ever screamed to be blended, it is those two. Given this scenario, it is no surprise that the state has stuck with the basic federal requirement that a grape name on the label requires that the wine be made from a minimum of 75% of the named varietal. Frankly, you should be thankful. With their naturally high tannin level and aggressive acidity, many 100% Cabernet Sauvignons are so severe they should not be wished on anybody but your worst enemies. And we believe that with very few exceptions, Merlot will always benefit from the amelioration that other grape types, even in small percentages, bring to a blend.

Major grape types

Simply put, Washington uses a wide variety of grape types in many climatic settings, from Riesling to Chardonnay, and from Cabernet Franc to Syrah. There are also exploratory plantings and bottlings of Sangiovese and Tempranillo, a welcomed addition in the sea of Cab and Chard.

One bright spot on the horizon is the rapidly increasing acreage of Syrah. If you ever get the opportunity to sample Washington State Syrah, do not hesitate. It is full-bodied but not overpowering, enrobed in a fruity-herbal-spice mix of dark plums, licorice, and black pepper. Yummy, and you will want to go back for more. Remember as well that wherever there is Syrah you are likely to find Grenache, which can be equally delicious, either on its own or as part of a blend with Syrah.

Lastly, Gewurztraminer deserves mention as a very enjoyable wine from this corner of the United States, sometimes produced dry or almost dry, other times left with a little sweetness to make it a bright, fruity summer white or an equally bright partner with Vietnamese or Korean dishes.

Climate

Let's be blunt. Washington is more than Seattle, that depressingly dark and rainy birthplace of depressingly dark grunge. There is an AVA called Puget Sound in the Seattle area, but it's a very small player. The hub of Washington State wine activity is eastward, inland, on the desert side of the Cascade Mountain range.

The Columbia River Basin has a sunny disposition, with a good two hours of sunlight more per day than the average California vineyard. But that does not make the region unrelentingly hot. Like most deserts, the entire area enjoys relatively cool nighttime temperatures, an essential element in quality wine production. Sun and heat may seem like advantages for ripening, but too much heat can produce both high sugars and low acids far too quickly in grapes that have not had enough time to fully develop all of their ripe flavor characteristics. They are like a young gymnast or violinist who shows precocious promise but never matures to an accomplished athlete or musician. Cool nighttime temperatures are an advantage, slowing down the vines' and grapes' development and allowing those grapes to enjoy every minute of the long daylight hours that are the blessing of the extreme northwestern United States.

We have to say it: size matters! The huge geographic area covered by Washington's AVAs means that there are many different, varied terrains in many different climatic pockets, with south-facing slopes offering more direct sun and heat for red grapes such as Cabernet Sauvignon, and cooler, north-facing slopes more suited to the delicate varieties such as Riesling. In many other grape-growing regions we might deride the possibility of several different grape varietals in the vineyards as a lack of direction instead of a rational determination of what will grow best. But in Washington State we have to applaud the broad variety of grapes that can be grown, with each one taking advantage of different climatic conditions. Variety can be the spice of Washington wine, and we say spice it up!

WineWise Washington AVAs

Currently, there are nine AVAs in Washington State. You very rarely see any wine labeled as simply "Washington State," mostly because almost all of the land that could possibly be planted to vineyards is covered by the huge Columbia Valley AVA and the AVAs that lie within it: Yakima Valley, Walla Walla Valley, Horse Heaven Hills, Rattlesnake Hills, Red Mountain, and Wahluke Slope. Adjacent to the Columbia Valley, on the Columbia River, which separates Washington from Oregon, is the much smaller AVA of Columbia Gorge, and toward the west is the Puget Sound AVA, which includes the cities of Olympia and Seattle.

COLUMBIA VALLEY

This is the big one, the AVA you are most likely to see on a bottle of Washington wine, simply because, at 17,000 planted acres (7,000 hectares), Columbia Valley produces more grapes than any other AVA in the state. It also produces a very broad array of different grape types from a seemingly endless variety of

climatic conditions, though we would still like to see more plantings of the lesser-known varietals. Columbia Valley is almost the "anti-appellation," representing everything that appellations are not supposed to be. It is too big and too diverse for anybody to make the claim that there is a Columbia Valley style. Since the creation of the Columbia Valley AVA in 1984, we have seen six other AVAs created within its boundaries, a sure—and welcome—sign that grape growers and wine producers are identifying and acting on geographic, topographic, and climatic differences.

That said, we would never suggest that you shy away from Columbia Valley wines. They are too plentiful and too good to avoid. By now, the savvy WineWise reader realizes that there are three main grape types that have captured attention in Columbia Valley—Cabernet Sauvignon, Merlot, and Riesling. And if you just cannot get enough Chardonnay, then by all means try the Chardonnay, too. With the immense size of the AVA, it is impossible to give specific information about climatic conditions, but if you read on the back label that the Cab or Merlot benefited from south-facing slopes that get the full impact of the sun, then go for it—it is unlikely you will be disappointed. Columbia Valley single-varietal versions of Cabernet Sauvignon and Merlot, along with Cab/Merlot/CabFranc blends, all offer well-tuned, ripe fruit with firm structure and refreshing acidity—they are assertive but not overpowering wines, playing their part as a partner with food, especially world-class Washington State lamb.

With Riesling, we are pleased to report that the last five years have seen an increase in the tonnage of Riesling harvested, and we hope that trend continues. Recently, this Riesling movement got a boost from a

Columbia Valley label.

partnership between Chateau Ste. Michelle, Washington's largest producer, and Dr. Ernst Loosen, one of the most respected Riesling producers in the world-famous Mosel Valley of Germany. The result of that partnership, "Eroica," is one of the finest non-German Rieslings produced anywhere, juicily ripe with a salivating freshness and slight mineral quality. We hope that the other already fine producers of Washington Riesling will respond to the challenge of this new standard. Picture yourself on an Olympic Penin-

sula waterfront (even in the rain) with fabulous local seafood and glorious local Riesling—ah, life is good!

The Ste. Michelle organization is also a leader in high-quality sparkling wine production at very reasonable prices under the Domaine Ste. Michelle label, and in the development of single-vineyard varietal red and white still wines. Indeed, it is no exaggeration to say that Ste. Michelle is a sort of mini-Washington unto itself. Having tirelessly promoted the state's wines with attractively priced single varietals

Washington State

- Columbia Gorge AVA (also in Oregon)
- Columbia Valley AVA (also in Oregon)
- Horse Heaven Hills AVA
- Puget Sound AVA
- Rattlesnake Hills AVA
- Red Mountain AVA
- Wahluke Slope AVA
- Walla Walla Valley (also in Oregon)
- Yakima Valley AVA

Oregon

- Applegate Valley AVA
- Chehalem Mountains AVA
- Eola Hills AVA
- Dundee Hills AVA
- McMinnville AVA
- Ribbon Ridge AVA
- Red Hill AVA
- Rogue Valley AVA
- Southern Oregon AVA
- Umpqua Valley AVA
- Willamette Valley AVA
- Yamhill-Carlton AVA

Map of the Washington State and Oregon AVAs.

The Red Willow Vineyard in Yakima Valley.

for many years, the company was so successful that it could branch out into bubbly production and high-end single-vineyard wines. That is essentially what all of Washington is about—well-made, affordable wines, plus some very fine top-notch specialties.

Additional relative bargains can be found from Hogue Cellars, Covey Run, and Columbia Crest—the Riesling and Gewurztraminer from any of those three are very enjoyable wines, very well suited to slightly spicy foods.

YAKIMA VALLEY

Although Yakima Valley was Washington's first AVA, it is now within the large Columbia Valley AVA. Even so, it has maintained its reputation as a premium site for the fuller-flavored red grape types such as Cabernet Sauvignon, Merlot, and Syrah. This is a reflection of the south-facing slopes situated to the north of the west-to-east-flowing Yakima River. These slopes provide plenty of warm sun during the growing season. They also allow for "air drainage" during the cooler months at the beginning and end of the season—this means that cold air will not sit still long enough to cause a frost that could damage the vines. A number of independent growers have developed excellent reputations for their vineyards, and large and small

wineries alike vie for the privilege to buy their grapes. One of the most well-known examples is Red Willow Vineyard. If you spot this name on a bottle of Yakima Valley wine, you will be in for a treat.

WALLA WALLA VALLEY

This is a special place. Being in the Walla Walla Valley, in the southeast interior of the state, is like being on an island ringed by a circle of mountains, far away from all other civilization. Not that Walla Walla is swank—it's downcountry and farmer-friendly. Most of the people who make the wines here actually get their hands dirty and callused in the vineyards.

It's hot and dry most of the time, and, once again, Cabernet, Merlot, and Syrah dominate the plantings, producing rich and ripe flavors of dark fruit, balanced by a refreshing streak of acidity. The local Blue Mountains provide some higher elevations at which grape varieties such as Gewurztraminer, Sangiovese, and Cabernet Franc do well in the cooler climate.

RED MOUNTAIN

This is Washington's smallest AVA, a modest 4,000 acres (1,600 hectares) in total, which is minuscule compared to most other AVAs in the state. Only about 800 acres (320 hectares) of that area are planted to vineyards, again with Cab, Merlot, and Syrah taking up the most room. This is not at all surprising. As a relatively lately designated AVA (2001), the area had already made its name for its warm, south-facing slopes, best suited to the fuller-flavored reds. With only that small acreage to play with, it is unlikely you will see any bottles labeled as Red Mountain Merlot unless you go to the source. However, if you do, remember that is what your credit cards are for—to enjoy the rare experiences that life throws at you, such as site-specific, well-made wine to be enjoyed with friends.

PUGET SOUND, COLUMBIA GORGE, HORSE HEAVEN HILLS, WAHLUKE SLOPE, RATTLESNAKE HILLS

The track record of these AVAs is spotty at best, with the final four having been designated only within the last three years. Still, Horse Heaven, Wahluke, and Rattlesnake all lie within Columbia Valley, and we hope all will continue the trend toward smaller, distinctive, quality-driven areas.

The stony soils of the Cayuse Vineyards in Walla Walla. (Washington Wine Commission)

Both Columbia Gorge (300 planted acres, 120 hectares) and Puget Sound (80 planted acres, 32 hectares) are geared more toward cooler-climate grape types such as Gewurztraminer, Pinot Noir, and Pinot Gris. Indeed, the Puget Sound area has such an unreliable climate that it has turned toward hardier varieties such as Madeleine Angevine and Muller-Thurgau. If you're in the area and you find a bottle of Madeleine Angevine, go ahead, buy a bottle and enjoy it on your picnic. While it won't stop the world, it's a fresh, fruity white, great in a casual way.

Further updated information about Washington State's AVAs and their wineries and wines can be found at www.washingtonwines.org.

Oregon

IN THE LATE 1960s and early 1970s, a number of disillusioned young men, unhappy about the mainstreaming and consumerization of their alternative, hippy lifestyle, left California. With no place farther west to move to, they headed north to Oregon and found new idyllic places for them to drop out. Among this happy band of wanderers were some California winemakers who had become similarly discontent with what they saw as too much emphasis on grape types and not enough consideration of soil and climate combinations.

Fortunately for us and for our *WineWise* readers, the wine industry has its fair share of mavericks and independents. The world benefits from their pioneer spirit in the form of new adventures and better wine. California had been concentrating on Cabernet Sauvignon and Chardonnay. These people wanted something else, and in Oregon they found the near perfect climate and soil conditions for Pinot Noir and related varieties. As a result of their efforts, the world now has another dimension of Pinot to consider, and all Pinot lovers are grateful for it. They have also raised the bar in terms of what is meant by quality Pinot Noir, not just for American Pinot but for the world. With Oregon as a model, Carneros was able to come into its own, New Zealand has developed its Pinot mecca in Central Otago, and the producers of the movie *Sideways* took us along on a humorous if puerile road trip in Santa Barbara's Pinot country.

Willamette Valley vineyards resting after a hard day's work.

Climate

Our general image of the climate in the U.S. Northwest—cloudy, gray, and rainy—is more applicable to the Oregon wine industry than to Washington State's. That is because the Oregon vineyards are located on the ocean side of the Cascade Mountains, so moisture picked up by westerly winds over the ocean is dropped as the air currents rise and cool when they hit the mountains. This classifies the Oregon vineyard climate as distinctly cool and maritime, especially in the northern part of the state. In that fairly uniform climate, the range of grapes that can be grown is limited mostly to cool-climate varieties such as Pinot Noir, Riesling, Chardonnay, and Pinot Gris.

As you move southward toward the border with California, temperatures are warmer on average, and cloud cover and rainfall diminish, allowing warmer-climate grape varieties to fare well, including Cabernet Sauvignon, Merlot, and even Syrah and Viognier.

Grape types

If you didn't know already, you will have guessed by now that Oregon is Pinot Noir country for most growers, winemakers, and wine lovers. Good Oregon Pinot delivers the kind of red fruit character that is associated with the grape, but it tends to be more in the cherry zone than raspberry or cranberry. It is a little denser and fuller than the average red Burgundy and is beautifully enhanced by clean, crisp acidity and firm tannins that take the wine a little beyond medium-bodied. Oregon's wine gurus obviously know how to grow the grape to achieve full, ripe character and how to make the grapes into world-class wines.

As important, Oregon's chefs and restaurateurs understand the versatility of Pinot Noir with Oregon's food bounty, matching the wine effortlessly with planked wild salmon or with lamb kebabs.

But there are other dimensions to the Oregon wine scene. The natural partner to Pinot Noir everywhere else in the world is Chardonnay, as evidenced in Champagne, Burgundy, and Carneros. But Oregon Chardonnay has had a hard time making a name for itself. Maybe that is simply because there is already an ocean of Chardonnay in the world. But that is not the whole story. Without getting too technical, within the Chardonnay group of grapes there are different strains with slightly different characteristics. The Chardonnay version that was originally planted in Oregon was brought directly from California, where it worked well in the warm climate. Transplanted to cooler Oregon, it did not fare well, producing wines that lacked the lemony zip that makes Chardonnay interesting. In the meantime, as the reputation for Oregon Chardonnay went into a nosedive, the fascination with Pinot Noir soared. In the last ten years, the acreage of Pinot has more than doubled, while plantings of Chardonnay have fallen by 30%. But the faithful still believe. They have researched strains of Chardonnay better suited to Oregon's cooler climate and longer growing season, and they are convinced they can make Chardonnay with verve and zip that will rival their best Pinot Noir for quality. Given the emphasis on Pinot Noir and the presence of Chardonnay, it shouldn't take a degree in winemaking to figure out that sparkling wine could be a good choice for Oregon, and sure enough, the Argyle winery has chosen to do just that, and very successfully, offering a line of high-quality bubblies made by the Champagne Method.

Looking for a viable white wine to partner with their benchmark red, Pinot Noir, the Oregon growers and their diehard fans embraced a most unlikely candidate that has now become a real winner—Pinot Gris. Undoubtedly, Oregon Pinot Gris benefits from its association with the Italian version, Pinot Grigio (some Oregon producers now use the Italian varietal name on their labels), but its star began to ascend long before the popularity of Pinot Grigio. Plantings of Oregon's "gray" Pinot have trebled in the last ten years, as growers and winemakers obviously see the grape and the wine as a quality alternative to a glut of poorly made, mediocre white wine in general. But beware—Oregon Pinot Gris is not your average Pinot Grigio. Good Pinot Gris, whether from Alsace or

Oregon Pinot Noir label.

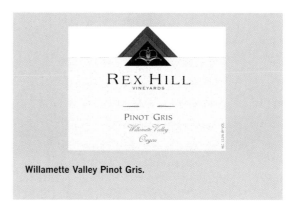

Willamette Valley Pinot Gris.

Oregon, will almost always display considerably more body and structure, with ripe melon flavors and a hint of orange scent. It is a beautiful wine to pair with freshly caught Northwest salmon, any other grilled firm-fleshed fish with pineapple-and-melon salsa, or spice-rubbed pork.

There are still those who believe that Riesling is a grape with great potential in Oregon, and certainly the climate seems to be conducive to great Riesling that displays ripe citrus fruit and zingy acidity with floral overtones. But acreage has decreased by one-quarter in the last decade, and we have yet to find a world-class Oregon Riesling. They tend to lack the delicacy and finesse that make Riesling special.

Moving away from the cool-climate grape types of the north, the southern part of Oregon tends to be far more varied in its plantings, with everything from Cabernet Sauvignon and Syrah inland to Riesling and Gewurztraminer nearer the coast.

Language of the label

With the early and modern history of Oregon being concentrated on single-variety wines such as Pinot Noir, Chardonnay, and Pinot Gris, it is no surprise that the local wine industry pushed for stiffer regulations concerning varietal labels. For any Oregon wine, if a grape type is mentioned on a label, the wine must contain at least 90% of that grape, as compared to 75% in the federal regulations. The one exception is that the minimum percentage remains at 75% for any wine labeled as Cabernet Sauvignon, mostly because, as our *WineWise* readers now know so well, Cabernet can almost always benefit from significant blending.

In addition, Oregon, like its neighbor Washington, has banned the use of all generic terms such as "Champagne" and "Burgundy."

AVAs

Oregon now has a total of fourteen AVAs, though seven of those have a very brief history, having been approved for use with the 2006 vintage onward. Two

Willamette Valley vineyards.

of the fourteen are relatively insignificant, being small portions of Walla Walla Valley and the tiny Columbia Gorge that extend into Oregon from Washington. The AVA that garners all the attention and has perhaps brought the most fame to Oregon is the Willamette Valley, which begins just south of the city of Portland, on the northern border of the state, and extends to just south of the state capital, Eugene, in the central coastal part of the state. Within the boundaries of the Willamette Valley AVA lie six of the seven new AVAs: Chehalem Mountain, Dundee Hills, Eola Hills, McMinnville, Ribbon Ridge, and Yamhill Carlton District.

The other AVAs with a lengthy track record are Southern Oregon, an umbrella AVA encompassing the smaller AVAs of Umpqua Valley (including the very recent Red Hill Douglas County AVA), Rogue Valley, and Applegate Valley.

WILLAMETTE VALLEY AVA

This is Oregon's most famous AVA, the one with all the glitterati of medal-winning winemakers, both maverick and mainstream. Whether it's the rocky sternness of the Yamhill sub-AVA, the iron and full-blooded style from Dundee and McMinnville, or the lighter fruitiness of Eola, there is something for every Pinot Noir disciple here. The richly textured Pinot Gris excels here as well, and the saints of Chardonnay continue to seek out the right plots that offer the cool climate and mineral soils Chardonnay loves.

For moderately expensive versions of Pinot Noir, Pinot Gris, and Chardonnay, we suggest the following producers—look for their basic line or perhaps the label that carries the appellation "Oregon" rather than "Willamette Valley": King Estate, Bridgeview, Eola Hills, Willamette Valley Vineyards, Domaine Drouhin, Erath, Sokol Blosser, Archery Summit, Rex Hill, Hip Chicks Do Wine, and Cooper Creek (certified biodynamic). Argyle's sparkling wine also fits in here.

For more expensive wines, try these best bottles: Adelsheim, Ponzi, Panther Creek, Eyrie, Chehalem, Beaux Freres, Ken Wright, Anne Amie, Amity, Benton Lane, Bethel Heights, Domaine Drouhin, Firesteed, Hamacher, Henry Estate, Panther Creek, St. Innocent, and WillaKenzie Estate.

Vineyards in Oregon's Dundee Hills. (Patrick Prothe; Wine Council)

SOUTHERN OREGON AVA (AND ITS SMALLER AVAS OF UMPQUA VALLEY, RED HILL DOUGLAS COUNTY, ROGUE VALLEY, APPLEGATE VALLEY)

As soon as you leave the Willamette Valley and travel south toward the other AVAs, the hubbub dies down. It's not that the growers and winemakers here do not have the conviction that they are doing a good job, but there is a noticeable absence of the grape patriotism that pervades the northern part of the state. Instead of "All Hail the Mighty Pinot" as anthem, the song is about diversity and differences. This is undoubtedly caused, at least in part, by a lack of uniform climate. The Willamette Valley AVA in northern Oregon is a relatively compact area, centered around the Willamette River, but the Southern Oregon AVA (and its smaller AVAs of Umpqua Valley, Red Hill Douglas County, Rogue Valley, and Applegate Valley) fans out to include protected, warmer inland river valleys as well as cooler coastal regions. As we have already mentioned, you will find everything planted here, from Riesling to Syrah, including northern Italian varieties such as Dolcetto and Spanish varieties including Tempranillo.

Both the Rogue Valley and the Applegate Valley are hemmed in by mountains that make for an overall warm climate favoring Cabernet, Merlot, Syrah, and the like. What will help them on the road to international recognition is a substantial difference between day and nighttime temperatures that keeps acidity levels high in the finished wines, making the flavors seem fresher and longer-lasting in the mouth.

Vineyard land is cheaper in southern Oregon, which makes for a greater probability of finding relative bargains or moderately expensive wines from producers such as Foris, Bridgeview, Hillcrest, Abacela (which specializes in Spanish and Italian varietals), Girardet, Spangler, Marshanne Landing (making "out of this world" Rhone and Bordeaux blends), Agate Ridge, Cricket Hill, Del Rio, Devitt, and Madrone Mountain (dessert wines).

New York State

BEFORE WE GET TO singing the praises of New York's best wines—and there is much to sing about—we need to give you the full picture, and in New York that picture is not completely pretty. Too much New York State wine continues to be made from native varietals, such as Niagara, Catawba, and especially Concord grapes (though most Concords are used for jams, jellies, and juices). We don't recommend these wines unless you like a grapey, jammy wine that really tastes more like overly sweet juice and harsh alcohol and not much else.

What we call "compromise wines" are made in the state from hybrid varietals—biological crosses of vinifera and native parents. Examples of prominent hybrids in New York State are Seyval Blanc and Vidal (white) and Marechal Foch and Baco Noir (red). The reason for hybrids in New York State: they are resistant to cold weather and plant diseases, and because of their parentage, they give an approximation of vinifera-quality wine. Wines made from these and other hybrid grapes can be tasty, but to be frank, just as often they can be bad, even nasty.

Today, we are happy to report that we've tasted great Hudson River Region Chardonnay that blows away a lot of California Chardonnay selling for more than twice the price. Many American Rieslings are not worth your time or money, but we believe that fine Finger Lakes Rieslings are among the best in the country. Cabernet Sauvignon, Merlot, and Cabernet Franc from Long Island have all garnered national and international attention, and the quality can be sublime. As with all regions, the reputation of the producer is important when purchasing, but few New York State wine producers are household names, so get ready to become WineWise about the best New York wines. Note that to get some of the best wines from small producers, you may have to visit the winery or make a virtual visit online.

AVAs

Currently, New York State has a total of nine AVAs.

NIAGARA ESCARPMENT REGION AVA

This is the newest AVA in the state, with six wineries and 400 acres (150 hectares) of vineyards. Bordering Lake Ontario to the north, this should be an area for Riesling, Chardonnay, and Pinot Noir to shine. Recommended producers are Eveningside Vineyards and Warm Lake Estate.

LAKE ERIE AVA

With a sea of Concord grapes covering 20,000 acres (8,000 hectares) in New York State (Lake Erie is a multistate AVA, containing parts of Ohio and Pennsylvania as well), growers in this region sell most of their fruit for grape juice and jelly. An exception to the rule among eight resident wineries that produce fruit wines and other novelties, Woodbury Winery produces good Chardonnay and Riesling.

Bully Hill, founded by the eccentric and creative Walter Taylor, produces wines in New York State's Finger Lakes wine region made mostly from hybrid grapes. Bully Hill labels feature Taylor's own humorous and witty artwork.

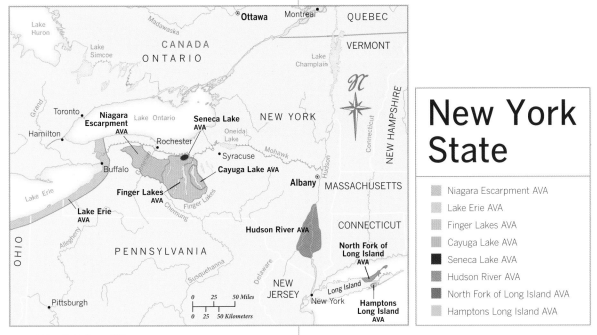

Map of New York State AVAs.

Legend:
- Niagara Escarpment AVA
- Lake Erie AVA
- Finger Lakes AVA
- Cayuga Lake AVA
- Seneca Lake AVA
- Hudson River AVA
- North Fork of Long Island AVA
- Hamptons Long Island AVA

THE FINGER LAKES AND TWO SUB-AVAS: CAYUGA LAKE AND SENECA LAKE

With more than 10,000 acres (4,000 hectares) of vineyards and about ninety wineries, the Finger Lakes (with its two sub-AVAs, Cayuga Lake and Seneca Lake) is the most important wine region in New York State, producing close to 90% of New York State's total wine production. Lakeside vineyard soils provide excellent drainage, and the moderating effects of Canandaigua, Keuka, Seneca, and Cayuga lakes control climatic extremes in the winter and summer.

Thanks to the pioneering work of the late Dr. Konstantin Frank (an émigré from Ukraine) and the late Charles Fournier (former president of Veuve Clicquot Champagne in France), vinifera grapes came to be accepted as commercially viable in the Finger Lakes region. Frank and Fournier forged an alliance that brought the entire New York State wine industry to a new level of quality.

Today, true Riesling lovers go nuts for Riesling wines from any of the Finger Lakes AVAs, especially the dry to semidry styles. Chardonnay and *methode champenoise* sparkling wines are also uniformly good

Hermann Wiemer has long been known as one of the best Riesling producers in the Finger Lakes wine region.

to excellent. The wines are good to great values, especially in whites and bubbly. The wineries of the Finger Lakes welcome hundreds of thousands of visitors every year, and several wineries have lovely tasting rooms, cafés, restaurants, and inns.

The best producers include Anthony Road, Atwater Estates, Chateau Frank (sparkling wines)

Konstantin Frank was a pioneering, quality-minded wine producer in the Finger Lakes; his efforts began in the 1950s. His winery, now run by his grandson Fred Frank, is one of a few American producers of Rkatsiteli, a delicious off-dry wine made from the grape of the same name.

Millbrook Winery is the leading producer of consistently high-quality wines in the Hudson River Region of New York State. Millbrook, whose reputation was established with good Chardonnay and Pinot Noir, is the only producer of the Italian varietal Tocai Friulano in New York State. The wine is crisp, fresh, dry, delicious, and quite affordable.

and Dr. Konstantin Frank's Vinifera Wine Cellars (still wines), Chateau Lafayette Renau, Fox Run, Glenora, Hazlitt 1852, Heron Hill, Hunt Country, Keuka Springs, Knapp, Lamoreaux Landing, McGregor, Rooster Hill, Keuka Overlook, Prejean, Red Newt, Salmon Run (second label for Dr. Frank, extremely good values), Sheldrake Point, Standing Stone, Swedish Hill, Wagner (fourth-generation growers, winery and brewery on site), and Hermann J. Wiemer (extraordinary wines and vinifera vines nursery).

THE HUDSON RIVER REGION AVA

All three *WineWise* authors live in the Hudson Valley, and so we would love to heap praise on all 500 acres (200 hectares) of our local vineyards and all twenty-five of our local wineries. Unfortunately, we can't. There are some gems, but there is still too much Seyval Blanc (a hybrid grape), some of it good, some not so good, produced here. The major producer of high-quality wine, especially Chardonnay, Pinot Noir, Cabernet Franc, and the historically Italian varietal Tocai Friulano, is Millbrook Winery (which, in fairness, has an owner with much deeper pockets than the other producers along the Hudson).

Other reputable producers of mostly vinifera-based wines include Whitecliff Vineyards and Rivendell Winery. Producers that do a good job with some vinifera, but also hybrids and fruit wines, include Alison Wines, Adair Vineyards, Baldwin Vineyards, Benmarl Winery (with some very good red hybrid-based wines), Brimstone Hill, Cascade Mountain, Clinton Vineyards, and Stoutbridge Winery.

LONG ISLAND AVA AND THE TWO SUB-AVAS: THE NORTH FORK OF LONG ISLAND AVA AND THE HAMPTONS, LONG ISLAND AVA

Long Island is probably the most sophisticated of all of New York State's wine regions. Long Island vineyards are planted solely to vinifera grapes; no hybrids, no native jam-and-jelly grapes. If you look at a map of the world, you'll see that Long Island is at the same latitude as Bordeaux, so it is no wonder that Merlot, Cabernet Sauvignon, and Cabernet Franc are the focus of the Long Island wine industry.

Long Island does have an inherent problem that it is unlikely to overcome: the cost of land and lack of agricultural land.

Lenz is a major Long Island wine producer, and the winery consistently produces very fine white, red, and sparkling wines from grapes grown in its own vineyards.

Considering that the expansion of Long Island's wine industry is limited, it has come a long way over the last thirty years or so (the first winery, Hargrave, was established in 1973). In the early 1980s, when there were fewer than a dozen wineries on Long Island, we can remember going to tastings and spitting out the wine not because it was the professional thing to do but because it was the only thing to do. However, as the vines aged and professional vineyard managers and winemakers came on board, the wines improved quickly.

In addition to the traditional Bordeaux varietals, Long Island produces good Chardonnay, some nice Gewürztraminer and Riesling, and is beginning to dabble in Syrah. The overwhelming majority of Long Island's vineyards and wineries are located in the North Fork AVA (about thirty wineries), with a smattering in The Hamptons AVA (just three).

Recommended producers include Bedell, Castello di Borghese, Channing Daughters, Corey Creek, Duck Walk, Lenz, Lieb Family, Macari, Martha Clara, Osprey's Dominion, Palmer, Paumanok, Peconic Bay, Pellegrini, Pindar, Pugliese, Raphael, Schneider, and Wölffer Estate.

For more information on New York State wines and wineries, or to buy wines (especially from the small producers without wide distribution), go to Uncork New York at www.newyorkwines.org.

chapter 6

Way down south
South America

Wines from Chile and Argentina are immensely popular in the United States wine market. In particular, Cabernet Sauvignon and Sauvignon Blanc wines from Chile as well as Malbec and Torrontes wines from Argentina have captured our imaginations and palates.

We often think of South American wines as basic wines that provide good value, and that's okay because there is an important place for such budget-based wines. But we need to take another look at the quality of these wines because although we can still find drinkable varietal-labeled wines from Chile or Argentina for about ten bucks, we can also find memorable, singular, expensive wines—both white and red—that are helping to redefine what it means to be a South American wine.

Let's take a look at the wines of Chile and Argentina. We think you'll find there's a lot to learn and a lot to enjoy about the wines from these two countries. When it comes to South American wines, if you're looking for bargains, you've found your region. If you're looking for a burgeoning quality-based wine region, you'll be glad you're here, too.

Let's start with a trip to Chile . . . ¡Vamos!

Chile: Bigger, better, and bargains

CHILE, the fourth-largest importer of wine to the United States, makes some wonderful wines and has established a solid reputation in the U.S. wine market for good value and quality, producing wines made mostly from internationally known varietals with good track records: Cabernet Sauvignon, Merlot, Chardonnay, and Sauvignon Blanc.

Chile has also had success with the Carmenere grape, a varietal with its ancestral roots in Bordeaux, where it is currently just about nonexistent. Chilean winemakers love to work with Carmenere, producing both varietal wines and Carmenere blends, usually partnered with Cabernet Sauvignon.

Chile entered the American market with a bang, providing drinkable wines at highly affordable prices, sometimes less than $5 per bottle. Those days are gone, but WineWise wine shoppers still should have no problem finding many Chilean wines priced under $10, however. Chile has not confined itself to bargain wines, however. Increasingly, we see quite a few truly expensive wines from Chile on retail shelves and on wine lists. Some of these wines are produced solely by Chilean winemakers, while others are made in partnership with French and American producers.

For Chile to find a toehold in the American luxury wine market, ironically it has to overcome its reputation as a supplier of bargain brands to appreciative and responsive wine consumers looking for value. Think about it: when you're out to dinner and want a special—and expensive—wine, is Chile the first place you think about? In most cases, unless the diner is a patriotic Chilean or has experience with a luxe Chilean import, he or she is thinking California, France, Italy, maybe Spain, or even Oregon Pinot Noir. For most of us, when it comes to expensive wines Chile is not even on our radar screen.

Concha y Toro's Don Melchor vineyard in Chile's Maipo Valley, at the foot of the Andes Mountains. Don Melchor Cabernet Sauvignon is one of the finest wines produced in the Southern Hemisphere. (Photo courtesy of Banfi Vintners)

Chile probably doesn't need *WineWise*'s help to sell its well-made value-driven wines. In the basic "fighting varietal" (fighting for retail shelf space with other $12-and-under wines), Chile is doing perfectly well, thank you. Whether or not Chile will become a major player in luxury wines is currently an unanswered question, but the ultra-premium Chilean wine industry believes it has the goods and will continue to produce these extraordinary wines, hoping to reach a larger audience.

The language of the label

Chile, like all New World wine producers, uses varietal labels for the overwhelming majority of its wines, which makes it easy for consumers to buy Chilean wines. If a varietal name appears on a label, the wine must be made from at least 85% of that named grape. Other labels are proprietary—fantasy names, just like some of the best-known wines from California ("Opus One," "Insignia," etc.). Here you'll find labels that read "Alpha M," "Domaine Paul Bruno," "Almaviva," "Clos Apalta," and so on.

Chile's vineyards cover a vast area of the country and are centered in the country's numerous river valleys. In the not-so-distant past, too many grapes were being harvested in these vineyards, and the overcropping led to diluted flavors. The best producers, realizing that they are now in a highly competitive international wine market, have abandoned this practice, and the overall quality of Chile's wines has markedly improved.

In addition to the name of the grape and the name of the producer, you may sometimes find on the label terms such as "*especial*" (the wine is aged a minimum of two years), "*reserva*" (at least four years of aging), or rarely "*gran vino*" (six years minimum). Beware the term "*reserva especial*," a marketing phrase with no legal meaning.

Of course, the names of Chile's wine regions will appear on wine labels. When a region (*denominacion*) is named, at least 85% of the grapes had to be harvested in that region. At right are the names of Chile's major wine regions and subregions that you're likely to find on labels.

Chile
Wine Regions and Subregions

Aconagua and Casablanca
■ Aconagua Valley
▥ Casablanca Valley

Central Valley
■ Maipo Valley
■ Rapel Valley
■ Curicó Valley
■ Maule Valley

Southern Region
■ Itata Valley
▥ Bío Bío Valley

Wine regions of Chile.

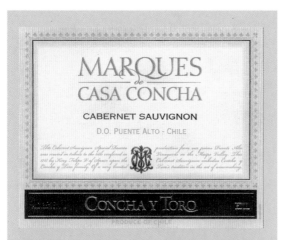

Marques de Casa Concha Cabernet Sauvignon is a single-vineyard estate-bottled red wine from the Puente Alto wine region of Chile. This is an excellent wine, with a moderate price (under $20).

Wine regions in Chile's Valle Central

The Maipo Valley is the most famous wine region here, with a reputation for good to excellent Cabernet Sauvignon, Merlot, and Carmenere. Also look for Puente Alto, a Maipo subregion with vineyards that produce stellar Cab and Merlot.

The reputation of the Rapel Valley, a reliable source of Cabernet Sauvignon, has been eclipsed by its subregion, the Colchagua Valley, where several boutique wineries and international partnerships sprang up starting in the 1990s.

Wine regions in Chile's Aconcagua Valley

Aconcagua grows a lot of Cabernet Sauvignon, Merlot, and Carmenere, and it has also become the focus for several international wine projects, anchored, of course by Cabernet Sauvignon and blends. The Aconcagua subregion of the Casablanca Valley benefits from the cool breezes and fog generated by the nearby Pacific Ocean and has become the most prized

denominacion for white wines, in particular Sauvignon Blanc, Chardonnay, and a bit of Gewurztraminer. These whites have up until now been obscured by the Cab-centric nature of the Chilean wine industry and are still good-to-great values ($8 and up), but we predict that this will not be the case much longer, so check them out now. The new and promising close-to-the-ocean cool-climate Aconcagua subregions of Leyda and San Antonio are producing fine examples of Sauvignon Blanc, Chardonnay, and—perhaps most important for varietal diversity in Chile's wine industry—Pinot Noir.

Chilean wines: The current picture

If it were not for the worldwide popularity of Cabernet Sauvignon, it's quite possible there would be no modern Chilean wine industry. Cab is the grape that defines Chilean wine and represents baseline quality for almost all of Chile's wine producers, especially those who seek export markets.

Most of the Chilean Cabernet Sauvignon in the $10-and-under category is made to satisfy thirsty, price-conscious consumers who like their wines to be fruit-driven, clean, and medium-to-full-bodied but without any hint of arch, bitter tannins. Chile produces these wines in abundance, and we recommend them for informal meals featuring either white or red meat, as well as richer pasta dishes or a meaty pizza. The wines can be enjoyed immediately and will be fine to drink for two or three years after you purchase them. These value-driven wines have a big presence in U.S. retail markets and are likely to show up on wine lists of informal bistros and bars that serve food, as well as a growing number of chain and theme restaurants across the country.

Our field research reveals something you really need to know about Chilean Cab: for a few dollars more—say, between $15 and $20—you can find wonderful, complex, ageworthy, *terroir*-driven Chilean wines that will knock your socks off. Some of the wines are estate-bottled or are made from grapes har-

Aurelio Montes is one of the best winemakers in Chile. He produces wines that sell for well under $10 to well over $100. His "Alpha" series sells for under $20, his "Alpha M" series for more than $50.

The Errazuriz "Don Maximiano" Estate, owned by the Chadwick family, produces fine single-vineyard Cabernet Sauvignon, Merlot, Syrah, and this Sauvignon Blanc.

vested in a single vineyard. If you love good Cabernet Sauvignon, these wines really deserve your attention.

Merlot has a checkered history in Chile due to misidentification—intentional or otherwise—of the grape, confusing it with Carmenere. All that stuff has come to an end, and Chile is producing some very good Merlot, mostly in the international, juicy, touch-of-sweetness style.

Carmenere has become Chile's own grape, and we are seeing more varietal-labeled Carmenere in the market, mostly at attractive prices. We like Carmenere, which is kind of a Cab/Merlot cross rolled into one grape, but find it a little too hollow or simple to carry a wine on its own. Carmenere is a great blender with Cabernet Sauvignon, however.

Chile has always produced a bit of Syrah, but with this varietal's growing popularity, often under the guise of its other name, Shiraz, watch for more Chilean Syrah to enter the U.S. market. Be the first in your neighborhood to taste one, especially the expensive but extraordinary Montes "Folly," with label art by Ralph Steadman.

White wines live in the shadow of Chilean reds, but this is changing, and not all that slowly. As people get off the Cabernet bandwagon, get back on, and then get off once more, Chilean Chardonnay grown in cool-climate regions is beginning to generate international buzz, and we've tasted some good wines at affordable prices. We're happy to report that the buzz generated by Chilean Sauvignon Blanc is even louder, and with good reason: Chile's best Sauvignon Blanc wines are classics, with refreshing lime juice and green fruits, real depth of flavor, lovely texture, and incredible food-friendliness, especially with fish. Right now, prices are still attractive, but they are sure to go up.

Our favorite producers

Much like Australia, many Chilean wine producers make "product lines" of wines that begin with inexpensive entries, include some moderately expensive choices, and go all the way to really costly. We'll identify some of the wines in each of these categories.

In the category of bargain and super-bargain producers from Chile (under $13) are Alfasi (kosher), Apaltagua, Aresti, Caliterra, Canepa, Casa Julia, Casa Lapostolle, Casillero del Diablo, Concha y Toro, Cousino-Macul, Echeverria, Luis Felipe Edwards, Errazuriz, Frontera, Hacienda El Condor, Haras de Pirque, Mapocho, Montes, MontGras, Morande, La Playa, Root:1, Santa Alicia, Santa Ema, Santa Carolina, Santa Rita "120," Sunrise, Tarapaca, Miguel Torres, Undurraga, Los Vascos, Veramonte, Walnut Crest, Xplorador, and Yelcho.

Moving up a notch, to wines that are moderately expensive to expensive (about $15 to $35): Carmen

A site-specific unfiltered Carmenere from Chile, from a single block of a single vineyard. Carmenere is an important red grape, both for blending with Cabernet Sauvignon and as the grape for its own varietal-labeled wines.

Many people told Aurelio Montes that it was "folly" to try to make a good Syrah in Chile. He proved them wrong by growing his grapes on a mountain estate in the Apalta Valley and making an extraordinary (and very expensive) wine from those grapes.

"Reserve," Casa Lapostolle "Cuvee Alexandre," Cono Sur (very good Pinot Noir), Concha y Toro "Marques de Casa Concha" (fine estate-bottled Cab and Merlot from Puente Alto), Concha y Toro "Terrunyo," Cousino-Macul "Finis Terrae" and "Antiguas Reserva," Luis Felipe Edwards "Dona Bernarda Coleccion Privada," Errazuriz "Grand Selection," Haras de Pirque "Elegance," Matetic, Montes "Alpha," La Playa "Maxima," Santa Ema "Catalina," Santa Rita "Medalla Real," Sincerity (from biodynamic vineyards), Miguel Torres "Cordillera" and "Manso de Velasco," Valdivieso "RSV" and "Single Vineyard," Los Vascos "Reserva," and Veramonte "Primus."

For wines that are truly expensive ($35 and up), try Almaviva, Antiyal (from biodynamic vineyards), Casa Lapostolle "Clos Apalta," Montes "Folly" and "Alpha M," Concha y Toro "Don Melchor" and "Amelia," Domaine Paul Bruno, Errazuriz "Don Maximiano," Santa Rita "Casa Real" and "Triple C," Valdivieso "Caballo Loco," and Los Vascos "Le Dix."

Some bubbly is produced by Valdivieso; go for those wines made by the *methode champenoise*: Brut Nature, Extra Brut, Grand Brut, and Grand Demi-Sec.

Argentina: Wines that know how to tango

UNTIL RECENTLY, Argentina was a sleeping giant of the wine world. In the last five or six years, however, Argentina's wine industry has awakened and, at least in the U.S. export market, become as lively as the night life in Buenos Aires. The wines are as delicious as a dish of *churrasco* (barbecued beef on skewers) with *chimichurri* (a garlic/parsley vinaigrette) and as seductive as the tango.

Argentina is the fifth-largest producer of wine in the world and the largest producer in all of South America, producing far more wine than its neighbor Chile. But until the current generation of the country's best winemakers decided that Argentina should have an international presence based on both quality and value, Argentines seemed content to produce a river of wine for domestic consumption. The country's best wines were reserved for the wealthiest of its forty million citizens. On the most basic level, this marketing strategy worked, because Argentines consume more wine per capita than any other country in the world, except for tiny Luxembourg. Even today, more than 70% of Argentina's total wine production is consumed by thirsty Argentines.

Most of Argentina's vineyards are located in the western part of the country, where the Andes Mountains (which border Chile) provide cool air currents that benefit the climate in the vineyards. Running north to south, the prime grape-growing regions create a strip of more than 12,000 square miles [20,000 square kilometers.] The topography of Argentina's vineyards is varied, encompassing valley floors, mountaintops, and everything in between.

Almost all of Argentina's high-quality red wines and many of the whites that we find in the U.S. market are sourced from the gigantic Mendoza region—60,000 square miles [154,000 square kilometers with 62,500 acres (25,000 hectares)] of vines in central Argentina—the largest wine region in the Southern Hemisphere. Another important wine-growing region for whites is Cafayate, located in the northwest province of Salta. Cafayate's best cool-climate vineyards are sited at about 5,000 feet (1,500 meters) above sea level.

Just about all wines produced in Argentina that are exported to the United States are *vinos finos,* considered the best wines that the country has to offer. *Vinos finos* represent less than 15% of Argentina's wine production. Despite the fact these are elite wines, you can find extraordinary values among the many Argentine wines now available in the U.S. market, including very good wines in the $8 to $20 range.

The language of the label

Like wines from other New World producers, the great majority of Argentine wines feature varietal labels. There's nothing to confuse the consumer on the label, and often the only Spanish wording is the name of the wine producer and sometimes the name of the grape.

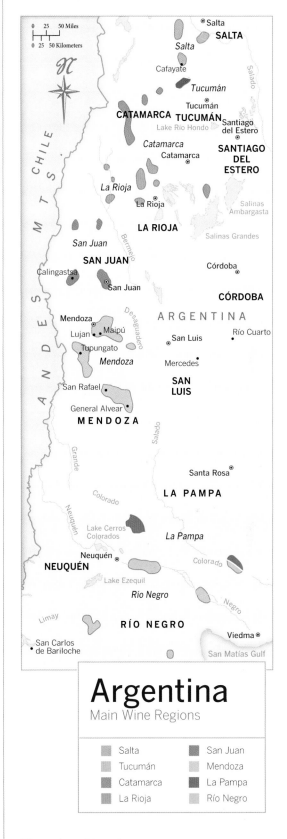

Argentina
Main Wine Regions

Salta		San Juan
Tucumán		Mendoza
Catamarca		La Pampa
La Rioja		Río Negro

Wine regions of Argentina.

Get to know Malbec

Argentina produces wines from many of the international varietals (Chardonnay and Cabernet Sauvignon, for example), and because of the country's Hispanic and Italian history and culture, winemakers also produce wines made from Italian varietals, such as Sangiovese and Nebbiolo (see page 182). But Argentina has captured the hearts and taste buds of wine lovers around the world with one red grape: Malbec. A classic blending grape in Bordeaux, Malbec is the primary varietal of Cahors, a red wine produced in the southwest of France. However, more Malbec is grown in Argentina than anywhere else on the planet.

In Argentina, Malbec is produced as a single-varietal wine and also often appears labeled as either Cabernet Sauvignon/Malbec or Malbec/Cabernet Sauvignon, depending on which varietal dominates the wine. These red blends are terrific—full-bodied, balanced, and well structured, all in a tasty nexus of black fruits. But we are even more enthusiastic about single-varietal Malbec from Argentina, because it is a unique tasting experience. Argentina's best Malbecs are incredibly earthy and powerful, but with a beautiful balance of fruit, acid, and tannins that makes them wonderful accompaniments to a meal.

It has been said, only partly in jest, that Argentina really doesn't have a cuisine; it has beef. Like so many jokes, this one is grounded in reality. Argentines consume more beef per capita than anyone else on the face of the earth, and the quality of the meat from their grass-fed cattle is legendary. We can't think of too many wines that enhance the flavors, textures, and the aromas of a perfectly prepared beef dish as well as or better than Malbec from Argentina. As with so many other Argentine wines, you can find Malbec at different price points, but don't shy away from entry-level wines that cost less than $10, especially if you're new to the varietal; they can be really enjoyable.

Finca Ferrer's Malbec Vineyards in Mendoza, Argentina.

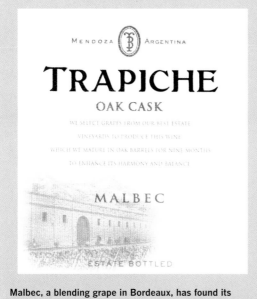

Malbec, a blending grape in Bordeaux, has found its true home in Argentina, where it is the most important varietal. Quality is good to excellent at all price levels. This Trapiche Malbec sells for under $12 and is a very good wine and a very good value.

Susana Balbo is one of the leading winemakers of Argentina; her name on the label is a virtual guarantee of quality. Her Torrontes is fresh, fruity, off-dry, affordable, and delicious.

A wonderful white: Torrontes is terrific

Although Argentina has made its current international reputation based largely on its success with red Malbec, it also produces wonderful white wines from the Torrontes grape. Still little known by all but the WineWise, Torrontes is beginning to gain a stellar reputation by word of mouth. We love the unique flavor of Torrontes: the zippy green apple acidity of Sauvignon Blanc coupled with the exotic spice of Gewurztraminer. What Malbec is to beef, Torrontes is to fish and white meats. This is a wine that can handle spicy food, too; jerk chicken comes to mind, or stir-fried tofu Szechuan style.

The best sites in Argentina to plant Torrontes are found in the high-elevation, cool-climate vineyards of Cafayate. Luckily, you don't have to climb mountains to enjoy this wine, and you don't have to pay for the trip, either. Most Torrontes is currently priced in the $7 to $20 range, but when word gets out about this luscious wine, expect the price to go up—we hope not as high as its vineyards in the Andes.

Some of the best Argentine producers are Alamos, Alta Vista, Altos las Hormigas, Balbi, Susana Balbo, BenMarco, Valentin Bianchi, Caro, Nicolas Catena, Clos de los Siete, Crios by Susana Balbo, Finca Flichman, Funky Llama, Gusto, Huarpe, Kaiken, Hermanos Lurton, Melipal, Monte Lomas, Montes, Navarro Correas, Norton, Peñaflor, Don Rodolfo, Familia Rutini, Salentein, Santa Julia, Ricardo Santos, Tango Sur, Terrazas de los Andes, Trapiche, Trumpeter, Weinert, and Zuccardi.

chapter 7

Way down south
Australia, New Zealand, South Africa

In addition to South America, the Southern Hemisphere is very well represented in the wine world by the nations of Australia, New Zealand, and South Africa. Of those, New Zealand's wine industry is relatively young when compared to the other two, which boast grape-growing and winemaking records back into the 1700s. Our organization of these three nations into the same chapter is not meant to suggest that their wines are similar—each nation has its own idiosyncratic style. However, there are some common factors that are worth pointing out. In the Southern Hemisphere, the climate gets cooler as you head south, away from the equator. Also, the harvesting season for Southern Hemisphere grape growers is early March to late April, depending on exactly how warm or cool the location is. This means that the new wine from the most recent vintage in the Southern Hemisphere will appear on shelves about six months before the Northern Hemisphere versions. You should bear this in mind if you are looking for freshness and youthful vivacity in a wine, especially a white wine—a 2007 wine from the Southern Hemisphere is "older" than a 2007 wine from the Northern Hemisphere.

Australia

WHAT MAKES Australian wine so popular and so appealing? It is warm, friendly, inviting, full of ripe fruit, and so easy to drink. Before you get the impression that Australian wine is all about casual drinking or that Australia does not make serious wine, let us set the record straight. Yes, it is true that Australia does dominate the casual segment of the market—[yellow tail]® Shiraz sells more bottles than any other varietal-labeled red wine—but the Australians have been in the winemaking game for hundreds of years, and in that time they have developed some very special vineyard sites producing extraordinary wines that command very serious consideration.

Australians seem to have the best of all worlds. They figured out several decades ago what the average modern wine consumer wants—affordable, flavorful wines that suit a twenty-first-century casual lifestyle—and they have the land and the technology to do just that. That same land and winemaking knowledge have also allowed Australian winemakers to use specific plots of land with ideal climates to create wines of incredible depth, nuance, and complexity—wines to meditate on, not just consume. In addition, it's not all about Shiraz. Australia has a wealth of grape varieties and styles to offer: from simple, fruity Verdelho whites to yummy, luscious Cabernet Sauvignon; from clean, lean, acidic sparklers to complex ageworthy reds; even "stickies"—what the Aussies call their gorgeous late harvest or fortified dessert wines.

On this label the state of South Australia is shown as the origin of the grapes.

Language of the label

WINE NAME

Like all New World wine-producing nations, Australia uses varietal labels for most of its wines, as well as a few proprietary labels. The use of varietal labels has certainly been a major factor in Australia's rise to prominence in wine markets all around the world—the consumer recognizes what is in the bottle.

PLACE NAME

All Australian wine labels also give what's called a "geographic indication," telling the consumer where the grapes were grown. The place names are organized in a hierarchical system, ranging from the unbelievably large to the very small, including the monster area of Southeastern Australia and the individual state names, such as South Australia or New South Wales. Within each state, the Australian system then identifies wine "zones," "regions," and "subregions." Don't worry—this is essentially equivalent to the system in other nations, with smaller areas identified within larger ones, and higher price tags on wines from the smaller areas.

The umbrella area of Southeastern Australia includes the states of Tasmania, Victoria, and New South Wales, plus the southern part of South Australia and the southern part of Queensland. It is indeed a massive area of land, and the creation of this catch-all name allows for grapes to be grown and harvested anywhere within that region and then trucked to a major winemaking facility, where the resulting wine will be blended with other wines from elsewhere in the region. It is this practice that has allowed Australia to continuously produce their affordable and attractive midrange wines that have so dominated the market. They are well represented by brands such as Yellow Tail, Little Penguin, Banrock Station, Greg Norman, Jacob's Creek, Alice White, Leasingham, Oxford Landing, Stonehaven, Black Opal, Woop Woop, and others, as well as by major producer names such as Orlando, Hardys, Wynns, Lindemans, Penfolds, Rosemount, Seppelt, Wolf Blass, McWilliam's, and Yalumba. Later in this chapter, we will highlight the most important regions in the states of South Australia, New South Wales, Victoria, Tasmania, and Western Australia.

Australia

Western Australia
- Swan Valley
- Perth Hills
- South-West Coastal Plain
- Margaret River
- Lower Great Southern Region

South Australia
- Clare Valley
- Riverland
- Adelaide Plains
- Barossa Valley
- Eden Valley
- Adelaide Hills
- McLaren Vale
- Langhorne Creek
- South Fleurieu

- Padthaway
- Wrattonbully
- Coonawarra
- Mount Benson
- Robe

Victoria
- Murray Darling
- Swan Hill
- Henty
- Grampians
- Pyrenees
- Bendigo
- Geelong
- Sunbury
- Macedon Ranges

- Mornington Peninsula
- Yarra Valley
- Central Victorian High Country
- Goulburn Valley
- Glenrowan
- Rutherglen
- Ovens Valley
- King Valley
- Gippsland

New South Wales
- Murray Darling
- Swan Hill
- Pericoota

- Riverina
- Tumbarumba
- Canberra District
- Hilltops
- Cowra
- Orange
- Mudgee
- Hunter
- Hastings River
- Shoalhaven

Queensland
- Granite Belt

Tasmania
- Launceston
- Hobart

New Zealand
- Wine regions

The wine regions of Australia and New Zealand.

LEGAL REQUIREMENTS

Like other nations, Australia requires minimum percentages to be met if certain terms like grape variety appear on the label. The principal requirements are:

- grape type: a minimum of 85% of any named grape variety must be used in the wine; if two grape types are listed, such as Cabernet/Shiraz, the first listed variety must be the dominant partner
- place name: a minimum of 85% of the grapes must come from any named place
- vintage: a minimum of 95% of the wine must come from grapes grown in the year stated

SPECIAL TERMS

Australia has a history of using certain label terms such as "Bin 25" or "Show Reserve," so these terms are defined. To claim "Show Reserve," the wine must have been a medal winner at a major wine competition, of which there are many in Australia. "Reserve Bin" may be used to denote a wine of demonstrably better quality than the ordinary version of the same wine, while some producers will use different bin numbers to identify different styles or origins of the same grape variety.

Grape types

In general, three grape types rule in Australia—Chardonnay in whites and Shiraz and Cabernet Sauvignon in reds. The prominence of Chardonnay and Cabernet Sauvignon is not at all surprising—that is the route that most non-European nations followed when pursuing their own wine path, at least in the late 1900s. But the recognition that Shiraz enjoys all around the world derives from Australia's production and promotion of this wine, which is made in a distinctly Australian style. Let's be clear: Shiraz is Syrah. Vines were shipped from France's Rhone Valley to Australia to be planted in the 1700s. To be sure, it has taken on its own characteristics in its new environment in much the same way that Australia's original immigrants developed their own national character in their new homeland. Compared to Rhone Valley Syrah, Australian Shiraz usually shows riper black

Aussie-style Riesling can be very enjoyable.

fruit character, with a warm, sensual, mouth-filling softness and roundness, something that the entire world has come to appreciate.

Standard Aussie Chard and Cab are made in much the same style as Californian versions—big flavors, ripe fruit, medium to high use of oak, lower acidity, and higher alcohol than European versions. That is the general picture; there are some differences from state to state, usually related to climatic variations. Just as Cabernet Sauvignon is often blended with Merlot in other parts of the world, in Australia it's Shiraz that most often partners with Cab. In fact, historically there was not much Merlot planted and produced in Australia, though the last decade has seen an increase in plantings, bringing it to the third-most-planted variety after Shiraz and Cabernet Sauvignon.

A nod of recognition, even reverence, should be given to Riesling, Sauvignon Blanc, and Pinot Noir, all three relatively limited in plantings, and all three demanding some specific growing conditions to show off their best profile. Both Riesling and Sauvignon Blanc have developed a particular Australian style—not as "green" as New Zealand, not mineral like in the Loire Valley, definitely ripe, even a little headstrong, but with enough emphasis on freshness and acidity to show a bright vivacity.

In many parts of this book, we encourage you to wander off the beaten path, to venture into unknown or unusual territory, for we believe it is there that you will find the best bargains and the best value. Just like the Tin Man, the Scarecrow, the Cowardly Lion, and Dorothy, you may even find your heart, your brain, your courage, and your home! The land of Oz offers many opportunities to do that with grapes such as Semillon and Verdelho, made as very different but equally fascinating styles of wine (see the "New South Wales" section, page 126, for more details). Also, it's unlikely that you have ever tasted red sparkling Shiraz—the wine equivalent of the ruby slippers—but in their inimitably irreverent way, the Aussies do it, and some of it is being shipped here. Sparkling Shiraz is produced all over Australia, wherever Shiraz grows. Some available brand names of sparkling Shiraz are Peter Rumball, Black Bubbles, and Lorikeet. And don't forget to look for an increasing presence in our market of Australian Champagne method sparklers, made from Chardonnay and Pinot Noir in any of the cool-climate regions of Oz.

Regions

If you have been an occasional and/or bargain-focused Aussie wine drinker, you have probably been drinking mostly wines from Southeastern Australia; as you continue to explore, all of the states and regions within the enormous Southeastern Australia appellation offer plenty of opportunity to branch out and try other wines.

SOUTH AUSTRALIA

This state produces more wine than any other, and it is renowned for some world-class wines from specific regions such as Barossa Valley, Eden Valley, Clare Valley, Langhorne Creek, McLaren Vale, Adelaide Hills, Coonawarra, and Padthaway.

Barossa Valley and Eden Valley. Situated just to the northeast of the city of Adelaide, the Barossa Valley and the Eden Valley are partners in producing very fine versions of both Shiraz and Riesling, an unlikely combination that is explained only by the planting of the Riesling vines at higher elevations to ensure crisper acidity. What makes these wines unique in the world of Riesling is a very attractive fully ripe citrus quality, replacing the German delicacy and floral aroma with more fruitiness. They are still obviously Riesling, but a very Australian interpretation of the grape. Grab some yabbies (Australian freshwater crayfish) or Louisiana crawfish and a bottle of Eden Valley Riesling, and the world begins to look a whole lot sunnier.

To talk about the potential of Shiraz in this area, all one need do is remember two names: Penfolds Grange and Henschke Hill of Grace. If you have never

The sun-blessed vineyards of the Barossa Valley.

St Hallett

Faith

Shiraz

BAROSSA

Dark, ripe fruit flavors are typical in Barossa Valley Shiraz.

tasted these two wines, trust us—they represent the pinnacle of Aussie Shiraz. When you decide to climb to the top of the Shiraz price mountain, you will be amply rewarded with wines of ripe black fruit, structure, complexity, a suave smoothness, and a long, balanced finish that will keep you well satisfied long after every mouthful. It's worth remembering as well that whenever Shiraz does well in any region, its Rhone Valley partner Grenache will probably do well too. Look out especially for old-vine versions of Grenache and Shiraz, either as individual wines or blended. If another Rhone Valley player, Mourvedre (the Aussies call it Mataro), is included, the wine may be given the easy name of GSM—now that's keeping wine simple! These wines are really autumn and winter wines, warming and comforting, and their dark, ripe fruit flavors and fuller body work extremely well with comfort foods such as bean-and-chorizo stews and pot pies.

For relative bargains from these areas, look for Wolf Blass, Peter Lehmann, Black Swan, Jacob's Creek, Pewsey Vale, Yalumba, McWilliam's, Angove's, Penfolds, Paringa, and Rosemount Estate.

Moderately expensive versions come from Saltram, Grant Burge, and St. Hallett.

Clare Valley. Further north, the Clare Valley also showcases the two extremes of Riesling and Shiraz, with a substantial dose of Cabernet Sauvignon thrown in for good measure. Again, it is differences

in elevation of the vineyards that make this unlikely pairing possible. There seems to be a Clare Valley characteristic, though, and that is a graceful silkiness to the wines, especially on the reds after a bit of age. Clare Valley is best known for its Riesling, however, and with good reason. Most are medium-bodied, fresh, and fruity, with a pleasant dose of minerals for a hint of complexity on the palate. For Riesling lovers, reputable producers of relative bargains include Annie's Lane, McWilliam's, and Leasingham. Moderately expensive to very expensive versions include Mitchell, Jim Barry, Petaluma, and the highly esteemed Grosset, whose Polish Hill Riesling is incredibly delicious and even ageworthy.

McLaren Vale and Langhorne Creek. McLaren Vale and Langhorne Creek are just to the south and southeast of the city of Adelaide, respectively, and they both have a giant reputation for Shiraz and Cab wines that combine ripe black fruit character with a spiciness of black pepper and a solid core of tannins, though the fruit is so abundant that the tannins never seem to get in the way. Moderately expensive versions come from Metala, Wirra Wirra, d'Arenberg, Andrew Garrett, McWilliam's/Mount Pleasant, and Ingoldby. Even if the label does not show McLaren or Langhorne as the place of origin, but gives only the state name of South Australia, it is a fair bet that the wines from these producers contain a large percentage of grapes from those areas. Any of the above Shiraz wines are a good partner to grilled 'roo—yes, the Australians eat kangaroo (most often farmed, not wild), usually the loin section that runs down the center of the back. It is a tasty red meat, slightly gamy, and anything similar would be a good substitute.

Adelaide Hills. Directly to the east of Adelaide are the Adelaide Hills, which have become well known for their versions of Chardonnay, particularly from the Piccadilly Valley subregion, where the Petaluma winery has proven that Australia can make world-class Chard, with muted wood treatment, ripe flavors of apple and citrus, and an elegant, smooth finish. In addition, Brian Croser, the founder of Petaluma, handcrafts a very fine sparkling wine from this area under his own Croser label, using Chardonnay and Pinot Noir.

The cool climate of the Adelaide Hills is also conducive to good development of clean flavors in Sauvignon Blanc, with moderately expensive versions offered by Shaw + Smith as well as by Leland Estate. Truly expensive wines—sublime examples of Sauvignon Blanc, Chardonnay, Pinot Gris, and Riesling for whites, and exciting Pinot Noir and Merlot for reds—are produced by the famous Henschke family winery in the Adelaide Hills.

Coonawarra and Padthaway. Much further south of all these regions, and closer to the south coast of South Australia, lie the regions of Coonawarra and Padthaway. If you have heard anything about Aussie wines, you might have heard of Coonawarra, hailed for many years as Australia's rival to Bordeaux based on the excellence of its ageworthy Cabernet Sauvignon wines. Coonawarra's Cabs are often blended with other Bordeaux varieties but usually are labeled simply Cabernet Sauvignon. Their distinctive blackcurrant fruit with dried leaf and eucalyptus aromas certainly make them stand out: they also age very well if that is your thing—a twenty-year-old version tasted recently still surprised us with fresh, dense black fruit alongside cigar box aromas and an earthy mineral character. Coonawarra Cabs are very capable partners with leg of lamb, a dish frequently seen in the region. The reputation of Coonawarra puts most of its wines in the moderately expensive to very expensive category, with good versions from Hollick, Lindemans, Mildara, Haselgrove, Brand's of Coonawarra/McWilliam's, and Wynns Coonawarra Estate.

With land at a premium in Coonawarra, the region of Padthaway was developed as an alternative, but it turns out to be better suited to Chardonnay as a variety. Padthaway Chardonnay tends to show riper, more tropical, pineapple fruit than the Piccadilly Valley versions, but still with good balancing acidity. Relative bargain wines come from Stonehaven, with moderately expensive versions from Browns, Lindemans, and Padthaway Estate.

Clare Valley Riesling vines.

NEW SOUTH WALES

While South Australia has always been home to a broad range of grape types and their wines, the state of New South Wales has tended to favor white grapes and wines, a curious fact since the state generally experiences a warm, humid climate that would not normally lend itself to grape growing of any kind, certainly not white grape growing. But careful vineyard management has produced some excellent results over the centuries, especially from the state's primary region, Hunter Valley.

Hunter Valley. Chardonnay and Semillon dominate the entire region, though in the lower part of the valley, closer to the ocean, Shiraz and Cabernet also cover significant acreage and produce some outstanding wines. Hunter Valley wines are famous for their rich lusciousness, a quality that comes across in the whites as tropical fruit, so Hunter Valley Chardonnay is more about pineapple and ripe melon than apple and citrus.

If you have never tried a Semillon wine, a Hunter Valley version would be a thrilling initiation. The genius of Semillon is a natural ripeness and high acidity, so you are likely to find ripe melon and orange notes, with crisp citrus acidity when the wine is young. Semillon is one of those wines that collectors love to age, so turn yourself into a collector and let a couple of bottles of Semillon sit around for five years or so—then try one of them. You will be struck by a honey and marmalade aroma with a background of lanolin and ground nuts. On the palate, the wine comes across as distinctly dry, with notes of dried fruits and a silky smoothness—a terrific accompaniment to a blue cheese, walnut, and pear salad. If you don't like it, forgive us; you will have to admit that it was fun and exciting to try!

Hunter Valley Shiraz and Cabernet Sauvignon wines display typical ripe fruit character of dark plums and blackcurrant, offset by some sturdy tannins that diminish with age, when the wines take on a more complex aroma of leather and dried leaves. For a refreshing and novel change, treat yourself to a glass (or, better still, a bottle) of Verdelho from Hunter Valley and discover a bright, aromatic wine full of citrus character—very refreshing on a warm, humid day, and the perfect foil to blood-orange salad.

Moderately expensive Hunter Valley producers include Rothbury Estate, Tyrell's, McWilliam's, and De Bortoli.

VICTORIA

Victoria has more wineries than any other Australian state, now approaching four hundred, and the state remains a strong contender for recognition, embracing its glorious past and an exciting future. That past is well represented by the ongoing presence of Goulburn Valley's Chateau Tahbilk, active since the 1860s and still making world-class Cabernet Sauvignon, and by the mysteries of Rutherglen "stickies," made from Muscat and Muscadelle. Meanwhile, the future seems safe in the hands of cool-climate Pinot Noir, Chardonnay, and sparkling wines from Yarra Valley and Mornington Peninsula.

Goulburn Valley. Despite some very favorable agricultural land, this region struggles in terms of the number of wineries, and even today there are really only two major producers. Chateau Tahbilk is steeped in tradition, making incredibly complex Cabernet Sauvignon wines in the same way they did a hundred years ago—simple but amazingly effective methods. An aged Chateau Tahbilk Cabernet Sauvignon will raise your spirits and your hope for humanity—if we can make wines like this, surely we can save the planet! The other major producer is a relative newcomer. Mitchelton originally gained fame for an impressive version of Marsanne—impressive because very few other producers in the world make a single-variety version of this white Rhone Valley grape, and because it hits the drinker with a wonderfully scented, floral nose and a tropical fruit salad flavor. Again, their Chardonnay is not to be sneezed at, and their GSM blend can be outstanding.

Rutherglen and Glenrowan. Wine regions may get tired of always being associated with one style of wine, but that is the nature of appellations: they do what they do best—at least, we think they should. And any attempt to make the land and the climate do something else is likely to result in lukewarm reception. Such is the case with both Rutherglen and Glenrowan, which have become inexorably linked

Yarra Valley vineyards.

with "stickies," deliciously sweet but nimble fortified wines made from late harvest Muscat or Muscadelle grapes, labeled according to the grape used.

These are spiritual wines, made for reflection and designed to reveal the wonders of the world. In small quantities as dessert or at the end of a grueling day, they reward the drinker with wondrously succinct flavors of dried apricots, white grapes, and peaches—the Muscat also reveals a noticeable raisin and prune dimension. By nature of their limited quantity, these wines can appear very expensive, but what they offer in return may in fact mean that they are relative bargains, as evidenced by the wines of Stanton & Killeen and those of All Saints.

Yarra Valley. Long hailed as one of Australia's most promising wine regions, Yarra basks in the luxury of a cool climate and mineral-rich soils that seem well suited to a variety of grape types, but particularly to Pinot Noir and Chardonnay. That means, of course, that those grapes are made into single-variety wines and are also used in the production of Champagne method sparkling wines. The Pinots and Chardonnays are less about weight and oak and more about clean, bright fruit, balanced with high acidity (and light tannins in the Pinot). The finesse and elegance displayed by all of the resulting wines is seen by some as a welcome relief to the sometimes ponderous nature of sun-drenched Shiraz and Cabernet Sauvignon. Perhaps capitalizing on that philosophy, a number of Yarra producers also

make Shiraz and Cabernet Sauvignon (usually blended with Cabernet Franc or Merlot), but in a noticeably more restrained style than some of the warmer, more northerly regions, emphasizing clean berry fruit, higher acidity for freshness, and a leaner finish, rather than mouth-filling richness. Moderately expensive versions are offered by Coldstream Hills, St. Hubert's, Yarra Ridge, Yarra Yering, and Yeringberg, while very expensive versions will be found from De Bortoli and Mount Mary.

Mornington Peninsula. Like the Yarra Valley, this is a noticeably cool climate—chilly mornings and evenings, even in the summer growing season—and, once again, Pinot Noir and Chardonnay reign, almost supreme. We have spent a lot of ink in this book bashing overripe and overoaked Chardonnays, so it is a relief for us, and we hope for you, to find Chardonnays from places such as Mornington and Yarra, where the emphasis is certainly on fruit, but on just-ripe fruit that has reached its pinnacle of flavor over a long, cool growing season and is therefore balanced by fresh acidity and enhanced by skilled winemaking that produces a peaches-and-cream softness of texture. So pleasant!

For Pinot Noir, ripe raspberry and cherry notes are matched by an earthy mineral character, while vibrant acidity and tannins seem to "lift" the wine in the mouth as it heads toward a long, give-me-some-more finish.

Given the peninsula's cool to moderate climate, it is perhaps no surprise that Pinot Gris/Pinot Grigio is also grown here in fairly large quantity and with success, producing wines with the kind of structure and flavors found in Oregon's versions of the same grape—leaning toward some fullness and roundness in the mouth, with distinctly ripe apple, pear, and melon flavors, countered by refreshing acidity. Moderately expensive versions come from Tuck's Ridge, Massoni, and Dromana Estate.

TASMANIA

The island state of Tasmania is about one thing—cold growing seasons that demand cool-climate grape varieties, especially Chardonnay, Pinot Noir, and Riesling. For consumers, that means some scintillating single-variety versions of these wines, plus some very exciting Champagne method sparklers from Chardonnay and Pinot Noir. The combination of long hours of sunlight and cooler temperatures means the opportunity for the grapes to develop fully ripe flavor profiles while maintaining fresh, vibrant acidity—just perfect for those varieties. The sparkling wines of Tasmania are among some of the best we have ever tasted, with finely defined flavors and a crisp acidity matched by a reassuring richness on the tongue. These wines may be hard to find but are well worth the search.

Relative bargains can be found from Ninth Island (a second label of Pipers Brook), and Jacob's Creek produces a sparkler for less than $15, while moderately expensive versions come from Dalrymple, Lalla Gully, Heemskerk, Bream Creek, Clover Hill, and Elsewhere (yes, that's the winery name). The very expensive Jansz sparkler is worth every penny.

WESTERN AUSTRALIA

Not only are the wines of Western Australia a continent away from their southeastern countrymen in terms of distance, but there is a major shift in style as well, with the generally cooler climates of the southern tip of Western Australia providing very different growing conditions from most of Southeastern Australia. The exposed nature of that corner of the continent and the cooling winds from the Indian Ocean are major players in those cooler conditions. The two big regional names here are Margaret River and Great Southern, with its subregion of Mount Barker.

Margaret River. By any measure, Cabernet Sauvignon is the No. 1 grape and wine here, often blended with Cabernet Franc and/or Merlot to produce a Bordeaux-type wine, much closer in style to the actual Bordeaux model than most of the Southeastern Australia examples. The Margaret River versions are less opulent, more modest perhaps, but no less interesting; firm and lean, they also show an elegant smoothness to counter the tannins and show off the ripe black currant fruit. That same leaner style is also apparent in the small quantities of Shiraz made here, much closer to the French style, with more peppery and gamy qualities, rather than being awash in abundant fruit.

In the white wines, Chardonnay certainly benefits from the cool ocean winds and produces some fine lean versions, but this region also does wonderful things with Riesling, Semillon, and Sauvignon Blanc. The last two are frequently blended, again in the Bordeaux style. Moderately expensive offerings come from Cape Mentelle, Cullen, Evans & Tate, and Leeuwin Estate.

Great Southern. Again, Cabernet Sauvignon and Chardonnay are the most planted grapes, followed by Riesling, Shiraz, and Merlot (for blending). For something more exotic, some Great Southern wineries have found good vineyard sites for cool-climate Pinot Noir and Sauvignon Blanc, both of which approximate the style of the New Zealand versions of those grapes—unmistakably ripe, but with fresh, lively acidity for freshness. Even more exotic and fun are the Verdelho wines with their seductive fruitiness, a simple indulgence in naive charm. The relative rarity of Great Southern wines makes them moderately expensive, but good versions can be found from Jingalla, Mad Fish, Ferngrove, Fonty's Pool, Goundrey, and Plantagenet.

New Zealand

AT THE VERY LEAST, New Zealand deserves fame and recognition for focusing attention away from Chardonnay in the 1980s when the world most needed that diversion. This was accomplished by the wild and ebullient style that New

Zealand winemakers gave to their Sauvignon Blanc, which one wine writer at the time described as like bathing in a vat of lime Jell-O. Undoubtedly it was boldly different—loads of fresh green fruit, but obviously ripe, backed up by mouth-watering acidity that kept the flavors lingering forever.

But New Zealand winemakers have shown no sign of resting on their Sauvignon Blanc laurels—they want to prove to themselves and the world that their vineyards produce world-class wines from several places and a range of grape types. Certainly, if you love New Zealand's very particular Sauvignon style, there is plenty of it to keep you happy. But there is much more to discover.

As the world's southernmost grape-growing area, New Zealand enjoys a combination of climate and sunlight similar to that found in Germany and Washington State. The growing season is cool and long, with extended hours of daylight well into the latter part of the growing season, meaning that the grapes have the chance to reach full physiological ripeness without the sudden rush of sugars that push growers to harvest early in warmer climates. Most New Zealand growing areas enjoy maximum "hang time," with grapes left on the vine well into the fall months. At the same time, another characteristic of being far from the equator has an especially beneficial effect: the temperature swing between day and night is more exaggerated, with warm to hot temperatures during the day and cool, even cold temperatures at night. It is the low nighttime temperatures that keep the freshness and liveliness in New Zealand wines, with acidity levels in the grapes actually boosted overnight to counter the acid loss during the day. Add to this New Zealand's unique feature—it is a long, thin two-island nation where the climatic features already mentioned are emphasized—and you have a recipe for success in the modern wine world.

Language of the label

WINE NAME

New Zealand fits right in with other New World wine producers in that it labels most wines by varietal. All varietally labeled wines must contain a minimum of 75% of the named variety, but in practice most single-varietal wines are made from 100% of the named variety. If two or more grape varieties are named on the label, they must appear in decreasing order of the percentage used—if a wine is labeled as Cabernet Merlot, there must be more Cabernet than Merlot. Some wines carry a proprietary or brand name, especially when the wine is a blend of two or more grapes, but the grape variety mix is usually included somewhere on the label. Blended wines from New Zealand are most frequently made from the Bordeaux grape mix of Cabernet Sauvignon, Merlot, and maybe Cabernet Franc and Malbec.

PLACE NAME

Surprisingly, the use of geographic indicators on New Zealand labels is not yet fully defined or controlled by legislation—the applicable laws are still working their way through the system. But New Zealand winemakers do include place names on labels to indicate the origin of the grapes used in the wine, and consumers have no real reason to suspect gross dishonesty in the use of place names. There are ten designated grape-growing regions, though in some cases the official name has changed over time. The ten regions are:

North Island	South Island
Northland	Nelson
Auckland	Marlborough
Waikato/Bay of Plenty	Canterbury
Gisborne	Central Otago
Hawke's Bay	
Wairarapa	

Grapes

Like a familiar Agatha Christie mystery, New Zealand assembles the usual cast of characters, so there really is no mystery—although the lead role in this case is Sauvignon Blanc, and Chardonnay is relegated to a supporting role. Over the last ten years, acreage of Chardonnay has increased to a little more than double, while Sauvignon Blanc now occupies seven times more acreage than in 1997. It was Sauvignon that blazed the trail for the Kiwis, and they were quick to recognize its potential. Almost all New Zealand Sauvignon Blanc is made in the style discussed in Chap-

Marlborough Sauvignon Blanc has become New Zealand's flagship wine.

ter 2 on page 25, though some are more minerally than others.

Having developed that forthright, fresh, zingy style for Sauvignon Blanc, winemakers were quick to realize that they could apply a similar philosophy to other white varieties. Enter the vibrant yet graceful starlet Riesling, which in New Zealand has fresh fruit nuances of kiwi in the aroma along with ripe citrus. The grace comes from a well-defined streak of acidity that allows some of the very best examples to show off distinct mineral notes to great effect—a core of firmness inside the ripe fruit.

That philosophy is adapted to Chardonnay and Pinot Gris by concentrating on retained acidity and restrained use of oak, allowing the natural apple and lemon flavors of Chardonnay and the rich sensual texture of Pinot Gris to shine through.

In red grape varieties, the surprise star is Pinot Noir, with a staggering tenfold increase in acreage in ten years, and that is attributable not just to fashion or to pigheaded winemakers who will make Pinot Noir or die trying. No, the increase here is valid. It is because New Zealand really does have pockets of climate, topography, and soil structures that favor Pinot.

The other red variety that has shown some interesting movement is Syrah, with a tenfold increase in acreage in ten years.

Regions

We have listed some producers at the end of each regional section. Remember that many wineries will often bring fruit in from other regions, and will always label the wine according to where the grapes were grown. In that model, Giesen is listed as a Canterbury winery, but its most available wine in the United States is Marlborough Sauvignon Blanc.

NORTH ISLAND

The regions of Northland, Auckland, and Waikato/Bay of Plenty rarely show up on our shelves, so we will concentrate on the other regions.

Gisborne. The real gem in Gisborne's tiara (it's not really a crown) is Chardonnay, especially when made in the style that many more consumers seem to want—bright, fresh, simple, and fruity, with little oak influence. That said, there are a few producers, such as Corbans, who know how to use high-quality fruit from prime vineyard locations to make wines that will age well and gracefully for ten years or more. Occasionally there is an interesting Gewurztraminer or Semillon, but they usually require more conducive climate patterns than Gisborne offers.

In addition to Corbans, Millton is a highly reputable producer.

Hawke's Bay. In contrast to Gisborne's wetness, Hawke's Bay boasts sunshine—lots of it. And yet it is not that hot, the majority of the vineyard areas being cooled by sea breezes through most of the growing season. As one more testament to its adaptability, Chardonnay also does well here, though a Hawke's Bay Chard usually shows a lot more depth and "oomph" than a Gisborne version, kind of like comparing a sliced chicken breast on romaine lettuce with a spit-roasted chicken with all the trimmings.

The notion that Hawke's Bay produces good Cabernet Sauvignon persists, though some growers believe that the region is not consistently warm enough to ripen Cab fully every year. There are some select vineyard sites that do achieve success, and the region continues to receive praise for its Bordeaux blends, with Merlot playing an increasingly important role in some blends, along with Cabernet Franc. The Te Mata red blends are especially noteworthy, and expensive.

There are plenty of other grapes being grown here, and we are likely to see more and more attempts at Pinot Noir and even Syrah from Hawke's Bay, some of which will be good.

Notable producers include Te Mata, Kim Crawford, Trinity Hill, and Ngatarawa.

Wairarapa. This region includes the smaller district of Martinborough, which will also show up as a geographic indication on labels and is probably better known in wine circles than Wairarapa. Whether we are talking Wairarapa or Martinborough, the topic is likely to be Pinot Noir, Sauvignon Blanc, or Chardonnay. The Martinborough district was one of the first in New Zealand to be recognized as having Pinot potential, and that potential has been delivered in wines that show well-developed dark red fruit character and some of the warm, earthy undertones that Pinot drinkers love. Martinborough Sauvignon Blanc has won over admirers with its extra suggestion of ripe stone fruit underneath the zippy acidity and citrus notes. Wines to look out for come from Ata Rangi, Palliser Estates, Martinborough Vineyards, and Dry River Wines.

SOUTH ISLAND

Nelson. It is difficult to pick any particular grape variety as the star of Nelson, but the region does an excellent job of producing the cool-climate array of Sauvignon Blanc, Chardonnay, and Riesling, all of which display the cleanness and greenness we have come to expect of New Zealand wines. Notable producers include Seifried, Denton, and Neudorf.

Marlborough. Probably everybody who has ever spoken the words "Sauvignon Blanc" knows about Marlborough. This was the place that started it all in terms of the world's acceptance of Sauvignon

Blanc, with a style that is instantly recognizable as bracing acidity behind ripe fruit with an undertone of grassiness and gooseberry flavors.

As good as the Sauvignons are, we should not limit our consideration of Marlborough only to that variety, since there are some equally outstanding—perhaps even better—Rieslings with a finesse and elegance that are rarely seen from other Southern Hemisphere versions of that grape. Equally interesting are the Chardonnays, with a lean edge and an understated use of wood, and the future holds promise for some leanly structured Pinot Noir that will offer a different emphasis than most boldly fruity New World versions.

You should take the opportunity to try any of these wines, especially from producers such as Montana, Brancott, Cloudy Bay, Selaks, Villa Maria (winery located in Auckland), Corbans, Allan Scott, Framingham, Nautilus, Seresin, and Vavasour.

The Marlborough region is also enormously important for growing Chardonnay and Pinot Noir that are used in *methode champenoise* sparkling wine production. Prominent labels of high-quality sparklers include Deutz, Chandon, Lindauer, Pelorus, and Amadeus.

Canterbury. By now our devoted and savvy *WineWise* reader will have figured out that as we continue to head southward we will see a continuing concentration on familiar cool-climate varieties. Such is certainly the case with Canterbury, where Chardonnay, Riesling, and Pinot Noir are all major players, along with a good smattering of Pinot Gris. Some of the Chardonnay and Pinot Noir head off to sparkling wine production, but there are also some very fine versions of those wines in their own right. From the right vineyard location and in the right winemaker's hands, Riesling and Pinot Gris from here can reach stellar quality, with an astounding depth and purity that many other producers of those grapes would do well to use as a model. Canterbury producers to watch include Pegasus Bay, Giesen, and Waipara Springs.

Central Otago. To date, all the attention here is focused on Pinot Noir, with much critical acclaim heaped on these wines from wine writers all around the world. The Pinots from Central Otago tend to show riper, denser dark red or even black fruit than many French Burgundies, but there is a meaty, chewy quality to the wines, without excessive intensity. That is something that many people love about Pinot Noir—authority without power. You like it because it suggests rather than dictates. Among the good and great producers are Two Paddocks, Felton Road, Mt. Difficulty, and Olssens.

South Africa

SOUTH AFRICA is a land of contrasts, especially within the hundred miles from the east, south, and west coastlines that define this wine land. It is situated at a crossroads of climatic and cultural influences that have helped to define South African history and its wines. Climatically, both the Atlantic and Indian oceans impact the region, bringing dry or moist, hot or cold air, depending on the season and the prevailing winds.

It is easy to make the assumption that South Africa's location at the southern tip of the continental mass of Africa makes it a cool grape-growing area. But the general picture is a warmer climate. Cape Town itself sits at 34 degrees latitude, which is only just within the accepted northerly limit of grape growing in the Southern Hemisphere. However, the varied landscape also provides for contrasts in climate, with pockets of cool, even cold grape-growing areas provided by elevation, proximity to the ocean, or shelter from warm winds. That wide variety of climatic conditions allows South Africa to make a broad range of wine styles, from cool-climate Sauvignon Blanc to warmer Rhone styles such as Syrah and Grenache.

Grape types

In addition to the usual gathering of international grape types, South Africa has two unusual claims to fame—Chenin Blanc and Pinotage. Chenin Blanc is South Africa's most widely planted grape type, a claim that can be made by no other wine nation in the world. Historically, the grape was used in South

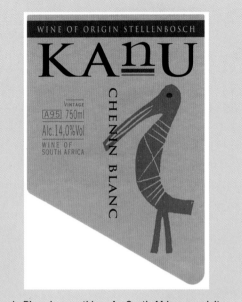

Chenin Blanc is something of a South African specialty.

Africa for the production of inexpensive fortified Port- and Sherry-style wines destined for the British market, both in the British Isles and their colonies. With the decline in that market and restrictions on using the terms "Port" and "Sherry" on South African wine labels, the growers of this grape have had to find another outlet. Given that the broad plantings of this variety often ended up on flat, fertile lands, making undistinguished wine, it has been difficult to generate much interest in the variety.

But the intrepid WineWise consumer need not be a slave to the fashions of the masses and the uninitiated. Relatively inexpensive South African Chenin Blanc produced in a dry style can be a fascinating wine and is extremely food-friendly. Its flavors of melon, pear, and hazelnut and its naturally high acidity make it a very useful wine to have on hand. Try it with lobster or smoked trout and you will wonder why more places around the world do not make this wine. Watch for the word "Steen" on some labels: it is a South African synonym for Chenin Blanc.

Pinotage is South Africa's own wine grape. It was created by a South African settler by crossing Pinot Noir with the southern French variety called Cinsaut. The WineWise reader may immediately recognize that Pinot Noir is a cool-climate grape type. Cinsaut, on the other hand, is a warm-climate variety. What the intrepid settler seems to have attempted was the creation of a grape type suited to South Africa's climate and growing conditions. Certainly, no other place in the world has adopted this unusual variety as a mainstay of its wine industry, and that should tell you something. Even today, with a revitalization of the South African wine industry well under way, Pinotage wines themselves remain something of a mystery and a glassful of contrast, capable of greatness but often disappointing.

In addition to those two unusual characters, the usual range of international grapes is found in South Africa. Chardonnay is made in an attractive cool-climate style when the right growing conditions can be found, producing a crisp wine with just a hint of oak and flavors of apple and citrus. Occasionally a producer will also go toward a fuller, more tropical style.

Sauvignon Blanc has earned a good reputation here thanks to its treatment at the hands of the right growers and winemakers. With an overall warm climate, it is not hard to find sites that will produce Sauvignon Blanc grapes with ripe citrus flavors, but the truly exceptional wines come from areas where there are cool influences that lengthen the growing season and keep acidity levels high. The result is not only a bright lime and gooseberry character, but also an element of green leaf or nettle. Try a glass with blanched asparagus and a drizzle of butter—your day will look brighter.

Cabernet Sauvignon has long claimed its rightful place in South Africa as a grape capable of producing some superb wines, and Merlot has more recently been adopted both as a blender with Cabernet and as a single-varietal wine in its own right. The style of these red wines tends to be warmly ripe, but with attenuating acidity and tannins that seem to make the wines more complete. Cabernet Franc is also frequently used in blends with Cabernet Sauvignon and Merlot.

Many producers of South African wine have won great acclaim for their Syrah/Shiraz and Grenache wines, and with good reason. These grapes and their wines are ideally suited to the general growing conditions in South Africa, and they seem to easily reach full ripeness, which translates into warm, dark fruit flavors with a touch of spice in the glass—a wonderful accompaniment to lamb stew on a cool autumnal evening.

Language of the label

WINE NAME

Like the other Southern Hemisphere wine nations, South Africa realized a long time ago the advantages of using grape variety names on wine labels to make their wines easily recognizable in the international marketplace. Some producers choose a proprietary name that can become well known as a brand: a good example from South Africa is the Goats Do Roam label—a cute play on the French wine name Cotes du Rhone—produced as a Rhone-style blend by Charles Back of Fairview wines. It has been a great success, attributable to the playfulness of the label and the quality of the wine. By the way, Fairview's farms also produce goat's-milk cheeses, so there really are goats on the property that . . . well, roam!

PLACE NAME

Again, like all other wine-producing nations, South Africa has a place name system equivalent to the United States' AVA system or Australia's geographic indicator system. In the South African model there are four main grape-growing regions that contain twenty-one districts. Occasionally you might also find the name of one of the country's fifty-three wards on a label. The wards are smaller areas, and most of them lie within the twenty-one districts. The four large regions are Coastal Region, Breede River Valley, Klein Karoo, and Olifants River. The wines from the Coastal Region and Breede River Valley, along with their better districts and wards, deserve some close attention.

Pinotage is unique to South Africa.

CERTIFICATION

All bottles of South African wine carry a neck strip indicating that the wine has been certified by the Wine & Spirit Board as authentic with regard to any information on the label such as grape variety, place name, and any specific claims. The certification is awarded only after rigorous tests, including tasting, have been administered. The presence of the certification strip confirms for the consumer that:

- If a grape variety is named on the label, the wine has been made using at least 85% of that variety

- If a vintage year is indicated, at least 85% of the wine originated from grapes harvested in the stated year.

- If a place name appears on the label, together with the phrase "wine of origin" or the abbreviation "W.O.," 100% of the grapes must have originated in that place.

- If the phrase "estate grown" appears on the label, the estate must be a single contiguous property, and all of the production processes must occur on the estate.

Simonsberg Mountain rises majestically over Stellenbosch vineyards.

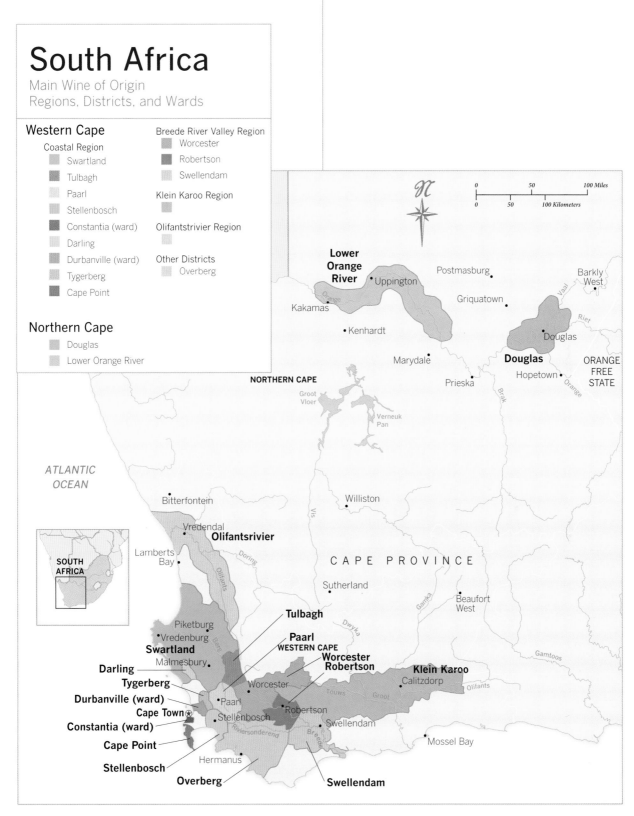

South Africa
Main Wine of Origin
Regions, Districts, and Wards

Western Cape

Coastal Region
- Swartland
- Tulbagh
- Paarl
- Stellenbosch
- Constantia (ward)
- Darling
- Durbanville (ward)
- Tygerberg
- Cape Point

Breede River Valley Region
- Worcester
- Robertson
- Swellendam

Klein Karoo Region

Olifantsrivier Region

Other Districts
- Overberg

Northern Cape
- Douglas
- Lower Orange River

South African wine regions.

Regions

COASTAL REGION

The defined grape-growing area of the Coastal Region stretches along the west coast of South Africa northward from Cape Town and inland to the towns of Paarl and Tulbagh, a distance of more than thirty miles. The area is undoubtedly warm, though there are pockets that are cooled by ocean breezes, depending on the time of year and the presence or absence of the impressive mountains that can channel cool air inland.

Within this region, the most familiar districts are Paarl and Stellenbosch, and those two place names can frequently be found on bottles of South African wine in this market. That should be reassuring, since both of these districts have a solid reputation for producing very good-quality wines. The districts of Darling and Tygerberg are also beginning to be players in the international market.

Paarl. This district contains four wards, three of which are becoming important as recognizable place names on labels: Franschhoek Valley, Wellington, and Simonsberg-Paarl. As reflected in its name and in the names of some of its wineries (such as L'Ormarins, La Motte, Dieu Donné), Franschhoek has a particularly strong historical French influence, and this can sometimes be seen in the profile of the wines, emphasizing a more reserved style instead of all upfront fruit. Whatever the ward, Paarl's mostly warm climate lends itself to the production of some fine Cabernet Sauvignon wines and Cab blends, as well as Syrah/Shiraz and Rhone blends. This is especially true from producers such as Fairview, Boekenhoutskloof (say it five times fast!), and Glen Carlou. At the southeastern end of the Paarl district rises the majestic Simonsberg hill, which provides elevation and cooler sites for Chardonnay, also produced by Glen Carlou.

Stellenbosch. Of all the districts in South Africa, this one contains some of the greatest estates, renowned for a few exquisite wines. This is because of the extremely diverse soil types and the varying climatic conditions that exist throughout the district, all made possible by the flow of cool ocean air from the south through mountain passes created by such ranges as the Simonsberg and Drakenstein hills. In the vicinity of these hills lie Stellenbosch's two most important wards—Simonsberg-Stellenbosch and Jonkershoek. The single estates mentioned in the "Certification" section earlier are particularly prevalent here and include some famous and very reliable names, such as Simonsig, Rustenberg, Rust en Vrede, Meerlust, Uitkyk, Warwick, and Kanonkop. Wines from those producers are all moderately to very expensive. Other very good producers making moderately expensive wines include Delaire, Mulderbosch, Ken Forrester, and Thelema.

Given the variety of climates and soils, the Wine-Wise consumer could spend many weeks working his or her way through the broad range of grapes and wines represented here, from the unrelenting integrity of Ken Forrester's Chenin Blancs to Mulderbosch's lean and austere Sauvignon Blanc and the complex conundrum of Rustenberg's Cabernet Sauvignons.

Darling. This cool area is situated fairly close to the Atlantic Ocean, just to the north of Cape Town, making the Darling district a favorite tourist destination. That alone could bring it fame and fortune, but the good news is that Darling can also produce some outstanding cool-climate versions of Sauvignon Blanc, especially from the Groenekloof ward. Darling Cellars is a representative producer of moderately expensive wines.

Tygerberg. The most important thing about Tygerberg is the Durbanville ward, a series of hills just to the northeast of Cape Town with a staggering view of the city and the ocean in the distance. This is another place where vineyards compete with developers who wish to build high-end residential housing for the wealthy suburbanites, and we are happy to report that a few hardy souls have mounted a tough resistance against further encroachment into vineyard territory. The very large Durbanville Hills winery along with smaller players such as Nitida and Biesjes Craal are doing an outstanding job producing fresh, vibrant, ripe versions of Sauvignon Blanc with distinct mineral elements, in addition to some well-

The vineyards of the Durbanville Hills.

structured and elegant Bordeaux-style wines from Cabernet Sauvignon and Merlot.

Constantia. This very famous and historic ward lies within the Coastal Region, just to the south of Cape Town, but is not situated in any district. It is an entity unto itself, and deservedly so, since much of the reputation of South African wines stands on the shoulders of Constantia. Historically famous for its dessert Muscat wines, the area is now recognized as a major producer of Cabernet Sauvignon wines and blends. Chardonnay also does well in the cooler vineyard sites. The three major producers of moderately expensive wines are Groot Constantia, Klein Constantia, and Buitenverwachting.

BREEDE RIVER VALLEY

The Breede River Valley wine region runs from the town of Worcester, about sixty miles inland from the Atlantic Ocean, in a southeasterly direction until the Breede River empties into the Indian Ocean on the south coast. It is sandwiched between the occasional mountains of the western Cape (such as Simonsberg and Drakenstein) and the far greater mass of the inland mountain range. The region contains an unlikely but very promising district, Robertson—unlikely because the relatively flat inland river valley is certainly warm if not hot, but promising because a few renegades have staked their future on the existence of cool climate pockets created by cold air that is sucked all the way from the Atlantic Ocean down through the valley toward the Indian Ocean.

Robertson. In the very heart of the broad sweep of the hot but fertile Breede River Valley, there are a few unique pockets such as Robertson, cool enough to create amazingly complex and mineral-laden Sauvignon Blanc wines, as reflected in Springfield Estate's top-ranking "Life from Stone," a brilliant and very expensive wine with fine apricot notes and the bright flash of flint aromas—a truly remarkable achievement and a memorable wine. Down the road from

The Life from Stone vineyard in Robertson.

Springfield, an equally adventurous maverick, Danie de Wet, has created the De Wetshof label, offering bright, fresh flavors of Chardonnay and Sauvignon Blanc through careful vineyard management and cold fermentation in stainless-steel vats. The wines of Van Loveren are equally impressive.

OTHER IMPORTANT AREAS TO WATCH FOR

Outside the four principal regions there are a few districts and freestanding wards of note, of interest mostly because the "Cape crusaders" who have developed them have moved into nontraditional areas to exploit specific climatic or territorial conditions. The following areas are particularly worthy of attention.

Overberg District (with Elgin Ward). One of several areas that have expanded the traditional vineyard area much further southward, the Elgin ward has produced some ripe and flavorful Sauvignon Blancs with vibrant fresh acidity, reflective of the cooler climate here. Paul Cluver is a good example.

Walker Bay. A little further south from Overberg, this area is snuggled into the southwestern tip of the Cape, with a wide ocean perspective making it particularly cool from the ocean breezes. In this environment, there is ample opportunity to produce truly cool-climate versions of Riesling, Gewurztraminer, Sauvignon Blanc, and Chardonnawy. Great work has already been done by pioneers such as the Hamilton Russell winery, and their moderately expensive wines are well worth looking for. Other fine producers include Bouchard Finlayson, Beaumont Wines, Southern Right, and Whalehaven.

Cape Agulhas (with Elim Ward). At the very southern tip of Africa, where the mighty Atlantic and Indian oceans meet, this newly defined area is making waves of its own with some remarkable cool-climate winemaking, especially a lean but vibrant Sauvignon Blanc. The Flagstone Winery version from the Elim ward is particularly impressive.

There is a world of pleasure to be found in the wines of South Africa, and the pleasure should be yours. It has certainly been ours.

chapter 8

C'est la vie
France

After a long and illustrious history in the wine industry, France now finds itself at a major crossroads, but every one of the traffic lights is flashing red. Rightfully proud of the path the nation blazed as the international standard-bearer for high-quality wines, today France is suffering from dwindling sales both in its domestic market and in foreign export markets. So what went wrong?

Wine drinkers all over the world have wised up and rebelled against what might be called the "domestic stigma," realizing that homegrown wines are not necessarily bad—and indeed can be wonderful—and that French wine is not necessarily better. Wine producers, especially those in the New World, realized that competing with French wines was a losing game. When winemakers in California and Australia stopped trying to copy French wines and began making fresh, appealing wines packed full of ripe fruit, they proved they could do that far better than the French.

The welcome message of fresh, fruity wines is communicated on the New World wine bottle, where the varietal label—the name of the grape—rules. Modern wine consumers readily understand what Pinot Noir and Chardonnay mean, while French place names such as Vosne-Romanee (wine made from 100% Pinot Noir grapes) and Meursault (a wine made from 100% Chardonnay grapes) remain practically meaningless.

In France itself, winemakers are confronted with a dwindling market as a new generation of young French people have turned their backs on the habits of previous generations. One recent survey estimates that in the past decade the amount of time spent on the average French dinner has dwindled from eighty-eight minutes to thirty-eight. If you add to that a vigorous anti-drinking campaign in the French media, it is no surprise that French people are consuming less wine.

In addition, some French wine producers have frequently yelled and screamed that they are hamstrung by archaic Appellation controlee regulations that require them to follow specific growing practices and to plant only certain grape varieties within a defined wine region (the red Bordeaux appellation, for example, that requires the use of mostly Cabernet blends but forbids the use of Shiraz). These producers have complained that such restrictions leave them with very little room for experimentation and innovation in a world that thrives on the new and the different. Despite numerous calls to overhaul the impractical rules and the heavy bureaucracy of the Appellation controlee system, very little has changed, and French wine producers continue to lose market share all around the globe.

Still, there is good news for *WineWise* readers. The quality wine producers of France will always turn out quality wines whatever the cumbersome and outmoded French regulations may dictate. There are plenty of intriguing and affordable wines from France's classic and lesser-known regions. In addition, many French wine producers continue to offer wines that are more restrained than their New World counterparts, a fact that often makes the Old World versions better food partners than the more obvious, fruit-forward style of the New World (see pages 280–303).

The overall picture

IN EUROPEAN TERMS, France is a large wine-producing nation, with a total of close to 2.5 million acres (1 million hectares) of vines turning out 145 million cases (50 million hectoliters) of wine per year, making France one of the two largest producers in the world (the other is Italy). That large amount of acreage planted with vines means that the vineyards span climatic ranges from cool to hot, producing everything from crisp, dry whites to full-bodied reds, along with sweet wines and a large variety of sparkling wines.

There are seven famous and classic wine regions in France: Alsace, Beaujolais, Bordeaux, Burgundy, Champagne, Loire, and Rhone. In addition, there are several lesser-known regions within the broad sweep of vineyards across southern France in the areas of Languedoc, Roussillon, and Provence.

In the pages that follow, we will introduce you to the more important white, rosé, red, and sparkling wines of each of these regions, as well as the landscapes and people behind them. But first a word on French labels.

Language of the label

FRENCH WINE LABELS present information that is common to all wine labels, which make them no more and no less difficult to read than any other nation's wine labels. What might be difficult for some of us is that the words are written in a foreign language—French—and, in many cases, familiar terms such as Chardonnay or Merlot do not appear on the label. But the following synopsis will help.

Company name

All wines labels include a company name, the producer of the wine. It might be a grape-growing estate, such as Chateau Latour, in Bordeaux, or it might be a family name, such as Louis Jadot, in Burgundy. In either case, since the reputation of the *negociant* or producer is often synonymous with the wine's quality, the name is prominently displayed on the main label, or perhaps on a neck label.

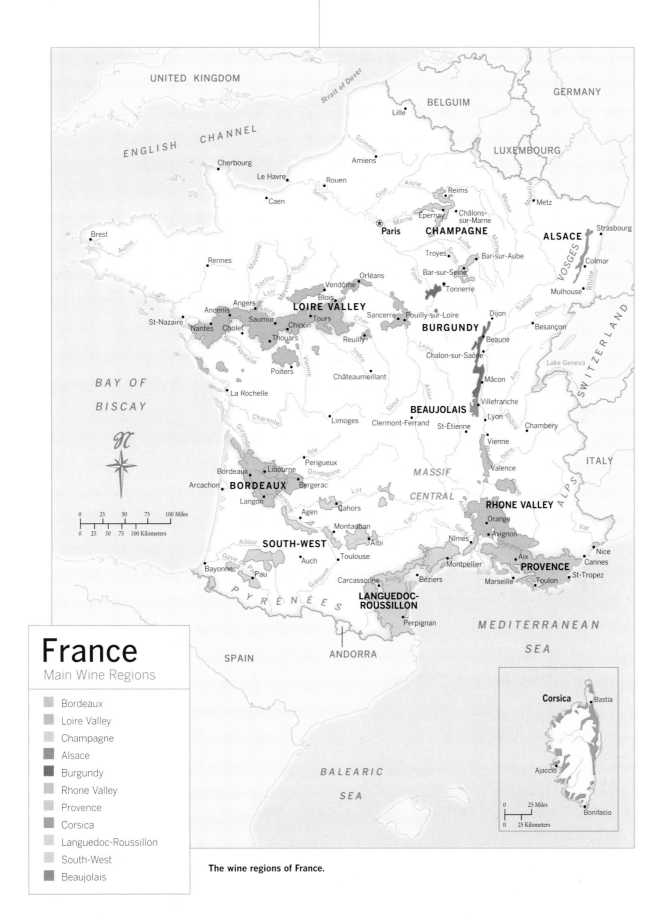

France
Main Wine Regions

- Bordeaux
- Loire Valley
- Champagne
- Alsace
- Burgundy
- Rhone Valley
- Provence
- Corsica
- Languedoc-Roussillon
- South-West
- Beaujolais

The wine regions of France.

Wine name

The company name and the wine name are the two most important pieces of information on any label. There are three broad possibilities for wine names: a branded name, such as Red Bicyclette; a grape variety name, such as Riesling; or a place name, such as Sancerre. The French use all three methods, but no label from any country is going to tell you directly if the name of the wine is a brand, a grape, or a place. The simple truth about French wine names is that it takes time, practice, and experience to recognize what is a place name, and then to be able to translate that into a grape variety or varieties.

The French system requires that if a place name is used on a label, only certain grape varieties grown in that place can be used to make the wine. Figuring

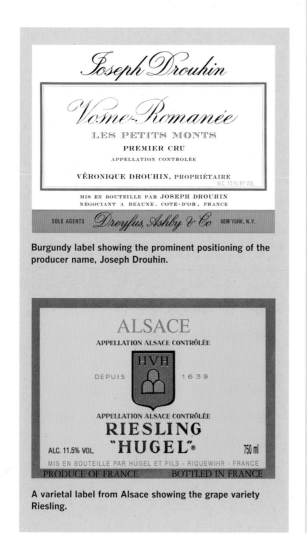

Burgundy label showing the prominent positioning of the producer name, Joseph Drouhin.

A varietal label from Alsace showing the grape variety Riesling.

this stuff out sounds a bit like work, right? Well, part of the beauty of French wines is that to learn about them you have to taste them. The more you taste, the more you learn. That's our kind of work (and we hope, yours too)!

In some cases, the name of a grape-growing estate is also the name of the wine. This is especially true in Bordeaux, with names such as Chateau Lagrange or Chateau Bonnet. Again, since the name of the wine is the hook that will draw in the customer, it is very prominently displayed.

Place of origin and appellation controlee

No matter what the size of the place of origin, it will always be identified on every French wine label. It could be as large as the entire nation, in which case the label will offer information such as the phrase *vin de table de France,* or it could be as small as a single vineyard (La Romanee, for example), in which case the French *Appellation controlee* system will come into play. By the way, from the modern consumer's perspective, the phrases *appellation controlee* and *appellation d'origine controlee* (AOC) are the same thing. We will take the easy way out and use AOC.

In most wine markets around the world, two levels of wine visibly represent France:

- *vins de pays,* wines from several large, defined regions, with very few regulations about what grape types can be used
- AOC wines from both large and small defined areas, with very specific restrictions on which grape types can be used

French producers want to capture a share of the New World wine market, so many *vins de pays* are labeled with a grape variety name. Chardonnay, Merlot, and Syrah, among others, are especially popular in the international market. In fact, Georges Duboeuf, who made his reputation as the leading producer of AOC Beaujolais wines, has become one of the leading players in the *vin de pays* varietal label game. Duboeuf has bucked French tradition completely, cashing in on the Australian version of the grape name and label-

What is this AOC?

In most wine-producing countries, "appellation" has come to mean a defined, named grape-growing region, such as Napa Valley or Bordeaux. In the French system AOC is shorthand for *Appellation d'origine controlee*, which translates as "controlled place-name

of origin." All that means is that if the producer uses a place name on the label and prints the words *Appellation controlee* on the label, there is a complete set of regulations that are supposed to be followed regarding grape-growing techniques and which grape varieties can be used. In addition, rules for some wines include restrictions on irrigation, permitted wine styles, minimum percentage of alcohol, and specifications on how the wine must be made. In all cases, the place name refers to the place where the grapes were grown.

ing his wine "Shiraz" instead of "Syrah." Whatever the name of the wine, all of these wines will be identified by the inclusion of the phrase *vin de pays* on the label, plus the name of the region where the grapes were grown. Prominent examples are *vin de pays d'Oc, vin de pays de l'Ardeche, vin de pays du Gard, vin de pays de l'Herault,* and *vin de pays des Cotes de Gascogne.* Oc, Ardeche, Gard, Herault, and Cotes de Gascogne are large grape-growing areas in southern France.

The vast majority of AOC wines in France are named after the place where the grapes grow (Vouvray, a village in the Loire Valley, is just one of hundreds of examples), and that place name is prominently displayed on the label (so the actual name of the wine is Vouvray). Underneath that place name, the phrase *appellation controlee* usually appears. That is a consumer's legal guarantee that the wine has been made according to the specific regulations for that place.

Remember that the phrase *appellation controlee* is a guarantee of authenticity, not a guarantee of quality. High-quality wines are made by the hard work of conscientious producers, not through some set of rigid regulations.

The major French exceptions to place-named wines are the wonderful wines of Alsace, named for the grape variety that is used to make the wine. So we can enjoy Alsatian Riesling and Alsatian Pinot Gris, just two examples of the varietal-labeled wines of Alsace. Those wines are still made according to AOC regulations and will carry the phrase *appella-*

A wine with the brand name Colombelle showing the *vin de pays* notation.

tion controlee on the label. If the grapes used to make the wine all came from a single vineyard, the name of that vineyard may appear on the label as well.

Indications of status

Five of France's classic wine regions (Alsace, Bordeaux, Burgundy, Champagne, and Loire) have adopted a system of indicating on the label the legal status of some of their best vineyards. Though the exact wording varies from region to region, the general picture looks like this: over time, certain vineyards have developed a reputation for consistently producing better grapes, and better wines from those grapes, than their neighbors. These vineyards have earned

Burgundy label showing *appellation controlee* notation.

Premier cru Burgundy label.

the title *premier cru* (first growth). In addition, of the several thousand vineyards in France, only a few hundred have earned the extraordinary status of *grand cru* (great growth). (In Bordeaux, things get a little tricky; the equivalent phrase is *grand cru classe*—classified great growth—with the highest level being *premier grand cru classe*—first classified great growth; see "Bordeaux," page 151.)

If all the grapes used to make a wine came from a *premier cru* or *grand cru* vineyard, that phrase will show up on the label. Still, the consumer needs to be wary. Any fool can take fabulous grapes from a great vineyard and turn them into terrible wine. *Premier cru* or *grand cru* is a sign that the wine might be great, truly memorable. Certainly it will carry a great, truly memorable price tag. But quality, as always, comes from the producer who has a reputation to uphold. In the regional sections that follow, we will be highlighting French producers that we think are consistent purveyors of high quality and whose wines can readily be found in most markets.

Other information

In addition to the three major signposts of company name, wine name, and place name, wine labels often include other bits of information, such as the legal name and address of the producer and importer, and the alcohol content. Sometimes descriptive phrases that are meant to tell us more about the wine can be found, such as *reserve* or *vieilles vignes* (old vines). As

far as we can tell, those particular phrases do not convey any specific legal meaning in France and can be used randomly and arbitrarily by producers.

Regions

Alsace

Alsace is at once a region that is wondrously varied but also unique in many ways. That variety and uniqueness are reflected in a melding of French and German culture that represents the region's history. With the exception of their exciting but restrained Riesling wines, the other, mainly white, grape varieties are presented in a rich, even full-blown style, tempered by high, refreshing acidity and an underlying touch of stoniness that can be very appealing. While Alsace focuses on whites, its full range of wines covers reds and sparklers, too.

Alsace has forgone the privilege of identifying *premier cru* vineyards in the region but does boast approximately fifty *grand cru* vineyards. If all the grapes used to make the wine came from one such vineyard, the phrase *grand cru* and the name of the vineyard may appear on the label.

Considering the modern international wine market, Alsace might hold a unique competitive advantage over other classic French AOC regions, since the overwhelming majority of its white and red wines display varietal labels.

WHITE WINES

Gewurztraminer and Pinot Gris. Alsatian wine producers are proud of a couple of wines they like to make in an opulent, almost decadent style: Gewurztraminer and Pinot Gris. Their rich, smooth texture is immediately appealing, in a sensual, gratifying way, but there is just enough restraint in the fresh acidity and underlying mineral quality that they do not become ridiculously blatant or blowsy. Of late we have seen a tendency for winemakers to leave more and more residual sugar in these formerly dry to off-dry wines, which we find regrettable, but we will not stop tasting them—they are still delicious.

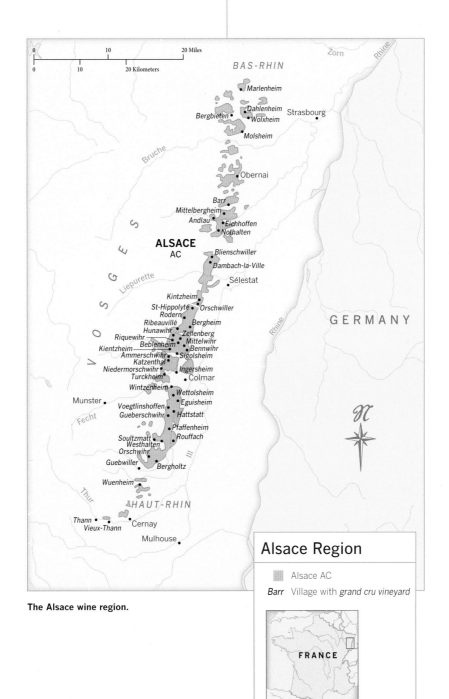

The Alsace wine region.

Alsace Region

▦ Alsace AC

Barr Village with *grand cru vineyard*

FRANCE

Riesling vines among the roses at Domaine Weinbach.

The assertive flavors and supple texture of Gewurztraminer and Pinot Gris make them delightful companions with the intense flavors of Alsatian cuisine, such as onion tart, cured pork dishes with cabbage (the famous *choucroute alsacienne*), braised game birds such as duck and goose, and foie gras. Their light sweetness, full fruitiness, and smooth texture also make them excellent accompaniments to Thai and Korean cuisine with their underlying heat and spice.

In years when the growing season provides a warm, dry autumn, winemakers will take advantage of the climatic conditions to produce a small quantity of very intensely flavored sweet wines, either as *vendange tardive* (late harvest) or as *selection de grains nobles* (botrytis-affected). To sip one of these rare and fairly expensive wines and reflect on the glories of a meal just enjoyed, or the wonders of life in general, is a truly sublime experience.

Riesling. And then there is Riesling. If Alsatian Gewurz and Pinot Gris are pushed in one direction, toward richness and opulence, Riesling is often pushed in the opposite direction, toward restraint, austerity, and subtlety, and we applaud the move.

Alsace's winemakers are creating delicious wines that show the extraordinary capabilities of all these grapes to their fullest potential.

Alsatian Rieslings are definitely dry—among the driest in the world—unless identified on the label as *vendange tardive* or *selection de grains nobles* (see above). In the dry style, the winemaker is forced into a corner since there is no camouflage of sugar to hide behind. The flavors have to be clean, pure, and vibrant, encased in an intriguing ensemble with balancing acidity. Nine times out of ten, Alsatian winemakers succeed in this goal with their Riesling wines. The most common descriptors for the aromas and flavors revolve around perceptions of citrus, from lime to orange blossom, backed by a slight hint of wet stone aroma. These wines may not take your breath away, but they will certainly make you sit up and say, "Oh! *That's* what Riesling can be like."

These lighter, less assertive styles of Alsatian Riesling lend themselves to pairing with salads, lightly poached or sautéed fish, or sautéed chicken with a light butter and wine sauce. It is also grand with smoked salmon or trout, oysters on the half shell, ceviche, or turkey sandwich leftovers from Thanksgiving.

Muscat. "Isn't Muscat a sweet wine?" you ask. In this world, usually it is. But Alsatian winemakers have their own world, and it has always included dry Muscat, a wonderful, intriguing concept since it combines the aromatic delicacy of ripe, grapey, almost tropical flavors with the sharp directness of a dry wine.

Alsatian Muscat is a beautiful accompaniment to sushi and sashimi and will shine when paired with a dry, crumbly cheese such as aged Cantal or the sharp tanginess of Conté or Emmental.

Pinot Blanc. With the grape types already discussed, the superlatives are easy to roll out. Pinot Blanc is more pedestrian, but that does not mean it should be avoided. It is a great choice—and often a great value—when you want something like Chardonnay but cannot face the overt oak that is so frequently a part of New World Chardonnay. Although Pinot Blanc may never shine, it is always a very well-made wine with ripe apple and pear characteristics. It is certainly a great sandwich and salad wine.

Blended White Wines. A number of producers in Alsace opt for a blend of white grape types to produce a style of wine known as Edelzwicker (noble blend). Their affordability and easy-drinking style make them very attractive if we are not looking for the more serious expression of a single grape variety. Two particularly attractive versions are "Les Crustaces" (as you can guess from the name, it's ideal served with crustaceans), produced by Dopff et Irion, and "Gentil" (a truly gentle but lovely wine), produced by Hugel.

SPARKLING WINES

Like the sparkling wines of other French regions (except Champagne), the bubblies of Alsace are called *cremant* wines, in this case Cremant d'Alsace.

They are made by the classic Champagne method (see page 3), using any one or a blend of Pinot Blanc, Pinot Gris, Pinot Noir, Riesling, and Chardonnay. Some of the finer examples take on the standard toasty notes that come with prolonged aging in contact with the yeast cells (see page 167), while others are more straightforwardly fruity. Try these delicious but simple wines with potato latkes and sour cream or with spicy pad thai—you will be surprised. While they may never scale the heights of great Champagne, they are an excellent alternative with which to impress company. They may be affordable, even inexpensive, but they are never cheap.

PRICES AND PRODUCERS

For many Alsatian producers, Pinot Blanc is their basic wine, and it is often the least expensive, making them WineWise bargains. The other wines in a producer's lineup will be priced accordingly, with the Gewurztraminer and Riesling wines more expensive. Some of our favorite producers include those on the list that follows. For some, we have included specific wines from their portfolio, including some of their best, which will almost always be more expensive than their good, basic wines. Note that some producers use the term *clos* with a name to indicate the grapes came from a single vineyard of that name (Clos des Capucins, for example).

Relative bargains include Pierre Sparr, Albert Mann, Blanck (Riesling "Rosenbourg"), Leon Beyer, Lucien Albrecht, and Willm (Cremant d'Alsace).

Moderately expensive choices include Trimbach (Cuvee Frederic Emile Riesling, Seigneurs de Ribeaupierre Gewurztraminer, Clos Ste-Hune Riesling), Schlumberger, Hugel (Jubilee Pinot Gris, Cuvee les Amours Pinot Blanc, and "Gentil"), Marcel Deiss, Mure (Clos St-Landelin), Dopff au Moulin, and Dopff et Irion ("Les Crustaces," Clos des Amandiers Muscat).

Producers whose wines are mostly expensive (and mostly worth it) include Zind-Humbrecht (any and all of their single-vineyard wines), Kreydenweiss, and Domaine Weinbach (Clos des Capucins Muscat).

Beaujolais

Beaujolais and its wines are easy to understand, easy to buy, and easy to love. With few exceptions, they are juicy, bubble-gum reds produced in a light style for easy drinking. A huge amount of red Beaujolais is produced, all of it made solely from the Gamay grape. A small quantity of white wine is also produced from Chardonnay.

The region of Beaujolais is situated between Burgundy and the Rhone Valley, marked by rolling

Vineyard of Gamay vines in Beaujolais.

Gamay vineyard in the northern Beaujolais Villages area.

granite hills and a warm climate that allows grapes to ripen easily just about every year (see Burgundy map, page 161). The friendliness and fruitiness of the wines are enhanced by a winemaking method that pushes fruitiness to the max. It is called carbonic maceration, which entails placing whole, unbroken grapes into a large stainless-steel vat and then enveloping them with carbon dioxide gas. In this "hostile" environment, the whole grapes use their own internal enzymes to try to consume the sugars. In the process they create alcohol, just as yeasts would. Basically, the grapes ferment from the inside out. Because this process involves very little movement or violent activity, the wines are lower in color and tannin levels, making them light and easy to drink.

In addition to the huge quantity of simple, fruity red wines, there are also some more intense red styles of Beaujolais, made by traditional winemaking methods, and well worth seeking out.

RED WINES

In truth, Beaujolais is all about red wines, from the fresh *nouveau* wine to ageworthy wines with greater depth and more complex flavors. Here are the basic styles of Beaujolais and the names to look for on their labels.

Beaujolais Nouveau. Every year, Beaujolais producers launch their *nouveau* or *primeur* wines on a "show me the money" schedule: grapes are harvested in September, the wine is made in October, and the bottles are sold on retail shelves starting the third Thursday of November, with cash in the bank in December. Although international excitement about the release of these wines has faded, they can still be fun to try. The irony is that when they are released in the fall, just in time for Thanksgiving, these Beaujolais Nouveau wines really don't have the guts—the body, the complexity—to successfully marry with our traditional holiday dinner. But if you can wait until April (when the price is likely to be heavily discounted) they make a great spring wine, chilled for a picnic or even for that first summer barbecue. Just beware that the wine has not lost too much of its zippy freshness.

Beaujolais Villages. This label name tells you that the grapes came from vineyards within thirty-eight villages, all located in the northern part of Beaujolais. Here, in vineyards rich in granite-based soils, the grapes tend to ripen more than elsewhere in the region. A good Beaujolais Villages wine should be bright, ripe, and full of fruit in its aroma, with a smooth texture on your palate.

The Best of Beaujolais. Wines labeled as Beaujolais Nouveau or Beaujolais Villages are juicy, enjoyable, inexpensive, and fun, perfect with a burger or a pizza. But we want to share our true excitement for some WineWise heavyweights, often referred to as Cru Beaujolais. These wines come from any one of ten villages in the Beaujolais region and are labeled with the village name. The vineyards within these villages are recognized as premium sites, and the depth of flavors, pigments, and tannins in the grapes respond very well to more traditional winemaking methods to produce full-flavored, structured wines, with darker colors and a more assertive, more complex set of characteristics. In many ways, they approach their Pinot Noir cousins to the north in Burgundy, with red berry, cherry, and plum flavors, and a touch of earthiness to add interest. The ten villages that have earned the privilege to use their name on the label are Brouilly, Chenas, Chiroubles, Cote de Brouilly, Fleurie, Julienas, Morgon, Moulin-a-Vent, Regnie, and St-Amour. Moulin-a-Vent and Morgon are usually the longest-lived of the ten *crus,* meaning that they can age about five years or more. The other wines are meant for early enjoyment.

Although Cru Beaujolais wines are more expensive than Beaujolais Villages (which often sell for less than $10), they still represent some of the great bargains in delicious red wine (priced from $10 to under $25). One of the reasons? Many American wine consumers have never heard of them, and for those who have, these wines have zero snob appeal. Cru Beaujolais is a secret hidden in plain sight, a largely undiscovered tiny gem, a true WineWise wine.

Hint: A bottle of St-Amour might be a good way to impress your lover on Valentine's Day, while Fleurie is the equivalent of a bouquet of flowers in a bottle. Good luck!

Producers whose wines are relative bargains include Pere Patriarche and Reine Pedauque. In the moderately expensive category are Paul Beaudet, J.-P. Brun, Chateau de la Chaize, Cheysson, Jean Descombes, Domaine des Ducs, Joseph Drouhin, Georges Duboeuf (by far the largest producer in the Beaujolais region), Henry Fessy, Sylvain Fessy, Foillard, Louis Jadot, Hubert Lapierre, and Thorin. A producer of more expensive wines is Raymond et Michel Tete.

Bordeaux

Almost everything to do with Bordeaux wine is big. The appellation area covers 285,000 acres (115,000 hectares), more than five times the size of Burgundy and eight times the size of Napa Valley. Making a living from grape growing in the region are twelve thousand growers whose grapes produce 850 million bottles of *Appellation controlee*/AOC wines each year. That's one big wine cellar.

The sheer size of everything means that Bordeaux has a finger in every pie—or a nose in every glass—of the wine business. They make white, red, rosé, sparkling, and even fortified wines. They can be sweet or dry, expensive or affordable. They boast some of the greatest wine names ever to grace a table, wines that show up on most people's top-ten list. They make excellent, very good, good, and occasionally even mediocre wines.

One of the reasons we can find very good and good, often from the same producer, is that Bordeaux

Aging cellar at Chateau Palmer.

chateaux (wine-producing estates) often have access to grapes from older, mature vines as well as grapes from recently planted vines. Most vineyards are in a constant state of flux, with older vines being replaced by younger ones on a regular basis. In general, grapes from young vines make wines that are less complex and have a sense of immaturity about them—they are less refined, less polished. Even the finest chateau will use grapes from younger vines to produce a "second-label" wine. For example, Chateau Lagrange produces a second-label Les Fiefs de Lagrange, which sells for about half the price of the "first-label" wine. Even though the raw material for the second-label wine may be less prestigious, it benefits from all of the expertise and experience that go into making Chateau Lagrange a fine wine. In this way, second-label wines from Bordeaux chateaux represent excellent value, and most of them can be enjoyed sooner, as they don't require as much aging as a chateau's flagship wine (see the list of second-label wines on page 157).

Another consideration for the range of qualities and prices is the diversity of the appellations. As in everything, the famous and the perceived best receive 90% of all the attention. In this way, the appellations of Medoc, Haut-Medoc, Pessac-Leognan, St-Emilion, Pomerol, and Sauternes receive the lion's share of all the publicity and media glare. Wines from those appellations are also the most expensive. But if we venture into the outlying appellations, the Bordeaux "satellites" of Premieres Cotes de Bordeaux, Cotes de Bourg, and Cotes de Blaye, we can frequently find very good wines at bargain-basement prices.

The big stats connected with Bordeaux wines continue: fifty-seven distinct appellations (whose official place names will appear on the label), nine permitted grape types, and four different classification systems that afford the status of *premier grand cru classe* or *grand cru classe* to a total of 170 chateaux. To beat a clear and easily navigable path through all of this, we will break down Bordeaux wines in the following manner:

- grape types
- appellations associated with white or red wine production
- comments on the status symbols of *premier grand cru classe* and *grand cru classe*
- descriptions of each appellation and some of its wines in more detail

GRAPE TYPES

Although there is a total of nine grape varieties permitted in Bordeaux wines, the heart and soul of those wines rest on two white grapes and three reds. For both dry and sweet white wines, Bordeaux winemakers use Sauvignon Blanc and Semillon, often blended together, though an increasing number of dry whites are 100% Sauvignon Blanc.

All the Bordeaux red wines are blends of two or more of the three major grape types—Cabernet Sauvignon, Merlot, and Cabernet Franc. To complement

Making wine from a blend of grape types

When wines are a blend of grape types, this is how they're made. Each grape variety is harvested separately and made into a single-varietal wine. If any oak aging is required, that also is done separately for each single varietal. After each wine has begun to show its potential character, blending begins. The different wines are blended to produce the best possible sum of their parts. This usually means that the exact blend is rarely the same from year to year—it is close, but there are variations. This allows the winemaker to take advantage of any single grape type that excelled during the growing season, using more of that grape type than usual. After the wines made from each grape type have been blended, the final product is allowed to age some more to marry together the various flavor and aroma components.

Merlot grapes in a Haut-Medoc vineyard.

this array of white and red grapes, Bordeaux boasts a wide variety of foods, including everything from oysters to lamb and beef.

MAJOR APPELLATIONS IN BORDEAUX

Remember that most appellation systems work on the basis of larger, more general appellations that contain smaller ones. The most general appellation here is Bordeaux. This huge appellation is authorized for the production of dry white and dry red wines. If a chateau's vineyards do not fall within a smaller appellation, the wine will be identified with the phrase *Appellation Bordeaux Controlee.* If the alcohol level is higher, there is also the possibility of using the phrase *Appellation Bordeaux Superieur Controlee.* In both cases, they are general Bordeaux wines, even if they carry a chateau name. Sometimes these wines can still deliver the Bordeaux pedigree of quality that many wine lovers seek, and at incredibly reasonable prices.

One very attractive feature of the basic AOC Bordeaux wines is that larger, internationally minded producers have begun using these wines as a testing ground for including the grape variety on the label. For now, this is true only for proprietary named wines, many of which have been made as single-variety wines, but the trend may eventually embrace the chateau wines. Examples of relative bargains in proprietary named, varietally labeled wines include "Premius" by Yvon Mau and "No. 1" by Dourthe.

Among the smaller appellations, the main dry white wine areas are Entre-Deux-Mers, Graves, and its subappellation of Pessac-Leognan. The two big-name sweet white wine appellations are Sauternes and Barsac. For dry red wines, the main appellations are Medoc, Haut-Medoc, Graves, St-Emilion, Pomerol, Premieres Cotes de Bordeaux, Cotes de Bourg, and Cotes de Blaye.

STATUS CLASSIFICATIONS

Four of the appellations of the Bordeaux region have classification systems. Of these, the two big guns date from 1855 and apply to numerous dry red wines of Haut-Medoc (plus just one red from Graves; the French never make it easy) and a small selection of the sweet white wines of Sauternes and Barsac. Back in those days, the wines listed in these classifications were considered to be the top-quality wines of those districts, and we would argue that, on balance, the classifications are still largely relevant today. Even if there are some new contenders, most of the elite wines included on the original lists still deserve their exalted place.

In 1959, the Graves district classification was introduced. The complete listings of these classifications can be found in *Exploring Wine* (it's written by us, too), or in any other good reference book on Bordeaux. The simple fact about all of these classifications is this: a Bordeaux wine that carries the phrase *grand cru classe* or *premier grand cru classe* on the label is considered to be a premium wine, and it will have a premium price tag. But (there's always a but) some words of warning:

- Bordeaux's Pomerol district has no classification system, and the magic phrase *grand cru classe* will never appear on a Pomerol label, but that does not mean they do not make superb wine there.

- Some unclassified chateaux happily use the unrestricted phrase *grand vin de Bordeaux* on their label, but they have never been classified.

- Comparing a *grand cru classe* wine from one appellation to a *grand cru classe* wine from another may not be comparing apples to apples, since the grape blend will be different, as will the growing conditions and climate. And remember, some of Bordeaux's *grand cru classe* wines are not as *grand* as others, but neither are their prices.

- The Graves classification refers to its wines as *cru classe* only, with no indication of *premier* or *grand*.

- The St-Emilion classification is revised every ten years. The most recent version (2006) recently survived a legal challenge from some unhappy producers who were not included or were demoted.

APPELLATIONS AND THEIR WINES

White Wines. ENTRE-DEUX-MERS. Wines from this appellation are all dry white wines made from Sauvignon Blanc, sometimes blended with Semillon. They will be labeled simply with the appellation name (Entre-Deux-Mers), or they may carry a chateau name if the grapes all came from one grape-growing estate. The area consists mostly of rolling uplands between the two major rivers Dordogne and Garonne. In recent years, most of the wines from this appellation have moved toward a fresh, simple, fruity style, often 100% Sauvignon Blanc with no wood aging. This makes them brightly attractive and appealing wines, great for light lunches and simple seafood dishes. When Semillon is included, the wines take on a riper tropicality and fuller body. Favorite producers of relative bargains include Chateau Bonnet, Chateau Ducla, and Chateau La Rose du Pin.

GRAVES. The Graves appellation lies on the west side of the Garonne River. Its dry white wines are indeed more serious—more grave, if you will—than their counterparts in Entre-Deux-Mers, but the name "Graves" refers to the gravelly soil that is typical of the area. The weightier style often comes from a higher proportion of Semillon blended with Sauvignon Blanc and a greater reliance on oak barrel fermentation or aging. The two white grapes are good partners, with the Sauvignon Blanc offering crisp acidity and fresh citrus or apricot aromas and flavors, while the Semillon provides greater roundness in the mouth

and more tropical fruit flavors. The fuller expression makes the wines good partners with pork, chicken, or turkey dishes, as well as with heavier seafoods with cream sauces.

Some of the respected moderately expensive chateaux include Chateau Berger, Domaine La Grave, Clos Lamothe, Chateau Landiras, Chateau Rahoul, and Chateau Haut La Croix.

PESSAC-LEOGNAN. For many, this is the aristocracy of dry white Bordeaux wines, representing the fullest embodiment of the Semillon and Sauvignon Blanc blend. The reverence paid to some of these wines is a reflection of why the French have historically claimed to produce superior wines. Like it or not, there are certain parcels of land where soil type, climate, daylight hours, grape variety, and the winemaker's hard work come together to produce something very special, something impressive and memorable. Situated in the northernmost tip of the Graves appellation, Pessac-Leognan is one of those places. A higher proportion of gravelly quartzite in the soil and the slope and lie of the land bring out a mineral quality in the wine, tropical but clean and vibrant fruit with a depth and complexity that is simply absent in most Entre-Deux-Mers wines.

Moderately expensive examples of these wines (around $30) are offered by Chateau Carbonnieux,

Botrytis-affected grapes.

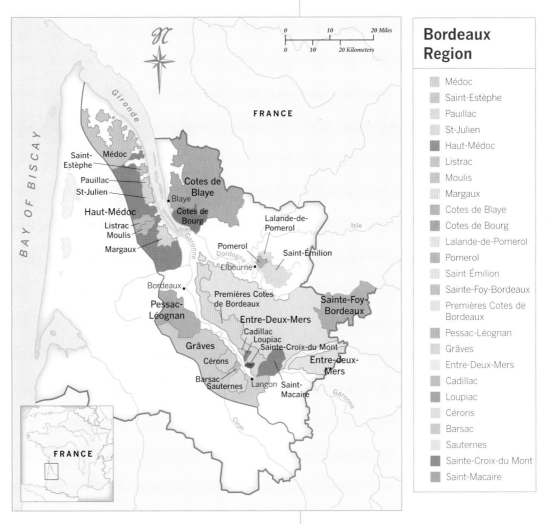

The Bordeaux wine region.

Bordeaux Region

- Médoc
- Saint-Estèphe
- Pauillac
- St-Julien
- Haut-Médoc
- Listrac
- Moulis
- Margaux
- Cotes de Blaye
- Cotes de Bourg
- Lalande-de-Pomerol
- Pomerol
- Saint-Émilion
- Sainte-Foy-Bordeaux
- Premières Cotes de Bordeaux
- Pessac-Léognan
- Grâves
- Entre-Deux-Mers
- Cadillac
- Loupiac
- Cérons
- Barsac
- Sauternes
- Sainte-Croix-du Mont
- Saint-Macaire

Chateau Bouscaut, Chateau Olivier, Chateau Couhins, and Chateau Smith-Haut-Lafitte. More expensive (around $50 and more) versions come from Domaine de Chevalier, Chateau Laville Haut-Brion, and the very rare (read *very* expensive) Chateau Haut-Brion.

SAUTERNES AND BARSAC. These sweet white wine appellations are at the southern tip of Graves, extending southward from the Garonne River. Indeed, the proximity to the river accounts for much of the success of these places as premium producers of sweet wines. The mists that typically sit on the river in the fall months move through the vineyards and encourage the settlement of the botrytis mold on the grapes as they near the end of the ripening stage. While most molds are ruinous to agricultural crops,

the botrytis mold helps to create some of the most sought-after sweet wines in the world.

The wines exhibit a distinctly honeyed aroma, with backgrounds of dried apricots, peaches, and pears. On the palate, they are richly textured and extremely sweet, but they are always balanced by an elevated acidity that leaves the mouth feeling fresh and clean, rather than sticky and cloying. The wines of Sauternes and Barsac were classified in 1855, with Chateau d'Yquem ranked above all others. It is still highly revered and highly priced at over $100 for a half bottle. Wines that are still very good but easier on the bank account include the moderately expensive wines of Chateau Suduiraut, Chateau Climens, Chateau Coutet, and Chateau Rieussec as fairly intense versions. Lighter but still impressive (and still mod-

Vineyards at Chateau Pichon Longueville.

erately expensive) styles come from Chateau Rayne-Vigneau, Chateau Filhot, Chateau Broustet, Chateau Nairac, and Chateau Lafon.

Red Wines. LEFT BANK: MEDOC AND HAUT-MEDOC.

Along with the wines of Graves, Medoc and Haut-Medoc wines are often referred to as Left Bank wines since the vineyards are situated on the left (west) side of the Gironde estuary and the Garonne River (see Bordeaux map). There is nothing particularly significant about that title other than its role in letting us know physically where the vineyards are. But the Left Bank moniker does give a clue as to the style of the wines, since the majority of them are produced with Cabernet Sauvignon as the dominant grape in the blend, with Merlot and Cabernet Franc playing second and third fiddle.

That weighting has a significant effect on the flavor profile of the wines. They tend to be tannic in their youth and full-bodied, with a depth and complexity of aroma and flavor. And they offer the promise of becoming softer and mellower with age. But exactly how complex, full-bodied, and ageworthy the wines are depends on exactly where they came from within Medoc or Haut-Medoc.

The Medoc and Haut-Medoc appellations (often informally referred to collectively as Medoc) make up a long but narrow strip of land stretching from north of the city of Bordeaux along the west bank of the

Gironde estuary toward the Atlantic Ocean. As you move northward from Bordeaux toward the ocean, the soil becomes more sandy and silty; this is the land of the official Medoc appellation. Closer to Bordeaux, in the official Haut-Medoc appellation, there are pockets of the famed stony, quartzite soil that makes certain vineyards shine. This is especially true around the villages of Margaux, St-Julien, Pauillac, and St-Estephe, and to a lesser extent in the villages of Moulis and Listrac. It is in these villages that most of the famed chateaux of the 1855 classification are found.

The general impression of a young Medoc wine from a prestigious chateau is firmness, tannin, and assertive but not forward black currant fruit. If you are ever offered the chance to taste an older Medoc wine, jump at it. But don't assume that you will automatically find the wine "better" than the young version. Older wines from anywhere are not necessarily better—they are different. Each person has to decide which style he or she prefers. As a Medoc or Haut-Medoc wine ages, it takes on a silky smoothness, but the flavors begin to fade and become more subtle, harder to detect. They are the flavors of dried fruit rather than fresh fruit, which is not everybody's preference.

Vineyards in the commune of St-Julien.

Medoc and Haut-Medoc wines that won't break the bank

The great and expensive wines of Medoc and Haut-Medoc are easy to identify: they are listed in the 1855 classification. But how can you find good wines to enjoy without pawning your grandmother's jewelry? We have compiled the following list, which includes:

- a selection of unclassified wines from Medoc
- a selection of unclassified wines from Haut-Medoc
- a selection of unclassified wines from the village appellations
- a selection of second-label wines of prominent chateaux

Rather than repeating the word "chateau" every time, we have listed just the chateau name. All of these wines qualify as moderately expensive.

Medoc unclassified	Haut-Medoc unclassified
Bellegrave	d'Arche
La Cardonne	d'Arcins
Castera	Bel Air
Greysac	Citran
Lafon	Coufran
Loudenne	Lanessan
Patache d'Aux	Larose-Trintaudon
Plagnac	Malescasse
Pontet	Segur
Potensac	Sociando-Mallet

Village unclassified	Village unclassified
d'Angludet (Margaux)	Le Crock (St-Estephe)
d'Arsac (Margaux)	Haut-Marbuzet (St-Estephe)
Labegorce Zede (Margaux)	Meyney (St-Estephe)
Siran (Margaux)	Ormes de Pez (St-Estephe)
du Glana (St-Julien)	de Pez (St-Estephe)
Gloria (St-Julien)	Phelan-Segur (St-Estephe)
Hortevie (St-Julien)	Clarke (Listrac)
Moulin de la Rose (St-Julien)	Fourcas Hosten (Listrac)
La Becasse (Pauillac)	Chasse-Spleen (Moulis)
Plantey (Pauillac)	Poujeaux (Moulis)

Second Labels

The chateau name is listed first, followed by the second-label name and the region or village in parentheses.

Chateau Cantemerle Les Allees de Cantemerle (Haut-Medoc)

Chateau Cos d'Estournel Les Pagodes de Cos (St-Estephe)

Chateau Grand-Puy-Lacoste Chateau Lacoste-Borie (Pauillac)

Chateau Pichon Longueville Les Tourelles de Longueville (Pauillac)

Chateau Pichon Longueville Comtesse de Lalande Reserve de la Comtesse (Pauillac)

Chateau Lafite-Rothschild Carruades de Lafite (Pauillac)

Chateau Latour Les Forts de Latour (Pauillac)

Chateau Ducru Beaucaillou La Croix de Beaucaillou (St-Julien)

Chateau Gruaud-Larose Sarget de Gruaud-Larose (St-Julien)

Chateau Lagrange Les Fiefs de Lagrange (St-Julien)

Chateau Leoville Las Cases Clos du Marquis (St-Julien)

Chateau Talbot Connetable Talbot (St-Julien)

Chateau Margaux Pavillon Rouge du Chateau Margaux (Margaux)

Haut-Medoc vineyards with the village of St-Estephe in the distance.

LEFT BANK: GRAVES. Like the red wines of Medoc and Haut-Medoc, the red Graves wines are generally dominated by Cabernet Sauvignon, but Graves offers something distinctly different. Medoc usually offers tight fruit and firm tannins, but a Graves wine always seems to entice with a note of delicacy and charm, which may be attributable to a higher percentage of Cabernet Franc in the blend, and/or a higher presence of sand in the soil. There are also several estates that concentrate more on Merlot than Cabernet Sauvignon.

Unfortunately, Graves wines tend to be underrepresented outside of France; if you find them, they provide an exciting glimpse of what else can be achieved in the world of Cabernet blends. That glimpse can be found in relative bargains from chateaux such as d'Archambeau, Le Bonnat, Haut-Mayne, de Landiras, Rahoul, and de Respide.

LEFT BANK: PESSAC-LEOGNAN. All of the best estates for red are clustered in this subappellation at the northern end of Graves, where there is a heavier concentration of the gravel and quartzite pebbles that seem to signify excellence in this region. Compared to the general Graves red wines, these wines offer more substance, with riper and deeper fruit. The renowned wines of Pessac-Leognan (all moderately expensive) will be labeled as *cru classe*, while the following chateaux offer relative bargains: Brown, de Cruzeau, La Garde, La Louvière, and de Rochemorin.

RIGHT BANK: POMEROL. In direct contrast to the Left Bank wines, where Cab generally dominates the blend, Right Bank wines are mostly about the soft, juicy Merlot, though, as we pointed out in our profile of Merlot on pages 43–46, the Right Bank is definitely capable of producing some thought-provoking versions of extraordinary depth and attraction. Perhaps to the dismay of the Medocains who have traditionally ruled the roost and run the market, the Merlot-based wines of the Right Bank have found great favor among knowledgeable and wealthy New World consumers. Despite the fact that Pomerol has no *grand cru* or *premier cru* designations, its most famous wine, Chateau Petrus, regularly outprices all of the other wines in Bordeaux. Undoubtedly,

the attraction of Right Bank Merlot wines is their rounder, more approachable style with softer tannins, particularly when young. The ripening season on the Right Bank is long and hot enough to ripen Merlot to perfection most years, though in Pomerol that forward fruit character in the wine is held in check by a mineral note, so that the wines are not all buoyant, one-dimensional black fruit. Instead you will find an intriguing palette of color and weight, with nuances of vanilla, toast, and earthiness. In addition, Cabernet Franc is used in heavier doses here, sometimes to the complete exclusion of Cabernet Sauvignon. An obvious conclusion from this is that while Bordeaux wines may show a family resemblance, there are notable differences among the siblings.

If you can afford them, it is hard to go wrong with a Pomerol wine. Perennial crowd pleasers include these moderately expensive selections: Beauregard, Certan de May, la Conseillante, La Fleur Petrus, Gazin, Lafleur, Plince, and de Sales.

As one of Pomerol's satellite appellations, Lalande de Pomerol often produces wines that approach the fruitiness and elegance of Pomerol itself, and usually at far more reasonable prices. True WineWise choices, these are some of the chateaux worth seeking out for relative bargains: Belles Graves, La Chenade, Les Cruzelles, La Fleur de Bouard, La Fleur St-Georges, Haut-Chaigneau, Moulin de Sales, and La Sergue.

Vineyards in the village of Pomerol.

Vineyard work in St-Emilion.

RIGHT BANK: ST-EMILION. Again, Merlot is dominant here, with Cabernet Franc playing a stronger role in the blends than Cabernet Sauvignon. The distinctive difference between Pomerol and St-Emilion lies in the limestone and gravel soil components in the latter that give St-Emilion wines a more noticeable mineral edge. In the generally warm, sunny conditions of this region, the Merlot ripens gracefully to its full potential, producing full, ripe, plummy characteristics.

If you want to go straight for the very expensive wines, that's not hard—the most highly revered chateaux in St-Emilion are Chateau Ausone, Chateau Angelus, and Chateau Cheval Blanc. The moderately expensive second labels of those three chateaux are La Chapelle d'Ausone, Carillon de l'Angelus, and Petit Cheval. Relative bargains are offered by Chateau Simard, Chateau Tertre du Moulin, and Chateau Fonplegade.

Wonderful St-Emilion look-alike wines that are relative bargains and are well worth searching out come from the four satellite appellations of Lussac-St-Emilion (Chateau Bel Air, Chateau des Rochers), Montagne-St-Emilion (Chateau Plaisance, Chateau Les Bardes), Puisseguin-St-Emilion (Chateau de l'Anglais, Chateau Lafaurie), and St-Georges-St-Emilion (Chateau St-Georges).

RIGHT BANK: COTES DE BLAYE, COTES DE BOURG, AND PREMIERES COTES DE BORDEAUX. For the real money-saving bargains in Bordeaux reds, these are the areas to look for. On occasion you will be rewarded with a wine that begins to approach the weight and elegance of a wine from a more "aristocratic" appellation. The majority grape is Merlot, providing ripe, supple fruitiness, and the varying depths of limestone soils will sometimes combine with the ripe Merlot fruit to produce a wine of distinction and class. There are no classification lists to worry about, so feel free to shop around and experiment—for less than $15 you will sometimes hit the jackpot. Good to very good relative bargains from Cotes de Blaye include Charron, Haut-Bertiniere, and La Raz Caman; from Cotes de Bourg, look for de Barbe, de la Grave, and Nodoz; and from Premieres Cotes de Bordeaux, seek out de Pic, du Juge, and La Bertrande.

Burgundy

Just as Bordeaux is big, Burgundy is small, with only 55,000 acres (22,000 hectares) in the appellation. Ironically, the Burgundy vineyards are owned and operated by nearly as many growers as Bordeaux, but that only underscores the small size of the plots worked by the Burgundy growers. Since most individual landholdings are so small, most growers cannot make their own wine, so they often sell their grapes to *negociants*, companies that buy raw material from several sources, make the wines, and label them with the most appropriate appellation according to the origin of the grapes. In Burgundy, as anywhere else, ultimate quality is in the hands of the producer/ *negociant*.

We will follow the same format with Burgundy as we did with Bordeaux, starting with grape types, then moving on to a list of the major appellations, with a discussion of any *premier cru* or *grand cru* designations, and concluding with a more in-depth look at each appellation and its wines.

GRAPE TYPES

Nothing is more simple than Burgundy grape types—Chardonnay for white wines, Pinot Noir for

Vineyards in the village of Mercurey.

red. Everybody can remember that. The problem, of course, is that those grape type names rarely show up on the label. The wines are named by place. So among the things we will emphasize in this section are some of the more important place names in Burgundy. From there, we will leave it up to you to figure out the color of the wine, and therefore the grape type. Remember that the Burgundy bottle is the one with the sloping shoulders (see page 13), and almost all Burgundy wines will have the name Burgundy or Bourgogne (French for "Burgundy") somewhere on the label.

MAJOR APPELLATIONS

Burgundy has several appellation levels, starting with the umbrella regional appellation of Burgundy (Bourgogne) itself. Within that large region, there are smaller regional and village-level appellations, and within the villages there are sometimes individual vineyard appellations of *premier cru* or *grand cru* status. As you progress from the large regional appellations all the way down to the single-vineyard

appellations, the permitted yield from the appellation is smaller. Fewer grapes from each vine and a correspondingly smaller quantity of wine should translate into a higher-quality wine. It will certainly translate into a higher price.

In summary, the structure of Burgundy appellations is as follows:

- The umbrella regional appellation, Burgundy (Bourgogne), is used for basic whites and reds from anywhere within the appellation.

- Regional appellations:

  - Chablis (whites only). Wines are labeled as Chablis if the grapes came from anywhere within the regional appellation; *premier cru* or *grand cru* may be added if the grapes came from a group of vineyards with that status. Wines may carry the name of a single *premier cru* or *grand cru* vineyard if the grapes are all from that vineyard.
  - Cote de Nuits Villages, Cote de Beaune Villages, and Cote de Beaune produce mostly red wines. Macon Villages produces white wines.

- Village appellations use the name of the village as the name of the wine. These individual villages fall within the areas of Cote de Nuits, Cote de Beaune, Chalon (officially called Cote Chalonnaise), and Macon (officially called Maconnais). We just want to make it WineWise simple for you—you can locate these areas and some of the villages within them on the Burgundy map on page 161.

- Single-vineyard appellations of *premier cru* or *grand cru* status. With the exception of Macon, every area has vineyards of *premier cru* status— in Cote de Nuits and Cote de Beaune, *premier cru* vineyards are sited in several villages. The words *premier cru* and the name of both the village (e.g., Vosne-Romanée) and the vineyard (Aux Malconsorts) will appear on the label. In Cote de Nuits and Cote de Beaune there are *grand cru* vineyards; on wines from these vineyards, the words *grand cru* and the name of the vineyard will appear on the label, but the village name will *not* appear.

APPELLATIONS AND THEIR WINES

White Wines. BOURGOGNE. Any wine that carries the AOC Bourgogne is the most basic type of Burgundy. Our comments about Chardonnay and Pinot Noir in Chapters 2 and 3 should alert you to the dangers of "ordinary" wine made from those varieties. But fear not—there are some gems out there that are relative bargains. Olivier Leflaive's white Bourgogne "Les Setilles" is particularly attractive, and Joseph Drouhin produces consistently reliable white and red versions carrying the "Bourgogne" designation, as do Vincent Girardin and Bernard Morey.

CHABLIS. Since Chablis is a white wine, and since Chablis is in the Burgundy region, the grape variety used is Chardonnay. But Chablis is like no other Chardonnay you have ever tasted. The standard approach for Chablis is to avoid wood, especially new wood, and to limit if not avoid malolactic

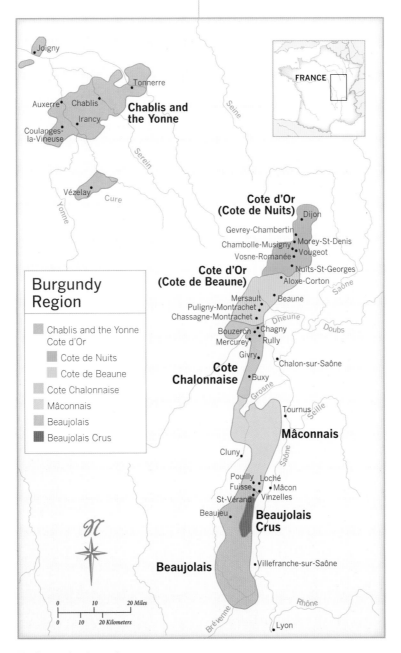

The Burgundy wine region.

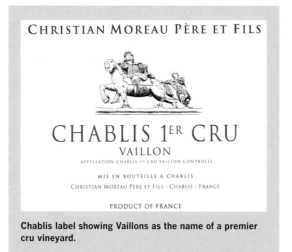

CHRISTIAN MOREAU PÈRE ET FILS

CHABLIS 1ᴱᴿ CRU
VAILLON
APPELLATION CHABLIS 1ᵉʳ CRU VAILLON CONTRÔLÉE

MIS EN BOUTEILLE A CHABLIS
CHRISTIAN MOREAU PÈRE ET FILS · CHABLIS · FRANCE

PRODUCT OF FRANCE

Chablis label showing Vaillons as the name of a premier cru vineyard.

fermentation (see page 7). The result is a lean, medium-bodied wine with green fruit and a pleasant tartness, very much like Granny Smith apples. For riper versions of Chablis, if your wallet is feeling too heavy and you need to unload some cash, you should look for the wines labeled *premier cru* or *grand cru*. The name of an individual vineyard, such as Vaudesir or Les Clos, will also appear on the label. These wines are much more complex, with smells of riper fruit, and a smoother texture on the palate.

Some of our favorite producers of Chablis include Christian Moreau, Verget, Dauvissat, Jean-Marc Brocard, Albert Bichot, William Fevre, and A. Regnard et Fils. From any one of those producers, the basic Chablis will be a relative bargain. The moderately expensive *premier cru* versions range from $35 on up, while the more expensive *grand cru* wines start at $45 and go up . . . and up and up.

COTE DE BEAUNE. In contrast to Chablis, the white (Chardonnay) wines of the Cote de Beaune appellation are more like what might be considered mainstream Chardonnay, and yet they are still a world away from standard New World offerings. The usual Burgundian approach is to highlight the characteristics of the grape from a specific place—wood and malolactic fermentation are secondary. White Burgundy, then, is more typically a medium-bodied wine with noticeable acidity to highlight ripe apple and pear flavors, with just a hint of wood in the background.

The Cote de Beaune and Cote de Beaune Villages appellations are used only for red wines, so the majority of Cote de Beaune white wines carry a village appellation and name, such as Meursault, with a small percentage coming from individual *premier cru* or *grand cru* vineyards.

Meursault, Puligny-Montrachet, and Chassagne-Montrachet are the most famous white-wine-producing villages of Cote de Beaune, and the most frequently seen on the U.S. market. When you want that special Chardonnay, a wine from any of those villages will be a good WineWise purchase. They are not "in-your-face" or "over-the-top" Chardonnays, like so many Californian and Australian versions. Instead, these white Burgundies draw you in with an alluring charm—they are gentle and kind.

If you want to go one or two steps higher, try any of the *premier cru* vineyard wines from Meursault, such as Les Gouttes d'Or, Les Perrieres, or Les

One of the gated entrances to the Montrachet vineyard.

Charmes. A pair of Puligny-Montrachet's better *premier cru* sites are Les Folatieres and Les Pucelles, while Chassagne-Montrachet's best includes Les Caillerets.

For *grand cru* vineyards, the villages of Puligny-Montrachet and Chassagne-Montrachet are the lucky guardians of what many consider to be the best Chardonnay vineyards in the world—a cluster of five plots that all include "Montrachet" in the name.

If there is any justice in the world, every *Wine-Wise* reader should get to try *grand cru* Montrachet at least once in his or her life. But reality intrudes in their impact on your purse. Village-level wines from Cote de Beaune fall into the moderately expensive category, with Chassagne-Montrachet and Meursault consistently priced around $40. For *premier cru* vineyards, think very expensive ($60), and for *grand cru*, double that, at least.

Some of the better Cote de Beaune producers include Bouchard Aine et Fils, Bouchard Pere et Fils, Joseph Drouhin, Louis Jadot, Louis Latour, Olivier Leflaive, and Bichot.

CHALON. The white wines of the Chalon area are generally less fine than their Cote de Beaune counterparts. While the better wines of Puligny or Chassagne might sing, Chalon wines just hum, but they carry a very pleasant tune. The wines from here have village names: for white wines the two main villages are Montagny and Rully. Occasionally you will find a Rully *premier cru* with a vineyard name such as Les Cloux on the label.

All in all, white Chalon wines are worth looking for and represent great value when you want Burgundian Chardonnay but cannot stretch your budget to the village wines of Cote de Beaune. Reliable producers offering relative bargains include Joseph Drouhin, Louis Latour, Andre Delorme, Antonin Rodet, and Olivier Leflaive.

MACON. The whites of the Macon area are refreshing, light- or medium-bodied Chardonnays, ideal reminders of how straightforward and simply enjoyable Chardonnay can be. Many wines are sold

Vineyards around the village of Chassagne-Montrachet.

WineWise special insight

Why does the word "Villages" keep showing up on labels? Several of France's wine-producing regions use this naming system, which consists of a region name (such as Macon or Beaujolais) followed by "Villages." In every case, what this means is that within

the region, a certain number of villages have been identified as having "better" vineyards, based on factors such as exposure to sun, soil types, drainage, or protection from wind. Those villages

then have the right to market their wine as Macon Villages instead of just Macon, or Beaujolais Villages instead of just Beaujolais.

WineWise readers will now know that a wine with a region

name plus "Villages" is usually better than a wine with just the region name, and the price difference is minimal.

The vineyards of Chateau de Rully.

under the collective appellation of Macon Villages, while some of the villages prefer to attach their own village name to Macon, such as Macon-Lugny or Macon-Vire. They are all relative bargains, fairly attractively priced.

Within the region, two villages have earned fame as stand-alone names on the label: St-Veran and Pouilly-Fuisse. St-Veran is much lighter in style and is best enjoyed soon after bottling. Pouilly-Fuisse should be a fuller, firmer wine, with ripe apple and wood notes, closer to a Cote de Beaune.

Good producers of Macon wines include Jean Thevenet, Joseph Drouhin, Louis Jadot, Georges Duboeuf, and Bouchard Aine et Fils.

Red Wines. BOURGOGNE. We already commented generally on red wine from the Bourgogne appellation (see above). It can be pretty good, drinkable, affordable, light- to medium-bodied Pinot Noir.

COTE DE NUITS. Cote de Nuits is all about Pinot Noir, from the regional appellation of Cote de Nuits Villages to village-level wines and individual vineyards at *premier cru* and *grand cru* level.

Cote de Nuits Villages wines can be pretty rough, and they are often too light and thin to handle a green, stemmy flavor that is the result of not enough sunshine to ripen the tannic compounds in the grape skins. What happens when vineyards are less than ideally situated is sometimes too clear. But if you have the means, village-level or higher wines can be very rewarding. A very fine red Burgundy offers a delicate balance of red fruit notes, fresh acidity to keep the wine lively, light to medium tannins, and a noticeable woodsy character that might remind you of mushrooms, potting soil, or dried leaves—something outdoorsy. It's what the French call *sousbois*, or "under wood." Such a clever word, and now it's part of your WineWise vocabulary.

The great villages of Cote de Nuits are Gevrey-Chambertin, Morey-St-Denis, Chambolle-Musigny, Vosne-Romanee, and Vougeot (notice that most of these village names have two words—see the sidebar on Montrachet, page 165). When you want to peek into the rarefied world of good, sometimes great French Pinot Noir, these are the place names to look for. From a good producer and in a good vintage, any village-level wine from any of the previously mentioned villages will deliver the goods. In many ways, it is stating the obvious to single out *premier cru* or *grand cru* vineyards to look for from these villages, but we'll do it anyway. For a complete list of all *grand cru* vineyard names in Burgundy, see a reputable reference book such as *Exploring Wine* by Steven Kolpan, Brian H. Smith, and Michael A. Weiss.

For any of the above, be prepared to take out a second mortgage, but also be prepared for a sublime

A Few *Premier Cru* and *Grand Cru* Vineyards in Cote de Nuits

Village	Premier Cru	Grand Cru
Gevrey-Chambertin	Clos St-Jacques Les Cazetiers	Chambertin Chambertin Clos de Beze
Morey-St-Denis	Clos de la Bussiere Clos des Ormes	Clos St-Denis Clos de la Roche
Chambolle-Musigny	Les Amoureuses Les Charmes	Musigny Bonnes Mares
Vosne-Romanee	Aux Malconsorts Les Chaumes	La Romanee La Tache
Vougeot	Les Cras	Clos de Vougeot

experience, one to be treasured and remembered for many years until you can afford the next one. To put things into perspective, a typical village-level wine from Cote de Nuits certainly falls into the moderately expensive category, around $45, while a *premier cru* version will push you into the very expensive category ($60 and up), and a *grand cru* wine will be double that and beyond.

For the WineWise Cote de Nuits bargain hunter, you can sometimes be rewarded by seeking out "lesser" villages such as Marsannay and Fixin, especially in a vintage year that had warmer growing conditions to get the grapes fully ripe.

Worthwhile producers of Cote de Nuits wines include Bouchard Aine et Fils, Bouchard Pere et Fils, Potel, Boillot, Bruno Clair, Faiveley, Louis Latour, Louis Jadot, and Dujac.

COTE DE BEAUNE. A red Cote de Nuits wine next to a red Cote de Beaune will usually show that the Cote de Beaune style is a little lighter, less sturdy, and more delicate than that of Cote de Nuits. The Cote de Beaune and Cote de Beaune Villages appellations tend to be used for wines that are relatively lightweight, sometimes too light to carry the tannins and acidity— they come across as green, not quite ripe. But the village-level wines and the *premier cru* and *grand*

WineWise special insight

What's all this "Montrachet this," "Montrachet that"? The villages that are today called Puligny-Montrachet and Chassagne-Montrachet were originally called just Puligny and Chassagne. They are right next to each other, and they share the glory of being home

to the fabulous single *grand cru* vineyard Montrachet (also called Le Montrachet). The boundary that separates the two villages goes almost through the middle of the vineyard. In the late 1800s, both villages legally changed their name to add the word "Montrachet," hoping to boost sales of all wines from the village, based on the reputation

of their most famous vineyard.

Anytime you come across a Cote de Beaune or Cote de Nuits two-word village name, such as Puligny-Montrachet or Gevrey-Chambertin, the original village name is the first word, and the second word is the name of a *premier cru* or *grand cru* vineyard in that village.

Premier cru villages include Nuits-St-Georges, Pernand-Vergelesses, and Auxey-Duresses (St-Georges, Les Vergelesses, and Les Duresses are *premier cru* vineyards). All other two-word village names refer to *grand cru* vineyard villages.

cru wines are another story. The prominent red-wine-producing villages are Aloxe-Corton, Beaune, Pommard, Volnay, and Chassagne-Montrachet. Of those, Beaune and Volnay offer a more floral and perfumed character in addition to the standard red berry qualities of Pinot Noir, while the other three villages provide a hint of meaty gaminess. Indeed, Chassagne-Montrachet red is a much-overlooked wine, worthy of attention for its depth of flavor and sense of completeness.

The only red *grand cru* vineyard in Cote de Beaune is Le Corton, in the village of Aloxe-Corton. Some of the *premier cru* sites from the above villages are:

Village	*Premier Cru* Vineyards
Beaune	Les Greves Les Bressandes
Volnay	Les Caillerets Clos des Chenes
Chassagne-Montrachet	Clos St-Jean La Boudriotte

As with white wines from Cote de Beaune, red village-level wines from this region of Burgundy fall into the moderately expensive category, with Beaune consistently priced around $40. For *premier cru* vineyards, think very expensive ($60), and for *grand cru*, double that at least.

For our money, some of the real gems of Cote de Beaune come from the underappreciated villages of Auxey-Duresses, Pernand-Vergelesses, Savigny-Les-Beaune, and Chorey-Les-Beaune, where, for around $25 to $30 (making it a relative bargain) you can find the delicate sensuality that makes Pinot Noir worth living for.

CHALON. Once again, the Chalon vineyards make highly acceptable versions of Old World Pinot at highly acceptable prices, around $18 to $25—moderately expensive, perhaps, but a relative bargain for Burgundy. The wines will carry a village name, and the principal red-wine-producing villages are Rully, Givry, and Mercurey, with *premier cru* vineyards in the first two.

Rosé Wines. Only one village in this area, Marsannay in Cote de Nuits, makes any appreciable quantity of rosé wine. It is situated at the northern extreme of the area, and the Pinot Noir grapes often don't reach the full level of ripeness for red wine production,

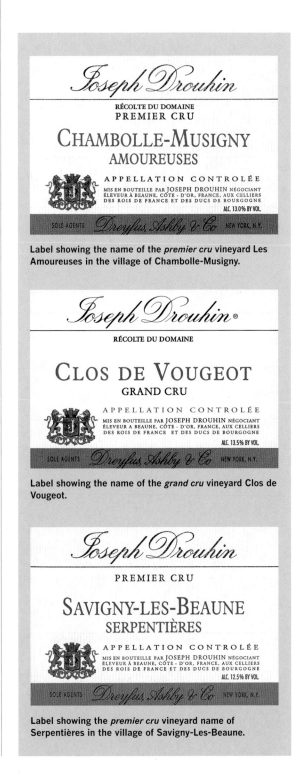

Label showing the name of the *premier cru* vineyard Les Amoureuses in the village of Chambolle-Musigny.

Label showing the name of the *grand cru* vineyard Clos de Vougeot.

Label showing the *premier cru* vineyard name of Serpentières in the village of Savigny-Les-Beaune.

The magnificent chateau in the Clos de Vougeot Vineyard. (Burgundy Wine Council)

but the resulting rosé wines are fruity and lively. The wines are labeled as Marsannay, and Domaine Clair Dau is the primary producer.

Sparkling Wines. Known as *Cremant de Bourgogne,* this is an important category for Burgundy producers. These are good wines, all made by the Champagne method. The favored grapes used by the better producers include the Burgundy mainstays of Pinot Noir and Chardonnay, with Pinot Blanc also used by some. The finished wines are well balanced, with fresh, lively fruit notes and good balancing acidity. At one-third to one-half the cost of Champagne, they are a worthy alternative.

Champagne

Ah, Champagne! A *vin de luxe* in the minds of most people, but the savvy *WineWise* reader will soon come to understand that there are many more daily uses for this wonderful beverage other than special occasions and celebrations. After all, what would brunch be without sparkling wine? We're not suggesting that you use the finest $250 Champagne to make a mimosa, but good Champagne with a late breakfast or lunch is a wonderful spirit lifter.

First of all, a distinction: real Champagne comes from the region called Champagne in northern France, and all other sparkling wines are just that—sparkling wines—though some of them are very fine. Sparkling wines made in the Champagne region of France must be produced by the *methode champenoise* (see page 3), and the wine must be made from one or more of the following grapes: Pinot Noir, Pinot Meunier, and Chardonnay.

Good Champagne is not only bubbly—it has a distinctive flavor profile, with slight variations depending on the house style of the producer and on the grapes used to make the wine. Many producers like to create a wine with a little yeasty aroma and flavor, something that comes across as (not surprisingly) bread- or dough-like, or toasty, even like brioche. That may seem weird in a wine, but in some ways it's sort of comforting, like the warm kitchen feel associated with baking. You will recall that the Champagne method gets bubbles into the wine through a second fermentation in the bottle. After the fermentation has finished, Champagne producers leave the wine aging on the yeast cells in the bottle for at least eighteen months (in fact, they are required to do this), and often longer. That is when the wine picks up these yeast aromas.

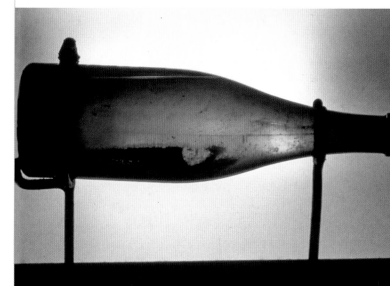

Yeast sediment collects on the lower side of the horizontal bottle after the second fermentation. (Photo courtesy of Frederic Hadengue, CIVC)

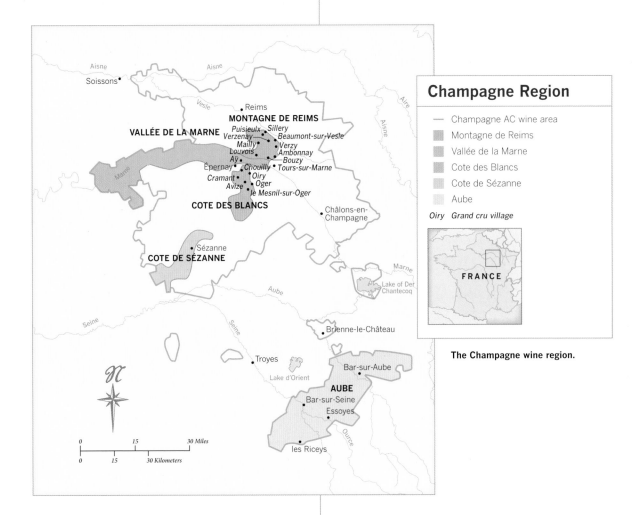

The Champagne wine region.

In terms of flavor profile, you can find anything from green apple and citrus to red berries as an aroma and even on the palate, depending on whether there was more Chardonnay (apples, citrus) used to make the wine or more of the Pinots (red fruits).

THE CHAMPAGNE LABEL

The label will not ordinarily tell you how long the wine aged in the bottle after the second fermentation. So getting to know which producer makes really toasty Champagne and which makes the lightly yeasty style means that you are just going to have to try several of them. However, there is a relatively rare style of Champagne that is labeled "recently disgorged" (*récemment dégorgé*), a sure indication that the wine stayed aging on the yeast cells for many, many years and will be very toasty (and very expensive).

As to grape varieties used, except for some specific styles, there will be no indication on most labels. Most producers make their standard Champagne by blending wines from all three grape varieties, and the proportion of each grape used depends on the producer. But sometimes you will see a label that specifies *blanc de blancs*, telling you that the wine was made entirely from white (Chardonnay) grapes. Important WineWise hint: the absolute association of Chardonnay with *blanc de blancs* is true only for Champagne. Other wine-producing areas all around the world may use the term *blanc de blancs*, but they may be allowed to use grapes other than Chardonnay.

So, what does the label always tell us? If the wine is truly Champagne, that term will show up on the label. It is the appellation the wine comes from.

In addition, the label will always provide an indication of the final sweetness level of the wine, ranging from bone dry to very sweet. The terms used have evolved over time, as the fashion for sweetness in Champagne has declined, and the English-language equivalent of the French phrases may appear misleading. However, we assure the *WineWise* reader that the following applications are accurate.

Dryness Level	Label Term
Bone dry	Extra brut, ultra brut, or brut sauvage
Dry	Brut
Off-dry, kiss of sweetness	Extra Dry
Lightly sweet	Sec
Sweet	Demi-sec
Very sweet	Doux

Note: Doux is very rarely seen on the U.S. market, though it is widely available in South America.

A final important label term is the use of the phrase *grand cru* or *premier cru* when the grapes have come from vineyards that have been classified as such. In fact, both of these quality designations are given to entire villages, so the grapes need only come from vineyards in a village that has been rated *grand cru* or *premier cru*. Not surprisingly, the village name will also appear on the label, such as Ay, Bouzy, or Cramant.

WHITE WINES/ROSÉ WINES

The vast majority of all Champagne is white, but many producers also make a rosé version. Rosé champagne can be made by making rosé base wines before the second fermentation takes place in the bottle.

Or you can make white sparkling wine all the way through and then use a little local red wine as the final *dosage* that is added to top off the bottle after the sediment is removed from the second fermentation (see page 3).

Whether the wine is white or rosé, Champagne comes in two versions—nonvintage (the norm) or vintage (the exception).

Nonvintage Champagne, especially nonvintage brut Champagne, is the bread and butter of all Champagne producers—it's what pays the bills. But that doesn't mean to say it's second-class stuff. In many ways, it is a vastly more remarkable product than vintage Champagne.

To make nonvintage Champagne, the winemaker has to balance several acts of blending on several different levels. He or she is blending different grape varieties, from different locations, to produce a base blend from the current harvest year. Then the winemaker has to blend in small portions of different wines from previous harvests so that the final finished product will taste exactly the same as the previous bottling from that producer. That is a remarkable achievement—consistency of style and flavor from year to year despite dramatic swings in growing conditions from one year to the next.

A cool start to the day in a Champagne vineyard.

In comparison, making vintage Champagne is relatively easy. Recognize first of all that vintage Champagne is not made every year: it is made only in those years when the quality of the grapes makes base wines that the winemaker believes can stand on their own, representative of the growing conditions that year. Even then, it is still a blended wine, made from different grape varieties grown in different locations, but all in the same year. From all of that you could rightly conclude that discerning Champagne producers make vintage Champagne relatively rarely, and when they do, it is only a small percentage of their total output. Even if they make vintage Champagne, they still have to keep up their regular nonvintage output. Beware the Champagne producer that has a vintage product from almost every year in a decade.

Thus each Champagne producer usually makes at least two versions of Champagne (nonvintage and vintage), perhaps also rosé versions of those, maybe a *blanc de blancs,* perhaps a recently disgorged and very often a top-of-the-line (usually vintage) product, their *cuvée de prestige* wine. The product line of a company such as Taittinger is fairly typical: nonvintage brut "La Française," vintage brut (produced only in some years), nonvintage sec "Nocturne," and vintage brut *blanc de blancs* "Comtes de Champagne"—their *cuvée de prestige* premium product.

If nonvintage Brut is the basic breadwinner for most Champagne producers, it follows that those wines are usually the least expensive in any producer's range, and everything else is priced accordingly. Our following pricing categories of producers reflects the standard price for their nonvintage Brut product. In some cases, we provide extra information about their vintage brut or *cuvée de prestige* wines.

Relative bargains include wines from the producers Nicolas Feuillatte, Paul Goerg, Lanson, Philipponnat (*cuvée de prestige* "Clos des Goisses" is about $100), Pommery (*cuvée de prestige* "Louise" at about $100), Laurent-Perrier, Mumm, and Perrier Jouët (*cuvée de prestige* "Fleur de Champagne" at around $220).

Moderately expensive wines come from the producers Billecart-Salmon, Charles Heidsieck (*cuvée de prestige* "Champagne Charlie" at around $140), Drappier, Gosset, Larmandier-Bernier, Bruno Paillard, Louis Roederer (*cuvée de prestige* "Cristal" around $220), Taittinger (*cuvée de prestige* "Comtes de Champagne" at around $140), Bollinger (*cuvée de prestige* "Grande Année" at over $100), Pol Roger (*cuvée de prestige* "Sir Winston Churchill" at about $150), Veuve Clicquot (*cuvée de prestige* "La Grande Dame" at over $100), Moet et Chandon (*cuvée de prestige* "Dom Perignon" at around $125 to $150).

Very expensive producers are Ruinart (*cuvée de prestige* "Dom Ruinart" at about $150) and Deutz. And at the truly expensive end of the range are Krug (*cuvée de prestige* "Clos du Mesnil Blanc de Blancs" at a breathtaking $600 to $700) and Salon (only available in vintage *blanc de blancs* "Le Mesnil" at about $200).

Loire

Situated in the northwestern quadrant of the nation, the Loire Valley is a huge wine region, radiating out from the banks of the Loire River, producing every type of wine imaginable, from several different grape types. But fear not—we have a few WineWise tricks to break the region down into easily manageable parts. First, the commonalities. Almost every year in April or May, one of the many wine magazines published around the world carries an article on the "wines of summer." They are writing about the wines of the Loire Valley, singing their praises for the light, zippy, refreshing character that graces most Loire Valley wines. Every summer, our consumption of a wine such as Muscadet (see below) goes up because it is a natural choice of wine on hot, muggy summer days—light, with refreshing acidity, not too much alcohol, and not a trace of wood. But more about that later.

We suggest that the *WineWise* reader thinks of the Loire Valley as a group of three wine zones—the West End, the Center, and the East End. For each of these areas we will discuss the principal wines and the grape types used.

WEST END

This part of the Loire Valley is closest to the Atlantic Ocean, whose climatic and culinary influences are all part of the wine heritage here. Here one wine dominates—Muscadet, a dry, still white. For those who love wine trivia, the official name of the grape type used is Melon de Bourgogne. But that will not help

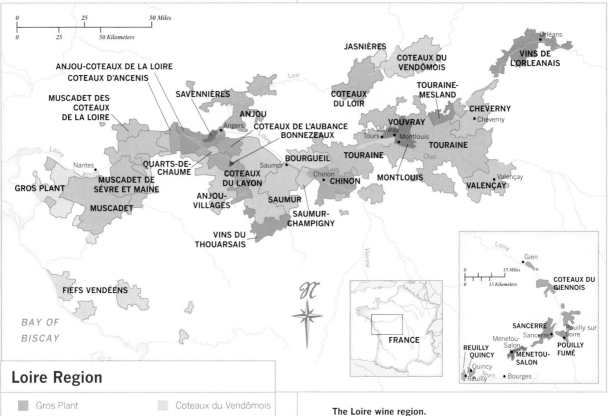

The Loire wine region.

Loire Region

- Gros Plant
- Muscadet
- Muscadet de Sévre et Maine
- Muscadet des Coteaux de la Loire
- Coteaux d'Ancenis
- Anjou-Coteaux de la Loire
- Savennières
- Quarts-de-Chaume
- Bonnezeaux
- Coteaux du Layon
- Anjou-Villages
- Fiefs Vendéens
- Vins du Thouarsais
- Anjou
- Coteaux de l'Aubance
- Coteaux du Loir
- Jasnières

- Coteaux du Vendômois
- Touraine
- Bourgueil
- Saumur-Champigny
- Chinon
- Saumur
- Montlouis
- Vouvray
- Touraine-Mesland
- Cheverny
- Valençay
- Vins de L'Orleanais
- Coteaux du Giennois
- Sancerre
- Pouilly Fumé
- Menetou-Salon
- Quincy
- Reuilly

you in the least, since you will never see it on a label. The wine is called Muscadet because that is how the local growers refer to the grape.

Whether you find Muscadet or Muscadet Sevre-et-Maine, the wine's characteristics are essentially the same—a high-acid, dry wine with green fruit character and a sense of smoothness on the middle palate. That smoothness comes from the practice of leaving the wine on the lees—the yeast sediment—in stainless-steel tanks after fermentation (the label will carry the phrase *sur lie*). This imparts a smooth texture to the wine, along with perhaps a bit of spritz—a gentle sparkle—and is a practice that most Muscadet producers use.

Muscadet is the archetypal seafood wine, shining with oysters on the half shell, but also very good with ceviche or cured herring. It is also a fabulous base for making a refreshing wine spritzer by adding a little lemon- or lime-flavored seltzer to the wine. This summer, promise yourself you will try a bottle.

Some of our favorite picks in the relative bargain category include Goulaine, Les Vergers, Domaine Sauvion, and Chateau de Chasseloir, with Chateau de la Ragotiere in the moderately expensive niche.

CENTER

There is a whole lot happening in this part of the Loire Valley. The Center makes every type of wine, from white sparkling to white sweet to red. But it can all be brought into WineWise perspective by concentrating on three grape types and by remembering that the wines are named primarily by place. Once again, you will need to kick your memory cells into high gear. The three main grape types are Sauvignon Blanc and Chenin Blanc for white wines and Cabernet Franc for reds.

Much has already been said about Sauvignon Blanc and its flavor profile (see page 24). Chenin Blanc is not widely known in the wine world, but it has found a home for centuries in this part of the Loire Valley, where it can produce sublime dry and sweet versions in different places, such as Vouvray and Saumur (see the map of the Loire Valley on page 171). Good Chenin Blanc will always display a touch of the aroma of honey and a nuttiness on the nose and palate. In addition, there is an attractive floral aroma and the flavor of melons. As with all Loire Valley wines, the Chenins from this area retain a high level of refreshing acidity, adding to their charm as summer wines, especially with poached or sautéed fish dishes.

So far we have referred to Cabernet Franc only as a junior partner to Cabernet Sauvignon or Merlot. But here it stands proudly on its own as the sole grape in a number of appellations, or it is the lead violin, while grapes such as Cabernet Sauvignon or Gamay play second fiddle in a blend. The 100% Cab Franc wines, such as Chinon and Saumur Champigny (see map on page 171), are seen more and more frequently on the U.S. market, and the viability of Cab Franc as a stand-alone wine is reflected in the copycat versions that can now be found from Napa to New York.

Loire Valley Cab Francs have the typically high acidity of the area, balanced nicely by aromas and flavors of ripe red berry fruits such as strawberry and raspberry. Here's a WineWise hint: their medium body, low tannins, and clean fruit style mean they can take a touch of chilling to keep them refreshing as a summer barbecue wine.

Mostly Dry White Wines. In the center there are four major villages that produce various styles of Chenin Blanc wines and two place names associated with Sauvignon Blanc. The Sauvignon Blanc areas are Touraine (the countryside surrounding the city of Tours) and Cheverny. As the *WineWise* reader might by now suspect, these wines are refreshingly high in acidity but also bright with the green ripeness of kiwis and limes. The Touraine wines are usually labeled as Sauvignon de Touraine, while the Cheverny wines retain that village name as the name of the wine.

As for the Chenin Blanc villages, they are Anjou, Saumur, Savennieres, and Vouvray. Of those, Vouvray has been a perennial favorite on the U.S. market, but the others are now finding increasing space on store shelves and wine lists. We welcome that development, since the wines from these villages can be truly fine— they are the benchmark of great Chenin Blanc.

However, the WineWise consumer will still have some sorting out to do in terms of sweetness styles of the wines produced. Anjou Blanc is dry, as are Saumur Blanc and Savennieres. But Vouvray? Well, that's anybody's guess. Most Vouvray would fall into a category called "off-dry," showing a noticeable hint of sweetness. But it is all up to the producer. Some make their wines bone dry, while others prefer a medium sweet style. The only hint you might get on the label comes from a few French terms that might appear. *Sec* is dry. *Sec-tendre* indicates an off-dry style, while *moelleux* suggests a fuller sweetness, but not sticky sweet like late harvest wines.

As for prices, they range from relative bargains from Anjou (for example, from Domaine de Closel) and Vouvray (good producers include Goulaine, Domaine Pichot, and Domaine Bourillon) to moderately expensive from Savennieres (very well rep-

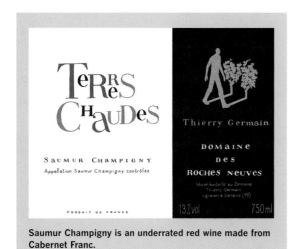

Saumur Champigny is an underrated red wine made from Cabernet Franc.

resented by Domaine des Baumard and Domaine de Closel). An expensive but very special wine from Savennieres is "Clos de la Coulee de Serrant."

Distinctly Sweet White Wines. Some areas of the Center specialize in sweeter Chenin Blanc wines, the result of either late harvest and/or botrytis (see page 9). A broad regional appellation is Coteaux du Layon, while the much smaller appellations of Bonnezeaux and Quarts de Chaume scale greater heights of intensity and balance. In quality, these wines are certainly the equal of good Sauternes from Bordeaux or good late harvest and botrytis-affected wines from California or Australia, but they are distinctly lighter, less syrupy, with a very high natural acidity that leaves the mouth feeling fresh and clean—a welcome relief after all that sweetness.

Here we get into the territory of moderately expensive to very expensive wines, with Domaine des Baumards and Domaine de Closel once again leading the pack.

Rosé Wines. At one time, rosé wines from the Loire Valley were the White Zinfandels of the wine world in terms of their popularity and widespread consumption. But things change, and now they are the alternative. They come in dry to medium-sweet versions and always display the kind of bright, fresh red berry fruit character that is so attractive in a good rosé. The key to the sweetness level is in sly nuances of labeling, so pay attention: the dry versions are called

The hilltop town of Sancerre.

Rosé de la Loire, while the semisweet versions are called Rosé d'Anjou or Cabernet d'Anjou.

You don't have to pay quite so much attention to price, as these rosé wines are all relative bargains.

Sparkling Wines. Made by the Champagne method, the sparkling wines of the Loire Valley offer excellent quality at competitive prices. Based on the Chenin Blanc grape type, they are distinctly different from Champagne and Champagne look-alikes but are well worth trying. A few different appellations and names are permitted, some regional and some village-specific. The terms *mousseux* or *cremant* indicate that the wine is sparkling. The appellations are Anjou Mousseux, Saumur Mousseux, Vouvray Mousseux, and Cremant de la Loire, and they all fall within the relative bargain or moderately expensive category.

EAST END

Separated completely from the other Loire Valley wine areas, and situated almost in the geographic center of the nation, the extraordinary "island" of Sancerre and Pouilly-Fumé produces dry white wines from the Sauvignon Blanc grape. Once held up as the guiding light for all Sauvignons, this area now faces stiff competition from New World competitors, especially New Zealand. In the face of that competition, it is encouraging to see that the presence of these wines in the market is not decreasing. While these wines do not have the juicy freshness of New Zealand Sauvignons, they offer a layered complexity that includes

Methode traditionelle sparkling Saumur is a great alternative to Champagne.

Vineyards below the commune of St-Andelain in the appellation of Pouilly.

a bracing level of acidity, aromas, and flavors of ripe citrus fruits, and an intriguing minerality.

Relative bargains from Sancerre include the wines of Fournier, Jolivet, Domaine des Berthiers, and Domaine de la Perriere. Relative bargains from Pouilly-Fumé are well represented by Michel Redde.

In the moderately expensive category for Sancerre we recommend the wines of Henri Bourgeois, Lucien Crochet, and Domaine Thomas, and for Pouilly-Fumé we suggest Ladoucette and Serge Daguenau.

A number of East End wines are getting increasingly expensive, but they are well worth trying. In the very expensive category we include Alphonse Mellot, Clos de la Poussie, Vacheron, and Cotat for Sancerre, and Didier Dagueneau for Pouilly-Fumé.

Rhone Valley

Geographically and stylistically, the Rhone Valley is divided in two. The northern Rhone concentrates on Syrah for reds and Viognier, Marsanne, and Roussanne for whites. The southern Rhone blends numerous grape types for white, rosé, and red wines. In both parts of the Rhone Valley, appellations range in size from regional, such as Cotes du Rhone, to village, such as Cornas or Gigondas. The climate of the entire valley is usually thought of as at least warm if

not hot, resulting in fuller-flavored wines with high alcohol levels, ripe fruit flavors, and lower acidity. In the north, the terrain is steep and rugged, while the south offers a gentler landscape with rolling hills and valleys.

WHITE WINES OF THE NORTH AND SOUTH

First of all, the standard WineWisdom is that the Rhone Valley is red wine country. However, the general appellations of Cotes du Rhone and Cotes du Rhone Villages (see the sidebar on page 164) cover both white and red wines that are the "basic" Rhones. For whites the standard blend includes Grenache Blanc, Clairette, dashes of Marsanne and Roussanne, and a host of others. Though the basic whites are just that—basic—they are still excellent buys, usually costing less than $10, and always delivering sound and reliable flavors of ripe fruit and medium body.

The more specific white wine appellations of the north are Condrieu, Chateau Grillet, Hermitage, Crozes Hermitage, and St-Joseph. In the south, Chateauneuf-du-Pape is the primary single-village white wine appellation.

Condrieu and Chateau Grillet are 100% Viognier wines and are the basis of the current fascination for that grape in various parts of the United States. A description of their style can be found in Chapter 2, page 34.

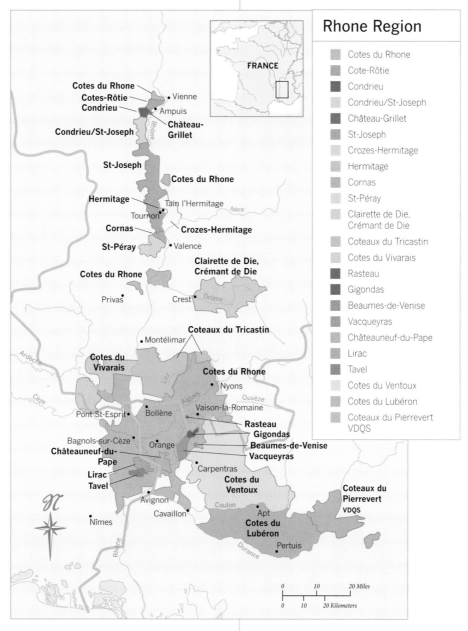

The Rhone wine region.

Of the single-village white wine appellations mentioned above, you are most likely to find St-Joseph. Other than Condrieu and Chateau Grillet, they are all Marsanne/Rousanne blends, though white Chateauneuf-du-Pape also includes many other grape types. With ripe stone fruit flavors of peach and apricot backed up by citrus peel and a noticeable earthiness, these whites can be extremely enjoyable in their youth, when they show their best fruit character.

RED WINES OF THE NORTH AND SOUTH

This is where the Rhone Valley really comes into its full glory. There is something deeply satisfying about the warmth and generosity of these wines. Both the northern and southern parts of the Rhone provide excellent examples of the sunnier side of French reds. The northern Rhone is Syrah country, but these wines are not the heady, jammy fruit bombs labeled as Syrah or Shiraz from California or Australia. Northern

Cornas Vineyards.

Rhone Syrah wines certainly show ample ripe fruit, but they are much leaner, and often the fruit character is equally matched by elements of peppery spice, earthy minerality, herbal notes such as rosemary, and even a sense of meaty gaminess.

The south relies on blends of numerous grapes, most notably Grenache, Syrah, and Mourvedre. Again, these wines are not your average GSM blend from anywhere else. Yes, they have delicious, mouth-filling ripe flavors, but there is also a sense of structure and poise gained from the tautness of tannins and a streak of acidity.

Our comments in the section on white wines about the basic appellations of Cotes du Rhone and Cotes du Rhone Villages carry even greater weight with regard to red wines. Almost all of the red wines from these regional appellations come from southern Rhone vineyards and are made from the standard GSM blend, possibly with the addition of other less well-known varieties, such as Cinsaut. They are wines of exceptional value: sound, reliable, and enjoyable. They are a safe haven that you know you can always return to and find a pleasant experience—a true WineWise choice.

All relative bargains, the Cotes du Rhone and Cotes du Rhone Villages appellations are very well represented by the following producers. For Cotes du Rhone (from the south, dominated by Grenache):

La Chasse du Pape, Coudolet de Beaucastel, Caves des Papes, Chapoutier, Clos du Caillou, Les Garrigues, Domaine Gramenon, Domaine de l'Ameillaud, Domaine du Pesquier, Perrin Reserve, Patrick Lesec, Mont-Redon, Les Monticauts, St-Cosme, and Tardieu Laurent. For Cotes du Rhone (from the north, dominated by Syrah): Jean-Luc Colombo "Les Abeilles," Domaine de la Solitude, Guigal, and Jaboulet ("Parallele 45"). For Cotes du Rhone-Villages (from the south, dominated by Grenache): Alary, Louis Bernard, Andre Brunel, Cave de Cairanne, Chateau du Trignon, Domaine de Coste Chaude, Domaine Santa Duc, Domaine St-Luc, Domaines de la Guicharde, Domaines Perrin, Guigal, Patrick Lessec, Gabriel Meffre Laurus, and Mas de Boislauzon.

Included in this experience are the relatively unknown wines of Cotes du Ventoux, Cotes du Luberon, and Costieres de Nimes. Usually reds made in a very light, fruity style, they are at the lower end of the price scale but the upper end of the satisfaction scale if you enjoy clean, straightforward red fruit flavors without the power and insistence of dark, heady jamminess.

The smaller appellations of the northern Rhone include Cote Rotie, Crozes-Hermitage, Hermitage, Cornas, and St-Joseph. The special characteristics of the Syrah grape are exceptionally well presented in all these wines, especially Cote Rotie, Hermitage, and Cornas versions. The wine of these appellations climbs to the very pinnacle of Syrah in all its beauty and excellence. As the WineWise reader has no doubt guessed, these wines will cost a pretty penny, but they

Cornas wines are fine examples of Syrah.

provide the kind of experience that will remain with you always as a measure of what great wine can be.

The offerings of the Crozes-Hermitage and St-Joseph appellations are lighter, less dense, and less intense; they are also more wallet-friendly.

The smaller appellations of the southern Rhone include Chateauneuf-du-Pape, Gigondas, and Vacqueyras. In effect, these are village names, and the name on the label reflects the fact that the grapes came from vineyards in and around the named village. The exact blend used depends on the village, but also on the producer. When French guidelines list a number of grapes approved for use in an appellation, the producer can use any number of the grapes in whatever proportion he or she sees fit. In general, most of the wines from these areas are dominated by Grenache, supported by Syrah and Mourvedre. With greater emphasis on Grenache, the southern reds tend to be rounder, softer and smoother in the mouth, more juicy, and more immediately satisfying.

For moderately expensive but very good wines from the north we suggest you look for producers such as Jaboulet, Chapoutier, Jean-Luc Colombo, Combier, Jean-Michel Gerin, Guigal, Tardieu Laurent, Albert Belle, and J.-L. Chave. Bear in mind that the exact cost will depend on the exact appellation—Hermitage and Cote Rotie will push you into the very expensive range, if not above it.

The popularity of the southern Rhone style, encouraged by the American wine media, has meant that prices have risen from merely moderately expensive to very expensive for wines such as Chateauneuf-du-Pape. Even so, you may want to bite the bullet and open your checkbook sometime to find out what it is all about. If you do, try some of the following: Chateau de Beaucastel, Chateau La Nerthe, Chateau Fortia, Domaine de Mont-Redon, Clos des Papes, and Chateau Rayas. If you choose to stay moderately expensive, then head for Gigondas, while Vacqueyras may afford you the occasional relative bargain (look for Chateau de Montmirail in both Gigondas and Vacqueyras).

Chateauneuf-du-Pape vineyards.

ROSÉ WINES

It may seem a contradiction to suggest that the hot, rugged terrain of the Rhone Valley can produce tantalizingly light and fresh rosé wines, but it is true, and the *WineWise* reader can figure out why this would be so—in the heat of summer, the local population has very little interest in the heavy, full reds they produce, but they would die for the vibrant berry freshness of an ice-cold rosé. And they have plenty to choose from. The regional Cotes du Rhone and Cotes du Rhone Villages appellations cover rosé wines, as does the village specific name of Tavel. Most importantly, these are refreshingly dry versions of rosé wine, even if they are moderately expensive. Chateau d'Aqueria produces a very reliable version.

Despite the stigma that pink wines seem to carry in this nation, we urge the more tolerant WineWise consumer to try them, especially in the summer when our climate demands just what these rosé wines were designed for. They are great picnic wines, delicious with a range of sandwiches, with cold smoked fish or cold cuts, and with bouillabaisse on a warm summer evening.

Languedoc, Roussillon, Corbieres, and Provence

Situated in the south of France, Languedoc, Roussillon, Corbieres, and Provence bathe in unrelenting heat for much of the summer. Cinsaut and Carignan grapes are important players in the production of red and rosé wines, with the reliable GSM trio offering

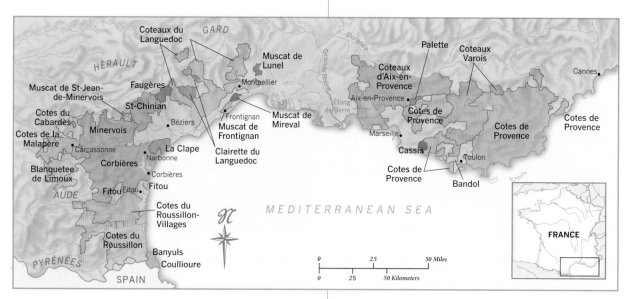

The wine regions of southern France.

support. For white wines, Grenache Blanc, Bourboulenc, and Clairette are the likely candidates. Any discerning WineWise consumer will recognize very quickly that there is much mediocrity among the wines of these regions, but occasionally there is a beacon of light. Such beacons can be found both within the broad regional appellations such as Coteaux du Languedoc and in the smaller appellations such as Minervois or Bandol. Whatever the appellation, red wines dominate, both in quantity and in quality.

For the *WineWise* reader, the real excitement might be the *vins de pays* category, which offers the consumer the chance to buy with ease and confidence, since producers are labeling their wines with grape variety names known all around the world, as opposed to obscure place names that mean very little to anybody. In some cases, wine producers from other regions have purchased old run-down vineyards in this area that had been planted with the older, high-yielding varieties such as Carignan and Cinsaut, and they have replanted with the much more marketable varieties such as Merlot, Syrah, Chardonnay, and so on. The resulting wines have international appeal at everyday, even bargain basement prices. Reliable producers of *vins de pays* include Georges Duboeuf, Reserve St-Martin, Fortant de France, and Val d'Orbieu.

WHITE WINES: LANGUEDOC, ROUSSILLON, AND CORBIERES

These regions offer a few examples of fresh, lively, fruity whites, especially from villages such as La Clape and Pic St-Loup, whose names will appear on the label. White Corbieres can also be very refreshing, especially when made in a slightly green style, with lots of lemony, mouth-watering acidity. The cleanliness of these wines comes from a concentration on stainless-steel fermentation and no oak aging. Provence offers a few inspired but expensive ($30) whites such as those produced by Domaine Ott in the Cotes de Provence appellation. In addition, there are the always enjoyable Cassis whites made from Clairette, Ugni Blanc, and Marsanne. But again, they are expensive.

At the other end of the scale are the wines labeled as Mas de Daumas Gassac, which do not fall within the AOC system because the producers use unapproved grape varieties such as Chardonnay in their white wine blend. Careful site selection and land management, hands-on vineyard and winery work, and diligent attention to detail put these wines at elevated ($50) price levels. But they also show what can be achieved in terms of quality, flavor development, and pure enjoyment.

RED WINES: LANGUEDOC

Within the large Coteaux du Languedoc appellation, the villages of St-Saturnin and La Clape stand out as superior red wine producers, offering clean red fruit character and a structure of light tannins and acidity. But it is the single estate of Mas du Daumas Gassac that captures most of the attention for its non-AOC wine based on Bordeaux varieties that create a richly pleasing but structured wine at an equally impressive price point (read very expensive).

The appellation of Minervois also offers some exciting possibilities, especially from producers such as Chateau Helene. Of all the up-and-coming appellations in the south of France, this would be our WineWise pick for value in the relative bargain category. Slightly less intense versions can also be found in the neighboring appellation of St-Chinian, especially from producers such as Chateau Coujan and Clos Bagatelle.

RED WINES: ROUSSILLON

The most likely finds here will fall under the regional appellations of Cotes du Roussillon and Cotes du Roussillon Villages. The fruity, slightly peppery reds are generally enjoyable quaffers, but producers such as Chateau Mosse and Chateau La Casenove make wines of denser fruit character and sturdier structure.

RED WINES: CORBIERES

Offerings from the Corbieres appellation show up fairly frequently in our stores at very attractive prices, but the WineWise consumer will do well to pick and

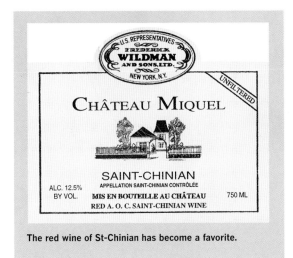

The red wine of St-Chinian has become a favorite.

choose and experiment. Occasionally you will find something that moves beyond rough and rustic to show a streak of softer, rounder fruit and an attractive concentration and length of flavors.

RED WINES: PROVENCE

The reds of Provence are often bolstered by the inclusion of Cabernet Sauvignon in the blend, giving the wines a bit more backbone. Within the Cotes de Provence appellation, Domaine Ott and Chateau Vignelaure are important and reputable producers, while in Les Baux de Provence the estate Mas de la Dame makes outstanding wines. Some equally astounding reds come from the Bandol appellation. They can be unrelenting in youth but will soften with age to show a softer side of ripe fruit. The best of these wines are not inexpensive, but they are unique, age-worthy, and unusual.

ROSÉ WINES

Whereas almost all of the southern French areas use the base blend of Grenache, Mourvedre, Cinsaut, and Carignan to make rosé wines, it is the large region of Provence that dominates production, regularly churning out almost half of France's rosé wines. Too often they can be dull and uninteresting, the result of grapes that have seen too many hours of sunshine. But from good producers such as Domaine Ott you will find the kind of fresh red berry character that makes good pink wine such a treat.

chapter 9

Andiamo
Italy

The wines of Italy have never been better, and the presence of Italy in the world wine market, especially the United States, has never been stronger. And yet Italian wines continue to be among the least understood of all European wines, perhaps because there are so many of them, possibly because their labels can be challenging to consumers, or maybe because of the introduction over the last two decades of extraordinary wines from almost every one of Italy's twenty provinces.

It was not so long ago that a bottle of Chianti in a wicker basket was considered to be a better candleholder in a dorm room than a wine, and sometimes with good reason. Today the wines produced in Tuscany's Chianti regions are exciting, delicious reds that are truly food-friendly. At the same time, Italy's "Super Tuscan" wines, a sometimes paradoxical mix of ultra-classic and ultra-modern wines produced in an international style, have taken the wine world, especially fine restaurants, by storm.

The Piedmont region in northwest Italy has built a solid and universal reputation on traditional wines produced in a modern world. There is a virtual revolution in quality taking place in the vineyards and wineries of Italy's southern and island provinces of Sicily, Sardinia, Puglia, and Campania. The white and red wines from the multicultural provinces of Italy's northeast—Alto Adige and Friuli–Venezia Giulia, with their German, Austrian, and Slavic heritages—have helped to redefine what it is to be an "Italian wine."

While much of Italy is enjoying a rebirth of wine quality and wine diversity, the anchors—classic wines of the Piedmont, Tuscany, Veneto, and Umbria regions—create a sense of historical and cultural continuity. Improvements and innovations in both vineyards and wineries in these classic regions allow them to compete on a world scale. Both large producers and artisans are working to create a new portrait of Italian wines, a work of art that may be grounded in classic techniques but with an image whose sensibility is postmodern.

Add it all up and you begin to see that although Italy is an ancient wine culture and the largest producer and exporter of wine in the world, its modern wine producers have embraced a new paradigm based on quality wine that's made to compete in a global market.

Welcome to the new world of the Old World: Italian wines!

The grapes of Italy: A bit of a challenge, but so much fun

I TALY PRODUCES WINES from hundreds of different grape varietals, some of which you've heard of, many of which you haven't. While Italy makes oodles of good wine from international varietals—the usual suspects of Chardonnay, Merlot, Cabernet Sauvignon, and so on—the backbone of Italian wine production is the country's own collection of vines. Here's our list of Italy's most important grapes, alphabetically arranged, with a few notes on each.

Red grapes

Of the ten grapes listed here, the two most heralded, the most "noble" of all Italian red wine grapes, are Sangiovese and Nebbiolo. As you become more familiar with Italian wines, you may want to learn a little bit more about some of the others, too.

- **Aglianico:** Grown mostly in the regions of Campania and Basilicata, this vine was brought to Italy by the ancient Greeks. Produces mostly powerful reds.

- **Barbera:** The second most frequently planted grape in Italy, it shines in the Piedmont region, where Barbera produces medium-to-full-bodied, delicious reds with refreshing acidity.

- **Cannonau** (Italy's name for Grenache; see page 56): The most important red grape for the quality red wines of Sardinia, its earthy, medium-to-full-bodied flavors have begun to catch on in the United States.

- **Corvina:** From the Veneto region, Corvina is the most important grape in the blend that makes one of Italy's best-known lighter reds, Valpolicella, and ironically Italy's most full-bodied red, Amarone.

- **Dolcetto:** Grown mostly in the Piedmont region, this grape produces fruit-forward, easy-to-drink wines, but with deep red color.

- **Nebbiolo:** Considered one of Italy's two most "noble" grapes (the other is Sangiovese; see below), Nebbiolo reaches its powerful zenith in the Piedmont region, where it is represented by extraordinary wines, particularly Barolo and Barbaresco. It is also an important grape in Lombardy, where it ends up in no less delicious but somewhat simpler wines, such as Inferno and Grumello.

- **Negroamaro:** Grown throughout southern Italy and islands, it is represented best by deep, rich, earthy red wines from Puglia.

- **Nero d'Avola:** The "Syrah of the south," this grape shines in Sicily, where its wines can be dark, dense, and wild, great with hearty food.

- **Primitivo** (it's really Zinfandel—see page 53): Along with Negroamaro, Primitivo is one of the two most important grapes in Puglia, making now-popular wines that are fruity, balanced, and full of sunshine.

- **Sangiovese:** One of the two most "noble" red grapes in Italy and also the most planted, it achieves its full potential in the Tuscany region,

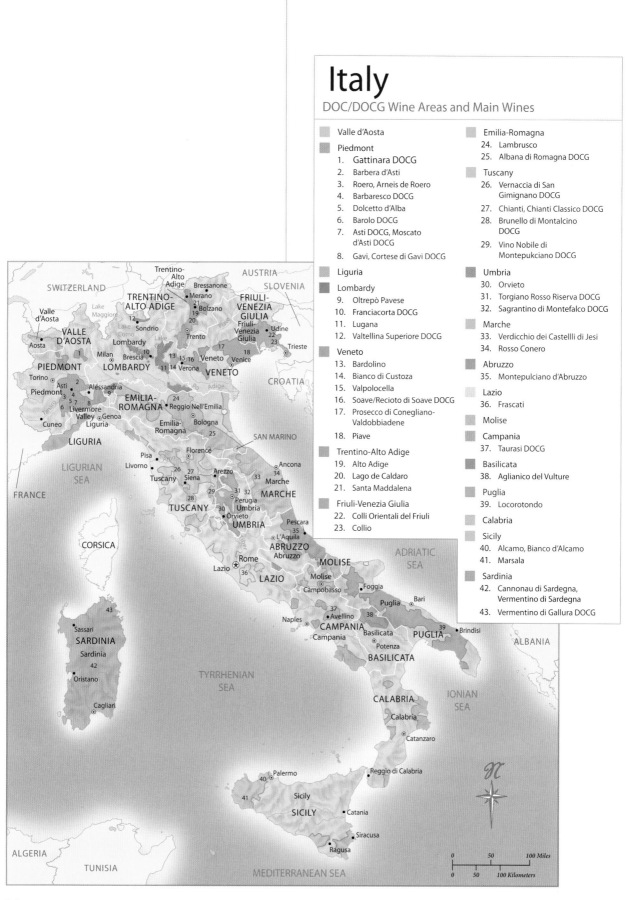

Italy
DOC/DOCG Wine Areas and Main Wines

Valle d'Aosta

Piedmont
1. Gattinara DOCG
2. Barbera d'Asti
3. Roero, Arneis de Roero
4. Barbaresco DOCG
5. Dolcetto d'Alba
6. Barolo DOCG
7. Asti DOCG, Moscato d'Asti DOCG
8. Gavi, Cortese di Gavi DOCG

Liguria

Lombardy
9. Oltrepò Pavese
10. Franciacorta DOCG
11. Lugana
12. Valtellina Superiore DOCG

Veneto
13. Bardolino
14. Bianco di Custoza
15. Valpolocella
16. Soave/Recioto di Soave DOCG
17. Prosecco di Conegliano-Valdobbiadene
18. Piave

Trentino-Alto Adige
19. Alto Adige
20. Lago de Caldaro
21. Santa Maddalena

Friuli-Venezia Giulia
22. Colli Orientali del Friuli
23. Collio

Emilia-Romagna
24. Lambrusco
25. Albana di Romagna DOCG

Tuscany
26. Vernaccia di San Gimignano DOCG
27. Chianti, Chianti Classico DOCG
28. Brunello di Montalcino DOCG
29. Vino Nobile di Montepukciano DOCG

Umbria
30. Orvieto
31. Torgiano Rosso Riserva DOCG
32. Sagrantino di Montefalco DOCG

Marche
33. Verdicchio dei Castellli di Jesi
34. Rosso Conero

Abruzzo
35. Montepulciano d'Abruzzo

Lazio
36. Frascati

Molise

Campania
37. Taurasi DOCG

Basilicata
38. Aglianico del Vulture

Puglia
39. Locorotondo

Calabria

Sicily
40. Alcamo, Bianco d'Alcamo
41. Marsala

Sardinia
42. Cannonau di Sardegna, Vermentino di Sardegna
43. Vermentino di Gallura DOCG

Italy.

where it is the backbone of every traditional (and some nontraditional) reds. Styles of wines made from Sangiovese can range from a simple, light-bodied Chianti to a memorable, complex, deep meditation wine, Brunello di Montalcino.

White grapes

Although over the last twenty years Italy has produced some killer whites, it is still known mostly for its red wines. Of the white grapes listed below, the one that almost everybody knows is Pinot Grigio. The other grapes on the list either are really important to broad-based Italian winemaking or are grapes you should get to know.

- **Falanghina, Fiano, and Greco:** Luckily, these three wonderful grapes (Fiano and Greco were introduced by the Greeks) maintain our alphabetical approach. They also grow in the same district of Campania province, where they end up in beautiful, soulful whites that feature their names: Falanghina, Fiano di Avellino, and Greco di Tufo.

- **Malvasia:** Widely planted, it serves many uses and exhibits several names, but it is at its best in Sicily, where it produces a lovely, rich sweet wine, Malvasia delle Lipari.

- **Moscato:** Italy produces extraordinary examples of wines from the Muscat grape, most of them sweet with irresistible peach overtones. Some of the best examples are from the Piedmont region: Moscato d'Asti (a bit bubbly) and fully bubbly Asti (formerly Asti Spumante; spumante means "sparkling").

- **Pinot Bianco and Pinot Grigio** (Italy's name for Pinot Blanc and Pinot Gris; see Chapter 2, page 32): Pinot Grigio is grown and produced almost everywhere, with the best examples produced in the cool northwestern regions, especially Friuli. Pinot Bianco can be crisper and leaner, but often with more character, especially those wines from Alto Adige, also in the northwest.

- **Prosecco:** This grape lends its name to a charmingly refreshing and highly affordable spumante.

- **Tocai Friulano** (recently renamed just "Friulano" in Italy): Whatever you call it, this grape is capable of rendering some of the best wines in Friuli. It offers earthy minerality in a medium-to-full-bodied swirl of apples and pears.

- **Trebbiano:** When you take into account all of its variants, Trebbiano trumps Malvasia for the status of Italy's most-planted white grape. In the Soave region of Veneto and in Tuscan whites, Trebbiano can really add character to blended wines. In other regions, it grows like crazy (sometimes referred to as a "weed," it's so prolific) and is used as a largely anonymous blender.

- **Verdicchio:** Grown in Marche province, Verdicchio lends its name to wines that can be stupendous: full-bodied, with exotic aromas and crisp acidity, an often overlooked gem that shines when paired with rustic fish dishes.

- **Vermentino:** An important grape in Tuscany and especially in Sardinia, Vermentino, a coastal grape, produces another fish-friendly wine, with high acids to refresh the palate and pleasant hints of green grasses in the nose.

- **Vernaccia:** The best-known example of wine from this grape is Vernaccia di San Gimignano from Tuscany, a white that is delicate yet so satisfying with shellfish and seafood.

The language of the label

WE OFTEN hear folks complain about Italian wine labels, saying that they're hard to decipher. True enough. But with a bit of WineWise coaching, we can simplify these labels and help to remove any stress in choosing a good Italian wine.

Whatever info the label conveys, remember that when it comes to Italian wines, maybe more than any other country we can think of, the reputation of the producer is paramount. In Italy, that name on the label is often a family name, and it is not difficult to find producers whose families have been making wine for hundreds of years, or at least for several generations. At the same time, there's a new wave of Italian winemakers, a new generation of producers whose families might have just grown grapes up until now, or whose wine previously ended up as part of the anonymous blend of a regional wine co-op. These "new wave" winemakers are doing some pretty exciting things and establishing good reputations in Italy and in the world's export markets.

Once you're aware that the producer's good name is important, what are some other WineWise shortcuts to understanding an Italian wine label? Well, first off, you should know that there are four basic ways to label an Italian wine:

1. **Grape name:** Italian varietal labels, with the name of the grape only, are not that common in the U.S. market.

2. **Grape and place name:** This is a far more common label format, and what's easy to remember is that it's almost always the name of the grape first, the name of the place second. The grape and place name will be separated by a form of the Italian word for "from." Here are some examples:
   - **Dolcetto d'Acqui:** Dolcetto is a red grape, and the grapes grew in the Acqui district of the Piedmont region.
   - **Sangiovese di Romagna:** Sangiovese is a red grape, and the grapes grew in the Romagna subregion of the Emilia-Romagna region.
   - **Moscato d'Asti:** Moscato is a white grape, and the grapes grew in the Asti district of the Piedmont region.

3. **Place name only:** In the U.S. market, this is probably the most common form of Italian wine label you'll find. The label features just the name of the place where the grapes are grown. That place can be very small—perhaps the name of a small town, or huge—maybe the

name of an entire region, and everything in between. Some examples:
- **Chianti** is a red wine made from grapes grown anywhere in the Chianti region of Tuscany. Chianti Classico is made from grapes grown only within a certain subregion.
- **Soave** is a white wine made from grapes grown in the Soave district of the Veneto region.
- **Barolo** is a red wine made from grapes grown only in the Barolo appellation in the Piedmont region.
- **Franciacorta** is a sparkling wine made from grapes grown in the Franciacorta district of the Lombardy region.

Vigne Regali is the wine producer; "L'Ardi" means "bright and brave"; Dolcetto is the grape; Acqui is the place where the grapes are grown. A DOC wine (see page 187).

Spalletti is the producer; Chianti is the place where the grapes (mostly Sangiovese, in this case) are grown. A DOCG wine (see page 188).

Oreno is the proprietary name for this Sangiovese/Merlot blend produced in Tuscany. An IGT wine. (Courtesy of Kobrand Corporation)

4. **Proprietary name:** A fantasy name chosen by the producer to represent the "story" or "soul" of the wine. Sometimes these are names of a vineyard or some other piece of land, but just as often a wine is named for a person or an idea. There are dozens of these wines in the American market. Most, though not all, are produced in Tuscany (and these wines are collectively known as "Super Tuscans"). They include label names such as Ornellaia, Col di Sasso, Excelsus, Le Pergole Torte, Solaia, Tignanello, Cepparello, Oreno, and Lupicaia, among many, many others. (See page 194 for a representative list of Super Tuscan wines.)

The origin of the wine

JUST AS FRANCE has its own set of wine regions regulated by the government under its AOC laws (see page 144), so does Italy, but under its DOC laws. DOC is shorthand for *denominazione di origine controllata* (controlled denomination of origin). Under these laws you'll find four official levels of quality:

- *Vino da Tavola* (**VdT**): We see a minuscule amount of this wine in the U.S. export market, and when we do it is a perverse commentary on Italy's wine laws. You see, VdT is the most basic wine in Italy, wine made for the family or for the rural village, or wine you might drink with a straw from a paperboard container at an Italian McDonald's. It is supposed to be dirt cheap and usually is. What we see in this country are

older vintages of very expensive wines, mostly the "Super Tuscans," that had no place to go but to the *vino da tavola* category because they were made with perhaps some Merlot, Syrah, Chardonnay, or some other foreign interloper grape not permitted by DOC regulations. Go buy a 1990 Tignanello, a humble little VdT, for $500 a bottle. Crazy, huh?

- *Indicazione Geografica Tipica* (**IGT**): As the nontraditional wines of Italy caught on in the international markets, demanding high prices at retail and in restaurants, the Italian government realized that to keep these wines in the low-class VdT category was a bad idea, and they changed the law to accommodate these new Italian wines.

  The producers were kind of getting into this idea of being outlaws—making great wines essentially free of government regulation—so to convince them to play along, the government declared that VdT wines could no longer carry a vintage year on the label. Well, the truth is you can't sell a nonvintage table wine for big bucks. Starting around 1996, most of the producers of the expensive VdT wines changed their wine's quality classification to this new official category, IGT, in order to continue to produce fine, vintage-dated wines. So while that 1990 Tignanello is a VdT, the 2000 Tignanello is an IGT. Crazy, huh? (Oh, we already said that. But it still applies.)

Cabreo produces "La Pietra," a Chardonnay from Tuscany, which, because it is made from a nontraditional (not Italian) grape in a traditional place (Tuscany), is an IGT wine. (Courtesy of Kobrand Corporation)

The evolution (or intelligent design?) of an Italian wine label

Once you get the hang of an Italian wine label, you can decipher its "code words" with ease. Here, we're going to give some examples of how a simple label can become more elaborate. You'll notice that with every layer of added information,

the origin and/or style of the wine becomes clearer, allowing you to make an informed, WineWise choice. Here are some examples:

The Cecchi family's "Messer Pietro di Teuzzo" Chianti Classico Riserva is named for the man who owned the vineyards more than a thousand years ago. The vineyards that produce this DOCG wine are now part of the Cecchi estates.

Chianti: the general name of the DOCG zone in Tuscany; a red wine with little aging.

Chianti Classico: the term *classico* indicates the traditional heartland

of the region, usually with the best vineyard sites.

Chianti Classico Riserva: a wine from the traditional heartland with the best vineyards, and aged in accordance with Italy's wine laws. In Chianti Classico DOCG, the term *riserva* on the label indicates a minimum aging time of two years in a barrel and three months in the bottle before the wine is released. Note that there is no federal Italian standard for *riserva*. Aging minimums vary widely, depending on provincial laws for each DOC or DOCG wine zone.

Barbaresco: the name of the DOCG zone, located in the Piedmont province; a red wine aged at least two years.

Barbaresco Riserva: for *riserva* wines from Barbaresco, the minimum aging time is four years before the wine is released. Note: there is no federal Italian standard for *riserva*. Aging minimums vary widely, de-

Two excellent single-vineyard (Paje and Asili) Barbaresco *riserva* wines from the highly regarded cooperative Produttori del Barbaresco. Barbaresco is a DOCG wine zone within Italy's Piedmont region.

pending on provincial laws for each DOC or DOCG wine zone.

Barbaresco Riserva "Asili": A Barbaresco Riserva from the single vineyard (*vigneti*) Asili. This is a wine with a unique *terroir*, made in a seriously limited quantity. It will be more expensive than a Barbaresco Riserva and much more expensive than a Barbaresco.

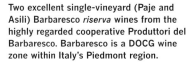

- *Denominazione di Origine Controllata* **(DOC):** The majority of Italian wine that you'll encounter falls into this category. There are hundreds of DOC zones. Again, they are the equivalent of the French AOC (page 144), and they are not so different from a U. S. AVA (see page 63). In essence, they are place names (sometimes grape and place names in Italy) that appear on the label. The DOC is a defined geographic area, and for each DOC the

government lists which grapes can be grown there and in some cases specifies approved vineyard and winery practices. While this is an outward sign of quality, remember that the DOC is awarded to a geographical zone (Valpolicella or Barbera d'Asti, for example), not to a particular producer. In Italy, as in the rest of the world, each producer's reputation is far more important than the designated DOC.

Vino Nobile di Montepulciano is a DOCG red wine from Tuscany, a Sangiovese-dominated blend. This wine, made by Carpineto, is a *riserva*, meaning that the wine has been aged longer in barrel and bottle than a wine that is not designated as *riserva*.

Falanghina, a delicious dry white wine from the Campania region of southern Italy.

- *Denominazione di Origine Controllata e Garantita* **(DOCG):** This is a category of Italian wines that have been elevated from DOC because the regions in which they are produced are considered special and unique. The criteria for elevation include quality, history, improvement, and, frankly, contribution to Italy's wine economy. Currently, there are more than thirty DOCG zones. We will go into more depth about their grape types, flavor characteristics, food affinities, and prices when we explore "The Major Wine Regions of Italy" (below).

The major wine regions of Italy

WHEN IT COMES TO WINE, it's been said that Italy is not so much a country as it is one big vineyard. This cliché is only a slight exaggeration. Wine abounds from all twenty provinces that constitute Italy (and the twenty-first, the Vatican, makes wine, too, although not from water as far as we know). The export market is chock-a-block with fine Italian wines, many from wine regions and provinces that ten or fifteen years ago were written off as suppliers of vapid, bitter, thin VdT wines for local consumption, with no hope that they would enter the export market to stellar reviews and consumer acceptance.

Following the lead of the classic regions that have always had an important presence in the U.S. market, the "new" wines of Italy may not really be new at all, but rather the product of better vineyard management and better winemaking. Many of the wines that have caught fire here are made from ancient grapes, but winemakers, both young and old, have adopted modern methods to make their wines technically and aesthetically better; in other words, the end product tastes good. At the same time, an increasing number of producers in just about all of Italy's wine regions have been successful with both white and red wines made from popular international varietals, or blends of Italian and international grapes.

So gaze upon our WineWise gazetteer of Italy's most famous—and most promising—wine regions, complete with the names of the best producers.* (Note: We have intentionally left out the wine regions of Liguria, Molise, and Valle d'Aosta, none of which currently have a significant presence in the U.S. export market.)

* When you see the actual labels of these wines, some of the producers' names may be preceded by certain words or phrases, such as "Azienda Agricola" (a wine estate), "Cantina" or "Cantine" (a winery), "Castello" (a wine estate with a feudal castle on site), "Fattoria" (a name for a winery, often connected to traditional and historic wine estates), "Podere" (a small, historic farm estate), and "Tenuta" or "Tenute" (a large wine estate).

Italy produces many wines made from popular international varietals, such as this Merlot from the Veneto region, made by Zonin.

Central Italy

TUSCANY

DOCG Wine Regions

Brunello di Montalcino, Carmignano, Chianti, Chianti Classico, Morellino di Scansano, Vernaccia di San Gimignano, Vino Nobile di Montepulciano

Important DOC Wine Regions

Bolgheri, Bolgheri Sassicaia, Moscadello di Montalcino, Pomino, Rosso di Montalcino, Rosso di Montepulciano, San Gimignano, Sant'Antimo

The wine of Tuscany is a perfect subject for an entire wine book, but don't freak out—we're not going to go that far. We'll just say that once you are bitten by the Tuscan wine bug, you'll want to taste more and more of the region's wines.

Over the last twenty years, Tuscan winemakers have revolutionized Italian wines, and this revolution has spread throughout the wine world. No longer content to produce passable wines that were accepted with minimal expectations by Italy and other countries in Europe, the best Tuscan winemakers set out to dramatically improve their traditional wines, and at the same time turn tradition on its ear (see the sidebar "Super Tuscans," page 194). The revolution is ongoing, and some traditionalists feel that many producers have gone too far in rejecting Tuscan wine history, ritual, and custom. Whatever the prognosis,

it's undeniable that the revolution is an exciting and vibrant movement in Tuscany.

Back to tradition for a moment. Even the most revolutionary Tuscan winemaker would agree that without the Sangiovese grape there is no Tuscan wine industry. Tuscany's most famous red wines—the wines that brought the revolutionaries to the party—rely on Sangiovese. All of Tuscany's esteemed red DOCG wines are based on Sangiovese, and many of the region's "new" red wines—"Super Tuscans," a term with no deep meaning, invented by wine writers—are either 100% Sangiovese or use it as part of a blend with international varietals such as Cabernet Sauvignon, Cabernet Franc, Merlot, and Syrah. (White "Super Tuscans" often employ Chardonnay and Sauvignon Blanc, either as single varietals or blended with Italy's indigenous varietals.)

Let's take a look at the wines that have made Tuscany famous.

Chianti. At one time the image of this wine was so bad that the name for the traditional wicker baskets wrapped around Chianti bottles, *fiasco*, entered the English language as a term meaning something that's all screwed up. Those days are gone. You can still find the old style of Chianti in the old fiasco, but you're far more likely to find a wine in a bottle reminiscent of red Bordeaux or California Cabernet Sauvignon. And the changes are not just cosmetic. Today's Chianti, especially Chianti Classico, is delicious and sooooo food-friendly. You can buy a fruit-forward wine labeled as just "Chianti" from a good producer for about $10 to $15 (good with veggies, fish, or meats); Chianti Classico, which we consider a true WineWise value, starts at about $12 and stops before $25 (a little more power, acidity, and complexity in this wine; food can be a bit heartier), and Chianti Classico Riserva starts at about $16 and climbs to about $40, depending on vintage and producer (a powerful and complex wine, great with braised and grilled meats). Also look for Chianti Rufina, Chianti Colli Senesi, and other wines featuring the name of any of the eight Chianti subregions—great wines with extremely reasonable prices.

Vino Nobile di Montepulciano. It's a mouthful to say, but Vino Nobile di Montepulciano is also a mouthful of delicious wine at an affordable price,

Central Italy
Main DOC/DOCG Wine Regions

Emilia-Romagna
1. Colli Piacentini
2. Gutturnio
3. Lambrusco
4. Colli Bolognesi
5. Trebbiano di Romagna
6. Albana di Romagna DOCG

Tuscany
7. Montecarlo
8. Chianti DOCG
9. Chianti Classico DOCG
10. Carmignano DOCG
11. Pomino
12. Vernaccia di San Gimignano DOCG
13. Bolgheri
14. Brunello di Montalcino DOCG, Rosso di Montalcino
15. Vino Nobile di Montepulciano DOCG, Rosso di Montepulciano

16. Morellino di Scansano DOCG
17. Bianco de Pitigliano
18. Parrina
19. Elba

Umbria
20. Colli Altotiberini
21. Colli Perugini
22. Torgiano Rosso Riserva DOCG
23. Sagrantino di Montefalco DOCG
24. Orvieto

Marche
25. Bianchello del Metauro
26. Verdicchio dei Castelli di Jesi
27. Rosso Conero
28. Verdicchio di Matelica
29. Vernaccia di Serrapetrona
30. Rosso Piceno

Abruzzo
31. Montepulciano d'Abruzzo
32. Trebbiano d'Abruzzo

Lazio
33. Est! Est!! Est!!! di Montefiascone
34. Montecompatri
35. Frascati
36. Marino
37. Colli Albani
38. Colli Lanuvini
39. Velletri

Molise
40. Biferno

Central Italy.

The rolling hills of Tuscany.

often under $25 at retail. For that money, you get a world-class wine from a small collection of vineyards that is not as well known as the other red DOCG wines of Tuscany (that's good for consumers) but is irrepressibly delicious. The full-bodied wine is fragrant, with herbal and spice notes, moderate acidity, and mature black and red fruits on the palate. A fine and less expensive alternative to Vino Nobile di Montepulciano is Rosso di Montepulciano (DOC), made from grapes grown on less mature vines. The Rosso may be harder to find than its Nobile parent, but it's worth the search for both its quality and its value.

Carmignano. With Sangiovese as its base, Carmignano, a wine from the vineyards surrounding Florence, can include as much as 20% Cabernet Sauvignon or Cabernet Franc in the finished wine. This is a limited-production, elegant wine, with the aroma of rose petals and black currants, as well as wild black fruit flavors and high acidity. If you've never tasted Carmignano, it can be a revelation. Priced about the same as Chianti Classico Riserva (usually under $30).

Brunello di Montalcino. We've saved the biggest, baddest, boldest, and arguably the best wine for last; it is also the most expensive. Many people believe that Brunello di Montalcino is consistently the finest red wine produced in Italy. It is an extraordinary wine, certainly the most powerful example of wine made

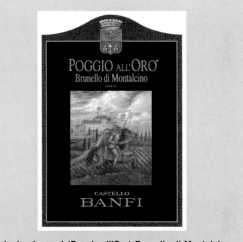

A single-vineyard (Poggio all'Oro) Brunello di Montalcino riserva (DOCG), which must, by law, age a minimum of five years before release. This expensive wine is made from 100% Sangiovese grapes. Tuscany's Castello Banfi is an astoundingly beautiful and historic estate of more than 1,000 acres/400 hectares.

from Sangiovese grapes; this is a wine that can and should age for years, and some of the *riserva* wines for a lifetime. Big and brawny but at the same time delicately balanced, Brunello di Montalcino is definitely a special-occasion wine, with retail prices starting at more than $50 and rising to the heavens for older, sought-after wines. On restaurant wine lists it is not uncommon for these wines to sell for $100 and up—way up. For those who can afford it, the experience of tasting a great Brunello di Montalcino is priceless.

There is good news for those of us who can afford only a "baby Brunello": Rosso di Montalcino (DOC). Like Brunello, Rosso is made from 100% Sangiovese picked in and around the same vineyards as the more esteemed wine, and made only by Brunello di Montalcino producers. For less than $30 at retail, you can enjoy some hints of Brunello in a wine that is enjoyable right out of the bottle, or within a few years—your choice. Rosso di Montalcino is among our top WineWise choices for value and quality.

Morellino di Scansano. The newest DOCG red from Tuscany is just now making a bit of a splash in the American market. Morellino di Scansano, from southern, coastal Tuscany, is made from 100% Sangiovese grapes and is an earthy, rich, and complex red. Morellino (one of dozens of alternative names for Sangiovese) is often priced under $25 and worth almost double the price. The *riserva* wines are more expensive (about $35) and are glorious.

Vernaccia di San Gimignano. A popular dry white wine from Tuscany is Vernaccia di San Gimignano, a DOCG of historical significance, produced in the vineyards surrounding San Gimignano, a medieval town perched on top of a hill. A light-to-medium-bodied wine, Vernaccia di San Gimignano marries well with seafood and shellfish.

Some of the Best Wine Producers

Chianti DOCG: Badiolo, Bellini, Borgo Salce, Cal del Vispo, Castellani, Donatella Cinelli Colombini "Fattoria del Casato," Geografico, Ghizzano, Parri e Figio, Petrolo, Spalletti, and Villa La Selva

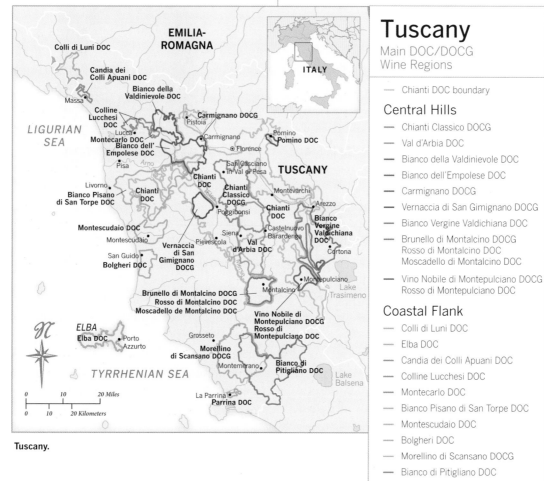

Tuscany.

Chianti Classico DOCG: Antinori, Badia a Coltibuono, Banfi, Barbi, Borgo Scopeto, Brolio/Barone Ricasoli, Cacchiano, Carpineto, Casa Emma, Castellare, Castello di Ama, Castell'in Villa, Cecchi, Le Corti, Felsina, Fonterutoli, Fontodi, Gabbiano, Grevepesa, Isole e Olena, Machiavelli, La Marcellina, La Massa, Melini, Monsanto, Nozzole, Poggerino, Querciabella, Querceto, Rampolla, Riecine, Ruffino, San Felice, Verrazano, Vicchiomaggio, Villa Cafaggio, and Volpaia

Brunello di Montalcino DOCG and Rosso di Montalcino DOC: Aleramici, Altesino, Antinori, Argiano, Castello Banfi, Barbi, Biondi-Santi, Camigliano, Campogiovanni, Caparzo, Casa Basse di Soldera, Casanova di Neri, Casato, Castelgiocondo/Frescobaldi, Castello Banfi, Cerbaiona-Salvioni, Col d'Orcia, Constanti, Corte Pavoni, Fanti, Fattoi, Fuligni, Gaja, La Lecciaia, Lisini, La Magla, Mastrojanni, Nardi, Pacenti, Poggio Antico, Il Poggiolo, Il Poggione, Salvioni, Solaria, Talente, and Val di Suga

Vino Nobile di Montepulciano DOCG and Rosso di Montepulciano DOC: Avignonesi, Boscarelli, Contucci, Fassati, Poliziano, Redi, Salcheto, and Valdipiatta

Carmignano DOCG: Ambra, Artimino, Cantagallo, and Capezzana

Vernaccia di San Gimignano DOCG: Falchini, San Quirico, Spalletti, Strozzi, and Teruzzi e Puthod

UMBRIA

DOCG Wine Regions

Sagrantino di Montefalco, Torgiano Rosso Riserva

Important DOC Wine Regions

Montefalco, Orvieto, Torgiano

Although landlocked Umbria lives in the shadow of its neighbor Tuscany when it comes to discussions of fine Italian wines, Umbria produces excellent wines of its own, the best of which are still a secret to the American wine public.

One white wine from Umbria has had great success in the United States: Orvieto. Look for Orvieto Classico, easy to find and a great bargain—about $10 to $12.

Lungarotti is a producer who has had great success with its Rubesco, a reasonably priced Sangiovese-Canaiolo red blend from the Torgiano wine district. Rubesco is a full-bodied, hearty, complex, but food-friendly red. Lungarotti also produces a more expensive DOCG version of this wine, made from a single vineyard site, Rubesco "Vigna Monticchio," a *riserva* aged for five years in the bottle before release.

Sagrantino di Montefalco is just beginning to gather steam in the American market. This extraordinary red is unique thanks to its singular grape,

Morellino di Scansano is a Sangiovese-based wine made from grapes that grow in the coastal Maremma region of Tuscany. Val delle Rose is a leading producer of this DOCG wine.

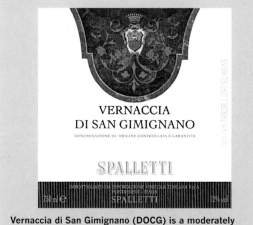

Vernaccia di San Gimignano (DOCG) is a moderately priced white wine that pairs well with fish dishes.

Super Tuscans

SASSICAIA

BOLGHERI SASSICAIA

Here is a list, a small sampling really, of the hundreds of "Super Tuscan" wines, both white and red. Mostly IGT, with a handful of DOC wines, most of them are quite expensive, with prices that start above $30 and quickly reach the stratosphere, but some are moderately priced, with six bargains (marked with an asterisk) thrown into this heady mix.

Sassicaia, one of the first "Super Tuscans." This very expensive red wine is at least 80% Cabernet Sauvignon and has won international acclaim. Sassicaia is one of several "Super Tuscans" produced in the Bolgheri wine region of Tuscany. (Courtesy of Kobrand Corporation)

Some of the Best-known "Super Tuscans"

Name of the Wine	Composition/Blend
White Wines	
Cabreo La Pietra	Chardonnay
Farnito	Chardonnay
Ghiaie Bianche	Chardonnay
Il Marzocco	Chardonnay
Serena*	Sauvignon Blanc
Terre di Tuffi*	Primarily Vernaccia
Torricella	Chardonnay
Trappoline*	Pinot Bianco/Chardonnay/Trebbiano/Malvasia
Vigna al Poggio	Chardonnay
Vigna Campo al Moro	Chardonnay (50%)/Trebbiano Toscano (50%)
Red Wines	
Borgoforte*	Cabernet Sauvignon/Merlot/Cabernet Franc
Brancaia	Sangiovese/Cabernet Sauvignon/Merlot
Brigante	Sangiovese (50%)/Merlot (50%)
Cabreo il Borgo	Sangiovese/Cabernet Sauvignon
Casalferro	Sangiovese
Castruccio Rosso	Sangiovese/Canaiolo/Colorino/Ciliegiolo

Name of the Wine	Composition/Blend
Centine*	Sangiovese
Cepparello	Sangiovese
Chiaie delle Furba	Cabernet Sauvignon/Cabernet Franc/Merlot
Col di Sasso*	Cabernet Sauvignon (70%)/Sangiovese (30%)
Colvecchio	Syrah
Cum Laude	Cabernet Sauvignon (30%)/Merlot (30%)/Sangiovese (25%)/Syrah (15%)
Desiderio	Merlot
Dogajolo	Cabernet Sauvignon/Merlot
Excelsus	Cabernet Sauvignon (60%)/Merlot (40%)
Farnito	Cabernet Sauvignon
Grifi	Sangiovese (50%)/Cabernet Sauvignon (50%)
Guado al Tasso	Cabernet Sauvignon (60%)/Merlot (30%)/Syrah (10%)
I Vigneti Geografico	Cabernet Sauvignon/Sangiovese
Il Pareto	Cabernet Sauvignon
Il Sodaccio	Sangiovese/Canaiolo
L'Eremo	Syrah
La Brancaia	Sangiovese (60%)/Merlot (35%)/Cabernet Sauvignon (5%)

Name of the Wine	Composition/Blend
Le Pergole Torte	Sangiovese
Le Volte	Sangiovese/Cabernet Sauvignon
Luce	Sangiovese/Merlot
Lucente	Sangiovese
Lupicaia	Cabernet Sauvignon/Merlot
Masseto	Merlot
Nemo	Cabernet Sauvignon
Oreno	Sangiovese/Merlot
Ornellaia	Cabernet Sauvignon/ Merlot/Cabernet Franc
Poggio alla Badiola	Sangiovese
Promis	Merlot (55%)/Syrah (35%)/ Sangiovese (10%)
Rosso dei Barbi	Sangiovese
San Leonardo	Cabernet Sauvignon/Merlot
San Leopoldo	Sangiovese/Cabernet Sauvignon
Sangioveto	Sangiovese
Sassicaia	Cabernet Sauvignon (at least 80%)/Cabernet Franc
Sassoalloro	Sangiovese
Schidione	Sangiovese/Cabernet Sauvignon/Merlot
Siepi	Sangiovese (50%)/Merlot (50%)
Solaia	Cabernet Sauvignon (80%)/ Sangiovese (20%)
Spargolo	Sangiovese
Summus	Sangiovese (45%)/Cabernet Sauvignon (40%)/Syrah (15%)
Tassinaia	Cabernet Sauvignon/Merlot/ Sangiovese
Tavernelle	Merlot
Tignanello	Sangiovese (80%)/Cabernet Sauvignon (15%)/Cabernet Franc (5%)
Tinscvil	Sangiovese/Cabernet Sauvignon
Vigna L'Apparita	Merlot
Villa Pillo*	Syrah

Sagrantino. Inky, full, and rich, with just the right acidity, it is one of the world's great wines. It is expensive and can be found mostly on fine Italian restaurant wine lists.

Some of the Best Wine Producers
Torgiano Rosso Riserva DOCG (from Lungarotti only) and Sagrantino di Montefalco DOCG: Adante, Alzatura, Antonelli–San Marco, Arnaldo Caprai, Colpetrone, Fongoli, Scacciadiavoli, and Tiburzi

Orvieto Classico DOC: Antinori, Barberani-Vallesanta, Barbi, Barone Ricasoli, Bigi, La Carraia, Cecchi, Coli, Fontana-Candida, Melini, Palazzone, Picini, Ruffino, Salviano, Straccali, and Le Velette

ABRUZZO
DOCG Wine Region
Montepulciano d'Abruzzo Colline Terramane

Important DOC Wine Region
Montepulciano d'Abruzzo

Montepulciano d'Abruzzo is a red wine that is enjoyable in its youth; it's quite fruity and easy to drink. Widely available in the United States, this wine is developing a good reputation among wine drinkers who enjoy a good, food-friendly wine (especially with barbecue and roasts) at a very reasonable price. It's really not necessary to go out of your way to find the DOCG version from the Colline Terramane district.

Some of the Best Wine Producers
Bove, Casal Thaulero, Cataldi Madonna, Citra, Contesa, Marina Cvetic, Gru, Masciarelli, Umani Ronchi, Valentini, and Valori

LE MARCHE
DOCG Wine Regions
Conero, Vernaccia di Serrapetrona

Important DOC Wine Regions
Rosso Piceno, Verdicchio dei Castelli di Jesi, Verdicchio di Matelica

Montepulciano d'Abruzzo (DOC) is an enjoyable, affordable, food-friendly, medium-bodied red. Zaccagnini Masciarelli is a leading producer.

Lungarotti has long been Umbria's most famous wine producer in the U.S. market. Rubesco is a brand name for Lungarotti's Rosso di Torgiano (DOC), a Sangiovese-based blend that is both ageworthy and affordable.

The most famous wine in Marche is Verdicchio; about twenty million bottles are produced each year, and Verdicchio is second only to Soave (from Veneto) as the most imported Italian white wine in the U.S. market. Verdicchio is so accessible, so reasonably priced, and of such high quality that it qualifies as a true WineWise bargain. A medium-bodied dry white with an herbaceous nose and green apple acidity to refresh the palate, Verdicchio at its best shows off a bit of hazelnut in the finish to add some complexity. A great match for fish and poultry, styles of Verdicchio range from clean and crisp to versions that are more about minerals and earth.

Two reds from Marche have made some small inroads in the United States. Rosso Conero (DOCG), and Rosso Piceno (DOC), based on Sangiovese, are both appealing, medium-bodied wines meant to be drunk young, within three to five years of vintage. These are great pasta wines that would also be just as happy accompanying a grilled salmon as marrying with white or red meat dishes.

Some of the Best Wine Producers

Verdicchio dei Castelli di Jesi DOC and Verdicchio di Matelica DOC: Belisario, Bisci, Bonci, Bucci, Colonnara, Coroncino, Fazi Battaglia, Garofoli, Luchetti, Marroti Campi, Martinetti, Mecella, La Monacesca, Montalto, Montecappone, San Biageo, San Lorenzo, Santa Barbara, Sartarelli, Tavignano, Terre Cortesi Moncaro, Umani Ronchi, Vallerosa Bonci, and Zaccagnini

Rosso Conero DOCG and Rosso Piceno DOC: Boccadigabba, Le Caniette, Colonnara, Ercole Velenosi, Fazi Battaglia, Garofili, Grifoni, Lanari, Montalto Rosso, Montecappone, Moroder, Saladini Pilastri, Serenelli, Le Terraze, Umani Ronchi, Tavignano, and Velenosi

LAZIO
Important DOC Wine Regions
Est! Est!! Est!!! di Montefiascone, Frascati

In the American market, just as it is in the Italian capital city of Rome, Lazio is all about Frascati, an inexpensive, fruity, fragrant, simple, crisp, light, and dry wine. Frascati works well as an accompaniment to light, simple dishes, especially fish, or deep-fried artichokes, a historic staple of Rome's Jewish ghetto. Often overlooked, Frascati is one of our favorite wines for warm weather, when you want to sip something that does not demand your attention but is tasty, especially when dining al fresco.

Est! Est!! Est!!! di Montefiascone is the stuff of Italian legend. The wine has zippy acidity and lovely aromatics, and those found in the American market are pleasant, especially with fried foods.

The legend of Est! Est!! Est!!! di Montefiascone

It goes like this: A twelfth-century German bishop, Johann Fugger, was traveling to Rome. Fat Fugger had his chief of staff travel ahead of him to mark the door of the best establishment in each town with the word "Est!" (This is it!), their own shorthand for "The wine is good."

When Fugger's advance man got to the village of Montefiascone, he wrote "Est! Est!! Est!!!" on the door of the local inn. Fugger's 900-year-old tomb is on display in the old village church.

Some of the Best Wine Producers

Frascati DOC: Casale Mattia, Castel de Paolis, Colli di Catone, Conte Zandotti, Fontana Candida, Gotto d'Oro, Pietra Porzia, Rashi, San Marco, and Villa Simone

Est! Est!! Est!!! di Montefiascone DOC: Cerveteri, Falesco, Mazziotti, and Mottura

Verdicchio from Le Marche has long been a popular Italian white wine in the United States and at its best can be medium-to-full-bodied and complex. Fazi Battaglia is one of the best-known producers of estate-bottled Verdicchio dei Castelli di Jesi (DOC).

Orvieto is a medium-bodied, refreshing dry white wine that can be sourced from vineyards in both the Lazio and Umbria regions of Italy. Orvieto, a good match with seafood, is a WineWise bargain.

Northwest Italy

PIEDMONT
DOCG Wine Regions
Asti/Moscato d'Asti, Barbaresco, Barbera d'Asti, Barbera del Monferrato, Barolo, Brachetto d'Acqui (alpha), Dolcetto di Dogliani, Superiore, Gattinara, Gavi/Cortese di Gavi, Ghemme, Roero

Important DOC Wine Regions
Barbera d'Alba, Dolcetto d'Acqui, Dolcetto d'Alba, Dolcetto d'Asti, Dolcetto di Diano d'Alba, Freisa d'Asti, Freisa di Chieri, Grignolino d'Asti, Grignolino del Monferrato, Langhe, Nebbiolo d'Alba, Piemonte

Lovers of Italian wine who don't think that Brunello di Montalcino (see "Tuscany," page 189) is Italy's finest wine usually come down on the side of one of two famous DOCG reds from the Piedmont region as their first choice: Barolo or Barbaresco. While we will never settle this argument among these three big wines, we can say without fear of contradiction that Barolo and Barbaresco, both made from 100% Nebbiolo grapes, are extraordinary wines that

Northwest Italy

Main DOC/DOCG Wine Regions

Valle d'Aosta
— Valle d'Aosta

Piedmont
— Carema
— Gattinara DOCG
— Ghemme DOCG
— Erbaluce di Caluso,
  Caluso Passito
— Barbera d'Asti DOCG
— Roero, Arneis
  di Roero DOCG
— Barbaresco DOCG
— Barolo DOCG
— Dolcetto d'Alba
— Asti DOCG, Moscato
  d'Asti DOCG
— Brachetto d'Acqui DOCG
— Gavi, Cortese di Gavi DOCG

Lombardy
— Oltrepò Pavese
— Franciacorta DOCG
— Lugana
— Riviera del Garda
  Bresciano
— Valtellina Superiore DOCG

Liguria
— Rossese di
  Dolceacqua
— Cinqueterre

Northwest Italy.

beautifully represent the traditions of Piedmontese winemaking. But Piedmont is about more than two great red wines.

Piedmont (*Piemonte* in Italian) is steeped in a tradition of *terroir* in the vineyards and production of officially classified DOC and DOCG wines made from Italian varietals (there are no newfangled IGT wines from Piedmont, the only wine region other than its teeny-tiny neighbor Valle d'Aosta not to have any). Piedmont is considered by many to be the true home of classic Italian wines, yet it is a region that is not standing still.

It is with their native varietals—Nebbiolo, Barbera, and Dolcetto among the reds, Cortese, Arneis, and Moscato among the whites—that Piedmont's wines shine, creating a brilliant luster to attract the wine world.

Piedmont borders France and Switzerland; the views of the Alps from Piedmontese vineyards are majestic. This is one of the coolest wine regions of Italy, and Piedmont's best wines exhibit searing acidity to refresh the palate in its whites, sparklers, and lighter reds, and balance the complex structure and tannins of its biggest reds.

There is an old Piedmontese expression: *Il vino e rosso* ("Wine is red"). That belief certainly doesn't allow much wiggle room. Of course Piedmont winemakers do produce white wines, but most of them live in the shadow of the region's famous reds. Let's look at those reds and then survey the most popular whites.

Barolo and Barbaresco. Barolo and Barbaresco are red wines produced from 100% Nebbiolo grapes grown in the vineyards surrounding the small city of Alba: Barolo to the south of the city, Barbaresco to the north. In the old days, Barolo, known as the "king of Piedmont's wines," was almost always the more powerful wine that needed more time to age, to tame the rustic, wild, sometimes harsh tannins in the wine. Barbaresco, the "queen," was in those days the more delicate of the two wines, although it still needed plenty of aging to achieve balance. Today, these wines are largely gender-neutral, with Barolo often more delicate than a Barbaresco, and a Barbaresco just as likely to be as powerful or more powerful than Barolo.

Barolo and Barbaresco call into question much of what we think we know about powerful, tannic wines. We usually assume that such blockbusters must be deeply colored, bordering on black, especially when young. Yet both of these wines, because they are made from the thin-skinned Nebbiolo grape, start life as medium-red in color, losing some of that color and taking on orange highlights as the wine ages. What a pleasant surprise it is to taste Barolo or Barbaresco for the first time. The tannins grab you and hold on, but soon give way to background flavors of spiced and dried red fruits, especially dried cherries. The nose of Nebbiolo is also pronounced: spices, roses, tar, and the earthy and exotic aromas of *tartufo bianco*, the white truffles that grow wild in Piedmont. These are wines that call for hearty foods without elaborate sauces or complicated, competing flavors.

Keep it simple—grilled steak, roast duck, or braised lamb shanks served with potatoes or polenta—and the wine will rapidly emerge as another flavor and texture component of the dish.

Barbaresco and especially Barolo are very expensive wines, and worth it. Best value: Produttori del Barbaresco (starting at under $35 retail, a bit more for some very special single-vineyard wines) and Ceretto "Zonchera" Barolo (about $45). Also look for the DOC wines Nebbiolo d'Alba and Lange Nebbiolo, which are great values (starting at about $15 to $20). They are a bit softer on the palate, a bit fruitier, and ready to drink within a few years of vintage.

A single-vineyard (Ovello) Barbaresco (DOCG) from Cantine del Pino, owned by Renato Vacca, a young winemaker.

A single-vineyard (Rocche) Barolo from Renato Ratti, a leading quality-driven producer. Marcenasco is a subdistrict within the Barolo DOCG. Renato Ratti's son, Pietro, is in charge of the vineyards, the ultra-modern winery, and making the wines.

Barbaresco vineyards in Piedmont.

Gattinara and Ghemme. Also based in Nebbiolo, but not necessarily made 100% from that grape, Gattinara and Ghemme are both DOCG red wines from the north of Piedmont. Cooler than the southern region that is home to Barolo and Barbaresco, these wines are produced from grapes with higher acid levels. It is difficult to ripen Nebbiolo here, so these wines are normally lighter than Barolo or Barbaresco, unless the growing season has been peppered with many dry, hot days. These wines are pretty: floral, perfumed, and delicate but substantive. They are normally about half the price of basic Barolo or Barbaresco.

Barbera d'Alba, Barbera d'Asti, Barbera del Monferrato. Barbera is the most-planted grape in Piedmont and the second-most-planted red grape in all of Italy (after Sangiovese). Barbera is planted in other parts of the world, but Piedmont is its ancestral home, and the region produces some of the world's best wines made from this grape.

Unlike wines made from Nebbiolo grapes, Barbera wines from Piedmont are moderately dark in color. They are generally medium-bodied and fruit-forward and always show off bright acidity, the trademark of virtually all good Piedmontese wines. These are fine examples of "crossover" wines, equally at home

in the company of grilled fish, white meats, red meats, pasta, pizza, or roasted vegetables. Again, the reputation of the producer is key. Barbera is considered the signature wine of Piedmont, so a good producer won't put his or her name on an inferior wine. These wines usually range from under $15 to about $25, with some more powerful wines that are produced and aged in small oak barrels and/or from single vineyards priced much higher, such as "Stradivario" from the esteemed Bava family, which sells for about $40.

Dolcetto d'Acqui, Dolcetto d'Alba, Dolcetto d'Asti, Dolcetto di Diano d'Alba, Dolcetto di Dogliani. Dolcetto is a light-to-medium-bodied dry red, with juicy berry flavors and high acidity. Often compared to Beaujolais from France because of its simplicity, Dolcetto is in fact a bit more complex. Still, this is a great "crossover" wine for a wide variety of dishes and can take a bit of chilling to bring out its fruit, especially in warm weather—a great wine for a picnic or old-fashioned family cookout. Dolcetto d'Alba, often produced by leading Barolo and Barbaresco producers, is the most widely available Dolcetto in the American market, but try any Dolcetto wine from Piedmont. An excellent value, with prices ranging from about $10 to under $25.

Brachetto d'Acqui. This is a sweet red wine, mostly produced in a light, sparkling style, that is a lot of

Barbera d'Alba (DOC), from the Gepin single vineyard, made by Albino Rocca, one of Piedmont's best producers. Barbera from Piedmont, with forward fruit and high acidity, is an excellent wine for a wide variety of foods.

fun, from its red berry color and frothing foam to its low alcohol content (about 8% to 10%) and flavors of fresh red fruits. It's the perfect match for dark chocolate and fresh fruit-based desserts, as well as a summer sipper. About $17 to $30 per bottle.

Gavi/Cortese di Gavi. Made from 100% Cortese grapes, this light-bodied DOCG dry white with refreshing, almost minty green, acidity can actually be called by three possible names: Gavi, Cortese di Gavi, and Gavi di Gavi. Well-chilled Gavi is an excellent match with seafood and shellfish, including cold dishes, such as a Nicoise salad. Usually produced as a still wine, we also recommend the slightly sparkling *perlante* version, Principessa Gavia, produced by Banfi. Retail prices for Gavi start at about $13 and will rarely exceed $25.

Roero Arneis. Red wines are made from Nebbiolo grapes in the Roero DOCG, located between the cities of Alba and Asti. However, Roero is best known in the United States for its white wines made from Arneis, an ancient grape supposedly of Greek origin, and the only white grape allowed to be labeled with the Roero DOCG. Arneis, with its aromas of flowers and hazelnuts, is an appealing light-to-medium-bodied white with moderate to high acidity. In the early 1980s, Bruno Ceretto and Bruno Giacosa, who realized the potential of Arneis, began to produce this wine, and they were soon followed by a select handful of Piedmontese winemakers. Roero Arneis is still a little-known "insider wine" but is high on our list of WineWise recommendations, and it's a very good value, with retail prices beginning at under $20.

Asti/Moscato d'Asti. The name of this shared DOCG actually represents two different styles of wine, both peachy-sweet and both made from 100% Moscato grapes. Asti used to be called Asti Spumante; the Italian word *spumante* means "sparkling." Because the wine is always presented in a Champagne-style bottle, allowing the consumer to easily figure out that it's got a lot of bubbles, it is now simply called "Asti." Moscato d'Asti is essentially the same wine, but with far less sparkle; it's made in the *frizzantino* style, which means "a little fizzy." Both wines are charming, fun,

and low in alcohol, from 5% to 7%. They're cheesecake wines, wines for fruit-based desserts, wines to sip and enjoy in warm weather, maybe by the pool or in the garden on a hot and muggy day when the only thought in your head involves cooling down.

Dolcetto is a great "crossover" red, a fine accompaniment to grilled fish, white meats, leaner red meats, and roasted or grilled veggies. Gigi Rosso makes a very good wine in the Dolcettto d'Alba DOC.

Gavi (DOCG) is a light-to-medium-bodied white. Perfect for fish, the wine is light, refreshing, and fun. Gavi is made only from Cortese grapes.

Moscato d'Asti (DOCG) is a light, frothy, refreshing, moderately sweet, low-alcohol wine, perfect to accompany cookies, cheesecake, or fruit-based desserts. Ceretto's "Santo Stefano" Moscato d'Asti is an elegant wine in an elegant bottle. Asti (DOCG; formerly Asti Spumante) is basically the same wine—but with more bubbles—in a champagne bottle.

Some of the Best Wine Producers

Barbaresco DOCG: Albino Rocca, Aldo Conterno, Ca' Rome', Cantina del Pino, Ceretto, Gaja, Bruno Giacosa, Fratelli Giacosa, I Paglieri, Marchese di Gresy, Mascarello e Figlio, Moccagatta, Musso, Pio Cesare, Produttori del Barbaresco, Prunotto, La Spinona, and Vietti

Barolo DOCG: Abbona, Alessandria, Elio Altare, Anselma, Batasiolo, Borgogno, Boroli, Brezza, Burlotto, Ceretto, Chiarlo, Clerico, Aldo Conterno, Giacomo Conterno, Corino, Einaudi, Fontanafredda, Gaja, Bruno Giacosa, F. illi Giacosa, Grasso, Manzone, Manzoni, Marcarini, Marchese di Barolo, Mascarello, Pio Cesare, Prunotto, Ratti, Revello, Rinaldi, Sandrone, Scarpa, Scavino, Settimo, Sottimano, La Spinetta, Veglio, Vietti, and Voerzio

Gattinara DOCG and Ghemme DOCG: Antoniolo, Bianchi, Cantalupo, Le Colline, Nervi, and Travaglini

Barbera d'Alba DOC and Barbera d'Asti DOC: Bartenura (kosher), Batasiolo, Bava, Bricco Mandolino, Giacomo Bologna/ Braida, Boroli, Cascina Castelet, Chiarlo, Conterno, Gaja, Negro, and Ratti

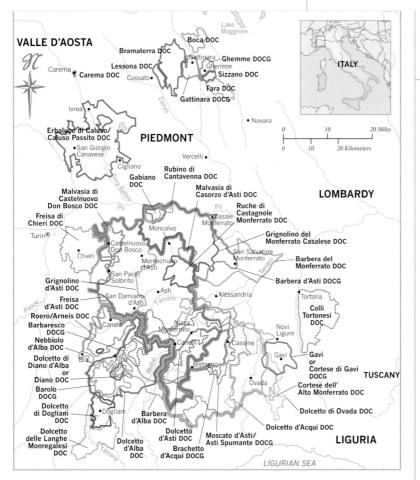

Piedmont.

Piedmont
Main DOC/DOCG
Wine Regions

Northern Piedmont
— Boca DOC
— Bramaterra DOC
— Lessona DOC
— Gattinara DOCG
— Ghemme DOCG
— Sizzano DOC
— Fara DOC
— Carema DOC
— Erbaluce di Caluso/Caluso Passito DOC

Alba
— Roero/Arneis DOC
— Nebbiolo d'Alba DOC
— Barbaresco DOCG
— Dolcetto d'Alba DOC
— Barbera d'Alba DOC
— Dolcetto di Diano d'Alba or Diano DOC
— Barolo DOCG
— Dolcetto di Dogliani DOC
— Dolcetto delle Langhe Monregalesi DOC

Southeastern Piedmont
— Gabiano DOC
— Rubino di Cantavenna DOC
— Grignolino del Monferrato Casalese DOC
— Freisa di Chieri DOC
— Malvasia di Castelnuovo Don Bosco DOC
— Malvasia di Casorzo d'Asti DOC
— Ruche di Castagnole Monferrato DOC
— Barbera d'Asti DOCG
— Barbera del Monferrato DOC
— Grignolino d'Asti DOC
— Freisa d'Asti DOC
— Moscato d'Asti/Asti Spumante DOCG
— Brachetto d'Acqui DOCG
— Dolcetto d'Asti DOC
— Dolcetto d'Acqui DOC
— Cortese dell'Alto Monferrato DOC
— Dolcetto di Ovada DOC
— Gavi or Cortese di Gavi DOCG
— Colli Tortonesi DOC

Dolcetto d'Alba DOC, Dolcetto d'Asti DOC, Dolcetto di Diano d'Alba DOC, Dolcetto di Dogliani DOC: Elio Altare, Azelia, Ceretto, Conterno, Einaudi, Gaja, Giacosa, L'Ardi, Mascarello, Pecchenino, Ratti, Sandrone, San Romano, and Vietti (Superiore is DOCG)

Gavi/Cortese di Gavi DOCG: Aurora, Banfi, Bartenura (kosher), Bava, Bersano, Broglia, Campo Verde, Chiarlo, Fontanafredda, Picollo, Pio Cesare, Gigi Rosso, La Scolca, Valditerra, Villadoria, Villa Sparina, and Volpi

Roero DOCG (whites using the Arneis grape): Bongiovanni, Broglia, Cascina Ca'Rossa, Ceretto "Blangé," Corregia, Deltetto, Bruno Giacosa, La Giustiniana, Monchiero Carbone, Negro, Pio Cesare, Poderi Alisia, Porello, and Vietti

Asti/Moscato d'Asti DOCG and Brachetto d'Acqui DOCG: Banfi, Bartenura (kosher), Giacomo Bologna/Braida, Bosca, Cascina Giovinale, Ceretto, Chiarlo, Cinzano, Contratto, Coppo, Costello del Poggio, Folonari, Gancia, Marenco, Martini e Rossi, Nando, Palazzacci, Santini, Saracco, Tosti, Vallebelbo, and Zonin

LOMBARDY
DOCG Wine Regions
Franciacorta, Valtellina Sforzato/Sfurzat, Valtellina Superiore (includes four subregions: Inferno, Grumello, Sassella, and Valgella)

Important DOC Wine Regions
Oltrepo Pavese, Terre di Franciacorta, Valtellina

Lombardy is often defined by its cosmopolitan capital, Milan, and its best wines are still a bit of a secret, except to the neighboring Swiss, who tend to think of these wines as their own and consume copious amounts of *vino di Lombardia*. More than half of Lombardy's wines are classified as DOC, and the only DOCG sparkler made by the *methode champenoise* (*metodo classico* or *metodo tradizionale* in Italian), Franciacorta, is produced here, with spectacular—and expensive—results.

Franciacorta, from Lombardy, is the only *methode champenoise* DOCG in Italy. Ca' del Bosco is a fine producer of Franciacorta, one of the best sparkling wines in the world.

The umbrella DOCG of Valtellina Superiore refers to four red wines sourced from vineyards located on the steep banks of the Adda River: Inferno, Grumello, Sassella, and Valgella. These wines are made almost entirely from the Nebbiolo grape, here called Chiavennasca. A WineWise favorite is Grumello ($20 to $35) because it consistently delivers the pleasure of a complex mélange of both black and red fruits with balanced tannins. For a less-expensive, less-expansive taste of what these wines promise, you can start with a Rosso di Valtellina, a DOC wine that sells for about $15.

Some of the Best Wine Producers
Franciacorta DOCG: Bellavista, Berlucchi, Ca' del Bosco, Contado Castaldi, Cavalleri, and Monte Rossa

Valtellina Superiore (Inferno, Grumello, Sassella, and Valgella): Fay, Nino Negri, and Rainoldi

EMILIA-ROMAGNA
DOCG Wine Region
Albana di Romagna

Important DOC Wine Regions
Lambrusco di Sorbara, Lambrusco Grasparossa di Castelvetro, Lambrusco Salamino di Santa Croce, Sangiovese di Romagna

In the American market, Emilia-Romagna is widely represented by one wine, Lambrusco, made from a red grape of the same name. Lambrusco can be made as a white, rosé, or red wine, and is often *frizzante* (semisparkling). A small amount of fine dry Lambrusco is available in the American market, but you really have to search for it.

While wine snobs mock the simplicity and popularity of fizzy Lambrusco, the original screw cap wine, we have found few wines that are a better match for the famous foods of Emilia-Romagna: Prosciutto di Parma cured ham and Parmigiano Reggiano cheese. Try all three—the wine, the ham, and the cheese—with some good bread and see if you don't agree.

Albana di Romagna is a white DOCG wine, most often dry when sold in the United States. There is nothing special about this wine on the palate, but it is a reliable, medium-bodied, tasty sip. We much prefer Sangiovese di Romagna, a well-made, fruit-forward, medium-bodied red that is extremely food-friendly and extremely well priced—a true WineWise value.

Some of the Best Wine Producers

Albana di Romagna DOCG and Sangiovese di Romagna DOC: Castelluccio, Celli, Umberto Cesari, Dantello, Ferrucci, Gregorina, La Macolina, Paradiso, Poggio, Poggio Pollino, San Patrignano, Tre Monte, and La Zerbina

Widely available Lambrusco producers: Caprari, Cella, Giacobazzi, Grasparossa, Riunite, and Zonin

Sweet tooth? Lambrusco is the mainstay of Emilia-Romagna's wine industry. In the United States we see mostly sweeter Lambruscos. Riunite, the category's brand leader, is made in many different styles and is exported throughout the world. Most Lambrusco wines are inexpensive and fun to drink.

Northeast Italy

VENETO
DOCG Wine Regions
Bardolino Superiore, Recioto di Soave, Soave Superiore

Important DOC Wine Regions
Bardolino, Bianco di Custoza, Lison-Pramaggiore, Prosecco di Conegliano-Valdobbiadene, Prosecco di Valdobbiadene, Soave, Valdadige, Valpolicella/Recioto della Valpolicella (includes Amarone)

Veneto produces more classified (DOC and DOCG) wines than any other Italian wine region, but it is best known in the United States for the white wine Soave, the sparkling wine Prosecco, and the reds Bardolino, Valpolicella, and Amarone. These are all classic Veneto wines that are made largely from classic Italian grapes. Veneto also produces plenty of Pinot Grigio, as well as reds and whites based on French varietals, especially Merlot.

Soave is a refreshing, pretty, straightforward quaffing white; Soave Classico, for just a few bucks more, can be more complex and provocative. Prosecco is a widely available, charming, and simple sparkler that's highly affordable (often in the $7 to $12 range)—a refreshing drink before a meal, or fun when paired with light, simple foods.

Bardolino and Valpolicella are both made from the same grapes; Corvina is the dominant varietal. Both of these reds are some of our favorite "crossover" reds, equally at home with meat, fish, pasta, and pizza. Look for wines from the Classico districts.

Ironically, Italy's most powerful wine, Amarone, is made from grapes grown in the same vineyards as the light-to-medium-bodied Valpolicella. The difference is that Amarone is made from *passito* grapes dried in the sun and then indoors over the winter. The grapes shrivel, becoming virtual raisins, and the resulting dry red wine is above 15% alcohol. There is a sweet version (somewhat lower in alcohol, but still potent stuff) called Recioto della Valpolicella.

Also, look for the *ripasso* style of Valpolicella. In this style, Valpolicella juice is "re-passed" over the lees—the spent yeast cells—of Amarone and then fer-

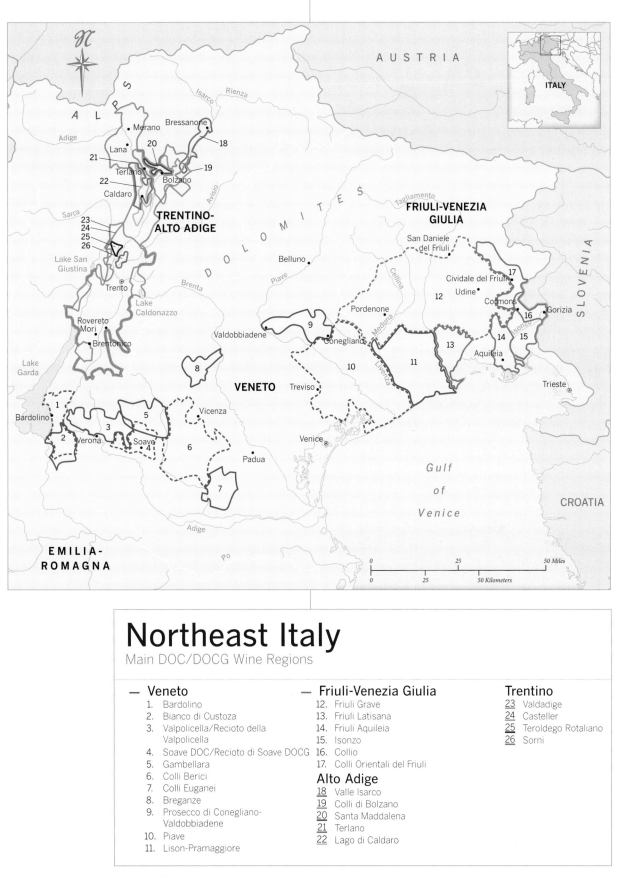

Northeast Italy
Main DOC/DOCG Wine Regions

— Veneto
1. Bardolino
2. Bianco di Custoza
3. Valpolicella/Recioto della Valpolicella
4. Soave DOC/Recioto di Soave DOCG
5. Gambellara
6. Colli Berici
7. Colli Euganei
8. Breganze
9. Prosecco di Conegliano-Valdobbiadene
10. Piave
11. Lison-Pramaggiore

— Friuli-Venezia Giulia
12. Friuli Grave
13. Friuli Latisana
14. Friuli Aquileia
15. Isonzo
16. Collio
17. Colli Orientali del Friuli

Alto Adige
18. Valle Isarco
19. Colli di Bolzano
20. Santa Maddalena
21. Terlano
22. Lago di Caldaro

Trentino
23. Valdadige
24. Casteller
25. Teroldego Rotaliano
26. Sorni

Northeast Italy.

Prosecco is a refreshing, fruity, sparkling wine, most often produced in a dry to semidry style, with moderate alcohol. It is wildly popular in the United States and makes a great aperitif before dinner, as well as a good partner with oysters, clams, and lighter seafood in general. Maschio dei Cavalieri produces an excellent Prosecco di Valdobbiadene (DOC).

Soave is the most popular Italian white wine in the U.S. market. Wines from the Soave Classico district tend to have a bit more depth, superiore versions a bit more alcohol. This is a Soave Classico Superiore from Bertani, a well-known producer in the Veneto region.

mented, creating a medium-to-full-bodied wine with luscious and complex flavors. The best known *ripasso* in the American market is the affordable Campofiorin, produced by Masi—a WineWise choice.

Some of the Best Wine Producers

Bardolino Superiore DOCG and Bardolino DOC: Bertani, Bolla, Boscaini, Guerrieri-Rizzardi, and Lamberti

Valpolicella and Valpolicella Classico DOC, Amarone and Amarone Classico DOC, and international varietals: Accordini, Aldegheri, Serego Alighieri, Allegrini, Aneri, Arano, Begali, Bertani, Bolla, Boscaini, Brigaldara, Brunelli, Castellani, Cesari, Domine Veneti, Fabiano, Masi, Musella, Nicolis, Quintarelli, Righetti, Rocollo Grassi, Le Salette, Tedeschi Tommasi, Trabucchi, Zenato, and Zonin

Soave Superiore DOCG, Soave DOC, and Recioto di Soave DOCG: Allegrini, Anselmi, Bertani, Bolla, La Cappuccina, Ca' Rugate, Gini, Graziano Pa, Fratelli Pasqua, Inama, Pieropan, Portinari, Pra, Santi, Sartori, and Zonin

Prosecco di Conegliano-Valdobbiadene DOC: Adami, Aneri, Bellenda, Canevel, Collalbrigio, Desiderio Bisol, Nino Franco, Maschio dei Cavalieri, Mionetto, Ruggeri, Santa Margherita, Valdo, Val d'Oca, and Zardetto

TRENTINO-ALTO ADIGE
Important DOC Wine Regions

Alto Adige, Teroldego Rotaliano, Trentino, Trento, Valdadige

This region borders Austria and Switzerland and combines two cultures: Alto Adige is officially bilingual (Italian and German). In fact, Italy's official alternate name for Alto Adige is Sudtirol. There is a real divide in the styles of many of the wines produced here as well. The entire region is, however, known for producing Italy's finest examples of Pinot Grigio.

Unlike the watery or merely serviceable wines that have flooded the American markets, fine Pinot Grigio from Alto Adige is sublime: a medium-bodied wine with a nose of tropical fruits wrapped in cashews and hazelnuts and a refreshing, mouth-watering flavor that is not at all simple, but lively and complex.

Alto Adige has made its reputation in the United States on Pinot Grigio, as well as whites and reds made mostly from popular market-driven varietals. Raise the bar for Pinot Grigio by tasting a great one from Alto Adige. Trentino (the traditionally Italian sector of this multicultural region) is best known for its excellent *metodo tradizionale* sparkling wines, as well as Teroldego Rotaliano, a wine that can be made as a rosé, as a light, accessible red, or as a full-bodied, hearty, ageworthy red.

Some of the Best Wine Producers

Alto Adige (Sudtirol) DOC and Valdadige DOC: Kettmeir, Lageder, Santa Magdalena, Santa Margherita, Tiefenbrunner, and Tolloy

Trentino DOC, Trento DOC, and Teroldego Rotaliano DOC: Cavit, Concilio, Ferrari, Foradori, Rotari, Pojer e Sandri, San Leonardo, La Vis, and Zeni

A single-vineyard Valpolicella Classico Superiore (DOC) from Veneto. Valpolicella is one of our favorite light-to-medium-bodied reds, easy-drinking, food-friendly, and affordable.

It seems as though Pinot Grigio—from Italy and other countries—is everywhere. One of the best examples of a fine Italian Pinot Grigio is this Alois Lageder "Benefizium Porer," a single-vineyard bottling from a leading quality-minded producer in the Alto Adige region.

By the time you read this label, the name of this Italian grape will have officially changed to simply Friulano. No matter—Marco Felluga and other high-quality producers in Friuli-Venezia Giulia will continue to make great white wines from this grape.

FRIULI–VENEZIA GIULIA
DOCG Wine Region
Collio Orientali del Friuli Picolit, Ramondolo

Important DOC Wine Regions
Colli Orientali del Friuli, Collio, Friuli Grave, Lison-Pramaggiore

Commonly called simply Friuli, this region borders Austria and Slovenia, and its wines, especially its whites, display that influence. Since the 1970s, when Friuli began to embrace low yields in its vineyards and high-tech methods for its wine production, the region's reputation for clean, delicious, food-friendly, varietally correct wine began to spread.

With the exception of its obscure DOCG sweet white, Ramondolo, which very few Americans (and even Italians) have tasted, international varietals rule in Friuli, especially Pinot Grigio, Pinot Bianco, Riesling, Chardonnay, and Merlot among reds. A fine medium-to-full-bodied white made from the native varietal Tocai Friulano (the name of which was recently changed to simply Friulano) has a healthy presence in the American market, as does the native red varietal wine, Refosco. The classic wine made from the Refosco grape is Refosco dal Peduncolo Rosso, a full-bodied, fruit-driven, violet-red wine, with flavors of damson plums and moderate tannins that create a pleasant, slightly bitter aftertaste, something akin to a hint of anise or black licorice. Refosco can easily age for five years. As it ages, its bouquet develops and features violets and dried fruits in the nose.

Today, Friulian whites and reds are major players in the international market. Prices vary, with some true values still available from larger producers, along with quite a few expensive artisan wines.

Some of the Best Wine Producers
Antonutti, Bastianich, Bollini, Borgo San Daniele, Castelvecchio, Colluta Friuli, Livio Felluga, Marco Felluga, Eno Friulia, Jermann, Lis Neris, Livon, Luisa, Luna di Luna, Pighin, Plozner, Rocca Bernarda, Ronchi di Manzano, Russiz Superiore, Mario Schiopetto, Tere di Ger, Vie di Romans, Villa Russiz, and Zamo

Southern Italy and islands

CAMPANIA

DOCG Wine Regions

Fiano di Avellino, Greco di Tufo, Taurasi

Campania, with a population of about six million people and famous for Mount Vesuvius and the cities of Pompeii and Naples (home to the best pizza in the world), produces only about 3% of Italy's wines, but what beautiful wines they are. Taurasi, the first red DOCG wine in southern Italy, made from the Aglianico grape, is sometimes known as the "Barolo of the South" for its power and complexity (and perhaps for its high price). The only two white DOCGs, Greco di Tufo and Fiano di Avellino, are full-bodied white wines with moderate acidity levels. Both wines marry well with fish stews, shellfish, and white meats, and are moderately expensive. Also look for varietal-labeled Falanghina, a wonderfully refreshing and mineral-driven medium-bodied white that is quite reasonably priced.

Some of the Best Wine Producers

Caggiano, De Lucia, Feudi di San Gregorio, Mastroberardino, Mustilli, Ocone, Terredora, Villa Matilde, and Villa San Michele

PUGLIA

Important DOC Wine Regions

Primitivo di Manduria, Salice Salentino

Another southern region that not long ago was known as Italy's largest producer of bulk, characterless wine, Puglia is going through a sea change in the way it thinks about and produces wine for the international market. Puglia's two best-known DOC reds are Salice Salentino and Primitivo di Manduria, the former made mostly from Negroamaro grapes, the latter from 100% Primitivo (Zinfandel). But Puglia produces not only medium-to-full-bodied red wines from Italian varietals grown in the red clay soils of the region but also whites made from Chardonnay, Sauvignon Blanc, and other international varietals.

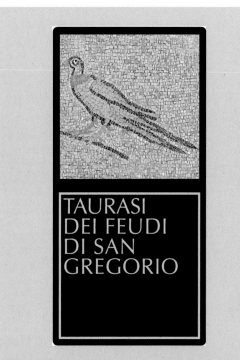

Taurasi (DOCG) is a full-bodied, ageworthy powerhouse that needs assertive foods such as roasts and stews. Feudi di San Gregorio produces excellent wines in the Campania region of Italy.

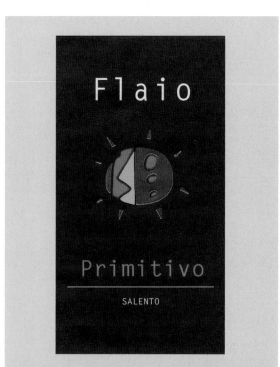

Primitivo is what Italian winemakers call Zinfandel. That's right: it's Zin. Primitivo is an important grape in Puglia, and wines such as this bottling by Flaio give Zinfandel lovers another wine to admire.

Southern Italy

Main DOC/DOCG Wine Regions

Campania
— Falerno del Massico
— Solopaca
— Greco di Tufo
— Taurasi DOCG
— Fiano di Avellino
— Ischia
— Capri

Puglia
— Aleatico di Puglia DOC (covers all DOC zones in the region)
— San Severo
— Moscato di Trani
— Castel del Monte
— Locorotondo
— Primitivo di Manduria

Basilicata
— Aglianico del Vulture

Calabria
— Cirò
— Donnici
— Savuto

Sicily
— Faro
— Etna
— Moscato di Siracusa
— Moscato di Noto
— Cerasuolo di Vittoria
— Alcamo
— Marsala
— Malvasia delle Lipari
— Moscato di Pantelleria and Passito di Pantelleria

Sardinia
— Vermentino di Gallura DOCG
— Moscato di Sorso-Sennori
— Oliena
1 Malvasia di Bosa
2 Vernaccia di Oristano
3 Arborea
— Mandrolisai
4 Campidano di Terralba
— Nuragus di Cagliari
5 Giro di Cagliari
5 Malvasia di Cagliari
5 Monica di Cagliari
5 Moscato di Cagliari
5 Nasco di Cagliari
— Carignano del Sulcis

Southern Italy.

Almost all of Puglia's export wines offer tremendous value and quality.

The appeal of Puglia has not been lost on Italian wine producers from other, more famous wine regions. Several have purchased large tracts of vineyard land and have built wineries in Puglia. The best known among these migrating winemakers is Piero Antinori, possibly the most famous wine producer in Tuscany, if not all of Italy.

Some of the Best Wine Producers

A Mano, Bortomagno, Candido, Cantele, Cantine Due Palme, Felline, Flaio, Leone de Castris, Li Veli, Masseria Pepe, Mocavero, Monaci, Pervini, La Pusara, Rivera, Rosa del Golfo, Salento, Sinfarosa, Cosimo Taurino, Vallone, and Vigneti del Sud/Antinori

BASILICATA
Important DOC Wine Region
Aglianico del Vulture

Basilicata, a region that produces only 1% of Italy's wine, is known in the United States solely for one wine made solely from one grape, produced solely in one DOC zone. That wine is Aglianico del Vulture, grown on the steep slopes of Monte Vulture. A full-flavored, deeply colored, often ageworthy red, this earthy wine can be a powerhouse, but it's always food-friendly with hearty dishes. Many producers currently offer American wine consumers great value, because the wine is not yet widely appreciated in the American market. Aglianico del Vulture, which is often priced under $15, is a true WineWise choice.

Some of the Best Wine Producers

Ars Poetica, Basilim, Cantina di Palma, Cantina di Venosa, Cantine Sasso, Consorzio Viticoltori del Vulture, d'Angelo, Eubea, Manfredi, Paternoster, Le Querce, Rosa del Golfo

SARDINIA
DOCG Wine Region
Vermentino di Gallura

Important DOC Wine Regions
Cannonau di Sardegna, Vermentino di Sardegna

Sardinia, an island of about one million inhabitants, lies about 150 miles/241 kilometers from mainland Italy. Over the last ten years, American wine consumers have begun to enjoy some very fine wines from Sardinia. Sardinia's most highly regarded white wine is Vermentino di Gallura, a dry wine from the far north that is the perfect accompaniment to the local *pesce alla griglia*, grilled fish in olive oil with fresh herbs. Vermentino di Sardegna is just a bit less expensive and easier to find.

Earthy, fruit-driven, full-bodied Sardinian red wines often feature the Cannonau (Grenache) grape. Cannonau di Sardegna and other Cannonau-based reds, sometimes blended with about 15% to 20% Merlot or Cabernet Sauvignon, are now widely available in the United States. These are great wines to enjoy with pasta, pizza, and meat-based dishes.

With steady improvement in whites and reds for the export market, Sardinia, previously a place for unexciting and predictable wines, is now on the wine world's map as a region to watch for quality and for excellent value.

Some of the Best Wine Producers

Argiolas, Cantine Sociale del Vermentino, Cantine Sociale Gallura, Cantine Sociale Santadi, Capichera, Contini, Gabbas, Mancini, Meloni, and Sella e Mosca

Cannonau is the Italian name for the Grenache grape, and the best producers in Sardinia, such as Sella e Mosca, are working wonders with this varietal to make truly exciting and delicious reds.

Planeta, run by a brother-sister team in Sicily, makes some of the island's best wines, both from traditional grapes and international varietals. Planeta's full-bodied red Cerasuolo di Vittoria (DOCG) is a blend of Nero d'Avola and Frappato.

Donnafugata is an excellent Sicilian producer. Its "Anthili" is a refreshing white, a 50/50 blend of Ansonica and Catarratto grapes that's great with fish and other seafood.

SICILY
DOCG Wine Region
Cerasuolo di Vittoria

Important DOC Wine Regions
Etna, Faro, Malvasia delle Lipari, Marsala

Sicily is the largest producer of wine in Italy and still produces a river of indifferent wine for local and regional consumption, but it is also one of the country's most exciting wine regions. This apparent contradiction resolves itself when we taste fine examples made from Sicily's own grape varietals—Nero d'Avola, Frappato, Nerello Mascalese, Catarratto, Inzolia, and Grillo, among many others—as well as fine examples of wines made from popular international varietals, especially Chardonnay, Cabernet Sauvignon, and Merlot. Some of the most interesting wines are produced from blends of traditional grapes, or from blends of those traditional varietals with the international grape varieties.

The reds of Sicily are rustic: earthy, full-bodied, and excellent when paired with red meats and hearty pasta dishes. Sicily's best whites are usually medium-bodied and display a distinctive seaside minerality that makes for an attractive match with fish stews and many other soulful seafood dishes. The region is famous for its fortified wine, Marsala, available in a wide range of styles. Sicily's best Marsalas can be hard to find in the U.S. export market.

Nero d'Avola from Sicily has become popular in the U.S. market, and it's easy to see why. A big, earthy, inky, food-friendly red that reflects the sunshine of Sicily in its ripe flavors, Nero d'Avola is a perfect match for hearty dishes such as rich stews.

Lately, we've also seen quite a bit of Inzolia, a white varietal from Sicily, in the American market. The best Inzolia wines have a fresh, fruit-driven flavor, with a subtle finish of hazelnuts. If we've piqued your interest, ask a knowledgeable wine merchant or sommelier to help you find a delicious Inzolia wine. The easiest one to find is a reasonably priced white produced by Corvo, and it's a good introduction to Inzolia. We love Inzolia-based wines with a wide variety of seafood.

Sicily's best wines are moderately expensive to very expensive, but there are many values to be had in both good whites and reds.

Some of the Best Wine Producers
Alvis-Rallo, Benanti, Colosi, Corvo/Duca di Salaparuta, COS, de Bertoli, Donnafugata, Fazio, Firriato Paceco, Florio, Hauner, Melia, Miceli, Palari, Pellegrino, Planeta, Settesoli, Spadafora, Tasca d'Almerita, and Torrevecchia

chapter 10

Olé
Spain

You've got no Wine Mojo if you're not drinking Spanish wines. Spain's winemakers are creating exciting wines from historically established vineyards and pioneering new areas. *WineWise* readers can savor sophisticated traditional Spanish wines or roll the dice and go off the time-honored track. If your budget is $5, $20, or $300 there is a Spanish wine that will delight you.

Sparkling Cava, fortified Sherries, and crisp dry white and rosé wines are often bargain priced and always food friendly. Both easy sipping and substantial reds are irresistible. Tempranillo and Garnacha are the nation's premier red grapes, but today they may be blended with international varieties such as Cabernet Sauvignon or Syrah, or bottled on their own.

In this chapter we will also provide WineWise readers with some of our favorite food pairings for the fresh young wines as well as the stately aged red Reserva and Gran Reserva wines of Spain.

We are fascinated by Spanish wines and are happy to share our excitement with *WineWise* readers. Try the wines of Spain and see if you don't catch the fever!

The success story of Spanish wines

FROM THE revolutionary culinary concepts of Chef Ferran Adria to the films of Pedro Almodovar and the architectural influence of Antoni Gaudí, all things Spanish have penetrated American culture. Spanish wines are no exception.

They seem to be everywhere, and in such volume that Spain is poised to take over the number three spot in amount of wine imported to the United States, behind Italy and France. We have done our fair share to contribute to this phenomenon, and we hope you will join us. Our refrigerators are always stocked with at least one bottle of Cava sparkling wine and a Spanish white as well. An inexpensive Spanish red is always close to our kitchens, and when we dine out, the reds are often a good choice, because of their reasonable prices and their affinity with the foods we are ordering. How did Spanish wine producers succeed in making Spanish wine a part of our everyday life?

Until the 1970s, most Spanish wineries—with the exception of those in the highly acclaimed Rioja region (see page 219)—made large quantities of rough and ready, inexpensive reds. An expanding Spanish middle class and Spain's subsequent entry into the European Union brought a more sophisticated approach to wine, and today wineries throughout the country are focused on making and exporting quality wines. Spaniards enjoy fine wine and food in restaurants and cafés, and as in many other nations, they are also choosing quality wines over quantity.

Spain has more acres of vineyards than any other nation in the world but ranks third in wine production after France and Italy. Why? First, many of the vineyards are dedicated to growing table grapes or grapes to make brandy. Second, yields in the finest vineyards are kept low to concentrate flavors in the grapes and in the finished wines.

Clearly, this country is home to some very hot regions that produce big, concentrated wines with lots of ripe fruit and a high alcohol content. Thoughts of Spain conjure up images of proud bullfighters in a hot, dusty arena, or exotic flamenco dancers on warm, sultry evenings. But Spain is not just about sun and heat. There are plenty of cooler locations at higher elevations and in coastal regions and river valleys, and they are turning out gorgeous wines with balanced acidity and without an overabundance of alcohol.

It is this attention to quality that is allowing Spanish winemakers to quietly build a reputation as producers of world-class wines, yet their relative anonymity is good news for *WineWise* readers. With a selection that includes refreshing bubblies and whites, bone-dry rosés, a range of reds, and fortified Sherries, this nation has a wine to suit every preference, occasion, and budget. Spanish wines are particularly enticing for two reasons:

- **Value.** Spanish wines offer some of the best quality for the price anywhere in the world. Most Spanish table wines are bargain priced (less than $10 a bottle for simple, fruity, everyday wines) to moderately priced (with many of the more complex versions under $35); more expensive wines are available for special occasions.

- **Quality.** Spain is home to many delicious, distinctive wines from both traditional and revolutionary winemakers who emphasize quality over quantity. More important to us than any label jargon is the integrity of the folks who make the wine, and so our most valuable (and oft-repeated) advice to *WineWise* readers is to buy wine based on the integrity of the producer. The best wineries will offer good wines at fair prices.

The grapes of Spain

SPANISH WINES incorporate many now-familiar international grapes, whose presence can be explained by simple geography. With one look at Spain's neighbor to the northeast, France, you'll understand the abundance of predominantly French varietals: Cabernet Sauvignon, Merlot, Syrah, Chardonnay, and Sauvignon Blanc are all represented in Spain. Its neighbor to the west, Portugal, is home to some of the same grape varieties as Spain, although they may have a slightly different spelling. For example, Spain's finest white grape, the Albarino, is known as Alvarinho in Portugal. The finest red grape, the Tempranillo, is known as Tinta Roriz in Portugal. The most celebrated wines of Spain are either single-variety versions or blends made from indigenous grapes. While some nations can claim dozens of important grape varieties, there are only a half dozen major Spanish types to learn about. Of course, where they are grown and how they are made can make a world of difference in the wines they produce.

Red grapes

The three most important red grapes are Tempranillo, Garnacha, and Monastrell.

TEMPRANILLO

Tempranillo is Spain's most famous and most planted red grape. *WineWise* readers can find simple fruit-forward Tempranillo-based wines at bargain prices or opt for the more complex wines at moderate to expensive prices. This thick-skinned, black-colored grape displays an array of flavors including red cherry, blackberry, licorice, and spices. It produces wines relatively low in alcohol (10.5% to 13%) and acidity. It also ages well, especially when blended with Garnacha, Graciano, and Mazuelo (see below) in the Rioja region. Some of the finest expressions of this grape come from wines produced in the Ribera del Duero region.

GARNACHA

Also known as Grenache in other countries, this is the second most widely planted red grape in Spain and one of the most planted in the world. Garnacha's popularity may be partially explained by its ability to ripen well in warm climates. Another reason is that Garnacha produces so many different styles of wine. It is our "jack in the box" grape, popping out of the bottle to say surprise! We have tasted semidry, light-bodied Grenache, as well as dry, full-bodied versions; both displayed the grape's characteristic strawberry and raspberry flavors. Delicious dry rosé wines are made with this grape in Spain as well. But what really turns us on are the old inky, "stinky" (in a nice earthy, leathery kind of way) Garnachas that are dark in

color and full in body. Some of the finest examples are made from vines that are more than forty years old. Some Garnacha-based wines are made for simple quaffing, while others are destined for greatness. For a heady example of all that Garnacha can be, look to the stellar reds of the Priorato region.

MONASTRELL

Known as Mourvedre in other countries, Monastrell is Spain's third most widely planted red grape. On its own, this grape produces medium-to-full-bodied wines with black fruit flavors. It also contributes high levels of alcohol, deep color, and good aging potential to blended wines. If you want more bang for your buck, seek out Spanish Monastrells from regions such as Jumilla.

Other red grapes native to Spain that you will encounter in the coming pages include:

- **Graciano:** Strictly a blending grape, Graciano makes wines that are low in alcohol. It provides acidity (freshness) and spicy aromas to the finished wine.

- **Mazuelo or Carinena (also known as Carignan in other countries):** Another blending grape particularly prominent in Rioja, Mazuelo bumps up the wine's color and tannins.

White grapes

ALBARINO

Spain's most important white varietal, this grape produces medium-to-full-bodied wines with complex aromas and flavors such as peach, citrus, cinnamon, and melon. Albarino wines from Spain's Rias Baixas wine region are delicious, especially with seafood.

MACABEO

Also known as Viura, this grape produces light, fruity wines with subtle floral aromas and flavors. Whether on its own or blended, Macabeo is the grape used in more than 90% of Rioja's white wines. Macabeo is a key component in sparkling Cava (see page 222), along with Parellada and Xarel-lo.

PARELLADA

Produces wines with floral and citrusy aromas and flavors that are high in acidity and low in alcohol.

VERDEJO

This high-acid grape displays aromas of apricots, citrus, melon, pears, and flowers. Verdejo wines from the Rueda wine region are exciting and affordable.

XAREL-LO

Produces wines with earthy and citrus aromas and flavors; gives richness to the Cava blends.

The language of the label

AS IN MOST European nations, the table wines of Spain may be sold by place name (e.g. Rioja), by varietal (e.g. Albarino), or by a fantasy name (e.g. Gran Vina Sol—"great wine of the sun").

The origin of the wine

Spanish wines are labeled according to government-controlled designations of origin. Listed in order of increasing quality, the designations are:

- *Vino de mesa* (table wine): These basic table wines are often blends of various grapes and regions. Most are inexpensive and consumed in Spain.

- *Vino de la tierra* (wine of the land): These wines express the character of a particular district. Both inexpensive and expensive wines are made in this category.

- *Vinos de calidad con indicacion geografica:* Quality wines with an indicated geographical area. After five years, these wines may be promoted to DO status (see below).

- *Denominacion de origen* (DO) (denomination of origin): The equivalent of the French AOC and Italian DOC, this designation covers about

Albarino by Morgadio is an example of a varietal-labeled wine.

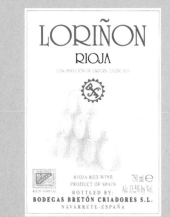

Rioja, Lorinon by Bodegas (winery) Breton is an example of a wine labeled by place name.

Dehesa la Granja, a Tempranillo-based red wine produced by Alejandro Fernandez is an example of a fine wine from an unclassified area.

sixty wine-producing regions. Penedes, Rias Baixas, and Ribera del Duero are examples of DOs whose name will appear on a label.

- *Denominacion de origen calificada* (DOC) (qualified denomination of origin): Similar to Italy's DOCG designation, this is reserved for truly superior wine regions. So far, the only DOCs are Rioja and Priorato.

The age of the wine

Spanish label terms are also based on aging the wine in barrel and in bottle. The benefit of aging is two-fold. Most importantly, the harsh tannins that may be present in a young wine diminish over time, so the wine develops a silky texture. In addition, aged wines develop more complex aromas; one can usually detect notes of earth, spice, or even vegetable alongside the primary fruit or floral aromas.

Terms you may find on the labels of DO and DOC wines to indicate age include:

- *Crianza:* Indicates a wine that is aged for a minimum of two years, including at least six months in small oak casks for most regions. Rioja, Ribera del Duero, and Navarra wines must have a minimum of a year in oak.

- *Reserva:* Red wines aged at least three years, including one year in barrel; producers of the finest reds will always exceed the minimum aging requirements. White *reserva* wines, aged at least two years, are rare.

- *Gran reserva:* Made only in exceptional vintages, gran reserva reds are aged at least five years (two years of these in barrel), although the finest wines may not appear on the market for eight to ten years. White *gran reserva* wines are rare and must be aged a minimum of four years.

Other label terms you might find

- *Cosecha:* Vintage wine. At least 85% of the wine is made from grapes harvested in the stated vintage. The unoaked *joven* (young) wine is, as the name implies, sold immediately and not aged in the bottle.

- *Roble:* Wines with just a kiss of oak and less age than a *crianza*.

- *Pago:* The *pago* designation for a single estate wine began in 2003. Wineries must apply to be allowed to use the *pago* designation.

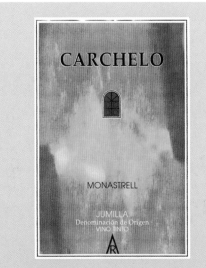

The Jumilla DO is one of our "off the beaten path" choices for great-value red wines.

Red *gran reserva* wines develop complex flavors from aging in the barrel and the bottle. Alejandro Fernandez produces a "Janus" Gran Reserva version of his Pesquera wine only in great vintages.

Once approved, a winery employing the *pago* designation can use whatever grape varieties they choose to grow on their estate. The *pago* wine must be fermented and aged at the estate. The wines may be released young or aged; it is entirely up to the estate making the wine. The jury is still out on how much impact the *pago* classification will have.

- Many *bodegas* (wineries) label each of their wines with different proprietary names to differentiate their styles. For example, La Rioja Alta winery (in—you guessed it—the Rioja region) offers a *crianza* called "Vina Alberdi," while its *reservas* are named "Vina Ardanza" and "Vina Arana." Its *gran reservas* are labeled "904" and "890."

Spanish wines: What's hot now

WHAT IS NEW AND HOT in the world of Spanish wines? On the white front, most winemakers have replaced their heavy, golden-colored whites with appealing, modern, lighter versions. Crisp, dry white wines produced in the Rias Baixas, Rueda, Ribeiro, and Chacoli wine regions have been embraced by American sommeliers and consumers alike. The wines are fresh and fruity, with a zingy acidity that pairs easily with a wide variety of foods. Spanish whites also tend to be lighter in texture and lower in alcohol than most New World Chardonnays, so they complement food rather than compete with it. In addition, most are inexpensive (under $15) to moderately priced (under $30).

Spain—most notably the region of Penedes—is also known for its inexpensive sparkling wines, or Cavas. Made using the quality-driven Champagne method (*methode champenoise*), Cavas are ideal for casual sipping, Sunday brunch, or even a day at the beach. New vineyards of Chardonnay and Pinot Noir are being planted alongside the indigenous Macabeo, Parellada, and Xarel-lo grapes to make Cava wines. Since the finest Champagnes in the world are based on Chardonnay and Pinot Noir, the potential for Cava producers to make even more elegant wines in the future is great.

Spanish whites and Cavas are pleasant partners to food or fine to savor on their own. But the inspiration for poets, musicians, and other romantics are the nation's reds, which are increasingly regarded as some of the most interesting and delicious in the world. Our survey of Spanish reds includes wines that range from the simple to the inspirational, from the bargain-priced to the very expensive. And while most whites and Cavas should be drunk within three years of their harvest, the best reds continue to improve over one or two decades.

Two regions producing some of Spain's hottest, most sought-after reds are Rioja—the nation's oldest recognized wine region—and the newer Ribera del Duero, located in the province of Castilla y Leon. The esteemed Tempranillo grape is the dominant varietal in both regions. The wines of Rioja are most often Tempranillo-dominated blends of indigenous grapes, while Ribera del Duero reds tend to be pure Tempranillo or blends with international grapes, such as Cabernet Sauvignon and Merlot. Simple red wines from Rioja or Ribera del Duero retail for about $10, with many fine wines priced under $25, but some of the extraordinary wines command prices from $50 to $400. Ouch! Talk about hot!

Perhaps slightly less well known (though not for long), Bierzo and Priorato are setting trends of their own. These wine regions have garnered international acclaim by resurrecting old vineyards and planting new vines in the best locations, producing some of Spain's most sensuous (and sometimes most expensive) reds. Their success has encouraged grape growers and winemakers throughout the nation to coax the best quality from their vineyards.

Today many newcomers are issuing challenges to the supremacy of Spain's most celebrated wine regions. Many hot new red wines creating a buzz are from the lesser-known areas of Toro, Calatayud, Campo de Borja, and Jumilla; their non-star status is reflected in their bargain to moderate prices, at least for now. Remember, some of the best values are open to WineWise adventurers who experiment with lesser-known grape varieties or venture to regions off the beaten path.

The major wine regions of Spain

AS THEY SAY IN REAL ESTATE, it's all about location. Spain is divided into a number of provinces; specific DO (or DOC) areas fall under the umbrella of each province. In the following pages, we will explore the better-known wine-producing DOs and DOCs, some notable up-and-comers, and good-value *vino de la tierra* country wines. *Salud!*

Northern Spain

PROVINCE OF LA RIOJA
DOC Region
Rioja

Rioja has the distinction of being Spain's oldest and most important fine-wine-producing region. Tempranillo is the star varietal here, and a typical red Rioja contains about 60% to 80% of that grape. Garnacha, Graciano, and Mazuelo complete the blend, producing wines that are truly unique and ageworthy. Some winemakers are now going beyond the native grapes, adding such international varietals as Cabernet Sauvignon and Merlot.

A "new wave" movement in Rioja is to craft very lush wines with a lot of new oak influence. These wines, which tend to be labeled with proprietary names, can be very exciting and delicious, but be warned: some new wave producers charge exorbitant prices—well over $100 or even $200 a bottle. On a daily basis, we prefer the bargain- to inexpensively priced Rioja wines.

Color is often an indicator of style as well as age, and this especially holds true for the wines of Rioja. Young reds tend to be a red cherry color and display black cherry and spice notes. Aged wines become a reddish brown and take on more complex aromas and flavors of earth, spice, leather, and mushroom.

Clearly the red wines of Rioja garner the most attention, and with good reason. Yet the region's dry whites and rosés are beginning to see an increase in popularity, mostly due to their accessibility: the wines are fresh, fruity, floral, and inexpensive. White Riojas shine as an aperitif or as an accompaniment to such *tapas* (little plates) as cold octopus salad, chickpea salad, or fresh sardines. Today most of the region's whites are made in a lighter style without oak. But lovers of oaky Chardonnays can still find some barrel-fermented versions, such as the superb example made by Muga for about $16.

The dry rosé wines of Rioja have undergone a similar makeover. They are dry, light-to-medium-bodied wines with strawberry and red cherry flavors and a bright, refreshing acidity. Marques de Caceres and Muga are two producers we suggest for bargain-priced rosés.

Riojas are wonderful food wines. The finest reds are best paired with simple dishes that do not compete with their complex flavors, such as a wild mushroom risotto or grilled lamb chops. Their less expensive counterparts allow you more leeway to experiment with ethnic foods, such as lamb kebabs or a gyro sandwich. Try one of the region's whites with fish tacos. Finally, the rosés shine when paired with a ham and Swiss or pastrami sandwich; they are also ideal partners for the local *lomo* (cured ham loin) or a spicy seafood gumbo.

We hope we've piqued your curiosity about this historical and much lauded region and that you're excited to see what all the fuss is about. Where should you start?

Some of the Best Wine Producers

Alma de Tobia, Artadi, Baron de Ley, Bilbainas, Ramon Bilbao, Bodegas Breton, Campillo, Castillo Labistada, Conde de Valdemar, Contino, CVNE, El Coto, Criadores, Faustino, Hacienda de Susar, Izadi, La Rioja Alta, Lan, Marques de Arienzo, Marques de Caceres, Marques de Grinon, Marques de Murrieta, Marques de Riscal, Martinez Bujanda, Montecillo, Muga, Palacio Remondo, Rafael Lopez de Heredia, Remelluri, Remirez de Ganuza, Senorio de San Vicente, Valenciso, and Vina Real

There are many other reputable Rioja producers to seek out; this is a mere fraction of that list. Young white, rosé, and red Riojas are bargain ($7.50) to inexpensively ($12) priced. *Crianzas* sell for $10 to

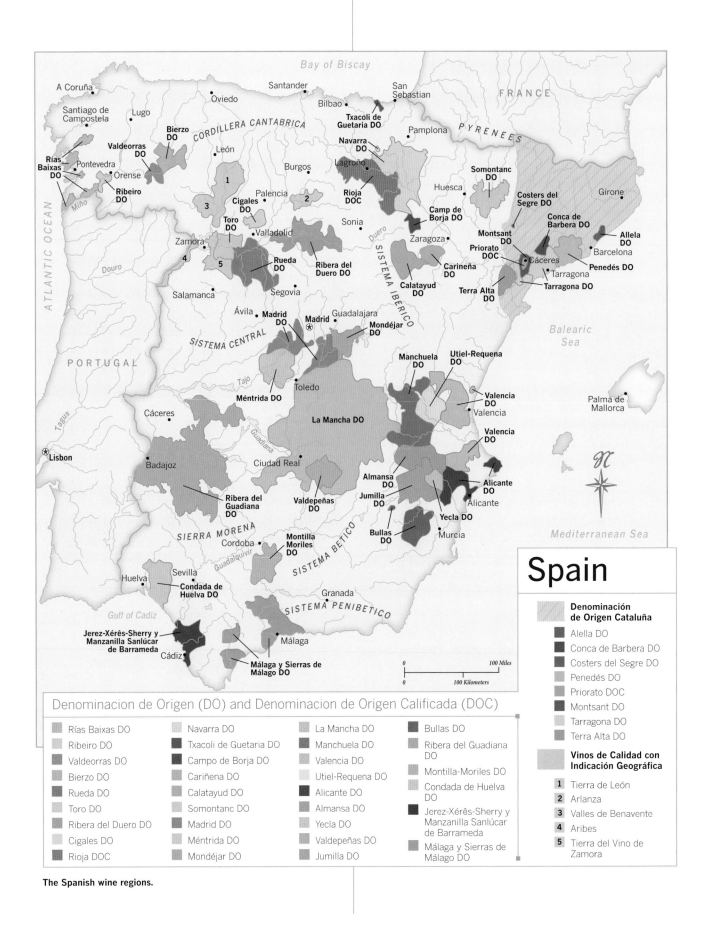

The Spanish wine regions.

Spain

Denominación de Origen Cataluña

- Alella DO
- Conca de Barbera DO
- Costers del Segre DO
- Penedés DO
- Priorato DOC
- Montsant DO
- Tarragona DO
- Terra Alta DO

Vinos de Calidad con Indicación Geográfica

1. Tierra de León
2. Arlanza
3. Valles de Benavente
4. Aribes
5. Tierra del Vino de Zamora

Denominacion de Origen (DO) and Denominacion de Origen Calificada (DOC)

- Rías Baixas DO
- Ribeiro DO
- Valdeorras DO
- Bierzo DO
- Rueda DO
- Toro DO
- Ribera del Duero DO
- Cigales DO
- Rioja DOC
- Navarra DO
- Txacoli de Guetaria DO
- Campo de Borja DO
- Cariñena DO
- Calatayud DO
- Somontanc DO
- Madrid DO
- Méntrida DO
- Mondéjar DO
- La Mancha DO
- Manchuela DO
- Valencia DO
- Utiel-Requena DO
- Alicante DO
- Almansa DO
- Yecla DO
- Valdepeñas DO
- Jumilla DO
- Bullas DO
- Ribera del Guadiana DO
- Montilla-Moriles DO
- Condada de Huelva DO
- Jerez-Xérês-Sherry y Manzanilla Sanlúcar de Barrameda
- Málaga y Sierras de Málago DO

$18, *reservas* for $15 to $26, and *gran reserva*, *pago*, and other proprietary top wines start at $25 and go up to $200.

PROVINCE OF CATALONIA
DOC Region
Priorato

Important DO Regions
Penedes, Monsant (other DOs include Terra Alta, Tarragona, Conca de Barbera, Costers del Segre, and Ampurdan–Costa Brava for dry wines and Alella for sweet wines)

Located in the northeast corner of Spain and including the city of Barcelona, this province is famous for artist Salvador Dalí, architectural genius Antoni Gaudí, musical inspiration Pablo Casals, and many celebrated chefs. The artistic temperament and creativity of the Catalans have resulted in fine food and wine that can rival those of any wine region in the world.

Together with the DOC region of Priorato, the eight DO regions produce everything from simple quaffing table wines and sparklers to some of the most expensive and sublime wines in the world. You may be able to source some good-value wines from the lesser-known DOs, but they may be hard to find.

So, we will focus mostly on the two most important regions of Penedes and Priorato, both well represented in the American market, in the coming pages.

Penedes. Penedes is home to many fine table wines as well as the majority of sparkling Cavas (see sidebar next page). The region's whites are pale, green and fairly low in alcohol with an apple-skin bouquet. The featured local white grapes, used to produce both table wines and sparklers, are Macabeo (also known as Viura in the Rioja region), Parellada, and Xarel-lo. French and German varietals also pop up here: Chardonnay, Gewurztraminer, Riesling, Sauvignon Blanc, and Muscat may be used on their own or in blends.

Penedes reds may be blended with international varieties, and they take well to oak aging.

The Torres family was instrumental in bringing modern grape growing and winemaking methods as well as the use of creative labels to the area. Their skillful use of both indigenous grapes such as Tempranillo and international varietals such as Cabernet Sauvignon helped to put Catalonian wines on restaurant lists and at tables all over the world. We applaud their inclusion of helpful information on the back label, such as the percentage of each grape used, where the grapes were grown, how the wine was made, how long

Spain's Tempranillo grape is blended with some Cabernet Sauvignon in the medium-bodied Coronas wine from Torres. This is consistently one of our best-value red wines from Spain.

Cava

Just as the word "Champagne" refers to the method used to make the wine, the grape types permitted, and the location of the vineyards, so "Cava" indicates the traditional Champagne method (*methode champenoise*), and the grape types used

Over 90% of all Cava comes from the Penedes region, although it may also be produced in other provinces. The majority of white Cava is made from the local white grapes Macabeo, Parellada, and Xarel-lo; flavors of Cava wines include citrus, apple, and toasted bread. Dry rosé Cavas have strawberry and raspberry flavors and are more full-bodied than white Cavas. As in Champagne, some fine Cavas are vintage-dated, but most are not.

Like those of its Champagne cousins, Cava labels will display the level of dryness. From driest to sweetest, Cava will be labeled in the U.S. market as extra brut, brut, extra dry, seco, semiseco, semidulce, or dulce, although most imported here are brut or extra dry. Serve extra brut, brut, and extra dry with savory foods. The sweeter wines are best with fruits and desserts.

Cava labels will also bear the term *reserva* or *gran reserva* to indicate more age and complexity. *Reservas* must be aged at least eighteen months before release; *gran reservas* are aged two years. The extra aging adds earthy flavors, such as mushrooms, to the fruit flavors of the wine. Aficionados of bubbly who find themselves in Spain should check out Barcelona's Cavateria restaurants, where many wines are available by the glass.

With prices starting under $10 a bottle, Cava is undoubtedly one of the wine world's greatest bargains. It may be served on its own or in cocktails such as the mimosa (sparkling wine with orange juice). The Cavas of the two largest wineries, Codorniu and Freixenet, are widely distributed in America. We also recommend the moderately priced Cavas made by some artisan producers.

Producers and their wines we recommend include Pares Balta, Castellblanch, Castell Roig, Cavas Domecq, Cavas Hill, Cavas Masachs, Paul Cheneau, Codorniu, Cristalino, Heretat Tinell, Ferret i Mateu, Freixenet, Gramona, Juve y Camps, Llopart, Mont Ferrant, Mont Marcal, Montsarra, Naveran, Albet i Noya, Parxet, Giro Ribot, Sarda, Segura Viudas, and Agusti Torello.

it was aged, its flavors, and suggested food pairings. It makes us wonder why so many of the world's wine labels offer only vague information or none at all.

Jean Leon is another Penedes producer who pioneered the use of varietal labeling and the planting of Chardonnay, Merlot, and Cabernet Sauvignon in the region's vineyards; prices for his wines range from $21 to $29.

Can Feixes is a top pick for its inexpensive ($13), tart, dry white blend.

Pares Balta, one of the region's brightest stars, produces delicious wines, from inexpensive to expensive, that are worth seeking out. Try their proprietary-labeled "Mas Irene"($20) blend of Cabernet Franc and Merlot or for a special occasion "Absis"($85), a lush and complex dry red blend of Tempranillo, Cabernet Sauvignon, and Syrah.

Other reputable Penedes producers include Albet i Noya, Rene Barbier, Mascaro, Masia L'Hereu, Masia Bach, Naveran, Sarda, and Valformosa.

Most Penedes reds can be found at inexpensive (under $15) to moderate (under $30) prices, but some expensive wines are available as well.

Priorato/Priorat. Speaking of Catalonian reds, does the name Priorato sound familiar? While it may not be as well known as California's Napa Valley, this DOC region is known to connoisseurs, collectors, and the young and the reckless as the source for many of Spain's most expensive and exotic wine treasures. The

Pares Balta has been producing Cavas and table wines for more than two centuries. The Blanc de Pacs crisp white wine made from organic indigenous grapes is a great value at $12.

Catalans' pride in their culture has encouraged them to use the local name for their region and drop the "o" off Priorato, so you may see "Priorat" on some wine labels.

Located in the highlands of the Mediterranean province of Tarragona, Priorato's vineyards are home to French varietals (Cabernet Sauvignon, Merlot, Syrah) as well as local grape types (Garnacha, Carinena). Historically, the wines produced in this warm inland region were rich reds that were known more for their potency and a hint of sweetness than for their sophistication. The quality revolution that began in the 1990s has proven successful, and today, in the pursuit of elegant and extraordinary wines, the grape varieties and winemaking techniques used in the region often break from tradition.

Many of the region's vineyards are on precipitous slopes that make harvesting difficult but oh so rewarding. These grapes contain a high level of acidity, which balances the high alcohol content and adds freshness to the wine. Although some wines are made with only Garnacha, it is common practice to blend it with the indigenous Carinena grape. Old Garnacha vines from low-yielding vineyards in this area make wines with more depth of color and flavor and a longer finish than inexpensive examples grown elsewhere. While simple Garnacha wines from other regions tend toward the one-dimensional, tasting merely of bright red fruit, fine Priorato versions deliver dark fruit, floral, and spice flavors in a rich package. Other red grapes used in the blended wines of Priorato include Cabernet Sauvignon, Merlot, Pinot Noir, and Syrah.

Time in costly new oak barrels adds to the body—and the price—of the more concentrated, age-worthy wines. In fact, the best reds can and should be aged for five to twenty-five years to allow their tannins to soften and bouquet to develop. Priorato reds range in price from about $20 to a select few priced at more than $300. Grilled meats, simply seasoned squab, and pasta with sautéed mushrooms are fabulous food partners for these wines.

Some of the Best Wine Producers

Ismael Arroyo, Arzuaga, Rene Barbier, Buil i Gine, Cartoixa, Clos Berenguer, Clos Erasmus, Clos Martinet, Costers del Siurana, Abat Domenech, Fuentes, Laurel, Legaris, Mas d'en Gil, Mas Igneus, Melis, Morlanda, Onix, Alvaro Palacios, Pasenau, Sangenis i Vaque, Scala dei, Trio Infernal, Vall-Llach, Valsotillo, and Vinicola del Priorat

Montsant. The grapes used in this DO are similar to those found in Priorato, as are the flavors of the wines themselves. However, Montsant is still a bit of a hidden gem, and some great-value wines can be found here. From the Els Guiamets winery, you can't go wrong with the medium-bodied "Les Tallades" ($14), made with native grapes and boasting fresh strawberry flavors, or the richer and more complex "Isis" ($22), with black pepper and raspberry flavors that tell the tale of the Syrah, Grenache, Carinena, and Cabernet Sauvignon that comprise it.

Another winner from the region is "Fra Guerau" (about $15) by Vinas del Montsant. This blend of primarily Syrah, Grenache, and Carignan is jam-packed with blackberry and earth flavors. Buil i Gine is also making excellent Montsant wines. Try the "Baboix" blend of Merlot and local grapes for $29. It has a medium to full body with red fruit and cinnamon flavors.

At the high end of the budget spectrum, you may want to treat yourself to the complex and memorable Peraj Ha'abib Flor de Primavera made by Capcanes. It is in the $40 to $50 range, and as an added bonus, it's kosher.

PROVINCE OF CASTILLA Y LEON
Important DO Regions

Bierzo, Toro, Ribera del Duero, Cigales, Rueda, Jumilla (part of the Jumilla DO is in Castilla y Leon, and the rest is in Murcia province; we will cover Jumilla in this section)

Bierzo. In this northwest corner of Castilla y Leon, grape pickers really earn their money, working at high elevations in the steep mountainside vineyards. Cool nighttime temperatures provide acidity to the supple red wines made from the local Mencia grape. The elevation of the vineyards, along with adequate rainfall and cooling winds from the Atlantic Ocean, allow this region to produce balanced, delicious wines with a refreshing acidity even in very hot years. In fact, we nominate Bierzo for DOC status due to the consistent high quality of its wines.

In general, Bierzo wines are marked by floral and fresh red cherry flavors and a medium to full body. Mencia may also be blended with Garnacha to add raspberry and strawberry flavors and ripeness. You do not have to break the bank to buy quality Bierzo wines: many fine examples can be obtained for under $20 a bottle—although several truly stellar wines are available for $100 or more. We suggest pairing Bierzos with simple grilled meats, roasted poultry, or game birds, as complex dishes might overpower the flavors of the wines.

Some of the Best Wine Producers

Adria, Cassar de Burbia, Descendientes de J. Palacios, Dominio de Tares, El Castro de Valtuille, Estefania, Luna Beberide, Pago de Valdoneje, and Joaquín Rebolledo

Toro. Toro is best known for its powerful, dry red wines made mostly from the Tinta de Toro grape. Garnacha plays second fiddle to Tinta de Toro and is never more than a quarter of the blend.

Toro reds tend to exhibit flavors of licorice, leather, and blackberries. The high tannins are best tamed by rich foods such as rack of lamb or vegetarian lasagna. As with most full-bodied reds, Toro wines open up and are easier to enjoy after being aerated for an hour. Prices range from inexpensive (under $15) to expensive ($70). Try a few and you'll see why we think this is a region to watch.

Some of the Best Wine Producers

Farina, Alejandro Fernandez, Liberalia, Gil Luna, Elias Mora, Numanthia-Termes, Estancia Piedra, Quinta Quietud, Rejadorada, Telmo Rodriguez, Torreduero, and Vina Bajoz

Ribera del Duero. The Duero River, known as the Douro when it reaches Portugal, moderates the temperature in this region. Tinto Fino and Tinto del Pais are the local names for Tempranillo. Here, the grape contributes more color and tannins than Tempranillo-based wines from other regions of Spain. Some blends contain Cabernet Sauvignon and Syrah, lending the wines a darker color and more body than most wines from the neighboring region of Rioja. Ribera del Duero reds are full-bodied and typically exhibit flavors of dark berries, plums, licorice, and dark spices. Plus, the overall high quality of these wines means that they are easy to find in retail shops and restaurants that sell Spanish wines. Prices range from $10 to $300, with older vintages of the region's finest checking in at an exorbitant $1,000 a bottle.

The bold wines of Ribera del Duero are traditionally served with lamb roasted in a wood-fired oven and Morcillo blood sausages, although a hunk of aged Manchego cheese is another appealing option. The richness of the cheese lessens the tannins in the wine while providing a pleasant contrast between salty (the cheese) and fruity (the wine). The wines are also a good choice to accompany a hearty vegetable stew or grilled meat.

Some of the Best Wine Producers

Aalto, Alion/Vega-Sicilia, Arzuaga, Balbas, Blason de Romera, Briego, El Lagar de Isilla, Alejandro Fernandez, Fuentespina, Lleirosa, Marques de Velilla, Pago de los Capellanes, Pagos de Quintana, Palacio, Prado Rey, Protos, Telmo Rodriguez, Secreto, Senorio de Nava, Valderiz, Valdubon, Valtravieso, Villar, and Vina Mayor

The refined reds of Ribera del Duero

Founded in 1864, Ribera del Duero's first high-quality winery, Vega-Sicilia, is still respected for its elegant red wines. Its top wine, Unico, is aged for more than a decade before it is sold. Tasted recently, a 1995 was still very youthful with flavors of red currant, cherries, licorice, and violets.

It is very full-bodied, very delicious—and very expensive (upwards of $300, depending on the vintage). The wines of Vega-Sicilia have prompted an epiphany for many wine drinkers, allowing them to experience how profound truly fine wine can be.

Valbuena, Vega-Sicilia's second-level wine, is released after only five years of age. It has a similar flavor profile and the same enticing velvety texture, at about half the price of Unico.

Vega-Sicilia's preeminent position was challenged by the Alejandro Fernandez winery in 1972 with a wine named Pesquera. When young, this wine has aromas and flavors of black fruits, wild herbs, and minerals. After a decade, it becomes incredibly rich and complex, with a bouquet that includes black tobacco, licorice, and sousbois (forest undergrowth), and flavors of black plums and grilled bell peppers. Both young and old Pesqueras have a long finish. With its finest vintages, Alejandro Fernandez will make "Janus" Pesquera, a fabulous wine inspired by and named for the Roman god of beginnings and endings. Perhaps "Janus" was meant to herald a new beginning of Ribera del Duero wines to equal the elegance of Vega-Sicilia.

Today there are many wineries that challenge the supremacy of Vega-Sicilia and Pesquera. Hacienda Monasterio's Ribera del Duero, which contains about 75% Tempranillo with a balance of Cabernet Sauvignon, Merlot, and a little Malbec, is medium-bodied with warm aromas of burnt embers, blueberries, and earth. Hacienda Monasterio also produces two expensive and sought-after wines produced only from Tempranillo grapes grown in biodynamic vineyards: Pingus and Flor de Pingus. Chocolate, black plum, tobacco, and licorice flavors elevate the tannic grip of Pingus; the silky-textured Flor de Pingus exhibits notes of blackberry, blueberry, and violets.

For a more floral example of the region, try Emilio Moro's single-vineyard Malleolus de Valderramiro, an admirable addition to the expensive category.

Cigales. This region produces mostly dry rosé wines from the Tempranillo and Garnacha grapes, though some dry red and white wines are made here as well. We really enjoy the medium-bodied rosés of Cigales. Typically a beautiful pale pink with tastes of ripe red berries and cherries, these refreshing wines are a perfect match for picnic food. Try one with a tomato salad, cold cuts, or fried chicken and you'll never look back. The Fuente del Conde Cigales rosé by Gonzalez Lara is a fine example for $9.

Rueda. In Rueda, white wine rules, and the queen bee is the Verdejo grape. Verdejo's sting lies in its high acidity, which makes it a lovely partner to acidic foods such as ceviche. Modern Ruedas are light and fresh with moderate alcohol. While Verdejo dominates, the wines may be blended with the native Viura or internationally popular Sauvignon Blanc.

Ruedas sell in the inexpensive (under $15) to moderate ($30) price range. Try the inexpensive ones with a Greek salad: the wine's light body will not overwhelm the greens, and its acidity will complement the acidity of the tomatoes, feta cheese, and citrus dressing. By contrast, moderately priced Ruedas are more full-bodied due to oak aging. These can stand up to grilled yellow peppers or grilled octopus as well as soft ripened cheeses. We suggest "Naia" by Aldial, "Martinsancho" by Angel Rodriguez, and the Rueda by Marques de Riscal, which are all inexpensive.

Jumilla. There are some great jewels to be mined from the lesser-known wine regions, and Jumilla in particular is a bargain seeker's paradise. If you are looking for an affordable red that is not wimpy, the wines of this region should be on your radar. Jumilla wines are most often blends. One of the primary components is Monastrell, with Merlot, Syrah, Cabernet Sauvignon, and/or Garnacha commonly added to the mix. Agapito Rico laid the foundation for other wineries in the region with its Monastrell-based "Carchelo." This bargain-priced wine ($9) is medium-bodied with lots of rich black fruit flavors. The winery's "Altico," a Monastrell/Syrah blend loaded with blackberry and black pepper flavors, is worth seeking out, especially at $15. Another of our favorite local wineries is Casa de la Ermita. We enjoy its Monastrell-based "Monasterio" ($10) as well as the crianza version ($15). For a treat, look no further than its pure Petit Verdot ($32), a grape commonly found in Bordeaux blends. If you think that's too much information, you are Wrongo Dongo! Sorry, that's just a playful local wine made by the winery Juan Gil ($10). We love wine producers that don't take themselves too seriously. Another fun local wine we enjoy is the Caracol Serrano for $9. This Monastrell, Syrah, and Cabernet Sauvignon blend is medium-bodied with lovely blueberry, black currant, and black fig flavors.

Other inexpensive to moderately priced Jumilla producers we suggest include Finca Luzon and Casa Castillo. El Nido winery makes expensive, complex blends of Jumilla based on Monastrell and Cabernet Sauvignon.

PROVINCE OF GALICIA
Important DO Regions
Rias Baixas, Ribeiro, Valdeorras

The province of Galicia—especially the DOs of Rias Baixas and Ribeiro—produces some of the best white wines in all of Spain. The Galician coastline attracted many Celtic immigrants, whose cultural influence is evident in the local music, where the *gaita*, or bagpipes, are prominent. The proximity of the Portuguese border is reflected in both the local language, Gallego, and the similarity of the white grapes grown in each country, especially Albarino, Loureiro, Treixadura, and Godello. The local seafood is among the most celebrated fare in all of Europe, and the white wines of Galicia have evolved to be in perfect balance with it. Unlike many overoaked Chardonnays produced around the world, the discreet use of oak barrels in the production of most of these wines allows them to coexist with (rather than dominate) the food.

Rias Baixas. Rias Baixas is home to the Iberian Peninsula's premier white grape, Albarino. Though the grape is difficult to grow and the wine painstaking to produce, pure Albarino wines have achieved

---

Vino de la Tierra de Castilla y Leon

Vino de la Tierra de Castilla y Leon wines come in both inexpensive, easy-drinking, light-bodied versions as well as complex full-bodied wines. Penascal makes a Tempranillo-based Vino de la Tierra with typical red cherry flavors that sells for a Bargain Alert! Price of $6 as well as a tart Sauvignon Blanc for $8.

Abadia de Retuerta is a state-of-the-art winery producing an entry-level "Rivola" red wine for $15, as well as a more complex "Cuvee Palomar" for $50. Both wines are oak-aged Tempranillo and Cabernet Sauvignon blends that offer floral and spice aromas and black fruit flavors. We also enjoy their Seleccion Especial ($20), which is a blend of Tempranillo, Cabernet Sauvignon, and Merlot.

Other Castilla y Leon producers we suggest include Hijos de Antonio Barcelo, Mauro, Dominio de Eguren, Ledas Vinas Viejas, and Femal. Prices range from bargain to expensive.

international acclaim. They are complex, medium-bodied, and redolent of flowers, peach, apple, citrus, and cinnamon. Wines labeled "Albarino" contain 100% of the grape, while those labeled "Rias Baixas" contain a minimum of 70%, with Treixadura and Loureiro added to the blend. Either way, the region's whites are a perfect match with fresh seafood. Rias Baixas blends are inexpensive (under $15), while pure Albarinos are moderately priced (most are well under $30). Looking for a bargain? Try the Nora or Vionta Albarino for about $15.

Some of the Best Wine Producers

> Agro de Bazan, Burgans, Casal Caeiro, Martin Codax, Condes de Albarei, Fefinanes, Fillaboa, Lusco, Mar de Frades, Morgadio, Nora, Pazo de Barrantes, Pazo de Senorans, Pazo Pondal, Valdamor, Villarei, and Vionta

Ribeiro DO and Valdeorras DO. These two regions produce delicious white wines that are rarely encumbered by heavy oak. Modern Ribeiro wines are made from a blend of Treixadura, Loureiro, and Godello. We recommend the "Gran Reboreda" by Campante ($16). This dry, medium-bodied wine is typical of the Ribeiro region with its lemon, mineral, and nectarine flavors. "Reboreda" by the same winery is not as concentrated as the gran wine, but it is a great value at $11.

Godello, the predominant grape of Valdeorras, produces dry whites with flavors of peaches and apricots. Our favorite examples are made by Godeval and Rafael Palacios.

The wines of Ribeiro and Valdeorras are light to medium in body and pair well with foods such as linguine with white clam sauce, falafel, or a seaweed salad. We encourage you to take advantage of the excellent value offered by these off-the-beaten-path wines.

PROVINCE OF ARAGON
Important DO Regions

> Calatayud, Campo de Borja, Somontano

The wineries of these fast-improving, lesser-known regions are shooting for success and offering tremendous quality for the price. The red wines offer differ-ent expressions of native grape varieties such as Garnacha and Monastrell but may also include international varieties such as Cabernet Sauvignon. A perfect example of a great value is "Borsao" ($9), a red from the Campo de Borja DO. A dry, light-to-medium-bodied blend of Garnacha and Tempranillo, this wine features appealing red fruit flavors and low tannins, making it an ideal wine to sip on its own or to serve at a buffet. However, for only $15 you can savor the winery's "Tres Picos." This wine is pure Garnacha, displaying concentrated strawberry, raspberry, and red plum flavors on a medium-to-full-bodied frame.

From the Calatayud DO, try Vina Alarba by Bodegas Castillo de Maluenda. This pure Garnacha has a similar character and price ($9) as the basic Borsao red wine described above. It is light-to-medium-bodied with bright red fruit flavors and can complement a pizza topped with roasted red peppers.

From the Somontano DO, we recommend Enate, a Cabernet Sauvignon/Merlot blend that retails for $15. Enate is medium-bodied with ripe black currant and plum flavors. Alquezar is another wine worth seeking out. This red is reminiscent of a good Beaujolais from France, with its charming flavors of fresh raspberries and loganberries. Vinas del Vero also produces solid reds and whites, including a delicious Chardonnay. Both the Alquezar and Vinas del Vero are under $10.

PROVINCE OF NAVARRA
Important DO Region

> Navarra

The Navarra DO is perhaps best known for the dry, inexpensive rosé wines it produces; these wines feature characteristic strawberry flavors and are medium in body. Rosés have a chameleon-like ability to adapt to a wide range of foods, and the wines of Navarra are a good example of this: seafood gumbo, jambalaya, and *jamon* (ham) all show off the best of the region. Garnacha is currently the dominant grape, although many new vineyards have been planted with Tempranillo, Cabernet Sauvignon, and Merlot. Prices for these rosés are typically under $15; you can also find some dry, medium-weight reds and whites at comparable prices. Our go-to producer in Navarra is Bodegas Julian Chivite. Under the "Gran Feudo" brand name, it produces both a rosé and a red crianza for about $11. Both are medium-bodied wines with bright red fruit flavors.

Some of the Best Wine Producers

Agramont, Castillo de Monjardin, Julian Chivite, de Sarria, Inurreta, Nekeas, Julian Ochoa, Palacio de la Vega, and Vinicola Navarra

Central Spain

PROVINCE OF CASTILLA–LA MANCHA
Important DO Region

La Mancha

The largest DO in all of Spain, La Mancha has been a source for the good, the bad, and the ugly of Spanish wines. Lucky for us, only the good are worth exporting to the Americas. Most of these Tempranillo-based wines are medium-bodied with red and black cherry flavors. Their simplicity makes them good candidates for pub fare; a Chicago pizza stuffed with sausage and pepperoni or a Philadelphia cheesesteak are cozy pairings. Try the Tempranillo wine by Bodegas Campos Reales ($9). It is a dry, medium-bodied red with the red cherry flavors typical of Tempranillo. And if you're looking for a refreshing dry rosé, try the Condesa de Leganza for under $10.

Some of the Best Wine Producers

Campos Reales, Condeza de Leganza, Dominio de Eguren, Alejandro Fernandez, Finca Antigua, Fontana, Marques de Grinon, Santa Quiteria, and Vinedos y Crianza

Southern Spain

REGION OF ANDALUCIA
Important DO Regions

Jerez-Xeres-Sherry and Manzanilla–Sanlucar de Barrameda

Jerez-Xeres-Sherry. Sherry is the unique fortified wine of Spain, and true Sherry can come only from the vineyards of Jerez (the nation's southernmost

Fino and manzanilla are dry styles of Sherry that are excellent as a before-dinner drink or with a wide variety of savory foods. Pedro Ximenez is a great wine to drink with Fig Newtons or dark chocolate brownies, or to pour over vanilla ice cream.

region is named after the capital of the province, Jerez—or Xeres—de la Frontera; "Sherry" is its bastardized English form). In 1996 the European Union formalized laws that prohibit other European nations from making imitations and calling them Sherry; now the fight is on to convince other countries outside Europe (such as the United States) to refrain from producing imitations under the name.

Sherry is one of the insider wines that most wine professionals love. Whether you are sipping a dry fino to pique your appetite or kicking back with some sweet Pedro Ximenez at the end of the day, we urge you to explore the wines of Jerez. They are interesting on their own, but Sherries really come to life when they are paired with food. And considering how much time and effort goes into the birth of a Sherry bottle, they are also wines of great value.

Growing the Grapes, Making the Wine.

Farmers can count on producing ripe grapes every year in the sun-baked region of Jerez. Over 90% of the region's vineyards are planted with the Palomino grape, which serves as the base for most Sherry. Sun-dried Pedro Ximenez (PX) and Moscatel provide sweetness and color to the base; they may also be bottled as single-variety dessert wines (see labels).

Sherry is a fortified wine, which simply means that clear brandy is added to the base wine. The fortification process also determines the presence or absence of the influential flor yeast, which affects the color and style of the wine. This native yeast is either encouraged to enter the barrel by keeping the alcohol level of the wine under 15% or avoided by fortifying the wine to a higher alcohol level.

Styles of Sherry.

There are three basic styles of Sherry: fino, amontillado, and oloroso. Fino wines spend their life protected by the flor and therefore have a pale yellow color. Olorosos receive no flor protection, and the resulting exposure to oxygen results in mahogany or dark-chocolate-colored wines. Between these two extremes are Sherries that are protected by flor in their youth but then are subjected to oxygen in later years. This process results in an amber-colored Sherry known as amontillado.

The flor yeast affects the color of Sherry wines. It forms a protective layer over fino and manzanilla wines, allowing them to preserve their pale color.

The pale and delicate fino is the most popular style of Sherry. A glass of fino is a great way to whet your appetite before a meal; it also makes a perfect accompaniment to tapas, the assortment of "little plates" of appetizers served in the region. We wish we could take all our *WineWise* readers to Andulucia's restaurants and go hopping from one tapas bar to the next for another cool glass of fino Sherry, another delicious morsel. Fortunately, you can still experience fino's flexibility by dining at one of the many exciting tapas bars and restaurants in North America.

Manzanillas are fino Sherries that come from the Sanlucar de Barrameda subregion of Jerez. The driest of all basic Sherries, manzanillas have a briny aroma because they are aged close to the ocean, and the oak barrels in which they are stored are influenced by salty sea breezes. Fino and manzanilla Sherries are always dry and are light to medium in body with 15.5% alcohol. They usually taste of salted almonds, with other common aromas and flavors (cashew, banana, apple, pear, and dough) reminiscent of a trip to a bakery.

Amontillado Sherries are slightly fuller and darker than finos, with just a hint of sweetness. Because they receive the benefits of both the flor protection and the exposure to oxygen, amontillados

The solera system

Once the Sherries are classified by type and style, they are placed in a solera, a fractional blending and aging system. Because the system consists of blending younger and older wines together, Sherries are nonvintage wines.

The solera system involves transferring wines through a series of several rows of barrels stored in tiers. Usually there are three to five barrels in a row. There may be three or four rows, so a solera may consist of twelve to twenty barrels.

Over time, about a third of the wine in each barrel is progressively transferred to a lower tier in its stack. Each time wine is transferred to a lower row in the solera, it is replenished with younger wine from the row above. This labor-intensive system moves the wines toward the bottom row of barrels in the original row. The *suelo* (floor level) contains the oldest blend of wines in the system, and by law, only a fraction of the wine in each of these barrels may be drawn off for sale each year.

The new wine of each vintage is introduced to the blend by placing it in the row farthest from the *suelo*. The beauty of the solera system is that over time, the younger wines contribute freshness to the older wines, and the older wines lend complexity to the younger wines. This blending of young and old enables winemakers to achieve a consistency of quality and flavor in each of their Sherries. As you can see, producing Sherry is an exacting process, truly a labor of love.

often develop to be the most complex of all styles of Sherry. Their signature aromas and flavors are varied and exotic, from nuts (hazelnut, Brazil nut, macadamia nut) to spice (clove, nutmeg, cinnamon) to fruit (quince paste, orange peel, papaya, yellow plum)—not to mention cocoa powder, caramel, butter toffee, and even soy/miso. These wines are medium-bodied, with an alcohol content of 16% to 18%. Try them with a hot mushroom soup in the winter or at a summer picnic with cold cuts and cheeses.

Oloroso Sherries are full-bodied and rich, with up to 20% alcohol. Whether dry or sweet, they are intensely aromatic and flavored. Dry olorosos, with aromas and flavors of mocha, orange, clove, ginger, and salted pecans, are considered the finest and can age for decades. The more common sweet olorosos offer flavors of black figs, Christmas fruitcake, molasses, cola, coffee, licorice, chocolate-covered raisins, beef consommé, mushrooms, pecans, and tamarind. Sweet olorosos are amazing over ice cream, though they are also wonderful served chilled in the summertime, as a dessert on their own.

Other Types of Sherry. Cream Sherries are sweetened by adding a rich sweet juice, wine, or paste to a base wine. Pale, medium, and rich cream Sherries are quite popular but are usually not as fine in quality as the olorosos made exclusively from dried Pedro Ximenez or Moscatel grapes.

A subcategory of amontillado, palo cortados, have the nose of an amontillado and the flavor and color of an oloroso and—no surprise—are slightly higher in alcohol. They are a little harder to find in America but are worth the search.

Designated-age Sherries of twelve, fifteen, or eighteen years have been aged a minimum of the age stated before they are sold. The longer aging results in amber-colored wines that have more interesting aromatics and flavors than wines bottled in their youth.

Very old Sherries (VOS) are aged a minimum of twenty years and therefore are quite complex and more expensive than standard Sherries.

Very old reserve Sherries (VORS) are aged a minimum of thirty years. Wineries producing VORS can only take one-thirtieth of a barrel to bottle each year! VOS and VORS are special-occasion wines offering a generous richness on the palate and a truly memorable array of flavors.

Serving Sherry. Sherry is traditionally served in a small glass the locals call a *copita* (cup), although any small wine glass will do. A standard portion is 2 to 2½ ounces (60 to 75 milliliters). Fino, manzanilla, and pale cream styles should be served well chilled from a refrigerated bottle. Amontillado, palo cortado, and dry oloroso should be served less chilled; you can warm it up by gently rubbing your hands on the glass. Pedro Ximenez, Moscatel, or cream Sherry can be served at room temperature.

As we mentioned earlier, the wide range of styles of Sherries means they can be served from the beginning to the end of a meal. Typically, the lighter-bodied dry finos and manzanillas are served before the medium-to-full-bodied dry amontillados. *Tapas* such as codfish-stuffed piquillo peppers, marinated octopus, grilled sardines, tortilla of egg and potato, slices of *jamon*, or a stew of chickpeas, sausage, and spinach are just a few dishes that locals have enjoyed with dry Sherry for centuries. However, *WineWise* readers should not limit their enjoyment of Sherry to Spanish foods, as we have enjoyed these wines with foods from around the world. Finos and manzanillas are nothing short of amazing with mu shu pork or eggplant with garlic sauce. Amontillados can be enjoyed with kung pao chicken, a whole roasted red snapper served over caramelized onions, or fried tempeh in a salad with a sesame-based dressing.

Sherry is a bargain, with some of the best producers offering their wines at prices starting well under $15 per bottle. Special bottlings can go as high as $60, but these are rare.

Some of the Best Sherry Producers

Barbadillo, Gonzalez Byass (famous for dry fino "Tio Pepe" and sweet "Noe"), Pedro Domecq (famous for dry fino "La Ina"), Hartley & Gibson, Harvey's, Hidalgo (famous for dry manzanilla "La Gitana"), Lustau (famous for dry fino "Puerto Solera Reserva" and dry amontillado "Los Arcos"), Osborne, Sanchez Romate, Sandeman (famous for medium-dry "Character"), Savory & James, Williams & Humbert (famous for medium-dry "Dry Sack" and "15-Year-Old Dry Sack"), and Wisdom & Warter

chapter 11

Apaixonado por
Portugal

Portugal is best known for its sweet fortified red Port wines. Since you probably drink more table wine than sweet fortified dessert wine, we urge you to take the first step on a journey to discover some of the tastiest wines on the planet. Portuguese wines offer great value, distinctive flavors, and some food pairing possibilities that are unique. This small country has more than 300,000 farmers carrying on a tradition of growing grapes to make wines for both a thirsty local market and for exports. Until the 1990s, only a handful of truly exceptional table wines were being produced in Portugal; today, many fine wines are being made from both indigenous and international grapes. The result is that Portuguese wines are more alluring to the WineWise consumer than ever before. Not only do they offer great quality for their price, but also the diversity is truly exciting: more than 200 indigenous grape types are used to make everything from sparkling wines to whites, rosés, and reds as well as fortified wines—a treasure trove waiting to be discovered.

If you have never drunk Portuguese wines, we suggest that your first glass should be a low-alcohol, dry, crisp, white Vinho Verde wine. Many of these charming wines cost under $10 a bottle. If a glass of Vinho Verde piques your palate and your interest, then try some of the easy-sipping light-bodied rosé and red wines from the Alentejo region that are also bargain-priced.

Once you are comfortable with the value wines of Portugal, take a step up to the moderately priced and more expensive complex, sinewy reds or unique fortified wines. Your safest bet for your first wine purchase in this group should be from the Douro region. One taste and you will wonder what took you so long to discover these fabulous wines. Or try some of the classic fortified wines of Portugal: true Porto, Madeira, and Moscatel de Setubal. The finest red and fortified wines possess so many nuances of flavor that a little taste is all you need to confirm that life is marvelous!

In this chapter we will take you on a tour through the best-known wine-producing regions and describe the styles of wines made there and mention some specific producers we respect. We will also take advantage of the wide range of wine styles made in Portugal to suggest some conventional and some wacky wine and food pairing possibilities.

The grapes of Portugal
Multiple personalities and names

For a fairly small nation, Portugal grows an amazing diversity of grape types. Portugal's vineyards are home to numerous international grapes: Chardonnay, Muscat, Cabernet, Merlot, and Syrah are all grown here. Yet, as is often the case around the world, it's the indigenous grapes that are instrumental in producing the most famous (and perhaps soon to be famous) wines of Portugal.

A quick review of the nation's native grape varieties reads like an Elmore Leonard mystery novel: there are Esgana Cao, the "dog strangler," and Borrado das Moscas, "fly droppings." One grape suffering from an identity crisis has a masculine name, Fernao Pires, in one province and a feminine name, Maria Gomes, in another.

Humor aside, Portugal is host to a number of "serious" grapes that are used to produce some of the country's finest—and most famous—wines.

Touriga Nacional

This important grape produces dark-colored, tannic wines with good acidity. Mulberries, plums, roses, violets, and spice notes are just some of the many flavors found in the wines from this noble grape. Some of the spice notes we often detect are cardamom, clove, and cinnamon. Although Touriga Nacional's springboard to fame has always been the Douro region, where it is a major component of both red wine and fortified Porto, it also produces some amazing wines in the Dao, Beiras, and Alentejo regions. This grape makes outstanding single-variety wines as well as delicious blends.

Tinta Roriz (Aragones)

Tinta Roriz (as it is known in the north of the country) and Aragones (in the south) are Portugal's names for Spain's finest red variety, Tempranillo. As in Spain, the grape is used to make single-variety wines as well as blends. Affordable wines based on this grape will have flavors of strawberries and be light-to-medium-bodied. Moderate to expensive wines have aromas of black fruits, dark spices, and licorice and are medium-to-full-bodied. If you are one of the many fans of Spanish wines, Tinta Roriz/Aragones wines are a no-brainer introduction to the pleasures of Portuguese red wines.

Language of the label

AS IS TRUE of most European nations, once you have a basic familiarity with Portugal's wine regions and grape types, reading their wine labels will be a piece of cake. Common to all labels is, of course, the producer, and a few terms will help you out here:

- *Quinta, palacio, casa, herdade,* or *solar:* a wine estate, similar to a French chateau.
- *Adega:* a winery.
- *Marques:* as in Spain, denotes a wine producer of noble heritage

A peek at Portugal's unique wine grapes

Aside from the Touriga Nacional and Tinta Roriz, here are some other popular red grape varieties you may want to get acquainted with.

- **Baga.** The thin-skinned Baga grape is the premier grape of the Bairrada region and can produce some of the greatest wines of Portugal. The wines are high in acidity and tannins, two ingredients necessary to make long-lived wines. Flavors of the wines are of black fruit, flowers, and spices.

- **Alfrocheiro Preto.** Lends aromas of spice and flowers to the red blends of the Dao region. Also produced as a single-variety wine with a medium body.

- **Jaen.** This grape, with scents of black pepper, blueberry, and fig, is a popular component in the blends of the Dao region. Also produced as a single-variety wine with medium body.

- **Castelhao.** This grape, also known as Periquita, is the most planted variety in Portugal. Wines based on Castelhao have charming flavors of raspberries and strawberries and are light-to-medium-bodied.

- **Trincadeira.** Also known as Tinta Amarela, this grape is a major component of the blended wines of central and southern Portugal. As a single-variety wine or in a blend, it offers black fruit aromas and flavors, color, and tannins. Inexpensive versions are medium-bodied and the moderately priced wines are full-bodied. Alentejo and Ribatejo are two regions where this grape soaks up lots of sunshine, resulting in wines with ripe fruit flavors.

Though known for its reds, the nation of Portugal produces some very fine whites.

- **Alvarinho.** Known as Albarino in Spain, this is considered by many to be the finest white grape variety in Portugal. Wines made from this grape are medium-to-full-bodied with a great balance of acidity and a seductive, aromatic bouquet of white flowers, peaches, and mango. Notable examples come from Vinho Verde in the Minho region. Wines made from Alvarinho are some of the most versatile wines for food pairing—in Portugal Alvarinho-based wines are often served with grilled sardines, one of the many seafood dishes based on codfish, the soup known as caldo verde, and local cheeses. For more suggestions, see page 297 in Chapter 14, devoted to wine and food.

- **Arinto.** Common to the Bucelas region, this grape is most prized for its vibrant acidity. It is available in both lightweight versions made in stainless steel and richer barrel-aged versions.

- **Encruzado.** The queen bee white grape of the Dao region is often anointed with expensive new oak. If you like full-bodied whites and want a break from Chardonnay, this is the Portuguese white wine you have been looking for. When used in blended wines from the Dao region, the grape contributes citrus, yellow plum, mineral, and nutty flavors.

- **Fernao Pires (also known as Maria Gomes).** This grape makes wines with trademark aromas of orange zest and pepper. It is the most-planted white variety in Portugal and used to make still and sparkling wines.

- **Trajadura.** Known for its citrus aromas, it may be found as a single-variety wine or in Vinho Verde blends.

- **Avesso.** Adds structure to the blends of Vinho Verde. It also produces fine single-variety wines with citrus flavors.

- **Loureiro.** Named for its aroma of bay laurel and flowers, this grape is available as a single variety or in Vinho Verde blends.

- **Malvasia Fina.** Grown in Douro, Madeira, and Dao. Whether this grape is used as part of a blended table wine or produced as a fortified wine, there are usually flavors of white flowers, kiwi, and pineapple.

- **Moscatel.** We admit it—we cannot resist the orange blossom and honey aromas of Muscat grape varieties. Try the precocious semidry white table wines from the Terras do Sado region based on Moscatel. Sensational aged fortified wines based on this variety are sold as Moscatel de Setubal.

A few additional terms you may encounter on Portuguese wine labels include:

- *Garrafeira,* used by some wineries to indicate additional aging before a table wine is released
- *Reserva, superior:* indicate riper grapes, producing wines with a little more alcohol to supply richness on the palate
- *Grande escolha* (grand selection) or *escolha* (selection): terms a winery may put on the bottles it believes represent its best efforts
- *Engarrafado na origem:* estate-bottled by the grower
- *Espumante:* sparkling

Next, Portuguese wine labels will include either the name of the grape, the place where the grapes were grown, both the grape and place name, or a proprietary name. The name of the grape is easy: Alvarinho, Touriga Nacional, et cetera. Most of us seem to be most comfortable choosing wines labeled by grape type (as opposed to place name), which explains the growing presence of varietal-labeled wines from Portugal.

The origin of the wine

The following terms are used to indicate the origin of the wine.

DENOMINACAO DE ORIGEM CONTROLADA (DOC)

Think of DOC wines as classic recipes to ensure a consistent style, similar to AOC in France and DOC in Italy. Just as we suggested in the French chapter, AOC and DOC are guarantees of authenticity, not quality. Of the thirty-plus DOCs, the most important include:

- **Vinho Verde, Bucelas:** dry white wines
- **Douro, Alentejo, Bairrada, Dao:** best known for dry reds, though rosé, white, and sparkling wines are also made in these areas
- **Moscatel de Setubal, Porto, Madeira:** best known for fortified wines

VINHO REGIONAL (VR)

There are eight regional wine areas, including Minho, Tras-os-Montes, Beiras, Ribatejo, Terras do Sado, Estremadura, and Alentejano. Winemakers are

An example of a wine labeled by place name. A blend of red grapes is used for this superb example of dry red wine from the Douro DOC.

Cortes de Cima is an innovative winery based in the Alentejo DOC. Their "Incognito" wine, which features a Bob Dylan quote on the front label and the word "Syrah" hidden on the back label, is a playful reference to the hesitancy of the local authorities to permit the use of Syrah grapes in Alentejo DOC wines.

allowed more freedom to use nontraditional grapes or blends in this category than at the DOC level.

VINHO DE MESA

These are the least expensive of Portugal's table wines; a vintage year will not appear on the label.

The overall picture: Some of the best wines

WE HAVE SUGGESTED time and again in *WineWise* to go off the beaten path for the best wine values, and Portugal is no exception. The Portuguese can boast of having a wide diversity of wine styles, including sparkling, still, and fortified wines with varying levels of sweetness, weight, and alcohol. If you're looking for alternatives to the world's most popular grapes or wine regions, we recommend exploring the unique wines of Portugal.

The major wine regions of Portugal

FOR A SMALL COUNTRY—it is roughly 520 miles (837 kilometers) long and 120 miles (193 kilometers) wide—Portugal features numerous geographic and climatic conditions, which have also played a major role in determining the styles of wines best suited to each area.

We offer *WineWise* readers suggestions for bargain wines (under $15), inexpensive to moderately priced wines (under $30), and moderately priced to expensive wines (over $30). We will also give prices of some wines we encourage you to try. The finest (and often the most expensive) examples will usually bear the label terms *reserva*, *garrafeira*, or *grande escolha* or have the name of a single grape variety and/or single vineyard.

Northern Portugal

MINHO
Important DOC Region

Vinho Verde

One of the easiest and least expensive Portuguese wines to find and drink is Vinho Verde (the name means "green wine"), from the province of Minho. Named for the Minho River, the province is influenced by the Atlantic Ocean and gets lots of rainfall, making the area quite verdant. These regional wines are often nonvintage and are best drunk as soon as they are released, while they are still "green" in color and taste. In actuality, the color should be a very pale straw yellow. If your Vinho Verde is gold, it is too old!

This wine is fruity, affordable, and plentiful. The Minho is Portugal's largest demarcated wine region, with most of the vines devoted to making these dry, crisp white blends. A number of varietals can contribute to the mix; the most typical are Loureiro, Trajadura, Azal, Pederna, and Avesso.

Vinho Verdes are light-bodied, low in alcohol (8.5% to 10.5%), and a little spritzy, so, unlike brawny Chardonnays, they will not increase the heat of fiery dishes such as hot chicken wings, spicy Thai seafood, or blackened catfish. Likewise, their acidity and efferves-

Quinta da Aveleda is a family-owned winery that produces delicious blended and single-variety wines at great value prices.

Lagares (stone troughs) are often used to get the maximum extraction of flavors, tannins, and color from the grapes before fermentation begins.

cence make a refreshing backdrop for steamed seafood or a salad with a citrus dressing, or to cleanse the palate from the richness of fried codfish fritters or falafel.

In addition to Vinho Verde's versatility with food, it has the added benefit of having a relatively low alcohol level. At a time when the alcohol level of many international wines has surged beyond 15%, Vinho Verde's lighter style makes it perfect for hot summer days. While most Vinho Verde wines are bargain-priced blends (with many well under $10), single-varietal wines are inexpensive to moderately priced ($12 to $25).

The finest of the single-variety wines is Alvarinho. Wines based on this grape are rich without being heavy, so they can handle grilled sardines, saffron risotto, or a roast chicken.

Some of the Best Wines and Producers

Bargain wines: Quinta da Aveleda, "Gazela," "Gatao," Broadbent, Famega, and Adega de Moncao (all under $10)

Inexpensive to moderate: Casa de Cello, Quinta de Carapecos, "Soalheiro," "Portal do Fidalgo," "Morgadio da Torre," Casa de Vila Verde, Quinta do Melgacao, Palacio da Brejoeira, Quinta do Ameal, and the celebrated wines of Anselmo Mendes such as "Muros Antigos."

THE DOURO VALLEY
Important DOC Regions
Douro, Porto

Douro. The Douro is one of the most beautiful wine regions in the world. What looks like a crazy patchwork quilt of vineyards is the result of various planting strategies on the precipitous slopes of the region. The Douro River (known as the Duero in Spain) moderates the area's climate. In an area where daytime temperatures can reach 115°F (46°C), achieving a balance of fruit, tannins, alcohol, and

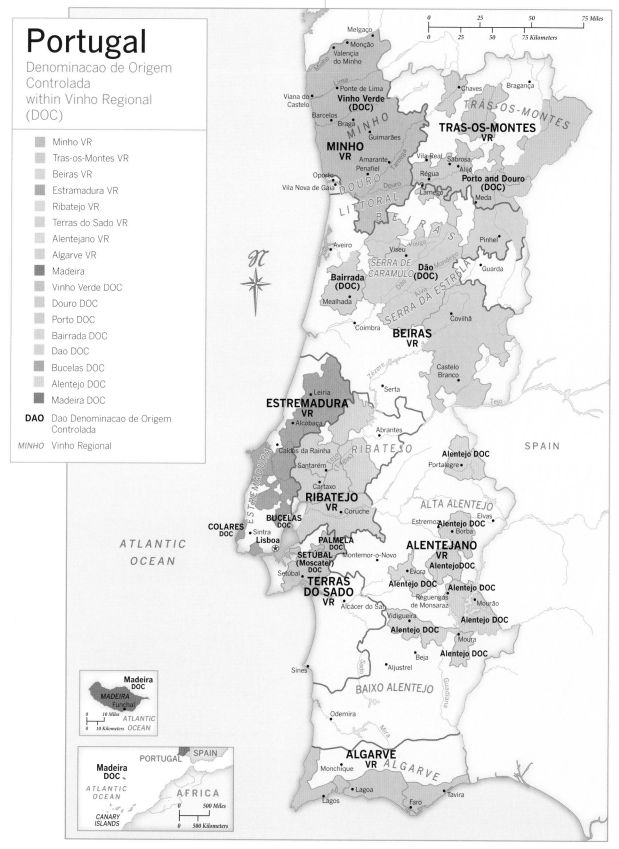

Portugal

Denominacao de Origem
Controlada
within Vinho Regional
(DOC)

- Minho VR
- Tras-os-Montes VR
- Beiras VR
- Estramadura VR
- Ribatejo VR
- Terras do Sado VR
- Alentejano VR
- Algarve VR
- Madeira
- Vinho Verde DOC
- Douro DOC
- Porto DOC
- Bairrada DOC
- Dao DOC
- Bucelas DOC
- Alentejo DOC
- Madeira DOC

DAO Dao Denominacao de Origem
Controlada

MINHO Vinho Regional

Melgaço
Monção
Valença
do Minho
Ponte de Lima
Viana do
Castelo
**Vinho Verde
(DOC)**
Barcelos
Braga
Guimarães
**MINHO
VR**
Amarante
Penafiel
Oporto
Vila Nova de Gaia
Chaves
Bragança
TRAS-OS-MONTES
**TRAS-OS-MONTES
VR**
Vila Real
Sabrosa
Régua
Alijó
**Porto and Douro
(DOC)**
Lamego
Meda
DOURO
LITTORAL
BEIRAS
Aveiro
Viseu
*SERRA DE
CARAMULO*
Pinhel
**Dão
(DOC)**
Guarda
**Bairrada
(DOC)**
Mealhada
SERRA DA ESTRÊLA
Covilhã
Coimbra
**BEIRAS
VR**
Castelo
Branco
Leiria
Serta
Zêzere
**ESTREMADURA
VR**
Alcobaça
Abrantes
Tejo
Caldos da Rainha
RIBATEJO
Santarém
Tejo
(Tejus)
Cartaxo
**RIBATEJO
VR**
Coruche
Alentejo DOC
Portalegre
SPAIN
**COLARES
DOC**
Sintra
**BUCELAS
DOC**
Lisboa
ALTA ALENTEJO
**PALMELA
DOC**
Montemor-o-Novo
Estremoz
Alentejo DOC
Elvas
Borba
**SETÚBAL
(Moscatel)
DOC**
Setúbal
**ALENTEJANO
VR**
Évora
AlentejoDOC
**TERRAS
DO SADO
VR**
Alcácer do Sal
Alentejo DOC
Reguengos
de Monsaraz
Alentejo DOC
Mourão
Vidigueira
Alentejo DOC
Sado
Alentejo DOC
Beja
Moura
Alentejo DOC
Sines
Aljustrel
BAIXO ALENTEJO
Guadiana
Odemira
Mira
**ALGARVE
VR** *ALGARVE*
Monchique
Lagoa
Lagos
Faro
Tavira

*ATLANTIC
OCEAN*

**Madeira
DOC**
MADEIRA Funchal
*ATLANTIC
OCEAN*
0   10 Miles
0   10 Kilometers

**Madeira
DOC**
*ATLANTIC
OCEAN*
CANARY
ISLANDS
PORTUGAL SPAIN
AFRICA
0   500 Miles
0   500 Kilometers

0   25   50   75 Miles
0   25   50   75 Kilometers

The wine regions of Portugal.

acidity proves a constant challenge to the area's winemakers.

Historically, the Douro was best known by collectors for expensive Porto fortified wines and only one fine dry red, Barca Velha by Ferreira. There were no challengers to its elite status until the 1990s, when competition appeared in the form of single-variety wines and blends, mostly of Touriga Nacional or Tinta Roriz. Today, less than two decades later, the lush, full-bodied dry red wines of the Douro are among the world's finest and have proved their elegance in many international competitions. The wines of the Douro are better today than ever before. And while many wineries hold on to certain traditions—some still tread their grapes by foot in *lagares* to get the maximum extraction of flavors, tannins, and color—others have taken modernization quite far, using robots to crush the grapes and extract the juice.

Douro reds range in price from inexpensive (about $12 and medium-bodied) to expensive (up to $100 and full-bodied), but don't be disheartened by the high ceiling: you can sample some wonderful examples of the region without emptying your wallet. Douro red wines display earth, game, mineral, and spice notes as well as a range of red and black fruits. The Douro's dramatic and supple wines are ideal with

(Photo courtesy of Quinta do Crasto)

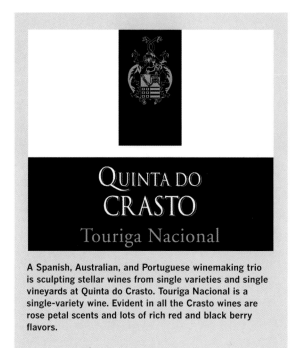

A Spanish, Australian, and Portuguese winemaking trio is sculpting stellar wines from single varieties and single vineyards at Quinta do Crasto. Touriga Nacional is a single-variety wine. Evident in all the Crasto wines are rose petal scents and lots of rich red and black berry flavors.

game birds, *cabrito* (goat roasted in a wood-fired oven), and many Indian vegetarian and meat dishes.

We adore the red wines of the Douro. The extensive list of suggested wines is our testimony to how excited we are for *WineWise* readers to try wines from this region.

Many of our favorite producers make a basic entry-level wine as well as more expensive *reservas* or single-vineyard wines. If there is a "brand name," it is followed by the producer's name.

Some of the Best Wines and Their Producers

Inexpensive: "Adriano" by Ramos Pinto, "Altano" by Symington, "Charamba" by Quinta da Aveleda, "Foral" by Aliança, "Vila Regia" by Sogrape, "Esteva" by Ferreira, Quinta do Portal, Quinta do Ventozelo, and Quinta do Cotto

Moderate to expensive: Quinta do Crasto, Quinta do Vale de Meao, "Quinta da Leda" and "Barca Velha" by Ferreira, "Redoma" and "Batuta" by Niepoort, "Pintas" by Wine and Soul, Quinta do Vale do Dona Maria, Quinta do Vallado, Quinta do Ventozelo, Quinta de la Rosa, Churchill Estates, Bago de Touriga

Gouvyas, "Quinta do Vale da Raposa" and "Quinta da Gaivosa" by Alves de Sousa, "Quinta dos Quatros Ventos" by Alianca, "Prazo de Roriz" and "Post Scriptum" by Symington, "Chryseia" by Prats and Symington, Poeira, "Xisto" by Roquette e Cazes, "Quinta das Pias" by Lavadores de Feitora, Passadouro, "Quinta dos Aciprestas" by Real Compania Velha, "Duas Quintas" by Adriano Ramos Pinto.

Porto: The One and Only True Port. California, Australia, and South Africa make some decent "Ports," but as the song goes, there "ain't nothing like the real thing, baby." Just as true Champagne and Sherry are wines of a specific place that must be produced in a traditional way, true Porto (sometimes labeled as "Port") has its own DOC and must come from the Douro Valley. Each bottle of Porto wine must pass rigorous quality tests before receiving the seal of authenticity.

Porto is the most successful fortified wine in the world. It is typically served as an after-dinner drink; it is also ideal with cheeses (such as an aged cheddar or Stilton), chocolate desserts, or a plate of dried fruits and nuts.

The process of making Porto is fairly simple. Before the fermentation proceeds to the point where all the sugar is converted to alcohol, the wine is transferred to casks containing clear grape brandy. The

Ruby Reserve wines such as the Bin 27 by Fonseca are an affordable alternative to Vintage Porto.

brandy's high alcohol kills off the yeast, resulting in a wine that is sweet, full-bodied, dark in color, and high in alcohol. The amount of time the wine spends in oak casks before it is bottled has a lot to do with the naming and styles of Porto wine. Wines that are bottled young are known as Ruby or Vintage Portos, and those that are aged longer in wood are known as Tawny Portos.

THE POWERFUL YOUNG WINES. Ruby Portos are fruity blends from young, nonvintage wines. At under $12, they are a good introduction to the pleasures of Porto.

Ruby Reserve Portos (formerly known as vintage character) are blended Portos with a little more age than Rubies. They have proprietary names such as Fonseca Bin 27, Sandeman's Founders Reserve, Warre's Warrior, or Graham's 6 Grapes. A simple Ruby or Reserve Porto is all you need to pair with Cherry Garcia ice cream or a fudge brownie, as the complexities of a more expensive wine would be lost alongside such rich desserts. Reserves are great value wines, costing about $20.

Crusted Porto is a wine made from a blend of years. The wine spends time in oak casks and then in bottle, where it throws a "crust" or deposit of sediment. Churchill and Smith Woodhouse are good examples that sell for moderate prices (about $30).

Late-Bottled Vintage (LBV) Portos are sourced from a single vintage and spend more time in cask and bottle than vintage Portos. At $25 to $30, they are moderately priced and can be a delicious alternative to the more pricey Vintage Portos.

Vintage Portos are sourced from the finest vineyards and are declared by a winery only when the harvest is of superb quality. On average, only three years in ten are declared vintage years. In their youth, Vintage Portos are packed with intense black fruit and floral flavors and have lots of richness and power on the palate. The wine mellows with age, becoming softer and more harmonious. If a wine could be described as Rubenesque, Vintage Porto would fit the bill. These wines are moderately to expensively priced ($35 to hundreds of dollars for older vintages) (see the sidebar "Act Your Age!").

Tawny Porto wines are lighter in body and lower in tannins than Vintage Portos. We enjoy these complex wines as an after-dinner drink or with a platter of aged cheeses, dried fruits, and nuts.

Single-Quinta Portos are made from the grapes of one vineyard and may be vintage or nonvintage. After spending less time in cask and bottle than Tawny Portos (see below), the wines of an individual estate may be sold. This category is a bit confusing, as the wineries have the option of making these wines from a mediocre harvest or from a very fine harvest. Unlike Vintage Portos, which are released in the third year, wineries may wait longer to release these wines than their vintage wines to allow more time to develop harmonious flavors. We recommend Quinta do Vesuvio, Quinta do Noval, Quinta dos Canais by Cockburn, Quinta da Foz by Calem, Quinta do Crasto, Quinta do Gaivosa, Quinta do Noval. Quinta do Seixo by Ferreira, and Taylor's Quinta de Vargellas Vinha Velha.

THE GRACEFUL AGED WINES. Tawny Portos are aged for at least six years in cask. Some Tawnies are made by blending white and red Porto, or by aging and blending Ruby Portos; these can be found at bargain prices, and quality is generally quite good.

Indicated-Age Tawny Portos are available in ten-year, twenty-year, thirty-year, and forty-year versions. These are based on an average minimum age of the blend of vintages in the bottle; the oxidation of the wines as they age allows them to develop a tawny color. The pigments and tannins also form sediment in the process, which is expelled by "racking," or moving the wine from barrel to barrel over time. Prices for Indicated-Age Tawnies range from moderate to expensive based on age (about $30 for the ten-year to over $100 for the forty-year). We believe the twenty-year versions are great values at about $40. They are some of the most sublime sweet wines in the world, adored for their exotic bouquet, flavors, and balance. Since the wines are not as tannic as the Vintage style, it is a lot easier to enjoy a second glass, or perhaps a third over time. Some of our favorite producers of ten- and twenty-year Tawny are Adriano Ramos Pinto, Barros, Calem, Delaforce, Ferreira, Quinta do Portal, Pocas, Taylor-Fladgate, Fonseca, Rozes, Offley, Royal Oporto, Graham's, Sandeman, Dow's, Warre's, and Cockburn.

Act your age!

Age is an issue in Porto for two reasons. First, older vines result in lower yields of grapes, which in turn results in more concentrated wines. Second, the amount of time the wine spends in cask and bottle before it is sold directly affects the naming of the wine and its character.

Vintage Portos, for example, are released between the second and third year, years after the grapes were harvested. Late-Bottled Vintage (LBV) Portos are released between the fourth and sixth years. Because they are bottled young and not exposed to much oxygen, both vintage and LBV Portos deteriorate quicker in the bottle than Tawnies, which are more resistant to oxygen. Once opened, the wines will begin to oxidize and should be preserved using a vacuum system or nitrogen to displace the oxygen.

Although tannic and full-bodied in their youth, Vintage Portos become suave and complex as they age, developing an opaque black cherry or deep purple color and flavors of black plum, blueberries, black figs, fruit, flowers, chocolate, and spices. You can cellar a great vintage Porto for fifteen, thirty, or even fifty years. Those from 1945, 1963, 1970, 1977, and 1994 are still delicious, while the 2000, 2003, and 2004 vintages all promise to be great wines when they mature.

Most Late-Bottled Vintage Portos employ a twist-off cap (with a short cork, often called a "stopper cork") and are meant for drinking within three years. Versions from Fonseca and Taylor Fladgate fall into this category. The LBVs with regular corks—such as those of Ramos Pinto and Niepoort—can be aged for at least twenty years. The flavors of these LBV Portos are quite similar to Vintage Portos, with black fruits, wildflowers, spices, and chocolate.

Ten-, twenty-, thirty-, and forty-year-old Tawny Ports are chestnut in color and display aromas and flavors of dried white fruits, flowers, and spices. They have medium tannins and are lighter in body than Vintage Portos. Portos are usually reserved for after dinner, but we suggest pairing a foie gras terrine appetizer with a fine Designated-Age Tawny. This may seem like a wacky combination, but trust us, it works.

Another bonus of Tawny Portos: they can be stored in a cellar for a decade, and once opened they will retain their basic flavors for a couple of weeks, unlike Vintage Portos, which deteriorate within a few days after opening them.

When pairing Portos with chocolate, match their intensities. Milk chocolate has an affinity with Tawny Portos, while dark chocolate complements Vintage.

Some well-known producers of ageworthy Port include: Adriano Ramos Pinto, Barros, Burmester, Calem, Churchill, Croft, Cockburn, Delaforce, Dow's, Ferreira, Fonseca, Graham's, Kopke, Niepoort, Offley-Forester, Pocas, Quinta do Crasto, Quinta da Gaivosa, Quinta do Infantado, Quinta do Noval, Quinta do Vale do Dona Maria, Quinta do Vallado, Quinta do Vale Meao, Quinta do Vesuvio, Rozes, Sandeman, Smith-Woodhouse, Taylor Fladgate, and Warre's.

Indicated-Age Single-Vineyard/Quinta Tawnies contain the name of an estate vineyard. Fine examples include Adriano Ramos Pinto's ten-year tawny from its Quinta da Ervamoira vineyard and its twenty-year tawny from the Quinta do Bom Retiro estate. Both are moderately priced.

Colheita Vintage Tawny Portos are from a single harvest and spend a long time in barrels before they are bottled. We recommend those of Niepoort, Calem, Royal Oporto, and Barros. They can be found at moderate to expensive prices.

Central Portugal

BEIRAS
Important DOC Regions
Bairrada, Dao

A Beiras regional label may be used by producers who want to blend grapes from both the Bairrada and Dao DOCs, or by those who want to break from the traditional "recipes" for those wines.

Luis Pato is one of Portugal's finest winemakers—a distinction awarded by both Portuguese and American critics. His single-vineyard Beiras wines in particular are worth seeking out: Quinta do Ribeirinho Primeira Escolha is a sophisticated wine with floral and wild berry flavors, while Vinha Barrosa has licorice and black fruit flavors. Also of note are Pato's *vinhas velhas* (old vine) whites and reds, a Baga/Touriga Nacional red blended wine, and an inexpensive sparkling rosé made from Baga. We also suggest the "Ensaios" white and red Beiras blends by Luis' daughter Filipa Pato. Her pure Baga "Lokal Calcario" from Bairrada DOC and the Touriga Nacional and Alfrocheiro Preto blend "Lokal Silex" from the Dao DOC are polished expressions of the grapes and their birthplace.

BAIRRADA
The Bairrada region produces sparkling, white, red, and rosé wines. The Baga grape dominates the vineyards of Bairrada. Bairrada wines are generous in body and acidity, with delicious black fig, blueberry, licorice, and floral notes. How can you tame the assertive tannins of Bairrada red wines? They pair well with hearty foods such as ribs, roast duck, or steak. *Leitao* is roasted baby suckling pig, and many Portuguese will drive a couple of hours just to savor this local specialty and enjoy the local wines. In the summer months they may drink a cool glass of bubbly *espumante,* but in the fall and wintertime red wines rule.

Bairrada red wines must be aged at least a year and a half before they are sold to allow the wine to become more harmonious. We believe that you can cellar their fine *garrafeira, reserva,* or single-vineyard wines for at least a decade and they will become even more balanced and complex. Our top Bairrada wines come from Quinta das Bageiras (the Garrafeira is sensational), Campolargo (try the "Termao"), Caves Messias, Alianca, and Marques de Marialva. The "Follies" line of wines by Quinta da Aveleda includes a Touriga Nacional we recommend.

Fernao Pires (also called Maria Gomes) accounts for the majority of the white grapes grown in the Bairrada region, whether used for dry table whites or *espumante* bubbly. These dry, medium-bodied wines often have a pleasant floral aroma and medium acidity. They are a good match for a Niçoise salad, lobster roll, or fried fish and chips.

DAO
Black grapes thrive in this mountainous region, and in fact two-thirds of Dao's production is red wine. The dominant grape is the Touriga Nacional. Most Dao reds tend to be medium in body, with softer tannins than their burly Bairrada cousins. They can coexist with a wide range of foods, from roast pork or roast chicken to red beans and smoked sausage.

For a super bargain, check out Sogrape's dry white and red blends labeled Grao Vasco ($7) or Duque de Viseu ($11). Our other favorite wineries are Quinta dos Roques, Quinta da Pellada, Quinta de Saes, Quinta da Cabriz, and Casa de Santar.

On the white front in Dao, blended wines are dry, medium-bodied, and inexpensive. They can be used as a cocktail or as a backdrop to foods such as a Caesar salad with grilled shrimp, crab cakes, or a BLT sandwich. *WineWise* readers looking for an alternative to Chardonnay should try the full-bodied single-variety Encruzado wines.

Southern Portugal

ESTREMADURA

Important DOC Region

Bucelas

The Estremadura region produces the largest volume of wine in Portugal, most of which is red wine. One of our favorite regional wines is "Touriz" by Casa Santos Lima. It is a mouth-filling blend, chock full of black fruit flavors, and it is rich on the palate with a long finish—a great value at about $18. But wait, there's more. Try their Alfrocheiro Preto for only $10. Violets, black raspberry, and black fig flavors are wrapped in a medium-weight package. Or if you want a full-bodied red wine with blackberry flavors, check out their varietal Sousao for $13. We also suggest wines based on indigenous and international grape varieties from Quinta do Monte d'Oiro.

BUCELAS

A region of note for the WineWise is Bucelas, which produces only white wines. These are mostly crisp whites based on the tart Arinto grape. To highlight the lemon flavors characteristic of Arinto, try serving them with a citrusy ceviche. Quinta da Romeira's wine is a great bargain at about $10.

RIBATEJO VR

Ribatejo produces the second-largest volume of wine in Portugal, most of it white. Fernao Pires is the major grape used for the inexpensive dry white blended wines of the region. As with the majority of Portuguese white wines, drink them young, while they're fresh. Our favorite dry whites from the region are the pure Arinto made by Quinta da Alorna and the Alvarinho/Sauvignon Blanc/Verdelho blend from Quinta da Lagoalva de Cima.

Conde de Vimioso, Quinta do Casal Branco, and Quinta da Lagoalva de Cima wineries produce fine local red wines made with indigenous and international grape varieties. Most Ribatejo blended red wines are medium-to-full-bodied with black fruit flavors. For a pure expression of the local Trincadeira grape, we suggest Casa Cadaval's tasty red wine for $16. Prices for most Ribatejo wines range from $7.50 to $25.

TERRAS DO SADO VR

Important DOC Regions

Moscatel de Setubal, Palmela

Terras do Sado wines are often blends of native and international varieties. Quinta da Bacalhoa and Jose Maria de Fonseca are the two top producers of the region. The latter is best known for their Castelhao-based wine, Periquita. This dry, medium-bodied wine with bright raspberry and strawberry flavors is one of Portugal's best values, at about $10 a bottle. Try Periquita with a turkey sandwich with cranberry relish, or with a slice of pizza.

Moscatel de Setubal. Moscatel de Setubal is a full-bodied, fortified wine produced from the white Moscatel grape in Portugal's Setubal region. Moscatel is the local name for the Muscat grape. It can be labeled as five, twenty, or twenty-five years and typically exhibits orange blossom and stone fruit flavors. Vintage Moscatel is complex, long-lived, and expensive.

These luscious sweet whites can be paired with blue-veined cheeses, fresh peaches, crepes Suzette, or a flan. J. M. Fonseca produces an entry-level, five-year-old wine called Alambre that sells for under $20, as well as a twenty-year-old Moscatel (about $70 a bottle).

Palmela. The most important native red varietal of the region is Castelhao. For white wines, Arinto, Fernao Pires, and Moscatel lead the pack. There are lots of unusual blends being crafted, and foreign grape types are widely planted.

Our favorite Palmela white, and one of our top Portuguese picks, is the dry Muscat "JP" ($12) made by the Jose Maria da Fonseca winery. Its hint of sweetness makes this wine a lovely contrast for the heat of a spicy shrimp curry and a complement to the fruit chutney served with it.

ALENTEJANO VR

Important DOC Region

Alentejo

The Alentejo is a very large DOC region and is home to some of the nation's finest and most complex red wines. It is also the largest source of corks in the world. Vineyards in the Alentejo are planted with both indigenous and international white and red grape types.

A bargain-priced dry white wine we suggest is the Monte Velho by Herdade de Esporao. This wine features fresh white fruit flavors and is only about $9. Serve it well chilled as a refreshing lunchtime accompaniment to the region's most famous dish, *carne de porco alentejano,* a stew of clams, linguica sausage, and pork topped with potato and onions. We also suggest their pure Touriga Nacional wine and their blended Reserva and Garrafeira red wines.

When the sun goes down and the air cools, we urge you to indulge in the red wines of the region. The dominant red grapes are Trincadeira, Castelhao, Aragones, and Alicante Bouschet.

The wine "pioneer" of the Alentejo is Joao Portugal Ramos. He has been a consultant for over a dozen other wineries and makes fine wines at his own property in Alentejo, as well as in Ribatejo and Douro. His basic easy-drinking light-bodied, inexpensive red wine to look for is Marques de Borba; there is also a medium-to-full-bodied *reserva* version.

Another accomplished winemaker in the Alentejo region is Luis Duarte of Herdade dos Grouse. We enjoy both their white and red wines.

For a traditional-style wine with leather and earthy flavors, try the "Cartuxa" by Fundacao Eugenio de Almeida. Or try the more international-style wines made by the Cortes da Quinta do Carmo, and Alianca wineries. Alianca's "T" is a medium-to-full-bodied red with soft tannins and a heady perfume of licorice, tobacco, mocha, and black fruits. At $50 a bottle, it truly represents the quality potential of Alentejo's red wines.

The Alentejo is known within Portugal for its delicious charcuterie products, whose smoky and salty flavors are a wonderful contrast to the region's fruity rosés and inexpensive reds. The moderately priced to expensive red wines of the Alentejo partner well with wild game dishes or aged cheeses.

White and rosé wines of the Alentejo usually sell for under $12. Red wines range from under $10 to $50.

Sercial is a dry fortified wine with high acidity. Serve about 2½ ounces chilled in a small wineglass.

MADEIRA

The island of Madeira is located off the coast of Africa. Madeira wines are fortified with clear grape brandy, then heated in tanks called *estufas.* Vintage wines are an exception; these are slowly warmed in *canteiros,* or oak casks, for twenty years. Then they are aged an additional two years in bottle before they may be sold. It boggles our minds to consider that Madeira winery owners must be patient and wait twenty-two years to be able to sell their vintage wines. Unlike most wines, which can be harmed by too much air, Madeira wines are purposely exposed to oxygen, giving them a nutty smell and taste. They are high in alcohol (about 20%) and high in acidity.

About 60% of the island is planted with the black Tinta Negra Mole grape, which is used for inexpensive, younger-style wines. However, the finest Madeiras are made from premium white grapes. The name of the grape appears on the label and indicates the wine's style: *Sercial* is the driest, *Verdelho* is semidry, and *Bual* and *Malmsey* are sweet. Madeira is made in a number of styles to suit every budget and mood. *Rainwater* is an affordable, lighter style we recommend for cooking; another type of inexpensive

Madeira is aged three years and may be labeled as finest, choice, or selected. We enjoy the reserve, which is aged five years before release and is priced at under $30. Old reserve (aged ten years) and extra reserve (aged fifteen years) come next in the hierarchy, then vintage Madeiras. *Colheita* vintage is aged five years in cask and one in bottle before sale, and classic vintage Madeira is aged twenty years in cask and then two in bottle before sale.

A standard portion of Madeira is 2½ ounces (75 milliliters). Sercial and Verdelho are excellent partners for savory foods. Their refreshing nature—Madeira wines are known for their high acidity—serves to cleanse the palate after rich foods such as seared foie gras, and their nutty flavor is a perfect complement to foods with nuts, such as satay of chicken or vegetable dumplings with a peanut sauce. We usually chill the Sercial and Verdelho wines unless they are accompanying a hot soup. Serve the Bual and Malmsey at cellar temperature [about 55°F (13°C)] or slightly warmer in the winter months) with nut-based desserts such as pecan pie, baklava, or chestnut and chocolate cake.

Some of the Best Madeira Producers

Blandys, Leacock, Cossart Gordon, D'Olivares, and Henriques & Henriques are the major wineries that export to America. Prices range from inexpensive to very expensive for old-vintage wines.

chapter 12

Essen und trinken
Germany and Austria

Groupthink pervades so many aspects of our lives. Despite our claim to be independent and individualistic, we veer more often than not toward conformity with the crowd. It took some carmakers longer than others, but every major auto producer, including Porsche and BMW, now offers SUVs as part of its lineup. And we are all familiar with the uniforms that teenagers have adopted over the decades, whether it's the 1960s jeans and leather jackets of Marlon Brando in *The Wild One* or the hip-huggers and layered look of every sixteen-year-old girl today.

The same group behavior is true in wine. However loudly we proclaim our desire to be different, social pressures push us to conform to Chardonnay, Pinot Grigio, and Shiraz. Not only are they easy to say and drink, but they also mark us as part of the cognoscenti. They are comfort names that allow us to drink without making a mistake.

But if you really want to show that you are not simply part of the herd, then the wines of Austria and Germany offer you plenty of choices. Fear not, dear *WineWise* reader: you will not be completely alone. Indeed, you will be part of that rare breed that is at the cutting edge of what is trendy, and you will have the added advantage of knowing that many of the wines are of good to very high quality. Austrian and German wines are particularly suitable to the new consumer because their labels usually carry a varietal designation, but you will not be confronted with an over-abundance of the usual suspects—Chard and Cab and Shiraz and PG—though you can find them if you want.

What the two nations' wines offer are high-quality examples of the neglected (Riesling), the overlooked (Gruner Veltliner), the unknown (Zweigelt), and some of the old standbys (Chardonnay, Sauvignon Blanc). For as long as we can remember, knowledgeable individuals in the wine business have been talking about the "Riesling renaissance," predicting that this noble grape will find a place in every wine drinker's heart. We love Riesling and are particularly enamored of Austrian and German Rieslings that embody everything truly remarkable about this grape and its wine (see pages 27–28). Austria's native grapes, particularly the white Gruner Veltliner, are especially expressive and individualistic. Indeed, German and Austrian winemakers offer the consumer the full range of wine styles, except heavy-handed use of oak. For a glimpse of the new and exciting possibilities from a new wave of winemakers in these countries, we will present a survey of their grape types and major growing regions. The point that we want to emphasize most about the wines of Germany and Austria is that they are not all sweet. Yes, these countries make beautifully structured and mesmerizing sweet wines, but their dry and off-dry versions are fine expressions of their environment and just as worthy of our consideration.

We have grouped the two countries in the same chapter simply because of some similarities of label language and their proximity to one another. For full coverage, we advise you to read the section on Germany before Austria.

Germany

Climate

As the northern partner in this duo, Germany has always been considered a cool, even cold grape-growing climate. Because of that, Germany has always been associated with lighter, lower-alcohol, more delicate white wines, with very little attention given to red grapes. As we have pointed out in other places in this book, an extreme latitude away from the equator may mean cooler temperatures overall, but it also

Germany has a long history of making wine. This wine press dates from 1801.

means longer hours of daylight during the growing season. And it is not just heat that ripens grapes. As long as there is daylight, the vine plant is working and the grapes are ripening. In the attentive hands of an understanding grape grower, the result is often a more balanced ripeness that will translate into a more harmonious, if delicate, wine. From that simple truth, we move to Al Gore's *An Inconvenient Truth:* the world is hotter, and that is affecting climate patterns, including Germany's. It is impossible to say right now what the long-term effects of climate change will be. Ironically, there is the possibility of colder winters that may cause devastating damage to some of the vineyards. But if it is simply a matter of warmer springs, summers, and falls, then we may see a long streak of riper, more alcoholic wines from Germany, as well as the establishment of a serious red wine industry where previously such an idea was unthinkable.

Language of the label

Historically, German wine labels have been a nightmare for the average consumer, even for average German consumers. We will not even try to explain the various systems that have been established over the years. We can only encourage our astute *WineWise* readers to retain a few German label words and their interpretation.

WINE NAME

Like all other wine-producing nations, Germany has its fair share of brand-name wines, many of which will be familiar to consumers. Those brands include the well-established examples of Blue Nun, Golden October, and Black Tower, but we should also mention a few new wave brand names such as Twisted River and Saint M. Whether established or new wave, labels on

Grans-Fassian produces a Riesling from the town of Trittenheim.

these wines will always provide regional information, and many will also give the grape variety used.

Away from the safety net of brand names, it is easy to develop a fear of falling when it comes to German wine names. Essentially, they are place names—either a village name, a vineyard name, or a combination of both. As with some other European wine-naming systems, it is sometimes impossible to tell from the label whether the name is a village or a vineyard, but here are a couple of hints.

1. If the wine name is two German words, and the first word ends in the letters -*er,* the wine is almost certainly named after a village *and* a vineyard, with the first word being the village reference and the second word being the vineyard. For example, a wine named Piesporter Goldtropfchen comes from a vineyard called Goldtropfchen in the village of Piesport. The wine is a Piesporter just like you might be a New Yorker or JFK wanted to be a Berliner.

2. If the wine name is one single German-looking word, there is no way from the label to tell if the wine is named for a village (in which case several vineyards might be the source of the grapes) or for one single vineyard. If it is from a single vineyard, probably your only indication will be the higher price.

S. A. Prum uses the brand name Essence for one of its Riesling wines.

From the perspective of the consumer, especially the adventurous consumer, the actual village and/or vineyard may be the last details to come to grips with. What are more important are the grape variety and the region, since those bits of information will directly open the window into the soul of the wine. Once you get familiar with what the individual grape types and regions offer, then you can begin to do more intense research into specific vineyard locations with books such as *The Atlas of German Wines* by Hugh Johnson and Ian Jamieson.

GRAPE VARIETY

Ninety-nine percent of German wine labels name the grape variety. As mentioned already, Germany has always concentrated on white grape varieties, and of those, the most revered is Riesling. When the climate cooperates, Germany makes superlative Riesling in many different styles, from bone dry through off-dry to lightly sweet and very sweet. In addition to the mighty Riesling, consumers in the United States can find examples of the white grape variety Muller-Thurgau that produces very pleasant, fruity, light-to-medium-bodied wines, but without the depth and grace of Riesling.

A little rarer are Germany's examples of Gewurztraminer, Pinot Blanc (Weissburgunder), and Pinot Gris (Grauburgunder or Rulander), providing greater impact of flavors and more body and substance in the

A *Qualitatswein* wine produced by Schloss Johannisberg using Riesling grapes grown in the Rheingau region.

wines. If warmer climates do become a fact of life, we can expect to see more of these varieties in the future. The same is true of Pinot Noir, though at the moment German Pinot Noir is still something of a crap shoot.

DRYNESS AND SWEETNESS LEVELS

Many German producers try to help the consumer by including on the label a notation of the relative dryness or sweetness of the wine. The two possible indications are:

- *Trocken*, meaning dry
- *Halbtrocken*, suggesting off-dry, or a little sweet

Special WineWise insight into German "quality" levels

If you have been wondering why we keep putting the word *quality* within quotation marks, you are WineWise beyond your years. Our reason is that the method behind the system is not really about quality at all.

It is true that the grapes for *Qualitatswein* and *Pradikaatswein* must be grown within specially designated "quality" wine regions—that is, the grapes cannot be grown just anywhere. But the whole system is really based on sugar levels in the grapes at harvest. In other words, the system is about how ripe (based on sugar content) the grapes were. As we have said all along, true, balanced ripeness is not just about sugar. And just because grapes come to the winemaker with high sugar levels does not mean that the result will be good-quality wine! So with that major caveat in mind, the WineWise consumer needs to interpret the other words that appear on the label.

However, if neither term is on the label, you cannot infer that the wine is sweet; you will just have to try it to find out. That can't be too painful, can it? Special WineWise hint: check the alcohol level on the label; if it is over 12.5%, it is probably a dry wine. Lower alcohol levels will indicate that the winemaker stopped the fermentation to leave residual sugar in the finished wine.

DESIGNATED "QUALITY" LEVELS

Germany has two levels of "quality" wines:

- *Qualitatswein*, which means "quality wine"
- *Pradikaatswein*, usually translated as "quality wine with special attributes." Until August 1, 2007, this category was formerly identified as *Qualitatswein mit Pradikat*.

Any wine with either of these labels will also identify the region where the grapes were grown and the grape variety.

For more information, see the sidebars on "quality" levels and on *Pradikaatswein*.

REGION NAME

For all *Qualitatswein* and *Pradikaatswein* products, the label will indicate which region the grapes came from. There are thirteen official grape-growing regions for "quality" wine in Germany, but, don't fret, the U.S. market rarely sees wines from more than five. The five, in order of presence on the U.S. market, are:

- Mosel-Saar-Ruwer
- Rheinhessen
- Pfalz
- Rheingau
- Nahe

Please note that from the 2007 vintage onward, the region name Mosel-Saar-Ruwer officially changed to just Mosel. Throughout the rest of this text we will refer to the region as Mosel.

Pradikaatswein, previously *Qualitatswein mit Pradikat*

Of all the wine words we have ever had to translate, this is perennially the most challenging. But let's cut to the chase: *Pradikat* is a ranking. In this case, the ranking is based on sugar levels in the grapes at harvest, not an assessment of the wine after it has been made.

Within the *Pradikaatswein* category, the rankings are:

- **Kabinett,** suggesting ripe grapes, based on sugar content; the wine should show ripe but not overripe flavors—there may still be some greenness to the flavors

- **Spatlese,** suggesting slightly overripe grapes, with fuller fruit flavors

- **Auslese,** indicating a wine made from specially selected, obviously ripe bunches,

giving a wine of solid flavors, complexity, and length

Any of the above wines might also come with the label indication of *Trocken* or *Halbtrocken*, giving an idea of the dryness/sweetness level of the wine. With the subsequent rankings of *Pradikat* listed below, there is so much sugar in the grapes at harvest that the wines will always be sweet.

- **Eiswein (Icewine),** made from grapes frozen on the vine (see page 9)

- **Beerenauslese,** rare and expensive, indicating a concentrated, sweet dessert wine made from very ripe or botrytized grapes (see pages 8–9)

- **Trockenbeerenauslese,** extremely rare and expensive, indicating all the grapes were botrytized to make a sinfully rich and decadent dessert wine (caution—drink responsibly in very small amounts)

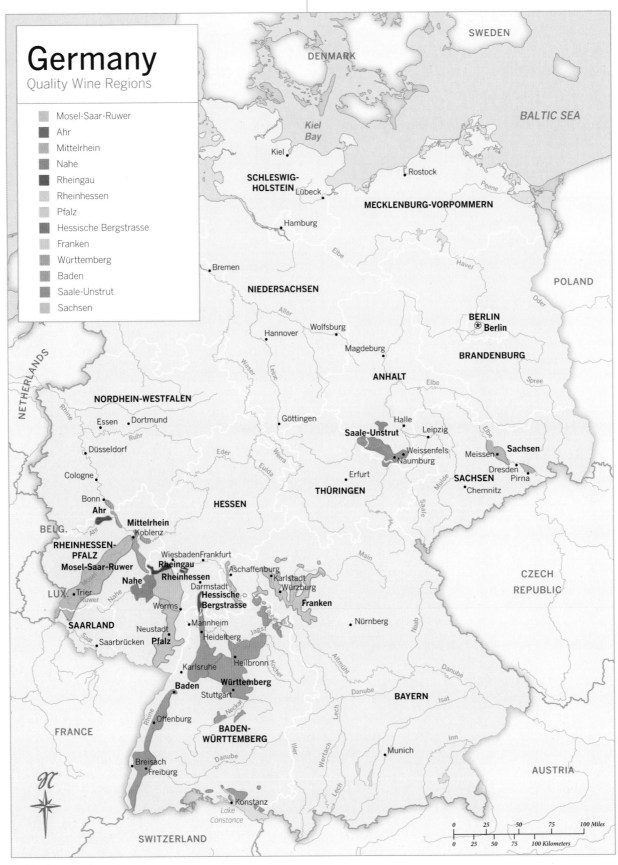

The German wine regions.

Where can quality be found? More WineWise insight

So if the *Pradikat* system with its rankings is all about sugar levels in grapes at harvest, and is not a reliable indicator of quality, what is the WineWise consumer to do?

With any agricultural product, quality cannot be legislated. It comes from the head, heart, and hands of the people who grow the raw material and process it. As always, we maintain that there are wine producers whose names are synonymous with quality. They have a vision and follow it through with integrity and honesty. We have included a representative selection of such producers within each regional commentary.

Other attempts by German wine producers to steer consumers toward quality products have taken two directions recently: the use of the terms *Classic* and *Selection* on the label, and the indication on a label that the grapes came from a premium vineyard site.

Classic and Selection

The term *Classic* indicates a vintage-dated, single-varietal wine that is "harmoniously dry" to the taste. The label will indicate the region of origin but cannot mention a village or vineyard name.

Selection wines must be made from grapes harvested by hand from a single vineyard, which must be named on the label.

Premium Vineyard Site

After a two-decade struggle promoting this concept, some German regions have recently allowed the inclusion on the label of various terms that denote that the wine came from a recognized high-quality vineyard, the equivalent of *premier cru* or *grand cru* from France. Regional notations for these very special wines include:

Mosel: *Erste Lage* (*Lage* is the German word for "vineyard")

Rheingau: *Erstes Gewachs* (first growth)

Rheinhessen: *Hochgewachs* (high growth)

Pfalz: *Grosses Gewachs* (great growth)

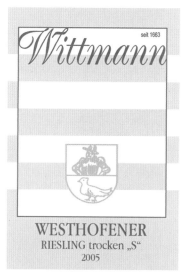

seit 1663

Wittmann

WESTHOFENER
RIESLING trocken „S"
2005

A Riesling Select label.

PRICE LEVELS

The relative prices of German wines are certainly a reflection of availability and the integrity of the producer. Within any one category of wine, there will be price variation. But for the most part, the relative bargains are to be found in the brand-name wines and at the *Qualitatswein* and *Kabinett* levels. *Spatlese* and *Auslese* wines will be moderately expensive to expensive, while the truly expensive group includes the three dessert wine rankings (*Beerenauslese, Eiswein,* and *Trockenbeerenauslese*).

Since any one producer will often make a range of wines covering several rankings from the same region, even from the same village or vineyard, our comments in the regional section will include listings of reputable producers without any indication of expense, unless there is something particularly noteworthy.

Regions

MOSEL

For decades this region has produced the archetypal German Rieslings—floral, delicate, lightly perfumed wines that walk a razor-thin line between acidity and sweetness while providing vibrant, fresh citric fruit flavors like a burst of lime sorbet. These wines are so well balanced that we never really notice that they are sweet or searingly high in acidity. Like a magnificent monarch butterfly, they bring great pleasure, and yet they are elusive, hard to pin down.

What makes all this possible is the sacred combination of climate, soil, and topography in the three river valleys that contain the Mosel, Saar, and Ruwer rivers. The rest of the magic lies in the steep river valleys that provide dramatic examples of south-facing slopes with slate as a major component of the soil. In many places, even the topsoil is slate. The delicacy of such wines makes them perfect as an aperitif, a before-dinner drink to whet the appetite. However, do not dismiss them as food wines. The foods would have to be delicately prepared, but Mosel wines work particularly well with lightly poached or lightly smoked seafood items. They are also the perfect choice for moderately spicy foods, especially Indian, Thai, Vietnamese, and Szechuan or Hunan Chinese dishes.

Notable producers are numerous. We particularly recommend the following: Fritz Haag, Willi Haag, Reinhold Haart, Johannishof, Keller, Reichsgraf von Kesselstatt, Kuhling-Gillot, Schloss-Lieser, Dr. Loosen, Egon Muller (all rare and expensive), von Othegraven, J. J. Prum, Selbach-Oster, Dr. H. Thanisch, and St. Urbans-Hof.

As we have mentioned before, the relatively light, green nature of wines from this region is reflected in the tradition of using green bottles. The wines from the regions discussed below have traditionally been marketed in brown bottles, reflecting their fuller body and riper fruit flavors.

RHEINHESSEN

Often dismissed as a sea of mediocre *Liebfraumilch*-style wines (like Blue Nun), the region of Rheinhessen has been making noise lately, and a very pleasant noise it is, created by the hard work and creative dynamism of a new generation of winemakers.

First, it has to be said that there has always been a handful of highly reputable producers of very fine

The village of Trittenheim on the Mosel River is surrounded on all sides by vineyards.

The village of Nierstein and its vineyards.

wines from vineyards around the village of Nierstein in the northeast corner of the region. Perched high above the Rhine River on east- and southeast-facing slopes, the wines from these vineyards project the ripeness of apricots and peaches as well as the minerality of the red sandstone that is clearly visible in that sacred enclave. Our advice would be never pass up the opportunity to taste or buy a Niersteiner (that's a wine from Nierstein, right?), especially if the vineyards involved are Holle, Hipping, Pettenthal, Paterberg, or Bruckchen.

But in the rest of this very large region, it is the sheer determination of the new mavericks who have turned their back on the ubiquitous and easy Muller-Thurgau and sought out special pockets of vineyard land suited to particular grapes. In addition, they are farming the vineyards completely with an eye to quality, restricting the yield per vine. The results, in some cases, have been nothing short of astounding—with Riesling, to be sure, but also with the unheralded Silvaner grape and the previously untried Sauvignon Blanc.

Notable producers (so far) include Bruder Dr. Becker, Groebe, Gunderloch, Heyl Zu Herrnsheim, Keller, Kuhling-Gillot, Villa Sachsen, Geschwister Scuch, Wagner-Stempel, Schloss Westerhaus, Winter, and Wittman.

PFALZ

Of the five regions we discuss here, Pfalz is the warmest on a regular basis, as evidenced by the frequent sightings of lemons and figs growing in various places throughout the region. Consequently, the wines show a good deal more ripe fruit character, even tropical fruit, creating a warm glow in the drinker, balanced by a good zip of acidity to bring us back to reality. Riesling is the most important grape here, especially in the more favored vineyard locations, but other grapes such as Gewurztraminer and the *drei* Pinots (Blanc, Gris, and Noir) have gained some ground and are drawing increased attention. However, we want to stress again that good Pinot Noir from anywhere in Germany is still something of a rarity.

The solid mouthfeel that these wines present, along with their fuller, clean flavors and high acidity, all make them especially well suited to the table. They make excellent accompaniments to baked fish or roast chicken, turkey, or pork, especially if those dishes include a spicy fruit note. But they are also very versatile, working well with the milder spice notes of

A cliff of Riesling vineyards at the western end of the Rheingau region.

To *Pradikat* or not

Some producers in various German regions have decided that there is an inherent flaw in the *Pradikat* system, with its rankings based on sugar levels in the grapes at harvest.

They argue that those sugar levels have nothing to do with quality and are often misinterpreted as an indication of the style of the wine. The assumption among many consumers is that the word *Spatlese* or *Auslese* on a label automatically means that the wine will be sweet. But if the sugars in the grapes are all turned to alcohol during fermentation, then even those wines can be dry.

To avoid at least some potential confusion, advocates of dry German Riesling often label their wine simply as *Qualitatswein,* even though the sugar levels at harvest would qualify their wine for *Pradikat* status. They believe that if they put one of the *Pradikat* rankings on the label, the consumer will automatically assume that the wine is sweet.

Backing up this claim to fine wine production is a long and glorious history of winemaking, exemplified by the elaborate chateaux at Schloss Johannisberg and Schloss Vollrads, and by the monastic influence of Kloster Eberbach. Indeed, Schloss Johannisberg has its own story to back up its claim that they invented botrytized wine (by accident, of course).

The "Discovery" of the Joys of Rot

According to Johannisberg legend, back in the eighteenth century the beginning of the grape harvest had to be approved by the local bishop, a prominent lord and landowner. Although the customary courier was sent off to the bishop's domain as usual, his return was somehow delayed, and the polite but puzzled grape growers refused to pick without permission. With the delayed return of the messenger, the grapes began to rot, much to the dismay of the growers, but still they held off. On the return of the courier (did nobody ever ask where he had been?), harvesting of the rotten grapes began, and the hapless growers let the fermentation proceed, only to "discover" the glories of wine made from grapes that had shriveled due to the onset of the mold. Is this story a candidate for Ripley?

biryani or masala dishes from India or the spicy peanut cuisine from Thailand or Korea.

Some of our favorite producers include Basserman-Jordan, Burklin-Wolf, von Buhl, and Pfeffingen-Fuhrmann-Eymael.

RHEINGAU

Mosel wines have their incredibly delicate balancing act that always makes them attractive; Pfalz wines can be deeply satisfying; but there is something spiritual, almost religious, about a good Rheingau—an exquisite marriage of clean, lean, laser-like fruit with a stony, mineral edge that is simply uplifting. The Rheingau area specializes almost completely in Riesling, made in a dry, austere style that is definitely a reflection of south-facing slopes and the red slate,

The messenger whose tardiness resulted in rotten grapes at the Johannisberg estate.

The Nahe River joins the Rhine, with the Rheinhessen vineyards on the left and the Nahe vineyards on the right.

sandstone, and schist soils. Both Robert Weil and Georg Breuer are particularly well-respected producers of this style. Fine Rheingau Riesling, whether dry or slightly sweet, is such a classically elegant wine that it really demands a classically elegant dish such as perfectly cooked Dover sole or tuna carpaccio.

Prime producers in Rheingau include Robert Weil, Georg Breuer, Verwaltung der Staatsweinguter Eltville (whose vineyards include Kloster Eberbach), Schloss Johannisberg, Weingut Johannishof Eser, Freiherr zu Knyphausen, Balthasar Ress, Schloss Vollrads, and Domdechant Werner'sches Weingut.

NAHE

Until recently, Nahe wines have not been much admired in the United States, perhaps because Mosel, Pfalz, and Rheingau are so much more famous and thus more marketable. But there are gems to be had here, especially if you can find some Riesling from the villages of Bad Kreuznach, Schlossbockelheim, or their nearby neighbors. These villages lie about mid-

point on the Nahe River as it winds its way in a particularly snaky slither northeastward to Bad Kreuznach. Here the volcanic soils give Riesling from the best (south-facing) vineyards a healthy dose of hard minerality that seems to perfectly set off the riper apricot and peach notes of this noble grape, especially in the company of sweetbreads.

Further north, the landscape begins to flatten out as the Nahe flows toward its confluence with the Rhine at the city of Bingen. Remember Hildegard, the abbess and accomplished composer? If only the beauty and serenity of Hildegard's music was matched by all of the wines from the lower stretches of the Nahe. Alas, that has not been the case, but increased plantings of the tricolor of Pinot grape varieties (Noir, Blanc, and Gris) may bring greater fame in the future. And who knows? You, *WineWise* reader, may be at the vanguard of this movement.

Preferred Nahe producers include Dr. Crusius, Diel, Emrich-Schonleber, Donnhoff, Kruger-Rumpf, Prinz zu Salm-Dalberg, and Tesch.

Austria

AUSTRIA HAS EMERGED as a scintillating wine personality of the twenty-first century, based primarily on its commitment to quality and its unabashed promotion of some unusual grape varieties alongside the usual cast of characters. It's like watching another formulaic Anthony Hopkins movie, and all of sudden Edward Norton comes onto the screen. As we have commented before, anywhere can and does make Chardonnay and Cabernet Sauvignon, but it's not every day of the week that you come across intriguing newcomers such as Gruner Veltliner (white) and Blaufrankisch (red). If you have not tried these gems so far, we encourage you warmly and heartily to get out there and do so. We are convinced you will thank us. If you have ventured down this path already, keep going, for there is much more to discover.

**LANGENLOISER
GRÜNER VELTLINER**

TROCKEN
QUALITÄTSWEIN L-F-153998

KAMPTAL-ÖSTERREICH
℮ 75cl - 12,5%vol

**ERZEUGERABFÜLLUNG
FRED LOIMER
A-3550 LANGENLOIS**

Gruner Veltliner wines have won many fans recently.

The Austrian grape-growing regions boast a variety of climates that allow for the full expression of these grape varieties and in a dry style, as well as some of the most highly sought-after sweet dessert Rieslings in the world.

Language of the label

Like German wine labels, Austrian versions are immediately consumer-friendly because they specify the grape type prominently. They also provide information about which growing region the grapes are from, and they use a very similar system of "quality" designation (note the quotation marks again) based on sugar levels at harvest. Occasionally there are also dryness or sweetness descriptions.

WINE NAME
Some Austrian producers stress the grape variety as the wine name, while others use the village and/or vineyard method that is also used in Germany (see pages 251–252). Even if the wine is named for the place (region, village, or vineyard), the grape variety will also be indicated.

GRAPE VARIETY
Currently the two most frequently seen Austrian wines in the U.S. market are Riesling and Gruner Veltliner. In a broad sense, Austrian Riesling has some similarities to the various German versions, ranging from steely, nervy minerality with green citrus fruit to rich, luscious, and stupefyingly sweet—there really is something for everybody. But Gruner Veltliner (the Gru Vee grape) is a world unto itself, like stumbling into an exotic Moroccan market in the middle of Fifth Avenue—slightly musky, perfumed, but always fresh, even prickly, with an Asian pear flavor and background of spicy white pepper.

Once again, the three Pinots—Pinot Noir (Spatburgunder), Pinot Blanc (Weissburgunder), and Pinot Gris (Grauburgunder or Rulander)—are making something of a splash here, and may even win acclaim as the climate picture continues to change. And there are a couple of old faithfuls in the guise of Chardonnay (Morillon), Sauvignon Blanc, Cabernet Sauvignon, and Merlot. As always, the latter two are sometimes made as single-varietal wines, but more often they are blended. But some of the real excitement lies in the unknown reds that Austria has embraced as its own—Saint Laurent, Blaufrankisch, and Zweigelt. They may never claim the throne from other, more rightful contenders, but they are certainly worth a look.

DRYNESS AND SWEETNESS LEVELS

The use of the terms *Trocken* and *Halbtrocken* have the same meaning as in Germany, dry and semidry, while the additional term *Halbsuss* will indicate semisweet, which would be noticeably sweeter than *Halbtrocken*.

DESIGNATED "QUALITY" LEVELS

Once again we are dealing with words on the label that convey an indication of "quality," though the words themselves are a direct reflection of sugar levels in the grapes at harvest. The system is the same as the German (see page 253), with these two differences:

- *Kabinett:* in Austria, *Kabinett* is not a ranking within the *Pradikat* system but is its own category, above *Qualitatswein* but below the *Pradikat* level
- *Ausbruch:* this is an additional ranking of sugar ripeness between *Beerenauslese* and *Trockenbeerenauslese*

Austria
Wine Zones and Regions

Niederösterreich
Wachau

Kremstal

Kamptal

Weinviertel

Donauland

Carnuntum

Thermenregion

Wien
Wien

Burgenland
Neusiedlersee

Neusiedlersee-Hügelland

Mittelburgenland

Südburgenland

Steiermark
Süd-Oststeiermark

Südsteiermark

Weststeiermark

The wine regions of Austria.

Label showing the district name of Wachau.

PLACE NAME

Austrian labels are almost obsessive about indicating the place where the grapes were grown. There are three large regions (Niederosterreich, Burgenland, and Styria), and each of these has smaller districts within them. If all of the grapes came from one of these smaller districts, that name will be indicated on the label. The most important and most frequently seen district names are Kamptal, Kremstal, and Wachau, all contained within the Niederosterreich region.

PRICE LEVELS

Given the quality and discovery factor surrounding Austrian wines, they are remarkably affordable. In addition to the *Qualitatswein* level, the Austrian *Kabinett* wines and some of the lower-ranking *Pradikaatswein* will easily qualify as moderately expensive if not relative bargains. As always, once you ascend to the dizzy heights of limited-production Icewine or botrytis-affected wines, the price will soar to the truly expensive level. There are some producers whose wines are rare and highly sought after and are therefore very expensive across the board.

Regions

NIEDEROSTERREICH (LOWER AUSTRIA)

With its holy trinity of the subdistricts Kamptal, Kremstal, and Wachau, this region commands a lot of attention around the world, especially for its dry versions of Riesling and Gruner Veltliner. The aromatic emphases of stone fruits and hard mineral edge are truly revelatory, and any one of the dry wines would be a valid candidate for some serious aging. Any opportunity you get to try a dry version from any one of these districts should not be passed by, especially if the wine is from a single vineyard such as Heiligenstein. But take care, and be prepared to be transported. Successful mission, Mr. Spock; beam us up, Scotty!

If you have to let food enter that ethereal picture, imagine the Riesling with poached turbot, and the Gruner Veltliner with pork medallions with pasta in a light tarragon cream sauce, or a stir-fry with Asian vegetables—equally out of this world.

We should also point out that when climatic conditions permit, the prized vineyards of these districts produce extraordinary dessert styles of Riesling that exhibit a purity of flavor that is hard to comprehend. It's like having a lifetime of good Riesling in a single glass.

One note about label terminology: the Wachau district retains slightly different terms on its labels, as indicated below.

General Austrian Term	Wachau Equivalent
Qualitatswein	*Steinfeder*
Kabinett	*Federspiel*
Spatlese	*Smaragd*

Further south, in the district of Thermenregion, there is a greater concentration on the red varieties of Pinot Noir and St. Laurent, the new *noir* in Austrian wine, and, for some, a viable alternative to Pinot Noir with similar characteristics. Of the two, St. Laurent tends to be a little fuller in body if treated well in the vineyard and winery, but both display what might be thought of as a New World profile—bright red to dark red fruit character, a little spiciness of black pepper, and an edge of earthy exotica. As such, they work well with dishes such as lamb kebabs or mushroom risotto.

Well-respected producers in this region include F. X. Pichler, Prager (both producers of some very expensive wines, but they are well worth it), Brundlmayer, Nigl, Lenz Moser, Weinrieder, Loimer, and Alzinger.

BURGENLAND

As a much warmer region, Burgenland concentrates more on red wines and white dessert wines—indeed, many authorities would cite the village of Rust in Burgenland as the mecca for sweet dessert white wine. The vineyards here seem to have no problem producing fully ripe grapes that have elevated sugar levels but also retain high levels of acidity to provide balance in the finished wines. A Ruster Ausbruch should certainly be on your list of things to try before you get beamed up for good.

For reds, the plantings include the indigenous varieties of Zweigelt and Blaufrankisch (Limberger or Lemberger in other places, including Washington State), as well as the international varieties of Caber-

net Sauvignon, Merlot, and Syrah. Of the two native varieties, the Blaufrankisch produces a fuller, darker wine with firm tannins and high acidity, a bit like the Barbera wines of Piedmont in Italy (see page 200), while the Zweigelt is closer to the Beaujolais wines of France (see pages 150–151) or Dolcetto of Italy (see page 200). Reputable producers in Burgenland include Kracher, Opitz (both almost entirely sweet wine production, very expensive and very worth it), Wenzel, Tremmel, Schrock, and Igler.

STEIERMARK (STYRIA)

This most southerly of the regions is home mostly to white grapes, especially Sauvignon Blanc, Chardonnay (sometimes labeled as Morillon), Pinot Blanc (Weissburgunder), and Pinot Gris (Grauburgunder). In that regard, this is an area to look for if you have been invited to a tasting or dinner and asked to bring a Sauvignon Blanc or Chardonnay. How much more fun to show up with a Styrian version rather than the too familiar New World regulars! Look for them and try them—you may find a winner. Some of these will likely come from one of the following producers: Polz, Domane Muller, Wohlmuth, Sattler, Koller, Platzer.

chapter 13

Up and coming
Canada and Greece

While there are many countries and wine regions that make some very good wines, not all of them have an important presence in the U.S. market. For example, the wines of Israel, Lebanon, Hungary, and Uruguay are all available, but on a nationwide basis, representation on store shelves and wine lists can be spotty. Likewise, good wines from Michigan, Idaho, Texas, and Pennsylvania, among many other U.S. states, are not always available outside of local or regional markets.

We've identified two countries—Canada and Greece—as "up and coming" in the U.S. wine markets. We like these wines a lot and encourage you to give them a try. The quality is good to great, they are a pleasure to drink with a good meal, and the prices are reasonable.

Canada: Cool wines with finesse

QUALITY CANADIAN WINES first came on the scene in the 1970s. Today, there are more than three hundred wineries making fine wines. With so many wine-producing nations competing for your attention and affection, Canada is probably not the first country that comes to mind. But if you believe the maxim that "less is more," then you should be checking out Canadian wines, eh?

First, a clarification: when we say "less is more," we are referring to the fact that most Canadian wines are neither high in alcohol nor full-bodied and heavily oaked. This means that when it comes to wine and food pairing, the wines coexist with rather than dominate a dish. Just like Canadian people, the nation's wines can finesse difficult situations with equanimity. *WineWise* readers will also discover that there are many Canadian wines that offer great value.

Due to cool growing conditions in Canada, wine grapes retain a high level of acidity, which translates to mouth-watering, food-friendly wines with bright fruit flavors. Still and sparkling Rieslings—whether dry, semidry, or sweet—are racy and luscious. Graceful Chardonnays and elegant Pinot Gris wines round out our list of best bets. You'll note that these are the same grapes found in the Burgundy, Alsace, and Champagne regions of northern France, but the Canadian vineyards are blessed with more sunshine hours than those European regions. Most of the vineyards are planted close to bodies of water, which helps to moderate any extremes in temperature.

Chardonnay, Pinot Gris, Pinot Blanc, Sauvignon Blanc, Semillon, and Gewurztraminer are the principal white varieties planted in Canada's vineyards, while most of the red wines are based on Pinot Noir, Gamay, Syrah, Merlot, Cabernet Sauvignon, and Cabernet Franc. In this chapter we will suggest several of our favorite producers of these grape types. Some of these wines are easy-drinking examples for every day; others have that special something that merits your attention.

In this latter category, look no further than the pinnacle of Canadian wines, Icewine (Ice Wine is one word—Icewine—on Canadian labels, just as in Germany, where the wine is labeled as "Eiswein.") Icewine just may be the greatest dessert wine around, and

Icewine is truly a treasure. These low-alcohol wines offer bright acidity and layers of white fruit flavors. Enjoy a glass as a refreshing end to a meal or with simple desserts such as a pear tart.

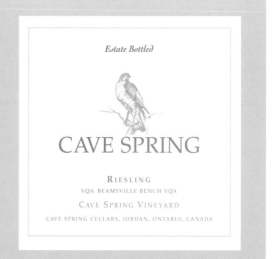

Riesling may be our favorite white grape. Cave Spring makes a lean, clean, fruity wine we enjoy on its own or with a variety of ethnic foods (see "Eat/Drink/Man/Woman: Wine and Food," pages 281–303). The grapes for this wine were grown in the Beamsville Bench subregion of the Niagara Peninsula DVA.

Canada is the world's largest producer of it. It is made by gently pressing grapes that have been naturally frozen on the vine. The frozen water remains behind, yielding a few drops of concentrated nectar from each grape. Icewines have a mouth-watering acidity that balances out their sweetness; as a result, they are never cloying and always alluring. They are usually sold in half bottles for about $40 to $75—pretty reasonable considering how little juice is taken from each berry.

Language of the label

Hooray! You do not have to take a wine course to understand Canadian wine labels. Most are labeled by varietal, which means that, by Canadian law, the wine contains at least 85% of the grape type named on the label. You may also encounter some fantasy- or proprietary-named wines, such as "Ping" by See Ya Later Ranch.

ORIGIN OF THE WINE

If a Designated Viticultural Area or DVA (such as Niagara Peninsula) appears on the label, a minimum of 85% of the grapes must come from that area. Aside from the hybrid white grape Vidal, which is used for some Icewines, all DVA wines must be made exclusively from *Vitis vinifera* grapes (the good stuff) planted within that DVA. The term *estate-bottled* guarantees that the grapes for the wine were grown in vineyards owned or controlled by the winery and that the grapes are 100% vinifera.

Note: Look for the Vintners Quality Alliance (VQA) sticker on the labels of Canadian wines. It's your assurance that 100% of the wine comes from the province listed on the label.

The major wine regions of Canada

Although a small amount of wine (as well as some delicious dessert ice apple ciders) is produced in Quebec and other provinces, in this chapter we will focus on the two provinces that produce the most wine, Ontario and British Columbia.

ONTARIO
Important DVA Wine Regions

Lake Erie North Shore, Pelee Island, and Niagara Peninsula (subregions such as "Beamsville Bench," within the Niagara Peninsula, may also be listed on labels)

About 80% of Canadian wines come from the province of Ontario; the vineyards that produce grapes for fine wine are in the southern portion of the province. Perhaps you have a mental picture of vast, snowy fields. In actuality, this is not the frozen tundra. It is part of a temperate zone known as the Carolinian Forest that stretches south to the Carolinas in the United States.

The climate in Ontario is comparable to that of Oregon or New Zealand; in fact, the Chianti vineyards of central Italy and those of the Niagara region are at the same latitude, the forty-third parallel. Here, the ambient temperature of the vineyards is impacted by their proximity to Lake Ontario and Lake Erie. In the spring, warm air rises from the land, drawing in cool air from the lakes. In the winter, the reverse is true: warm air from the lake rises, drawing in cool air from the land. This natural circulation system protects the vines from extreme temperatures.

The cool conditions allow the wineries to produce pure varietal wines that offer a direct expression of the vineyards' personality or *terroir*. Another benefit of the cool temperatures is high acidity levels, which extend the life of the wines.

It is this acidity that makes Canadian wines such good food wines. Consider Ontario Chardonnays, with their characteristic flavors of green apple and pear. Though medium-bodied when unadorned by oak, they become full-bodied when fermented or aged in oak. Try one with grilled swordfish with lemon butter and capers or even corn on the cob. What about fruity, light-to-medium-bodied wines with a hint of sweetness? Chenin Blanc, Gewurztraminer, and semidry Riesling wines may be used to contrast spicy, smoked, or salty foods. The hint of sweetness in these wines may also be used as a complement for dishes such as green papaya salad. The late harvest and Icewine versions of Riesling are even richer and more

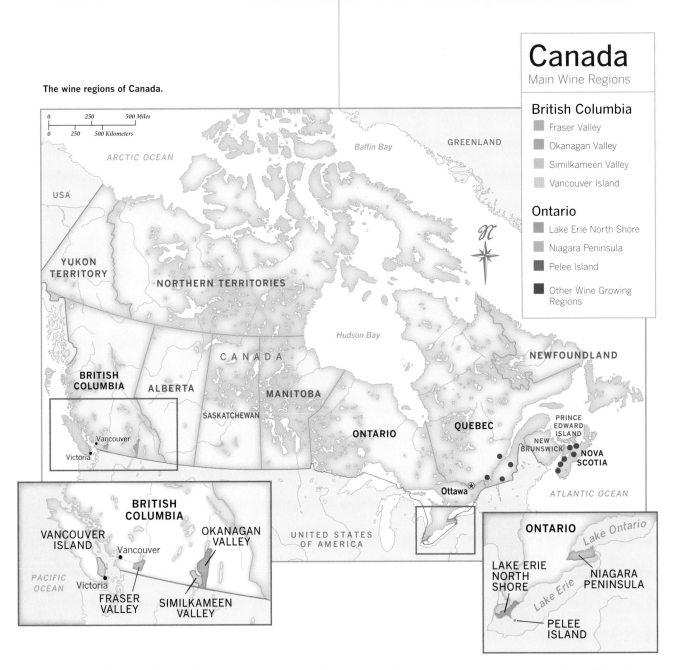

The wine regions of Canada.

Canada
Main Wine Regions

British Columbia
- Fraser Valley
- Okanagan Valley
- Similkameen Valley
- Vancouver Island

Ontario
- Lake Erie North Shore
- Niagara Peninsula
- Pelee Island
- Other Wine Growing Regions

complex. Flavors of honey, lychee nut, pineapple, and tropical fruits such as guava are retained by pairing these wines with a simple pound cake or apple pie. Of course, Icewines also can be enjoyed solo, as a "liquid dessert."

This province also produces a number of lovely reds. Elegant Pinot Noirs show all the bright red cherry, strawberry, and raspberry flavors you expect in their youth, taking on additional notes of mushrooms and tea with age. A perfectly grilled salmon steak with chopped tomatoes makes a lovely complement. The Beaujolais grape, Gamay, does well in Niagara, producing light-bodied, cherry-flavored wines with less complexity than Pinot Noir but at more affordable

prices. Gamays are a good match for Prince Edward Island mussels marinara. Cabernet Franc, a better choice for the climate than Cabernet Sauvignon, is also worth seeking out. The wine is medium to full in body, with charming red and/or black cherry flavors that showcase simply seasoned grilled red meats.

In 1974, Inniskillin was the first Canadian winery to be established since Prohibition. From the beginning, the founding team of Donald Ziraldo and Karl Kaiser focused on high quality rather than quantity. When their 1989 Vidal Icewine won a prestigious Grand Prize of Honor in a 1991 competition in France, it caught the attention of wine lovers around the world. Inniskillin continues to be one of the nation's finest winer-

The Niagara Escarpment protects many of Ontario's vineyards from cold northern winds. (Photo courtesy of Cave Spring Cellars)

ies, and we recommend its full line of wines. Another pioneer winery of the region is Cave Spring. Owned by the Penachetti family, Cave Spring was the first Canadian winery to emphasize gastronomy by opening a fine-dining restaurant, the Inn on the Twenty, at the winery. We enjoy its entire range of wines, especially when accompanied by food.

Most of Ontario's dry and semidry wines are inexpensive to moderately priced; some of the finer reds cost more, and the dessert-style late harvest and Icewines are always expensive.

In general, we believe Ontario excels with its white wines and lighter-style reds. If you are searching for full-bodied Canadian reds, then British Columbia can fill that bill.

We trust *WineWise* readers to be adventurous and seek out some of these flavorful wines. If you are traveling to Canada's largest city (Toronto) or to nearby Buffalo in New York State, you are within striking distance of the country's scenic wine regions. Until then, here are some wines we suggest you try.

White Wines: Dry and Semidry

Chardonnay: Cave Spring, Flat Rock, Inniskillin, Malivoire, Henry of Pellham, and Peninsula Ridge "Reserve"

Dry Sparkling: Cave Spring Brut, Henry of Pelham Blanc de Blancs

Gewurztraminer: Malivoire

Pinot Blanc: Inniskillin

Sauvignon Blanc: Creekside, Vineland Estates

Semidry Riesling: Cave Spring "Estate" and "CSV," Fielding "Rosamel Vineyard," Flat Rock "Nadja's Vineyard," Hillebrand Trius, Inniskillin, Vineland Estates "St. Urban Vineyard"

Vidal: Ancient Coast

White Wines: Sweet

Cabernet Franc Icewine: Inniskillin

Gewurztraminer Icewine: Birchwood, Inniskillin

Late Harvest Riesling: Cave Spring "Indian Summer"

Riesling Icewine: Cave Spring, Henry of Pelham

Vidal Icewine: Inniskillin, Konzelmann Estate, Lailey "Barrel Aged," Peller Estate

Vidal Sparkling Icewine: Inniskillin, Magnotta

Red Wines

Baco Noir: Henry of Pelham, Lakeview "Reserve"

Cabernet Franc: Inniskillin, Stratus, Tawse Family Estate, Thomas and Vaughan, Vineland Estate

Gamay: 13th Street "Reserve," Cave Spring "Estate"

Merlot: Lailey, Lakeview "Reserve Butlers Grant Vineyard"

Pinot Noir: 13th Street "Sandstone Reserve," Coyote Run "Reserve," Flat Rock, Henry of Pelham "Family Reserve," Le Clos Jordanne

BRITISH COLUMBIA
Important DVA Wine Regions
Okanagan Valley, Similkameen Valley, Fraser Valley, Gulf Islands, and Vancouver Island

The scenic beauty of the Coastal Mountains, Pacific Ocean, and verdant valleys make British Columbia an ideal place to live or tour. In fact, some of Canada's finest wines are produced in this region's vineyards. As in Ontario, it is the temperature-moderating effect of nearby water—in this case, the Pacific Ocean or Lake Okanagan—that aids the vines in achieving balanced ripeness in the grapes. Here too, many of the vineyards are located in the warmer southern portion of the province.

The wine scene in British Columbia is vibrant. New investments have brought more competition and wines to choose from, and as a result, the number of wineries has grown from fourteen in 1980 to over one hundred today. As established wineries gain wisdom from working their land and the vines mature, quality will continue to improve. The diversity of ethnic restaurants and the high quality of local foods also means there is room for a wide range of wine styles to accompany the food.

The region's vineyards are about equally split with white and red grapes. Ninety-seven percent are planted with the finest *Vitis vinifera* varieties; the balance is planted with hybrids. The comment "elegant" continually pops up in our tasting notes of BC wines. Leading the pack of our favorite whites are Pinot Gris and Chardonnay, followed by Pinot Blanc, Riesling, Gewurztraminer, and Sauvignon Blanc. Dry, medium-to-full-bodied Pinot Gris has the structure to showcase roasted chicken, lobster, or mushroom risotto. Or try a tart, juicy Sauvignon Blanc with raw oysters, another wonderful—and classic—pairing. Our go-to red is the cool-climate-friendly Pinot Noir; we also like the Cabernet Sauvignon, Merlot, and (as in the United States) Bordeaux-style "Meritage" blends of the two. Syrah, which most folks consider to be a warm-region grape, also does very well in British Columbia. Some wineries such as Sandhill are even making small lots of the Italian varieties Barbera and Sangiovese. Pair one of the region's Pinot Noirs with a gorgeous, meaty piece of fish—tuna, black cod, or salmon are all good choices. The full-bodied "Meritage" Bordeaux-style blends have the weight to stand up to wild game such as venison. Finally, full-bodied, peppery Syrah is a perfect complement for peppercorn-crusted steak—or, if you're slightly more adventurous, the Quebec meat pie known as *tourtiere.*

Within the five DVAs of British Columbia there are subregions, each with its own distinct character. Nk'Mip, for example, is located in the southern part of the Okanagan Valley. The low rainfall forces the vines to dig deep into the soil for moisture, and the resulting wines have an attractive mineral flavor. The Nk'Mip winery is North America's first aboriginal-owned winery, and we enthusiastically recommend its entire line of wines.

As in Ontario, prices of British Columbia wines range from inexpensive to moderate, with some of the noble red wines costing more and the dessert wines being the most expensive selections. Following are some of our favorites from the region.

White Wines

Chardonnay: Calona Vineyards "Artist Series Reserve," Cedar Creek, Laughing Stock, Stag's Hollow, Tinhorn Creek, Township 7

Chenin Blanc: Quails' Gate

Gewurztraminer: Gray Monk, Thornhaven, Tinhorn Creek, Wild Goose "Mystic River"

Pinot Blanc: Blue Mountain, Lake Breeze, Nk'Mip

Pinot Gris: Blasted Church, Burrowing Owl, Gray Monk, Lake Breeze, Mission Hill "Reserve," Red Rooster, Sandhill

Riesling: Gray Monk, Quails' Gate "Reserve," Red Rooster

Riesling Icewine: Gehringer Brothers, Jackson-Triggs "Proprietors' Grand Reserve," Nk'Mip

Sauvignon Blanc: Sumac Ridge "Black Sage Vineyard," Vineland Estate

Semillon: Lake Breeze
Sparkling: Sumac Ridge "Steller's Jay Brut"

Red Wines

Bordeaux-style "Meritage Blends":
Burrowing Owl, Cedar Creek "Platinum Reserve," Osoyoos Larose "Grand Vin," Sumac Ridge "Black Sage Vineyard"

Cabernet Franc: Hawthorne Mountain

Cabernet Sauvignon: Cedar Creek, Sumac Ridge "Black Sage Vineyard"

Merlot: Burrowing Owl, Cedar Creek "Platinum Reserve," Poplar Grove, Red Rooster, Stag's Hollow, Tinhorn Creek

Pinot Noir: Blue Mountain, Cedar Creek, Hawthorn Mountain, Mount Boucherie "Reserve," Nk'Mip, Quails' Gate, See Ya Later

Syrah/Shiraz: Burrowing Owl, Jackson-Triggs, Mission Hill, Sandhill "Small Lots"

Greece: Wines of antiquity and wines for today

WINE HAS ALWAYS been important to Greek culture. The Greeks have been getting together to drink wine, party, and exchange opinions since the seventh century B.C. They were also the first to develop and record organized vineyard strategies and fermentation methods, and in fact their farming, winemaking, and storage methods were adopted by the Romans. Wine was integral to the country's religious ceremonies, whether Christian, Jewish, or pagan. And perhaps most telling of all, the Greeks named a god after the wonderful liquid: Dionysus, the god of wine and merriment. Throughout Greek culture, wine was and is food for the body, mind, and soul.

This chapter will take *WineWise* readers beyond the world of Retsina and other rustic wines served in tavernas. We want to turn you on to the concept of *kerasma*—the pleasure of sharing food (and to us, wine *is* food) with friends and loved ones.

Are *you* ready to break free and venture outside the mainstream? Because here's the skinny: Greece is making some killer wines! A host of ambitious winemakers, many of whom studied and/or worked overseas, have brought back knowledge and techniques that have allowed the country to take giant steps forward. Advances in vineyard management and winemaking have resulted in wines of good value and distinction. Today, both traditional and "new wave" wines are being made from indigenous and international grape varieties.

The grapes of Greece

Greek wine drinkers need no longer look to imported wines to sample acclaimed international varietals. The usual suspects that first gained fame in France—Chardonnay, Sauvignon Blanc, Cabernet Sauvignon, Merlot, and Pinot Noir—are all planted here. The Greeks are also producing wines from grapes native to Italy (Sangiovese, Refosco), Spain (Tempranillo, Garnacha), and Germany (Riesling). While some are good and a few are very good, we feel that the majority of interesting and exciting Greek wines are based on the country's 300 unique grape varieties. Luckily, you only need to know a handful of them to start exploring the wonderful world of these wines.

THE REDS

- **Agiorgitiko** (also known as St. George): The most important red grape of southern Greece, it produces wines with aromas and flavors of black currant, strawberry, cherry, and plum. Bargain-priced versions tend to be medium in body, while the moderate to expensive wines are full-bodied.

- **Mavrodaphne:** This "black laurel" grape is used in blended dry wines to contribute dark color and blackberry flavors. When used to make sweet wines such as Mavrodaphne of Patras, it has a rich flavor of raisins, honey, and walnuts.

- **Xynomavro:** The finest grape of northern Greece. The name translates as "acid black," which is also a good indication of the grape's tart and tannic nature. Wines based on this

Greece
Wine Regions

1 Côtes de Meliton
2 Naoussa
3 Amyndeo
4 Goumenissa
5 Rapsani
6 Aghialos
7 Zitsa
8 Messenikolas
9 Nemea
10 Mantinia
11 Patra
12 Cephalonia
13 Limnos
14 Samos
15 Paros
16 Santorini
17 Rhodos
18 Peza
19 Dafnes
20 Archanes
21 Sitia

The wine regions of Greece.

grape have aromas and flavors of black pepper, blackberries, black olives, and tobacco. There is always a hint of tomato scent in the wine, and the further south it is planted, the more pronounced the sun-dried tomato flavor. We have served quality, aged Xynomavro-based wines to our friends, who often mistake them for the highly regarded wines of Burgundy from France or Barolo from Italy.

- **Mandelaria:** Supplies lots of color and tannins as well as some acidity to blended wines. The blackberry-scented grape is used in the rosés and reds of such regions as Rhodes and Santorini.

THE WHITES

- **Assyrtiko:** This is the principal grape grown on the island of Santorini, where it is used to make dry, age-worthy wines and sweet Vin Santos, both of which are high in acidity. The vines are quite unusual for where and how they grow—on a sun-baked island in the shape of a wreath. Young wines have discreet aromas of white pepper, ocean, mineral, and pear. With six to ten years of age, Assyrtiko wines develop flavors of caramelized pineapple and lemon or orange marmalade.

- **Moschofilero:** If we had to pick one grape to be the source of your first Greek wine experience, this is it. Seductive rose petal, honey, and ginger aromas are typically followed by tropical fruit flavors and a good balance of acidity. Its pink-colored skin means it can also produce rosé wines.

- **Malagousia:** This white grape has similar floral and tropical fruit flavors as Moschofilero but makes wines that are fuller in body.

- **Muscat:** If Greece is the birthplace of wine, this might be considered a native variety. Many historians suggest that Muscat was *the* original *vinifera* and that all of the fine grape varieties used today are its descendants. Muscat may have been first spotted in Persia, but it was the Greeks who successfully made wine from it. Regardless of its history, this grape produces highly aromatic wines that are more often sweet than dry. The heady smell of orange blossoms and honey is usually followed by a richness on the palate.

- **Robola:** Produces wines with notes of lemon, green melon, and minerality on the island of Cephalonia.

- **Savatiano:** The most widely planted white grape in Greece is a major component of Retsina wines. Savatiano is occasionally used to make good, medium-bodied wines with orange aromas, but it needs a blending partner to supply acidity.

- **Vilana:** Grown in Crete, it produces crisp, dry wines with green apple flavors.

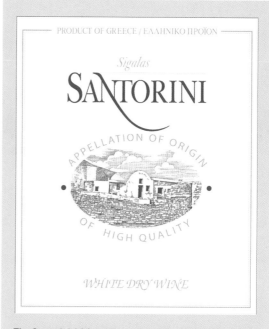

The Santorini AOC produces dry white wines with mineral, lemon, and pear flavors.

The language of the label

Greek table wines may be labeled in a variety of ways:

- by grape name, such as Moschofilero (European law stipulates that the wine must contain at least 85% of the grape mentioned)
- by place name, such as Nemea (a dry red) or Santorini (a dry white)
- by grape and place, such as Muscat of Samos (a sweet white)
- by fantasy or proprietary name, such as "Miden Agan" or "Fresco" (both are dry reds)

Sparkling wines use the ubiquitous terms to denote dryness or sweetness, such as *brut*. Some wineries label their sparkling wines with a fantasy or proprietary name, such as "Ode Panos" by Domaine Spiropolous.

Greek wine bottles will carry either the designation OPAP (*Onomasía Proeléfseos Anotéras Piótitos*) with a pink seal to indicate the wine is dry and of superior quality, or the designation OPE (*Onomasía Proeléfseos Eleghoméni*) with a blue seal when the wine is sweet.

The label may also contain the term *ktima,* which refers to a wine estate.

THE ORIGIN AND AGE OF THE WINE

The quality pyramid for Greek wines, in order of increasing quality, is as follows:

- *Oenos epitrapezios,* or table wines. These may have just a brand name or be a traditional wine such as Retsina.

- *Vins de pays,* a French term for country wines (also known locally as **topikos inos**). Looser rules for using both native and international grape varieties exist at this level. We will refer to the wines under this category as "TI" when we discuss the wine regions (below).

- The highest echelon in Greek wines is **appellation of origin wines,** modeled on the French AOC and meant to guarantee authenticity and maintain traditional "recipes" of grape content for the wines. We will refer to these wines as "AOC" when we discuss wine regions (below).

The terms *reserve* and *grand reserve* on AOC wines carry a legal responsibility to age the wines longer. White wines are aged a minimum of two years for reserve and three for grand reserve, while reds must be aged an extra year for those designations.

The wine regions of Greece

Wherever you travel in Greece, vineyards are part of the landscape. From the sun-soaked islands in the south to the cooler mountainous areas in the north, the nation's vineyards grow grapes for eating as well as for wine and brandy production.

Unlike most other European wine-growing nations, many of the Greek vineyards are planted with a northern exposure to avoid too much heat and to maintain acidity in their grapes (and ultimately their wines). Planting vineyards at higher elevations or by bodies of water is another tactic used by farmers to produce balanced wines.

In this chapter we will briefly discuss the regions, but our aim is to turn you on to our favorite wines so you can share our appreciation for the "new wines" of ancient Greece.

Prices are referred to as inexpensive (under $15), moderate (under $30), and moderate to expensive (over $30).

MACEDONIA
Important AOC Regions
Naoussa, Cotes de Meliton, Drama, Amyndeo, and Goumenissa

Important TI Region
Epanomi

The vineyards of this province benefit from enough rainfall to nurture the grapes so they are not "stressed out."

Naoussa AOC. We begin our survey with the most famous AOC of northern Greece, where the Xynomavro grape is grown on the foothills of Mount Vermio. Here the grape's natural acidity is heightened by being grown at such a high altitude. Just as Barolo is referred to as the "king of Italian reds," Naoussa is referred to as the "king of Greek reds." A typical Naoussa wine has an opaque dark red color and flavors of sun-dried tomato and black olives. The wines are aged a minimum of one year in oak, with

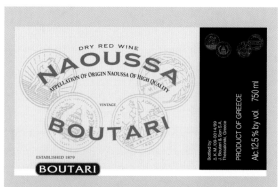

Boutari is Greece's largest wine company, and we highly recommend their entire line of wines. Naoussa is a medium-to-full-bodied red wine based on the Xynomavro grape.

reserve wines spending two or more years in oak before they are bottled and sold. Locals enjoy this red with lamb chops, and the black olive flavors make it a good complement to rabbit stew with olives. Prices range from inexpensive for medium-bodied versions to moderate for wines that are full in body.

Suggested Wine Producers

Boutari, Katogi and Strofilia, and Kir Yanni

Cotes de Meliton AOC. This region produces medium-bodied, crisp whites from the Assyrtiko, Malagousia, Roditis, and Athiri grapes. The medium-to-full-bodied red wines are based on the local Limnio grape partnered with French varieties such as Cabernet Sauvignon. They are inexpensive to moderately priced. We suggest the full bodied red Chateau Carras.

Epanomi TI. Domaine Gerovassiliou is one of northern Greece's finest wineries. Check out its dry Malagousia white for its charming flavor of ripe apricots. If red's your thing, the winery's full-bodied Syrah offers characteristic aromas of black pepper combined with earthy and gamy scents, followed by lots of black fruit flavors and richness on the palate. Pair the Syrah with steak crusted with black peppercorns. Domaine Gerovassiliou wines are moderately priced.

Drama AOC. Modern wineries have made large investments in this area, which is home to both native and international grape types. Chateau Nico Lazaridi, Domaine Costa Lazaridi, and Ktima Pavlidis are the region's leading wineries.

Amyndeo AOC. Alpha Estate is producing the type of wines that prompt people to ask, "Where is this from, and how do I buy some?" This winery makes sumptuous world-class red wines. Try the Xynomavro ($35), which is bursting with bright red berry flavors; the "Estate" blend ($37), with its notes of red cherry, cinnamon, and nutmeg; or the blackberry-rich Alpha "One" ($75). Grilled lamb chops, a Moroccan lamb tagine, or vegetarian stuffed red peppers are suggested pairings. Amyndeo is also home to AOC rosé wines

based on the Xynomavro grape. Our favorite is by Kir Yanni and it sells for $12.

THESSALY
Important AOC Region

Rapsani

Rapsani AOC. The iron and schist soils on the slopes of Mount Olympus give extra power to the wines produced here. We recommend the reserve by Tsantali ($21), which features a deep purple color and aromas and flavors of black tobacco, black pepper and black plums in a full-bodied package. Try it with richer foods such as a vegetarian seitan stroganoff or *pastitsio* (a Greek version of meat lasagna).

STEREA ELLADA
Important TI Regions

Attica, Atalanti

Attica TI. Dionysus' original stomping grounds were in this part of central Greece. Today both local and international grape varieties are grown here; unfortunately, the proximity to Athens has led to urban expansion and the uprooting of some of the ancient vineyards.

On the hillsides of Mount Gerania lie the vineyards of the Evharis winery. We enjoy its dry white blend of Chardonnay and Assyrtiko ($21). Evharis' finest red is a full-bodied, pure Syrah ($22) that contains rich black fruit flavors. Another winery worth seeking out is Semeli, named after the mother of Dionysus. Look for its floral-scented dry white blend "Orinos Helios" ($11).

PELOPONNESE
Important AOC Regions

Nemea, Mantinia, Patras

In his poem *The Iliad,* Homer made the first written reference to the Peloponnese vineyards, calling them "*ampeloessa*" or full of vines. The description is still true today. Tourists visiting Olympia, site of the original Olympic Games, should experience the magnificent Mercouri estate. Tasting their Roditis based

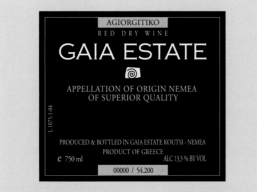

AGIORGITIKO
RED DRY WINE

GAIA ESTATE

APPELLATION OF ORIGIN NEMEA
OF SUPERIOR QUALITY

PRODUCED & BOTTLED IN GAIA ESTATE KOUTSI - NEMEA
PRODUCT OF GREECE

e 750 ml   ALC 13,5 % BY VOL

00000 / 54.200

The Gaia estate winery produces an excellent example of Nemea AOC red wine based on the Agiorgitiko grape.

"Foloi" white and their red wines in the beautiful gardens is magical.

Nemea AOC. Tourists flock to Nemea, which boasts the largest vineyard area in Greece. Just outside of Nemea is the city of Nafplio—the first capital of modern Greece. Wine and *mezze* flow at the outdoor restaurants in this charming town. In fact, the region's red wine is referred to by the locals as the "blood of Hercules" because it was here that he killed the lion.

The Agiorgitiko grape rules in this region, and it is used to produce dry rosés and dry to semidry reds

The vineyards of Nemea produce some of Greece's finest red wines. (Photo courtesy of All About Greek Wines)

that are medium to full in body. Vineyards are planted in the valley as well as on hillsides. Nemea wines possess aromas and flavors of black cherry, black currant, black licorice, tobacco, and black fig. Nemea is home to a number of talented, quality-driven winemakers, including Yiannis Tselepos, George Papaioannou and Georges Skouras. Their namesake wineries offer wines that speak of sunshine and elegance. We also suggest Gaia winery's ageworthy red "Estate" wine and their "Nobilis" Retsina white. The region's wines can be found at many price points.

Suggested Wine Producers

Boutari, Domaine Skouras, Domaine Tselepos, Gaia, Papaioannou, Pavilos, and Semeli

Mantinia AOC. Here the Moschofilero grape is planted at high altitudes, where the cool temperatures and sunshine result in wines with ripe fruit flavors balanced by high acidity. The sparkling and still white wines produced from this grape are delightful. Our two favorite Greek sparkling wines come from the Mantinia AOC. "Ode Panos" is a fine dry bubbly made by Domaine Spiropolous that has rose petal and orange zest flavors. The medium-bodied "Amalia" by Domaine Tselepos is also a standout, with notes of allspice, ginger, grapefruit, and pear.

You can seek out the lovely dry whites from these same wineries, or sample the white Mantinia from Antonopolous ($16), with its tastes of clove, nutmeg, tangerine, and rose petal water.

For a dry rosé, look no further than the Domaine Spiropolous ($11), with its unusual notes of rose petal, lychee, cherry tomatoes, and paprika.

Moschofilero-based wines are well suited to the salty-sweet profile of many Asian seafood or chicken dishes. Prices range from inexpensive to moderate.

Patras AOC. You'll find both dry and sweet wines in this lively, culturally significant region, almost all of which are inexpensive. Dry whites are labeled as Patras AOC; we suggest the lemon-and-grapefruit-flavored "Asprolithi" ($13) by Oenoforos Winery. Sweet wines include the white Muscat of Patras AOC and the red Mavrodaphne of Patras.

THE ISLANDS
Important AOC Regions

Cephalonia, Samos, Rhodes, Crete, and Santorini

Cephalonia AOC (Ionian Islands). One of the most beautiful and hospitable islands in Greece is Cephalonia. Here the most significant winery is Gentilini. The limestone soil, which produces many of the world's finest white wines, imparts a mineral flavor to the winery's Robola-based dry white ($15). Sashimi, crab, and lobster are good choices to highlight the lemon curd, green melon, and nectarine flavors.

Samos AOC (Aegean Islands). Sweet Muscat of Samos may be the nation's finest dessert wine. The local cooperative makes "Anthemis," which is aged five years in oak before it is sold ($28). With its decadent caramel, honeysuckle, and brown sugar flavors, this wine makes a wonderful dessert unto itself or marries well with cheesecake or apple pie with vanilla ice cream. Muscat of Samos wines are inexpensive to moderately priced.

Crete. Our favourite Boutari red wine is the full-bodied and complex "Skalani" blend of Syrah and Kotsifali grapes.

Rhodes AOC (Dodecanse Islands). This island's vineyards receive lots of sunshine and enough rainfall to prevent the vines from becoming parched. Athiri is the principal grape for the region's dry whites. Young Athiri wines taste of lemon and grapefruit, while older versions develop notes of honeycomb, aloe, and sesame. We recommend Athiri ($16) by Emery Estate. Emery also makes "Efreni" ($16), a sweet Muscat that could be served with dessert or enjoyed as an after-dinner drink.

Santorini AOC (Cyclades Islands). Santorini is an odd mix of ancient culture combined with the demands of the tourist trade. The lost world of Atlantis is said to be under the water near Santorini. Ruins and museums of antiquity on this island speak of the Minoan culture, with evidence of wine production

In Santorini there is a unique method of growing grapes. Vines are planted close to the ground and protected from direct sunshine by a wreath of branches and leaves. This technique is known locally as *ampelia*. Wines labeled as "Santorini" are crisp, dry white wines. "Vin Santo" is the term used for the sweet whites, which may be enjoyed as an after-dinner drink or paired with pastries such as baklava. (Photos courtesy of All About Greek Wines.)

dating back to the second century B.C. (Actually, the oldest wine press in the world, circa 1600 B.C., was found on the island of Crete.)

It's telling that this region is home to what many believe to be Greece's finest white wine. Santorini whites must be made from at least 70% Assyrtiko, which supplies lots of acidity to the blend, while the Athiri grape contributes fruit and vegetal aromas. In addition, while 95% of the world's whites are better when drunk within three years of their harvest date,

these wines improve with age—a decade for the dry whites and even longer for the sweet wines.

It is amazing that the grapes can survive—and thrive—in this hot, arid climate. There is little rainfall, so the grapes receive water via the moisture brought by sea breezes. As a result, the vineyards and the wines they produce are truly unique.

A top producer in the region, Sigalas, makes both a stainless-steel-aged white and one aged in oak; we prefer the clean flavors of the stainless-steel version. Aromas and flavors of lemon, cucumber, and green melon are enveloped in a medium-bodied wine with a long finish. Other fine producers in the region include Arghyros, Boutari, Santo, Orphanos, and Hatzidakis. Dry wines range in price from inexpensive to moderate.

Seafood reigns supreme in the region's restaurants and provides an ideal accompaniment to the region's wines. Fried mullet (*barbouni*) served with lemon, grilled swordfish steaks, and a Santorini salad with tomatoes and capers are some of the delicacies we suggest you pair with these dry whites. For vegetarians, a cool fava bean puree, hummus, or feta cheese also make a delicious accompaniment.

Vin Santo is a luscious dessert wine made from Assyrtiko and Ardani grapes dried on mats. Aromas and flavors typically include dried apricots, figs, and dates as well as caramel corn and tangerine. These are fabulous wines to accompany a *galaktaboureko* custard or a baklava pastry with nuts and honey. Vin Santo prices are moderate to expensive.

chapter 14

Eat/drink/man/woman
wine and food

We could consider it a duty, but it really is a pleasure to help our *WineWise* readers demystify the subject of wine and food pairing. Although there are no set rules, the "right" wine can elevate a humble meal into something truly memorable. We will provide some simple guidelines for achieving successful food and wine marriages; wine recommendations for a myriad of ethnic and American foods.

As you read this chapter, remember that pairing wine and food is fun, requiring only an adventurous spirit and a little common sense. So relax! Be experimental. After all, how bad can it be? You may just discover the next perfect combination, such as the classic example of a Sancerre white wine and goat cheese or a Bordeaux red wine and lamb. So grab a plate and a glass, and let's begin with some basic principles for pairing wine and food.

Basic principles

Complement or contrast flavors

Wine is simply a product made from grapes that are fermented. Grape types used to make wine have intrinsic flavors, and great winemakers allow the grapes to speak for themselves. Similarly, a great chef should not obscure the natural flavors of a just-picked, sun-ripened tomato. Working from these principles, we can emphasize specific flavors or play them off each other.

COMPLEMENTING FLAVORS

When we complement flavors, we are simply highlighting specific flavor characteristics in the wine by pairing it with foods that have similar flavors. For example, Cabernet Sauvignon typically features aromas and flavors of black currants and black olives. Syrah has distinct black pepper notes, and Zinfandel is known for its ripe berry flavors. Of course, these smells and flavors are affected by where the grapes are grown. Wines from the warmer New World regions (United States, Australia, Chile) usually have more forward fruit flavors than wines from the Old World (Western Europe). So an Aussie Shiraz will be chock-full of ripe fruit flavors, while a French Syrah will have less pronounced fruit along with notes of earth, game, or leather.

The key in complementing flavors is simply to play up these attributes. An unoaked Chardonnay-based Chablis from the Burgundy region of France, with its aromas and flavors of green apple, may be ideal for pork with a tart apple sauce or apple stuffing, while an oaky California Chardonnay is better suited to a cedar-planked salmon.

CONTRASTING FLAVORS

Another way to highlight a flavor characteristic in the wine is to play it off the food—for example, to balance spice with fruit. Smoked, spicy, and salty foods pair beautifully with wines that are semidry or dry yet fruity. Our mind can play tricks on us when it comes to discerning fruity from sweet. If every experience

(Photo courtesy of Culinary Institute of America, Hyde Park, New York)

you had smelling a strawberry was followed by sweetness on the palate, then the smell of strawberries will cause you to expect a sweet taste. But certain grape types that smell of strawberries, such as Grenache and Zinfandel, usually make dry wines that are fruity (as opposed to sweet wines). Here again, place plays a role, as New World examples of Grenache are more obviously fruity than their Old World counterparts.

So how do you contrast spice and fruit? The classic combination of prosciutto and melon is a good food example of this attraction of opposites. The juxtaposition of salty meat with the sweet melon is very appealing, and you'll notice this principle followed in many ethnic dishes. It is also why semidry wines such as Riesling, Gewurztraminer, and Chenin Blanc are often suggested in the ethnic food pairings found later in this chapter.

THE BEST OF BOTH WORLDS: COMPLEMENT AND CONTRAST

It may sound contrarian, but it is possible for a wine to both complement and contrast a dish. For example, staying with our prosciutto and melon appetizer, consider a Riesling from the Finger Lakes of New York or the Canadian province of Ontario. The semidry wine complements the sweetness of the melon while providing a contrast to the salt of the prosciutto. Or partner a German Riesling from Mosel-Saar-Ruwer with a spicy shrimp curry with mango chutney. The hint of sweetness in the wine offsets the heat of the curry, while playing up the sweet fruit in the chutney. The cold serving temperature of the Riesling also serves as a physical contrast to the heat of the dish and helps alleviate the spicy "buzz" on your lips.

Match intensities

The principle here is to match the body of the wine with the "body" (texture or richness) of the dish, ensuring that the flavor intensity of the wine and food are more or less equal. When enjoying wine with our meal, we want to be able to taste both the food and the wine and not sacrifice one to appreciate the other. For example, if you serve a big oaky Chardonnay with a delicate poached sole, the flavor of the fish will be lost. Likewise, if you pair a light-bodied red such as

Beaujolais with a hearty dish such as short ribs, the flavor of the wine will be lost. A harmonious pairing is based on balance. Most of the time, flavor intensity parallels the body of a wine: a lightly flavored wine tends to be light-bodied and delicate, while a full-flavored wine usually feels heavier in the mouth and is full-bodied.

White wines tend to be lighter than red wines, with those that are fermented and/or aged in oak barrels being more full-bodied than those that are fermented in stainless steel. Pinot Noir is a thin-skinned red grape that usually makes medium-bodied wines that are equal in power to full-bodied whites, such as barrel-fermented Chardonnays. Cabernet Sauvignon is a thick-skinned red grape that produces wines with a fuller body than Pinot Noir.

Another point to consider when evaluating a wine's intensity is price. Within the world of Cabernet Sauvignon, for example, inexpensive versions that retail for under $15 are generally not as rich or complex as moderately priced or expensive Cabs from the same growing region. For example, we enjoy the inexpensive Cabernet Sauvignon/Merlot blend by Concha y Toro from Chile. This wine is a great value, though not as full-bodied or as complex as the winery's moderately priced Marques de Casa Concha or its expensive Don Melchor Cabernet Sauvignon.

THE TOWER OF POWER

The Tower of Power classifies many of the world's most important wines by body. For ease of reference, the first tower lists wines by grape type; the second tower, by European place name.

There are a few things you should be aware of when reading the towers:

- Generally speaking, bargain-priced wines tend to be easy-drinking and lighter in body than moderately priced to expensive versions of the same grape or regional wine. Thus, a higher price tag often corresponds to more complex flavors and a more full-bodied example of the wine.

- You'll notice that some red and white wines overlap. In the table below, the medium-bodied reds line up next to the full-bodied whites, and the light-bodied reds correspond with the medium-to-full-bodied whites. In these cases, feel free to choose either red or white, or serve half portions of both. For example, pair a grilled salmon and Provençal sauce with a barrel-fermented Chardonnay or a Pinot Noir (or both). Or try a lamb carpaccio with a barrel-fermented Fumé Blanc and/or a Gamay.

Now that you know how to evaluate a wine's flavor intensity or body, how do you apply that to food? You're probably familiar with the age-old rule that dictates having only white wine with seafood and poultry and red wine with red meats. Although this maxim works, it limits the amount of fun you can have by experimenting with other choices. Consider how vast the world of seafood or red meats really is. Just as Cabernet Sauvignon comes in different levels of intensity, so do proteins. Let's look at them according to intensity or body.

Seafood/Fish

Most delicate: clams, crab, mussels, oysters, sole

Delicate: scallops, shrimp, perch, pike, trout, turbot

Moderately rich: bass, cod, cuttlefish, flounder, grouper, halibut, lobster, sea urchin, skate, snapper, squid

Tower of Power by Grape Type

New World	Red Wines	White Wines
Full bodied	Cabernet Sauvignon, Syrah/Shiraz, Petite Sirah, Mourvedre, Zinfandel	
Medium- to full-bodied red wines	Malbec (Argentina), Grenache, Tannat (Uruguay), Merlot, Cabernet Franc	
Medium-bodied red wines are equivalent to full-bodied white wines	Pinot Noir, Carmenere (Chile) Pinotage (South Africa)	Chardonnay (barrel fermented)
Light-bodied red wines are equivalent to medium-bodied white wines	Gamay and rosé or "blush" wines	Fumé Blanc (barrel fermented Sauvignon Blanc), Semillon, Viognier, Pinot Gris/Pinot Grigio (barrel fermented), Marsanne, Torrontes (Argentina), Gewurztraminer
Light-bodied white wines		Riesling, Chenin Blanc, Stainless Steel fermented Sauvignon Blanc

Tower of Power by European Wine Name

Here we offer some of the best-known wines; for others, we suggest you look in other chapters of *WineWise*.

	Red Wines	White Wines
Italy		
Full-bodied red wines	Amarone, Barolo, Barbaresco, Brunello di Montalcino, Carmignano, Sagrantino de Montefalco, Vino Nobile di Montepulciano, Aglianico del Vulture, Taurasi	

	Red Wines	White Wines
Medium- to full-bodied red wines	Chianti Classico Riserva, Salice Salentino, Barbera d'Asti or Barbera d'Alba, Cannonau di Sardegna, Teroldego Rotliano	Barrel fermented Chardonnay, Greco di Tufo, Fiano di Avellino
Medium-bodied red wines are equivalent to full-bodied white wines	Chianti Classico, Nero d'Avola, Primitivo, Dolcetto d'Alba or Dolcetto d'Asti	Chardonnay (barrel fermented)
Light-bodied red wines are equivalent to medium-bodied white wines	Chianti, Valpolicella, Bardolino, Grignolino, and rosé wines	Gavi, Arneis, Vermentino, Vernaccia di San Gimignano, Verdicchio, Friulano
Light-to-medium-bodied red wines are equivalent to light-bodied white wines	Bardolino, Chianti, Valpolicella	Gavi, Tocai Friulano, Vermentino, Vernaccia di San Gimignano, Frascati, Galestro, Orvieto, Soave
Very light-bodied white wines		Galestro, Soave, Frascati, Orvieto
France		
Full-bodied	Cornas, Cote Rotie, Hermitage, Chateauneuf du Pape, Cahors; Bordeaux wines from Pauillac, Graves, St-Estephe, St-Julien, Margaux, and St-Emilion	
Medium- to full-bodied red wines	Pomerol, St-Joseph, Chinon	
Medium-bodied red wines are equivalent to full-bodied white wines	Chambolle-Musigny, Vosne-Romanee, Gevrey-Chambertin, Volnay, Morey-St-Denis, Beaune, Morgon, Julienas, Moulin-A-Vent	Alsace Gewurztraminer, Pinot Gris, Muscat, or Riesling. Meursault, Puligny-Montrachet, Condrieu, Chassagne-Montrachet
Light-bodied red wines are equivalent to medium-bodied white wines	Fleurie, Brouilly, Beaujolais-Villages, and rosé wines from Provence	Pouilly-Fuisse, Pouilly-Fumé, Sancerre, Pessac-Leognan/Graves
Very light-bodied reds are equivalent to light-bodied white wines	Beaujolais Nouveau	Entre Deux Mers, Muscadet Sevre et Maine
Spain		
Full-bodied red wines	Ribera del Duero, Toro, Priorato, Montsant, Penedes blends with Cabernet Sauvignon or Syrah	
Medium- to full-bodied red wines	Rioja Gran Reserva or Reserva, Jumilla, Bierzo	
Medium-bodied red wines are equivalent to full-bodied white wines	Rioja Crianza, Campo de Borja, Navarra, Cigales, Yecla	Penedes Chardonnay (barrel fermented)
Light-bodied red wines are equivalent to medium-bodied white wines	Young Rioja red and Rioja or Navarra rosé	Albarino, Rias Baixas, Rueda, Penedes, Ribeiro, Godello from Valdeorras, Rioja (barrel fermented), Txacoli

Rich: black cod (sable), cobia, marlin, monkfish, octopus, sturgeon

Very rich: bluefish, eel, herring, mackerel, salmon, sardines, tuna

In assessing a food's level of intensity, texture is very important. A carpaccio of scallops would fall under the most delicate category, while whole scallops would be considered delicate. Likewise, smoked salmon or sashimi of salmon would be moderately rich, while a salmon steak would be very rich.

The bottom line:

- Serve the lightest styles of white wines with the most delicate seafood.
- Pair medium-to-full-bodied whites with seafood in the moderately rich, rich, and very rich categories.
- Light-bodied reds can be served with rich or very rich seafoods.
- Rosé and sparkling wines are another alternative for moderately rich or rich seafoods.

For example, very light-bodied to light-bodied whites (such as Riesling) will not overwhelm delicate oysters on the half shell, while seared tuna can be served with either a heavy white (barrel-fermented Chardonnay) or a light-to-medium red (Pinot Noir).

Poultry/Game Birds

Most delicate: chicken or turkey breast without skin

Delicate: chicken or turkey breast with skin

Moderately rich: chunks of chicken for stews, tacos, or stir-fries; chicken or turkey wings, thighs, or drumsticks; Cornish game hen; duck breast without skin; quail

Rich: chicken livers and gizzards, morsels of duck for stews or pastas, pheasant

Very rich: whole duck, goose, partridge

The bottom line:

- Pair the most delicate and delicate birds with light whites.
- Serve moderately rich or rich poultry preparations with full-bodied whites, rosés, or light-to-medium reds.

- Pair the very rich examples with full-bodied reds.

Veal/Pork

Delicate: thin medallions of veal or pork, sliced boiled ham

Moderately rich: chunks of veal for stews, chunks of pork for dishes such as souvlaki, loin of pork for roast

Rich: veal or pork chops, pork knuckles or trotters

Very rich: veal breast, veal shank (*osso buco*), pork ribs, *cocinella* (Spanish roast suckling baby pig)

The bottom line:

- Serve delicate preparations with light whites.
- Try moderately rich veal and pork dishes with medium-to-full-bodied whites and rosés.
- Pair rich and very rich foods with medium-to-full-bodied whites, rosés, or light-to-medium-bodied red wines.

Lamb/Beef

Delicate: carpaccio of lamb or beef, thinly sliced roast beef

Moderately rich: medallions of lamb or beef; slices of beef for tacos, fajitas, or subs (such as cheesesteak sandwiches)

Rich: leg or loin of lamb, filet mignon, hamburger, skirt steak

Very rich: lamb chops or rack of lamb, lamb ribs, New York strip, T-bone or porterhouse steak, short ribs

Two important considerations when pairing red meats with wine are the amount of marbling (fat) the meat has and how rare it is served. The more fat it has and the rarer it is, the richer it is—and the more full-bodied the wine required.

The bottom line:

- A filet mignon is leaner than a sirloin steak, so it can be paired with a full-bodied white, a rosé wine, or a medium-bodied red.
- A lean burger cooked well done needs a light-bodied red or a rosé.

- A rare T-bone steak is best with a full-bodied red.
- A rare to medium-rare rack of lamb with a powerful, full-bodied red is a classic marriage we adore.

So far it's pretty straightforward, right? Just to make it interesting, there are other factors you would do well to take into account besides the intensity and richness of the food. Cooking method, the sauce, the grain or starch served with the protein, and the vegetables contribute to the overall "weight" of the finished dish.

Cooking Method

Delicate: poaching, marinating (e.g., ceviche), steaming

Moderately rich: baking, sautéing, smoking, stir-frying

Rich to very rich: deep-frying, grilling, searing

The richness of salmon provencal is balanced by a full-bodied white such as an oak-aged Chardonnay, a medium-bodied rosé, or a medium-based "crossover" red wine such as Pinot Noir.

Sauce

Delicate: tomato water or lemongrass broth

Moderately rich: mango salsa, meunière (lemon butter), scampi style, yellow pumpkinseed mole

Rich: béchamel, chimichurri, coconut-milk-based sauces, cream-based sauces, Hollandaise, ketchup, mayonnaise, pesto

Very rich: beef gravy, demiglace-based sauces, Provençal

Grain or Starch

Very delicate: angel hair pasta, boiled potato, white rice

Delicate: baked potato, couscous, cellophane noodles, linguine, yellow rice

Moderately rich: barley, fettuccine or egg noodle pasta, hominy, kasha, mashed potato or roasted red potato, quinoa

Rich: cheese grits, gnocchi, home-fried potatoes, lasagna noodles, soba noodles

Very rich: french-fried potatoes, polenta, potato knishes or kugel, poutine (french fries with curd cheese and gravy)

Vegetables

Most delicate: celery, endive, iceberg lettuce, grape leaves, radishes, squash blossoms

Delicate: arugula, bean sprouts, bell peppers, bok choy, cabbage, hen-of-the-woods mushrooms, kale, oyster mushrooms, romaine or red leaf lettuce, salsify, spinach, Swiss chard, water chestnuts, yellow squash, zucchini

Moderately rich: black-eyed peas, broccoli, carrots, cauliflower, chickpeas (garbanzo beans), corn, edamame, fennel, green peas, oyster mushrooms, pigeon peas, radicchio, string beans, turnips, wood ear mushrooms

Rich: Brussels sprouts, butternut squash, chanterelle mushrooms, chayote squash (mirliton), green olives, okra, red beans, spaghetti squash, tomatoes, yucca

Very rich: beets, black beans, black olives, eggplant, porcini mushrooms, portobello mushrooms, shiitake mushrooms

Whether the vegetables are the side dish or the focal point of the meal, the textural richness is the most important consideration when balancing the vegetables' power with the wine.

You'll notice that the majority of the more delicate vegetables are pale in color, and as the colors increase in intensity, so do the flavors. In this way, the color of the vegetables often provides a clue as to whether a white or a red wine is appropriate. Red peppers, tomatoes, beets, and radicchio, for example, are all excellent choices to pair with red wines.

The cooking technique can also change the power of the vegetables. Red peppers, zucchini, and tomatoes all become richer when they are grilled or fried. Brussels sprouts and cauliflower pair well with a light-bodied white or rosé when steamed but require a full-bodied white or rosé (or even a light-to-medium-bodied red) when stir-fried, deep-fried, or sautéed.

As with fish and meats, the sauce can have a profound influence on the intensity of the vegetable and the wine needed to balance it. Adding red peppers to your cauliflower stir-fry or serving the cauliflower with a tomato sauce may encourage you to enjoy a red wine with the white vegetable.

For vegetarian proteins, apply the same principles you would for vegetables. Tofu, tempeh, and seitan are strongly influenced by cooking technique and the garnish or sauce that accompanies them. When butter, oils, or other fats are included in the preparation of vegetarian dishes, they raise the level of richness of that dish. The use of seeds and nuts—a vegan alternative to butter or dairy—also adds richness. Depending on the preparation, everything from light-bodied whites to rosés and even the heaviest reds can be served with vegetarian dishes.

Prioritize! What is the dominant flavor of the dish?

We've looked at how to choose a wine for a single element of a dish—the protein, sauce, or vegetable, for example. But consider a typical dish or course: you have a moderately rich protein, a light sauce, a rich vegetable, a very rich starch. How do you decide what the overriding component is and what approach to take when choosing a wine to accompany it? Sometimes one element of the dish, perhaps the sauce, is the most important factor to consider when choosing a wine. Complementing or contrasting that sauce—or matching its power—becomes a priority and trumps the pairing of the grain or protein on the plate. Other times, a special or unique component of the dish warrants the spotlight—for example, wild game or just-picked blueberries.

Use acidity and bubbles to cleanse the palate

There's a kind of wacky mathematics involved here, where $1 + 1 = 1$. When acidic wines are paired with acidic foods, the total impression of acidity is lowered and the other components of the dish are highlighted. Of course, it helps to know which grapes are naturally high in acidity.

WHITE WINES

Rieslings from cool growing regions (such as Germany, New York, and Canada) have a refreshing acidity that can reinvigorate the palate. The international varieties of Sauvignon Blanc and Chenin Blanc are almost always high in acidity, as are certain indigenous white grapes, including Albarino (Spain)/Alvarinho (Portugal), Arinto (Portugal), and Assyrtiko (Greece).

Since acidic wines in combination with acidic foods lower the impression of acidity on the palate, the wines from these grapes are delicious accompaniments to ceviche or dishes with acidic sauces. Citrus-based sauces or sauces with rice vinegar or balsamic vinegar are preferred. White, apple cider, white wine and red wine vinegars are too aggressive and make the wine taste sour, so if you must use them in a recipe, do so sparingly.

RED WINES

Always high in acidity is the Pinot Noir grape, which makes it such a wonderfully versatile food wine. Additionally, Italy boasts a number of high-acid red grapes, including Barbera, Sangiovese, and Nebbiolo. Just think of all those tomato-based sauces: the combination of fruit and acid in the tomatoes is a perfect match with the region's fruity, acidic red wines. A slice of pizza and a glass of Chianti demonstrate how the acidity of the wine complements the tomato and cleanses the palate from the richness of the cheese.

SPARKLING WINES

Good sparkling wines are usually sourced from cool growing regions that also produce high-acid table wines. Because of this, they have a remarkable effect when paired with food. Not only are they wonderful for heightening and then cooling down the flavors of hot, spicy dishes, but their effervescence cleanses the palate from fatty or rich foods.

Some of our favorite food-and-bubbly pairings include an egg salad sandwich or fish and chips with a Spanish brut Cava, linguine with pesto or Parmigiano cheese with an Italian Prosecco, chili dogs or a pastrami sandwich with a New World Blanc de Noirs, sparkling Shiraz, or sparkling rosé, grilled salmon or lamb chops with a California sparkling rosé, and lobster or caviar with a French Blanc de Blancs. For spicy-hot fare such as blackened fish, jerk chicken, or a Thai seafood curry, you want a hint of sweetness; go for the extra dry sparklers (not as dry as wines labeled "brut"). Spicy beef tacos or Korean beef with kimchee are fantastic with fruity brut rosé wines or sparkling White Zinfandel.

The default wines

Now that selecting a glass of wine to accompany your own dinner is a snap, what do you do if you're ordering a bottle for the table and everyone is eating something different? How do you please so many different tastes?

First, you can order sparkling wine. Not only is it festive, but its acidity makes it a great companion to a range of foods, and the bubbles reinvigorate the palate. Brut sparkling wines and Champagnes tend to be medium-bodied and the most versatile. If you're eating heartier fare such as salmon, tuna, lamb, beef, or even rich vegetarian dishes, order a full-bodied sparkling rosé or Blanc de Noirs. On the other hand, if the cuisine tends toward more delicate foods such as sushi, sashimi, or raw oysters, go for the light-bodied Blanc de Blancs.

We understand that not everyone is a bubblehead, so great alternatives to sparkling wines are medium-bodied table wines, which are unlikely to overwhelm (or be overwhelmed by) most foods. Our tried-and-true choices: for the whites, a dry Sauvignon Blanc or semidry Riesling, and for the reds, Pinot Noir or Grenache. (For a more complete list of medium-bodied wines, consult the Tower of Power charts earlier in the chapter.) If there are four or more in your party, we suggest ordering both a bottle of white and a medium-bodied red.

The progression of intensities: Horizontal and vertical pairings

Although we enjoy popcorn and Champagne in bed, that is not what we mean when we refer to a horizontal pairing. Rather, we're talking about matching one plate of food with one wine. A vertical pairing involves matching a series of wines with a succession of dishes. It is exciting to climb a ladder of intensities in both the foods and the wines served with them.

When planning a multicourse meal, you do not want to serve powerful foods and wines early on. The idea is to serve low-alcohol wines before fuller bodied high-alcohol wines, simple young wines before complex old ones, and dry or semidry wines before sweet ones. An expensive oaky Chardonnay or Cabernet Sauvignon early in the meal will overwhelm not only the palate but delicate appetizers or salads. Instead, we prefer to start with lighter-style wines of good value and revel in the anticipation of the more complex wines to come.

Red alert! Possible pitfalls

Beware of sweetness

Pop a grape in your mouth and then taste a dry Chardonnay. Or try some chocolate ice cream with Cabernet Sauvignon. Trust us, it's gross! The sweetness of the food robs the wine of its fruit, making it taste really awful. So how can we manage to pair dry Cabernet Sauvignon or Zinfandel with chocolate? The trick is to serve wines with obvious fruit flavors and fairly high alcohol levels, which contribute some sweetness. Also, the desserts should contain dark chocolate, which is richer and more bitter than the sweeter milk chocolate. The rule overall is that the wine must be at least equal in sweetness to the food.

This caveat doesn't apply just to desserts. These days we enjoy chicken fingers with honey mustard, fish with fruit salsas, honey-baked hams, coconut shrimp with chutney… the list goes on. You know to avoid most dry wines with this sweeter fare, but what does that leave? You have several options.

SEMIDRY WHITES

Riesling, Chenin Blanc, Gewurztraminer, Torrontes (from Argentina), Moschofilero, and Malagousia (from Greece), among other whites, are all fruity enough to hold their own against these sweeter foods.

ROSÉS

Don't be a wine snob! In the semidry category, check out American White Zinfandel, White Grenache, or White Merlot. Or experiment with dry yet fruity rosé table or sparkling wines from around the globe. We enjoy the dry rosés from the Navarra, Cigales, and Rioja regions of Spain. From Portugal, try Mateus or Lancer's semidry wines or a bone-dry rosé from the Alentejo. Australia makes some super Grenache-based rosés, and Greece offers the floral-scented Moschofilero as a rosé or a white. Most of these wines have the added benefit of bargain to inexpensive prices.

SEMIDRY BUBBLIES

Opt for extra-dry sparkling wines, which are a little sweeter than the popular brut style.

DRY, FRUITY, LIGHT-BODIED REDS

In California, look for Gamay by Beringer; Grenache by Bonny Doon; fun, inexpensive proprietary reds such as Lolonis' organic Ladybug or Francis Coppola's Rosso; or inexpensive Zinfandel by Barefoot Cellars, Mondavi/Woodbridge, Peachy Canyon, or Parducci.

French Beaujolais, based on the Gamay grape, is also a nice option. Try the lightest, simplest Nouveau style served with a light chill, or offer a finer cru Beaujolais, such as St-Amour, Fleurie, or Moulin-a-Vent, at room temperature. In this category, Georges Duboeuf and Louis Jadot wines are good quality, relatively inexpensive, and easy to find.

Italian wines that are dry and fruity include Valpolicellas by Masi or Sartori, or Bardolino by Bertani or Folonari.

Bargain-priced Australian Shiraz or Grenache blends are also appropriate, but the moderately priced to expensive versions of these grape types will be richer and too tannic for this sweeter fare.

Beware of very spicy and salty foods

The only time you should not match the power or intensity of wine and food is when the food is spicy-hot (rather than rich) or very salty. The high tannins of a full-bodied wine and high alcohol only exacerbate the heat. So forget your favorite oaky Chardonnay, Cabernet, or Shiraz and opt for lighter-bodied wines and/or wines with lower alcohol. The idea is similar to not getting caught up in another person's fiery words. Shouting back just fuels the fire; it's much better to take a step back and chill out. Instead of meeting fiery hot foods head-on with a big wine, take the road of less resistance with a light-bodied (or low-alcohol) wine, such as Vinho Verde (Portugal), Riesling (Germany), or Galestro (Italy).

Another unpleasant combination is very salty foods with full-bodied or high-alcohol wines. Sparkling wines or tart (high-acid) whites such as Sauvignon Blanc cleanse the palate from saltiness; the "briny" flavor of Manzanilla Sherry from Spain also can complement salty dishes. Although it has a fairly high alcohol level (15%), its salty flavors and high acidity work wonders with foods such as salt cod.

You can also contrast spicy, smoked, or salty foods with semidry or fruity wines, as mentioned earlier in the chapter (see "Complement or Contrast Flavors"). Chenin Blanc, Gewurztraminer, and Riesling, for example, are semidry whites that are usually lower in alcohol than Chardonnay. However, if you really love Chardonnay, choose one from a cooler climate such as New York, Oregon, or Canada. They usually have less alcohol than wines from warmer growing regions. Here's a fun experiment: compare an Australian Chardonnay from the cool Yarra Valley to the warmer Barossa Valley or Southeastern Australia. Or pit a Chablis from cool northern France against a Chardonnay Vins de Pays d'Oc from the warm south. You will notice a distinct difference in heat—in both taste and mouthfeel—between the two wines.

Semidry, light-bodied reds are another option. The wine police aren't watching you, so admit it—you like a little sweetness if you are just having a glass of wine instead of beer or a cocktail. Perhaps you are at hanging out with friends after work and need the perfect wine to pair with pigs in a blanket, spicy chicken wings, smoked almonds, or jalapeño poppers. If you crave a little sweetness, the Lambrusco-based Riunite (or another Lambrusco from Italy) is a fun wine to contrast spicy, salty, or smoked foods. Choose other light-bodied reds using the Tower of Power charts, and don't be afraid to chill them. The cool temperature is a great contrast to the heat on your lips.

Resist the urge to overcomplicate

Expensive foods or complicated fusion dishes are often best paired with simple wines.

Special or expensive ingredients such as caviar or truffles deserve to take center stage, and a moderately priced simple wine can act as a good canvas or backdrop for the food. The same holds true for "fusion" dishes, where a complex wine would only compete with the complex flavors of the dish, leading to confusion. In these cases, brut sparkling wine is a perfect choice. As we mentioned before, bubbles renew the palate and the spirit.

Beware of problem children

Several foods are notoriously hard to pair with wine. Here are some of the most common wine antagonists.

ASPARAGUS AND ARTICHOKES

These items may cause your wine to taste sweeter than it is. The solution is to serve the asparagus with a sauce that has some richness. For example, we serve steamed asparagus with a little butter, then partner it with a light-to-medium-bodied dry white such as a Sancerre from France or Blanc de Blancs sparkling wine. As for the artichokes, we adore oyster and artichoke stuffing on Thanksgiving Day. A dry rosé will not compete with the flavor of the artichokes; it also complements the sweet-tart cranberry sauce and is in balance with the flavor and intensity of the turkey.

SPINACH

This is the top vegetable side dish served at steakhouses, where most people order a full-bodied red such as a California Cabernet, French Bordeaux, Italian Barolo, or Spanish Ribera del Duero to match the intensity of the juicy steak. However, the tannic nature of such brawny wines will clash with the spinach, producing a very unappealing metallic flavor. To combat this reaction, order creamed spinach or a spinach timbale. The added fat will turn a negative

The low-down, nitty-gritty cheat sheet

When selecting a wine to pair with a meal, assess the wine using the following simple guidelines:

1. **Temperature at which you will serve the wine:** chilled, cool, or room temperature. Chilled wines can relieve and contrast the heat of spicy foods. Also, hot outside temperatures (or a day at the beach) may suggest a chilled glass of wine, whereas cold damp weather (or a day on the slopes) may have you thirsting for a big dry red or even a mug of glogg (a hot spiced wine cocktail).

2. **Body of the wine:** very light, light, medium, medium-full, or full. Use the body of the wine to balance a dish's power.

3. **Level of sweetness:** dry, semidry, semisweet, or sweet. The wine should be at least as sweet as the food.

4. **Level of acidity:** low, medium, or so tart you drool with pleasure. Acidic wines cleanse your palate of richness; they also pair well with tart foods.

5. **Level of alcohol:** low, medium, or high. Lower alcohol is best for spicy foods or salty foods.

6. **Level of bitterness.** Bitter wines are better than semisweet wines with earthy foods.

7. **Level of oak influence:** none, a hint, or so high you taste bark. Very oaky wines complement smoky flavors or grilled fish and meats.

8. **Level of complexity:** simple, interesting, or amazing. Truly complex wines shine when paired with simple foods, and vice versa.

9. **Major flavor(s) and aroma(s) of the wine:**

   Fruity—stone fruit, citrus, red or black fruit? Dried or fresh fruit?

   Floral—violets, lilacs, or roses?

   Spicy—dark savory spices (cumin, coriander), dark sweet spices (cinnamon, clove, ginger, nutmeg, allspice), or green herbs (rosemary, sage, thyme)?

   Peppery—white pepper, black pepper, or bell pepper?

   Smoky—embers in a fireplace or smoked meat?

   Other—gamy or leather aromas? Mineral?

   Pair wines with foods that have complementary flavors. For example, Syrah/Shiraz almost always smells and tastes of black peppercorn, making it a nice match for pepper-crusted New York strip steak. Likewise, the salted almond flavor of Manzanilla Sherry comes shining through when served with trout amandine.

10. **Wow factor.** Does the wine put a big smile on your face? If so, it's a keeper—experiment with a variety of foods. Part of the fun of pairing food and wine is that potential rush of excitement that comes from discovering an unorthodox but magnificent combination.

combination into a positive one. Employ a similar technique for broccoli rabe or broccolini by sautéing these vegetables with olive oil or butter and garlic, or toss in some bacon or pancetta, which will contribute fat to the dish.

GARLIC

The stinky bulb is much more wine-friendly when it is sautéed or roasted than when it is raw. It has a mineral flavor that can complement mineral flavors in a wine (such as Sauvignon Blanc) as well as some sweetness that can complement fruity or off-dry wines.

TAMARIND

The acidity and bitterness of tamarind can destroy the flavors of a fine wine. Try instead a dry rosé with dishes that have a strong tamarind flavor.

EGGS

Eggs have a protein-based richness that can wreak havoc with many wines. What does work with omelettes, frittatas, and quiches are Fino or Manzanilla Sherries from Spain, brut sparkling wines, or tart, semidry Rieslings from New York, Canada, or Germany, as well as dry, medium-to-full-bodied whites from Alsace, France.

INK

Cuttlefish or squid ink dishes clash with red wines, so pair with a light-to-medium-bodied dry white wine that doesn't have strong oak flavors. Albarino from Spain or Pinot Grigio from Italy are good choices for a black paella.

Cheese: Friend or foe?

You might think pairing wine and cheese is a no-brainer, hard to mess up. If only it were that simple. Once again, the possibilities for ambrosial combinations—and legendary disasters—are endless. After years of experimentation (and dieting), we have come to a few conclusions about pairing wine with cheese. The following is a simple guide and does not go into the myriad possible options.

Dry or semidry white wines and sparklers are usually the best choice to showcase the flavors of cheese. If the cheese is tart, such as a fresh domestic goat cheese or Greek feta, a tart (high-acid) dry white wine such as Sauvignon Blanc or a tart semidry white such as Riesling is ideal. Remember our wacky math? The acids in the wine and cheese negate each other, allowing the creamy flavors of the cheese to shine through.

An aged cheese such as Manchego (sheep's milk) or Reblochon (cow's milk) can handle medium-to-heavy-bodied whites such as an Albarino from Spain or Alvarinho from Portugal. This Iberian grape is also a good middle-of-the-road choice when serving an assortment of cheeses, as it tends to coexist with a variety of cheeses rather than dominate them.

Where does Chardonnay, the most popular dry white of all, fit into the equation? Chardonnay can work with cheese as well, but as you have seen, it is a grape with multiple personalities. The wine's style is largely dictated by where it is grown and how it is made, and this in turn affects the kinds of cheeses suited to the wine. In the Burgundy region of France, for example, the unoaked versions from Chablis are rather austere with a distinct mineral flavor, while the oaky Chardonnays from villages such as Meursault or Puligny-Montrachet are more complex and full-bod-

ied. The same holds true for California and Australia, where price is often an indicator of style. There is a plethora of popular, pleasant, simple Chardonnays that are dry and light-to-medium-bodied. After that, the more you spend—generally speaking—the more interesting the wine and the more "weight" on the palate. Try milder cheeses such as Edam, Swiss, or mozzarella with the lighter versions of Chardonnay (or try a Pinot Blanc from Alsace).

Aged cheeses such as Jack, Emmentaler, or cheddar have more pronounced flavors and are better balanced by fuller-bodied Chardonnays.

Smoked cheeses also fall into this latter category. Smoked Gouda, for example, is well suited to a big, oaky Chardonnay, as well as other full-bodied whites and (remember our Tower of Power charts) medium-bodied reds.

Sparkling wines have a natural affinity with cheese. A glass of delicate Blanc de Blancs or a medium-bodied brut with mild Mascarpone, gooey Camembert, or nutty Parmigiano is a beautiful thing. Demi-sec Champagnes are equally versatile. Their sweetness provides a great foil to a pungent peppercorn goat cheese, yet complements a Spanish or Portuguese cheese served with a sweet quince paste. In addition, demi-sec bubblies can hold their own against the sweet fresh fruits that accompany the cheese course, maintaining their fruit flavors.

As cheese ages, it loses moisture and becomes richer and saltier. This is where red wines come into play. Convention held that the tannins in red wine tame the fattiness of the cheese, and the fruit of the wine will contrast the saltiness of the cheese. Reds with high acidity, such as Pinot Noir, have the added bonus of cleansing the palate. We have seen many classic still-life paintings depicting a table with cheese, bread, and a big glass of red wine. Indeed, red wine has been enjoyed with cheese for centuries. However, recent scientific research has found that cheese destroys the flavor of most red wines. Whom do we believe?

It's a good thing we never read that report until this year. We have been enjoying pizza, cheeseburgers, and Gruyere-topped onion soup with red wines for a long time. Combined, the three of us have probably drunk 100,000 glasses of the "wrong" wine without knowing it! We have also been fortunate enough to travel to many wine regions where the local cheese is usually an ideal pairing with the local wine, which may be red. In Portugal's Douro Valley, for example, we savored a Portuguese Serra mountain cheese with a dry, full-bodied, tannic red and a sweet, fortified Porto. Both were fabulous. Why did these pairings work so well? Was it the amazing scenery of the region? The emotional connection from drinking wine at the site it was created? The excellent company at the table? Whatever the reason, we know it was a positive experience.

You can decide for yourselves where you fall on the red-wine-with-cheese debate by having a cheese tasting. For the wines, start with a sparkler, a white, a light-to-medium-bodied red, and a full-bodied red. Then try them with three different styles of cheese, such as cow's milk, goat's milk, and sheep's milk. Or select cheeses of different ages and different textures—for example, a fresh, soft, ripened cheese such as Brie, a semihard aged Fontina, and a young hard cheese such as a Pecorino Romano. Or for a cold winter day, compare an open-faced sandwich of Swiss raclette heated underneath the broiler with an American grilled cheese sandwich, saganaki (fried Greek Kasseri cheese), and a cheese calzone.

Another option is to pair regional wines with regional cheeses. Serve fresh mozzarella, Bel Paese, and Parmigiano Reggiano from Italy with a Prosecco (Italian sparkling wine), Vernaccia di San Gimignano (white), Chianti (medium-bodied red), and Barolo Riserva (full-bodied red). Or you can mix it up and sample those same Italian cheeses with affordable American wines, such as a brut sparkling wine, a Riesling, a red Zinfandel, and a Cabernet Sauvignon. Do not limit yourself to four types of wine or three cheeses: the more combinations you have, the more opportunities for a successful pairing.

The most difficult cheeses to pair with wine are the blue-veined cheeses. They are very salty and thus can clash with tannic red wines. Traditionally, blue cheeses are best paired with sweet table wines or fortified wines. Classic examples include French Roquefort with Sauternes or English Stilton with a vintage Porto from Portugal. Other matches we recommend are a Cabrales blue from Spain with a dry, salty-flavored Manzanilla Sherry, or an American Maytag or Point Reyes Blue with a Napa Valley Cabernet Sauvignon or Barossa Valley Shiraz from Australia. If the cheese is a crumbled component of a salad, then a medium-to-full-bodied dry white, such as a California Fumé Blanc, can work well. If the dressing has a bit of sweetness, such as a raspberry vinaigrette, Riesling complements the sweetness of the dressing while contrasting the saltiness of the cheese.

A world of flavors: Some magical matches from around the globe

WE ARE FORTUNATE to have access to ingredients and cuisines from all over the world. And with the increasing presence of fusion dishes and ethnic foods—and the myriad of flavors they offer—comes the chance to experiment with a diversity of wines. While some play it safe and just drink beer with ethnic foods, we prefer sparkling wines over beer, and you'll notice that many of our suggestions in this section include bubbly. Table wines can be a little more hit-or-miss, but we are willing to roll the dice and take some chances in pursuit of a heavenly pairing. When wine and food exalt each other, it's magic!

First, a couple of reminders about pairing wine with ethnic foods:

- Temperature of the wine is very important. Make sure your sparkling, white, and rosé wines are well chilled to refresh your palate. Serve simple inexpensive dry whites, rosés, and sparklers at 41° to 47°F (5° to 8°C); more complex whites and light-bodied reds can be served at 50° to 54°F (10° to 12°C), medium-bodied reds at about 55°F (13°C), and full-bodied reds at 59° to 64°F (15° to 18°C). Sweet still and sparkling wines are served at 41° to 47°F (5° to 8°C). Sweet fortified wines, such as Porto, should be served at room temperature. In each of these categories, serve the simpler wines at the lower range of the temperature spectrum and the more complex ones at the higher end.

- Simpler, often inexpensive to moderately priced table wines are the best backdrop for complex dishes, as very powerful, complex, expensive wines will create a tug-of-war for your attention.

- If the dish has a hint of sweetness, you're often better off with the riper fruit flavors of New World wines. If the dish has a more earthy profile, Old World wines with their vegetal or herbal notes are better complements.

We apologize that we cannot feature all the nations of the world or all the foods we enjoy in this section. However, our goal is to provide a general approach to pairing styles of wines with different regional or ethnic foods. Use these guidelines as a starting point, then go wild and experiment on your own. Substitute wines of equal intensity from other countries (refer to the Tower of Power charts), keeping in mind the wine antagonists we listed earlier in this chapter. And remember, when in doubt, you can rarely go wrong choosing a regional wine to accompany food from the same region.

Asia

Vietnam

Spring rolls: dry, light-bodied whites such as Soave (Italy) or Sauvignon Blanc (New Zealand); light sparkling wines such as Blanc de Blancs (United States)

Pho with beef: in the summer, full-bodied whites such as Chardonnay (United States); in the winter, light-to-medium-bodied reds such as Beaujolais (France) or Cabernet Franc (New York, other parts of the United States, or Canada)

Korea

Beef with spicy kimchee: dry rosé sparkling wines from United States or Spain (Cava); medium-bodied reds such as Barbera (Italy), Rioja (Spain), or Dao (Portugal)

Thailand

Pad thai noodles with seafood: light-to-medium-bodied, semidry whites such as Vouvray (Loire, France), Gewurztraminer (Alsace, France), Chenin Blanc (United States or South Africa, where it is known as Steen)

Coconut-milk-based seafood curry: dry, tart, medium-bodied whites such as Sauvignon/Fumé Blanc (Sonoma, California; Sancerre, France; or Menetou-Salon, France)

Indonesia

Chicken satay: dry fortified wines such as Amontillado Sherry (Spain) or Sercial Madeira (Portugal); semidry white such as Gewurztraminer (California, Washington, or Alsace, France)

Nasi goreng (fried rice with shrimp, chicken, and vegetables): crisp whites such as Rueda (Spain) or Gruner Veltliner (Austria); richer whites such as Semillon (Washington State or Australia)

China

Egg rolls: sparkling Prosecco (Italy); semidry whites such as Riesling (New York, Canada, or Australia)

Mu shu pork: semidry whites such as Riesling (New York, Canada, or Australia); medium-weight reds such as Merlot (Washington State), Carmenere (Chile), or Malbec (Argentina); or for a walk on the wild side, Fino or Amontillado Sherry (Spain)

Eggplant in black bean sauce: full-bodied reds such as Ribera del Duero (Spain), Douro (Portugal), Xynomavro (Greece), or Petite Sirah (Mendocino, California)

Szechuan scallops: semidry white such as Riesling (New York, Canada, or Australia), low-alcohol dry whites such as Vinho Verde (Portugal)

Japan

Sushi/sashimi: Sparkling brut (United States); dry Fino or Manzanilla Sherry (Spain); dry light-to-medium-bodied whites such as Verdelho (Australia) or Rueda (Spain); semidry whites such as Chenin Blanc or Gewurztraminer (United States)

Tempura: dry, tart white such as Sauvignon Blanc (Chile or New Zealand)

Chicken or beef teriyaki: fruity, light-bodied reds such as Gamay (United States or Beaujolais, France) or Valpolicella (Italy)

India

Samosa: sparkling brut (United States) or extra dry (Champagne, France), or dry, medium-to-full-bodied whites such as Marsanne (Australia or United States) or white Rhone (France)

Shrimp or lobster with mild curry sauce: full-bodied dry whites with forward fruit flavors such as a Chardonnay from Australia or an Encruzado from Portugal

Shrimp or lobster with spicy curry sauce and chutney: light-bodied, fairly low-alcohol dry white wines such as Vinho Verde from Portugal, or semidry white wines such as Riesling from Germany, the United States, or Canada; Vouvray (France)

Tandoori lamb with red lentil dhal: dry, full-bodied red wines such as Petite Sirah from California, Douro red from Portugal, or a Ribera del Duero wine from Spain

Europe

Italy

Since Italian is often cited as the most popular style of food in America, we will feature a more comprehensive list of pairings than for other nations.

Linguine with pesto: dry, tart whites such as Sauvignon Blanc (South Africa) or Vermentino (Italy)

Fettuccine Alfredo: dry sparkling brut (Franciacorta, Italy) to break through the richness or Chardonnay (Tuscany or California) to complement it

Spaghetti with white clam sauce: dry, medium-bodied Italian whites such as Vernaccia di San Gimignano, Orvieto Classico, or Pinot Grigio

Spaghetti with meat sauce: dry, medium-to-full-bodied Italian reds such as Chianti Classico or Barbera Superiore; Grenache blends (Australia or United States)

Meat lasagna: gutsy, dry, full-bodied reds such as Cabernet Sauvignon, Petite Sirah, or Syrah (California); Amarone or Aglianico del Vulture (Italy)

Veggie pizza: light-to-medium-bodied reds such as Valpolicella or Dolcetto (Italy) or Merlot (United States)

Everything pizza (loaded with meats and veggies): full-bodied reds such as Shiraz (Australia), Zinfandel (Mendocino or Sonoma, California), or Salice Salentino (Italy)

Calzone or white pizza: dry, full-bodied whites such as Chardonnay (California), Semillon (Australia), or Greco di Tufo or Fiano di Avellino (Italy)

Fried calamari with marinara sauce, or zuppa di pesce (seafood soup): dry rosé table or sparkling wine from Franciacorta, Italy; light-to-medium-bodied reds such as Chianti Classico, Sangiovese di Romagna, or Grignolino (Italy), Pinot Noir (New Zealand or Oregon), or an inexpensive Barbera or Zinfandel (California)

Chicken piccata: dry, light-to-medium-bodied whites such as Soave Classico or Gavi (Italy) or Semillon (Australia or Washington State)

Veal chop with wild mushrooms: dry, full-bodied, complex reds with at least five years' aging, such as Barolo, Barbaresco, or Brunello di Montalcino (Italy) or Pinot Noir (Oregon or France)

Osso buco served with a saffron risotto: full-bodied Italian Chardonnay (Tuscany or Friuli); medium-bodied Italian reds such as Merlot or Dolcetto; full-bodied Italian reds such as Carmignano or Barbaresco

Beefsteak Fiorentina: big Italian reds such as Brunello di Montalcino, Sagrantino di Montefalco, Carmignano, Taurasi, or Amarone

France

Pate de campagne: dry, medium-to-full-bodied French reds such as Gigondas or Minervois, or dry, medium-to-full-bodied whites from Alsace, France, or try Verdelho Madeira from Portugal

Choucroute (cabbage and charcuterie): dry or semidry, medium-to-full-bodied whites such as Muscat, Riesling, Pinot Gris, or Gewurztraminer (Alsace, France); semidry table or sparkling cold-climate Riesling (Germany, Canada, or New York)

Cassoulet (white beans with pork and duck): in the summer, dry, full-bodied whites such as Marsanne (California or Australia), white Cotesdu-Rhone or Coteaux d'Aix-en-Provence (France), dry French rosé (Bordeaux or Tavel); in the winter, full-bodied reds from southern France (such as Chateauneuf-du-Pape, Collioure, or Bordeaux), California Zinfandel (Paso Robles or Dry Creek)

Salade Niçoise: dry, Grenache-based rosés from California, Bandol (France), or Navarra or Cigales (Spain); dry, crisp white such as Sauvignon/Fumé Blanc (California)

Bouillabaise: dry rosés, blanc de blancs or brut sparklers, such as Cremant de Bourgogne or Champagne (France); full-bodied French whites such as white Condrieu or Cotes du Roussillon; medium-bodied French reds (Pinot Noir from the Burgundy villages of Marsannay, Pernand-Vergelesses, or Chorey-les-Beaune, or a regional Bourgogne)

Duck confit in a salad (as an appetizer) at room temperature: medium-bodied whites such as the Chardonnay-based Macon, St-Veran, or Pouilly-Fuisse (Burgundy, France) or a Pinot Gris (Oregon or Alsace, France)

Duck confit as a main course, served hot: bold French reds such as St-Estephe or St-Emilion (Bordeaux) or Cornas or Cote Rotie (Rhone Valley); full-bodied versions of California Zinfandel, Cabernet Sauvignon, or Syrah

Spain

Classic paella (with chicken and seafood): dry, medium-to-full-bodied whites such as Albarino, Ribeiro, or Rueda and Fino Sherry (Spain) or Chardonnay (California)

Roast suckling pig: in the summer, dry, medium-to-full-bodied white such as Albarino (Spain); in the winter, medium-to-full-bodied Spanish reds such as Rioja, Ribero del Duero, or Bierzo

Tapas or pixtos (an assortment of little plates or tastes): sparkling Cava (Spain); dry, fortified Fino or Manzanilla Sherry (Spain)

Portugal

Caldo verde (kale soup with linguica sausage): dry, medium-to-full-bodied whites from the Dao, Beiras, Bairra daTerras do Sado, or Bucelas regions (Portugal); light-bodied, low-alcohol dry whites such as Vinho Verde (Portugal)

Cabrito (baby goat cooked in a wood-fired oven): dry, full-bodied noble reds from the Douro, Beiras, or Alentejo regions (Portugal); Cabernet Sauvignon from Napa Valley (California)

Carne de porco alentejano (pork and clams with potatoes): in the summer, dry, medium-bodied Portuguese whites from the Alentejo, Ribatejo, or Terras do Sado regions; in the winter, light-to-medium-bodied inexpensive reds from the same regions

Greece

Moussaka: dry, full-bodied Greek reds such as Naoussa (Xynomavro grape)

Gyro or souvlaki sandwich: in the summer, dry or semidry Greek rosé wines based on the Moschofilero grape, or a dry rosé from California; in the winter, medium-bodied Greek reds such as Nemea (Agiorgitiko grape)

Spanakopita with tzatziki, or Greek salad with feta: dry, tart, local wines based on the

Roditis or Assyrtiko grape; tart Sauvignon Blanc (New Zealand, Australia, or South Africa)

Grilled octopus, mullet, or swordfish with olive oil: dry floral local whites based on the Moschofilero or Malagousia grape

Great Britain

Fish and chips (watch out for the vinegar, it can make the wine taste sour): tart, dry, medium-bodied whites such as Sauvignon Blanc (New Zealand); sparkling Cava (Spain)

Roast beef with Yorkshire pudding: dry, full-bodied, noble reds such as chateau wines from Pauillac or Margaux (Bordeaux, France); Australian Cabernet Sauvignon or Shiraz

Belgium

Moules frites (steamed mussels with Belgian fries): dry, light-bodied whites such as Muscadet (France) or Vinho Verde (Portugal); dry sparkling Cremant d'Alsace (France)

Waffles with strawberries and whipped cream: in the summer, sweet, sparkling (and low-alcohol) Brachetto d'Acqui (Italy); in the winter, the sweet, higher-alcohol Reserve Porto (Portugal)

Sweden

Gravlax: semidry, light-bodied whites such as cold-climate Riesling (New York, Canada, or Germany); dry, medium-to-full-bodied rosé Champagne (France)

Eastern Europe

Borscht (who knew that beets and wine could be so marvelous together, as long as the soup is not sweet): big dry reds such as Grenache or Grenache blends (California; Australia; Cannonau di Sardegna, Italy; Gigondas, France); Zinfandel or Petite Sirah from Mendocino, California

Chicken soup with matzoh balls: dry, full-bodied white such as Chardonnay (kosher versions are available from many nations); sparkling brut (Israel or United States)

Wiener schnitzel: dry, medium-to-full-bodied whites such as Pinot Gris from Oregon or Canada

Veal or beef gulyas (goulash): dry, medium-to-full-bodied reds such as Egri Bikaver (Hungary), Nemea (Greece), or Alentejo (Portugal)

Chicken paprikas: medium-to-full-bodied whites such as Marsanne (California or Australia) or a white Cotes du Rhone (France); medium-bodied reds such as Dolcetto (Italy), Pinot Noir (Santa Ynez Valley or Santa Maria Valley, California), or Egri Bikaver (Hungary)

Duck with red cabbage: dry, medium-to-full-bodied reds such as Mourvedre (California, or the Spanish version known as Monastrell), Zinfandel (California), Shiraz (Australia), or Salice Salentino (Italy)

Pierogis: dry, full-bodied white such as Chardonnay (California, or a French version such as Pouilly-Fuisse) or a Greco di Tufo from Italy; brut sparkling (California)

Africa

Morocco/Algeria

Vegetable couscous: dry, medium-to-full-bodied white such as Chardonnay (California); if you prefer a lot of spicy harissa, then a dry, light-bodied, low-alcohol Vinho Verde (Portugal) or semidry, low-alcohol Riesling

Lamb tagine: dry, fruity, medium-bodied red such as an inexpensive to moderately priced Zinfandel (California); semidry rosé such as white Zinfandel (California); or a dry rosé from Rioja, Spain

Ethiopia

Injera and wat (thin pancakes made of the grain teff, served with a spicy meat stew): dry, light-bodied reds that can be served with a light chill, such as Gamay (United States or Beaujolais, France) or Valpolicella (Italy); dry and semidry rosés (United States)

Middle East

Israel, Lebanon, Syria

Vegetarian mezze of tabouleh, fatouche, baba ghanoush, and hummus: dry, light-bodied whites such as Sauvignon Blanc (Israel) or a Lebanese blend such as Chateau Musar's wine from the Bekaa Valley; brut sparkling (California, Washington State, or Oregon); or a fruity white from Greece such as Moschofilero or Malagousia

Kefta kebabs or shawarma: dry rosé table or sparkling wines (United States or Australia); medium-to-full-bodied reds such as Cabernet Sauvignon blends (Israel, Lebanon, North Coast of California, Southeastern Australia, or Chile)

Americas and the Caribbean

Brazil

Feijoada: full-bodied reds such as Cabernet Sauvignon, Carmenere or Syrah (Chile), Tannat (Uruguay), or Toro (Spain)

Argentina

Beef chimichurri: full-bodied reds such as Malbec, Bonarda (Argentina), Cabernet Sauvignon, or Syrah from Argentina or Chile

Puerto Rico

Pernil of pork: in the summer, dry, medium-to-full-bodied whites such as Albarino

(Spain) or Chardonnay (Chile); in the winter, medium-bodied reds such as Merlot (California) or Campo de Borja or Jumilla (Spain)

Mexico

Pozole: if green pozole, dry, tart Sauvignon/Fumé Blanc (Mexico or United States); if red pozole, light-bodied reds such as Gamay (California or Beaujolais, France) or Moristel (Spain)

Red snapper Veracruz: dry, light-to-medium-bodied whites such as Sauvignon Blanc (Mexico or Chile)

Guacamole: rich, full-bodied Chardonnay (California) to balance the avocado's richness; tart Sauvignon Blanc (New Zealand or South Africa) or sparkling Cava (Spain) to cleanse the richness

Chiles rellenos: semidry whites such as Riesling (Germany); dry, fruity whites such as Torrontes (Argentina) or Moschofilero (Greece)

Beef tacos: dry rosé table or sparkling wines such as Cava (Spain); light-to-medium-bodied reds such as Merlot (Mexico or Chile) or inexpensive Tempranillo or Monastrell (Spain)

Lobster with huitlacoche (corn truffle) sauce: older brut Champagne (France); fine white Burgundy such as Chassagne-Montrachet (France)

Beef chimichangas, enchiladas, or fajitas: for mild preparations, full-bodied reds such as Cabernet Sauvignon or Mourvedre (California); for spicy-hot versions, rosé table or sparkling wines such as Cava (Spain) or a light-bodied red such as Gamay (California), served chilled

Jamaica

Curry goat: if served by itself, dry, light-to-medium-bodied reds such as an inexpensive Zinfandel (California); if served with a jicama salad or fruity slaw (as is customary), semidry whites such as Chenin Blanc

(United States; South Africa, where it is known as Steen; or Vouvray from the Loire Valley, France) or Riesling from New York, Washington, or Germany

Ackee: dry floral white with some richness such as Torrontes (Argentina), Malagousia (Greece), or sparkling Prosecco (Italy)

UNITED STATES
Down-Home American Cooking

After all those exciting ethnic foods, it seems appropriate to end this section with American comfort food. Following are some of the traditional foods we grew up with and the wines we enjoy with them.

Hamburger with all the fixings: Cabernet Sauvignon or Cabernet blend (California, Australia, or Chile), Zinfandel or Syrah blend from California

Hot dog: with mustard, an inexpensive Chardonnay (California), or a semidry Riesling from Washington State, New York State, or Germany; for a chili dog with onions and cheese, Zinfandel (California or Italy, where it is known as Primitivo)

Chile con carne: for mild versions, inexpensive Zinfandel (California); if super-spicy, semidry white Zinfandel (California) or a light red served chilled, such as a Gamay (California or Beaujolais Nouveau, France) or Bardolino (Italy) or sparkling rosé (California) or Cava from Spain

Pastrami sandwich: Blanc de Noirs or sparkling rosé (Oregon or California); a dry rosé such as Cigales or Navarra (Spain); a semidry Riesling (New York)

Mac and cheese: California Chardonnay to balance the richness, or California Sauvignon/Fumé Blanc to cleanse the palate

Fried chicken: dry, full-bodied California white such as Viognier or Chardonnay; sparkling brut from New Mexico, California, or a Cava (Spain)

Barbecued ribs: dry, full-bodied reds such as Zinfandel (California), Shiraz, or GSM (Grenache/Shiraz/Mourvedre

blend) (Australia) or Amarone (Italy); outdoors on a hot day, try a semidry white Gewurztraminer from Washington or California or sparkling rosé from California

New England clam chowder: New York Chardonnay or brut sparkling wine

Manhattan clam chowder or California cioppino: cool-climate Pinot Noir (New York or Oregon; within California, Russian River Valley, Carneros, Anderson Valley, Santa Ynez Valley, Santa Rita, or Santa Maria Valley), or a rosé Pinot Noir

Cajun/Creole

Seafood gumbo: dry or semidry rosé table or sparkling wine, such as Cava (Spain) or Cremant de Bourgogne (France)

Crawfish étouffée: medium-to-full-bodied white such as Chardonnay (Pouilly-Fuissé, Macon, or Rully from Burgundy, France); sparkling Blanc de Noirs (California) or Pinot Blanc (Alsace, France)

Jambalaya: dry or semidry Grenache-based rosé such as Tavel or Bandol (France) or versions from Navarra Spain or California.

Crawfish boil: dry, light-bodied sparkling such as Blanc de Blancs from Washington State or Prosecco (Italy); semidry whites such as Gewurztraminer, Riesling, or Chenin Blanc (United States)

Red beans and rice with sausage: medium-to-full-bodied reds with ripe fruit flavors such as Zinfandel or Petite Sirah (California), Shiraz (Australia), Bierzo (Spain), or Alentejo (Portugal)

Muffaletta sandwich: in the summer, dry, light-to-medium-bodied whites such as Vermentino (Italy) or Semillon (Washington State); in the winter, medium-bodied reds such as Merlot (Chile), Nemea (Greece), or a Penedes blend (Spain)

Pairing sweet wines with food

WHAT BETTER WAY to end a meal than with wine? There are two views of pairing sweet wines with food: You can treat the wine as the dessert, or you can serve it with fruit, cheese, or dessert. The ideal serving for sweet wine is 2 to 3 ounces (60 to 90 milliliters)—about half of the standard serving for table wine.

First, a quick lesson in identifying sweet wines and reading their labels. Whether table (still), sparkling, or fortified, sweet wines have their own vocabulary. Once you know a few key terms, however, decoding them is a snap.

Sweet table wines

These wines may be labeled by varietal, proprietary name, place name, or a combination of varietal and place name.

VARIETAL LABELS

These include the grape name along with country-specific terms that indicate the wine is made in a sweet style. For example:

- **In English-speaking nations:** late harvest, botrytis, or Ice Wine (Icewine in Canada)
- **In France:** vendange tardive or selection de grains nobles
- **In Germany:** Auslese, Beerenauslese, Trockenbeerenauslese, or Eiswein
- **In Austria:** Ausbruch, as well as the German terms above
- **In Italy:** recioto, dolce, or vin santo

The most common grapes to be made into sweet wines include Riesling, Gewurztraminer, Chenin Blanc, Semillon, and Muscat. In fact, the Muscat grape is used so often that the label may not include a term such as late harvest. (Portugal and the Alsace region of France do make some dry versions of this grape, so ask your wine shop or server to confirm it is sweet before buying the wine.)

PROPRIETARY NAMES

These may also be used to label sweet wines: Quady's "Electra" (California) and Maculan's "Torcolato" (Italy) are examples.

LABELS BY PLACE NAME

Just like their dry counterparts, many sweet wines from Old World regions especially are labeled according to place. The place will often provide the key to the grape type used. In Bordeaux, France, the wines of Barsac, Loupiac, Ste-Croix-de-Mont, Cadillac, and Sauternes are based mostly on the Semillon grape. These wines are all full-bodied, with the most expensive versions from individual chateaux. In the Loire Valley, Vouvray Moelleux, Coteaux du Layon, Bonnezeaux, and Quarts de Chaume are based on the Chenin Blanc grape. Italian sweet wines that honor their birthplace include Recioto di Soave (white) and Recioto della Valpolicella (red).

LABELS WITH GRAPE NAME FOLLOWED BY PLACE NAME

Sometimes the grape name will be followed by a word meaning "of" (de, d', di, etc.) and the place name, as is the case with a sweet Muscat from the Rhone Valley (Muscat de Beaumes-de-Venise) and the Cotes de Roussillon (Muscat de Rivesaltes) of France. Greece makes a delicious sweet wine called Muscat of Samos. From Italy, there is Moscato d'Asti, a charming, low-alcohol, spritzy white, as well as the medium-bodied Malvasia di Lipari.

SWEET SPARKLING WINES

The terms *sec, demi-sec,* and *doux,* used in the Champagne region of France to denote whether the wine is dry, off-dry, or sweet, respectively, are commonly employed in other nations as well. A proprietary name such as "Nectar Imperiale," a demi-sec Champagne by Moet et Chandon, may also be used.

SWEET FORTIFIED WINES

These wines are made by the addition of brandy, so they can pack a wallop of power and flavor. Although not all fortified wines are sweet, below are some of our favorite sweet fortified wines from around the world.

Italy: Marsala Dolce

Spain: sweet Sherries, including the varietal-labeled Pedro Ximenez and Moscatel, as well as the blended Cream-style wines

Portugal: true Porto can only come from Portugal's Douro Valley, although California, Australia, and South Africa are all producing fine wines in the style of Porto; Portugal is also home to Moscatel de Setubal and sweet Bual and Malmsey Madeiras.

United States/California: some good Port-style wines

Australia: famous for its "stickies"—sweet wines based on the Muscat grape—as well as some fine Port-style wines

Cyprus: Commandaria (an off-the-beaten-path bargain sweet wine)

Greece: Mavrodaphne of Patras, Muscat of Samos

Dessert pairing guidelines

Just because a wine is sweet does not guarantee a perfect marriage with dessert. We recently attended a dessert and wine pairing with twenty-five different sweet wines, and only by trial and error did we discover our favorite combinations. The lesson is that experimentation is key. Luckily, experimenting is half the fun. Following are some guidelines to get you started.

COLOR COUNTS

As a general rule, we like to pair sweet white wines with desserts that feature white to yellow fruits such as apples, pears, mangoes, peaches, nectarines, apricots, gooseberries, or bananas. Likewise, show off those red dessert wines with red- or black-fruit-based desserts (think blueberries, blackberries, raspberries, strawberries, plums, and cherries). For example, an Auslese or Eiswein Riesling from Germany is lovely with apple strudel, while blueberry pie is a wonderful partner for the black fruit flavors of a Late-Bottled Vintage Porto from Portugal.

GO NUTS

Oxidized sweet wines, such as Vin Santo (Italy, Greece) and Bual or Malmsey Madeira (Portugal), have a nutty flavor that perfectly complements nut-based cookies, cakes, or other desserts such as pecan pie, baklava (Greek nut pastry), almond biscotti, or even a Nutty Buddy ice cream bar.

EMBRACE THE RICHNESS OR REVIVE YOUR TASTE BUDS

Almost any style of sweet wine works with the following desserts: ice cream, custards, yogurt, crème caramel or flan, tres leches cake, cheesecake, and rice pudding. You just need to decide what you want the wine to do. If the goal is to refresh your palate and contrast with the richness of the dessert, choose a sweet sparkling wine. If you want to play up and extend the richness of the dessert, serve either a sweet table wine or a sweet fortified wine. Some of the same guidelines apply here as for savory pairings: complement the flavor of an apricot cheesecake with a sweet white, such as a Tokaji Aszu from Hungary. You can also match intensities. For a light, fluffy cheesecake, try a sweet, light-bodied white—perhaps a Moscato d'Asti from Italy. A dense and sinful cheesecake, however, calls for a richer wine, such as a Sauternes or Muscat de Beaumes-de-Venise from France.

A WORD ABOUT CHOCOLATE

If a chocolate dessert is more bitter than sweet (i.e., based on dark chocolate), then a rich Cabernet Sauvignon, Shiraz, or Zinfandel is one way to go, though it's not our favorite choice. We prefer sweet fortified wines that will balance the richness of the chocolate, such as true Porto from Portugal or Port-style wines from California or Australia. An alternative is the red, effervescent Brachetto d'Acqui from Italy; the bubbles break through the richness of chocolate.

Perhaps the dessert has a secondary component that can indicate a pairing. Chocolate-dipped strawberries and Black Forest cake have red fruit flavors in addition to the chocolate—a good match for the Portos and Brachetto mentioned above. Likewise, orange-flavored, fortified Muscats are wonderful play pals for a chocolate-orange mousse.

Another factor when pairing chocolate desserts is texture—how thin or dense are they? The dense texture of a chocolate terrine demands an equally powerful wine, so a sweet fortified wine such as a Malmsey Madeira from Portugal or a Pedro Ximenez Sherry from Spain are our go to wines of choice.

THE WINE MUST BE AT LEAST AS SWEET AS THE DESSERT

If the wine is less sweet than the dessert, you will be left with a bitter aftertaste. Needless to say, it is best to avoid ending a meal with bitterness. Remember that people's impression of sweetness varies, so if someone recommends a Riesling with dessert, make sure it is a late harvest, botrytis, or Ice Wine style.

REGIONAL WINES ROCK WITH REGIONAL DESSERTS

Over time, certain wines have proven to be fabulous with local desserts. One classic example is hazelnut biscotti with the local Vin Santo of Italy; another incredible combination is Pedro Ximenez Sherry poured over vanilla ice cream—hedonistic heaven! We also nominate apple pie and New York State late harvest Riesling as a marriage made in heaven. It's our contribution to a regional sweet ending.

chapter 15

The good life
living with wine

For us, as for many *WineWise* readers, wine is a good part, a fun part, sometimes even a profound part, of daily life. In this chapter, we'll be sharing some thoughts about wine tasting at home, the "seasonality" of some wines—light whites in warm weather, hearty reds in cold—special wines for special occasions, and the evolution of the wine container—screw caps on bottles and swapping bottles for boxes.

What we hope you'll glean from all of this is that wine fits with the patterns of modern life, whether it's just a glass of wine with dinner, a little bit of a reward at the end of a tough day, or making just another meal a heightened, even special, experience.

And of course, the theme that runs throughout this chapter is that wine is a gift from nature that is meant to be shared with friends and family, expanding our conversations and humor and bringing us closer to one another.

Wine tasting: Do try this at home

NOT SO LONG AGO, a professional wine-tasting panel at the Twenty-eighth International Eastern Wine Competition in Corning, New York, was unanimous in their opinion: they all preferred one California Shiraz over almost 2,300 other wines, awarding the winner a "Double Gold" medal. The wine they embraced, a Charles Shaw Shiraz, sells for $1.99 to $3.99 at selected Trader Joe's stores across the country, and will forever be remembered in the annals of American wine commerce as "Two Buck Chuck." Chuckie beat out wines selling for less than $10 to more than $60 per bottle. Chuck's Chardonnay also won "Best Chardonnay in California" at the 2007 California State Fair Wine Competition, receiving a score of 98 out of 100 points, beating 350 other wines, with price tags topping out at $120. This kind of thing happens more often than you might imagine and far more often than professional tasters want to admit, talk about, acknowledge, and—last, but surely not least—make public.

When we told some friends about the results of this tasting, each of them (1) gave us a withering glance, as if to lump us with this group of frauds and phonies, (2) got close up in our faces and laughed really loud, and (3) said, "Anyone can do that," referring to the total lack of acumen on part of the *poseur* tasters. We had to turn away, and reflexively started doing the "perp walk" made famous on the evening news by dope dealers, crooked politicians, and disgraced corporate executives.

As if the majority of the American public did not already think that "wine professional" was another term for "can't get a real job," we have a dirty little secret about professional tasting that we want to share. Many professional tasters—*but not us*—believe that the job of the professional wine taster is to find the faults with the wine. For those who look only for faults, professional wine tasting is a bit like finding all the reasons *not* to award your Cub Scout son his merit badge (he forgot to kiss Grandma) or *not* to let your daughter play outside with the other kids (she didn't clean her room). In case of a tie between wines, taste again, and look for the one that metaphorically didn't practice her clarinet for an hour each day or didn't do his homework right after supper.

We don't agree with this stance, and when we taste on the job, pleasure is paramount. Maybe we're naive in our approach, but we want to taste wines that excite us, wines that make us want to yell "Yes!"

The real fun of tasting wine is tasting for pleasure, not for punishment. And the best place to do this is at home, with friends, in a relaxed atmosphere of conviviality and generosity. Tasting wine at home is fun coupled with a bit of self-guided education. Ouch. Don't worry—in this case the education mimics the learning curve that began with the awkward pleasures of your first kiss and grew exponentially into sensual subtlety: the confident strut, the irresistible smile.

How to begin? What wines? How many wines? How expensive are the wines? What glassware? What room? Outside or inside?

Wait! The most important factor is the people. You can taste some of the most glorious wines in the world, but if you taste them with miserable people, guess what? The wines will taste miserable, too. You want to invite friends who enjoy the company of other people, have a sense of humor, don't judge others harshly, don't want to be the "expert" but have something to say. Finally, invite friends who are moderate drinkers. Wine tastings are not for lushes, who can diminish or even ruin the experience for everyone else. *Tasting* is the operative word.

Once you've put together your guest list, start to think about the wine. Some basics:

- *Use wineglasses.* Don't use clear plastic cups, which make the wine taste like clear plastic cups. Most people don't have enough glasses, so here's a hint: rather than burdening your guests with a request to bring glasses from home, check out the local party rental folks. You'll be surprised how inexpensive it is to rent two or three racks of glasses—not necessarily great glasses, but all of them the same size and shape, and racked together for convenience and to avoid breakage.

- *Provide spit cups and napkins.* Tasting involves four steps: looking (judging the color of the wine), smelling (the nose of the wine), tasting (sampling a small amount of wine and swishing it around in the mouth), and spitting. That's right, part of tasting is spitting the wine into a spittoon or spit cup. While you're at the party place renting glasses, pick up a sleeve of 16-ounce (480-milliliter) paper cups, and place one at every setting. You may not be able to enforce spitting at a home wine tasting, but especially if your friends are driving away from the tasting, you can certainly encourage it. A couple of good-quality paper napkins should be placed at each setting, too.

- *Bread and water.* Water should be plentiful and available. A few bread baskets filled with crisp sliced baguettes and/or individual plates with water crackers should be available for cleansing the palate between wines. Make sure the bread or crackers are as neutral-tasting as possible: no brioche, croissants, or flavored crackers because these will have a dramatic impact on the wine's taste.

- *Tasting mats/tasting sheets.* On your home computer you can make a simple or an elaborate and creative tasting mat, or if you're truly inspired, you can design your own.

If you are tasting the wines blind, obviously the wines will be identified by number only. If you know what wines you are tasting, list them by name. It helps your guests to be consistent in how you list the wine. We recommend listing each wine this way:

1. Product
2. Special attribute, if any
3. Producer
4. Subregion, if any
5. Region, if any
6. State (U.S.) or country
7. Vintage, if any (write "NV" if nonvintage)

Examples

Pinot Noir (1), Reserve (2), Robert Sinskey (3), Carneros (4), Napa Valley (5), California (6), 2005 (7)

Chianti Classico (1), Reserva (2), Banfi (3), Tuscany (5), Italy (6), 2005 (7)

Shiraz (1), Peter Lehmann (3), Barossa Valley (4), South Australia (5 and 6), 2000 (7)

(It would be redundant to write "South Australia, Australia," as most people can figure this one out. If they can't, well, then you probably don't want them at your tasting.)

Wine tastings may be a prelude to or part of a festive meal, outdoors or indoors. (Photo courtesy of Iron Horse Winery)

Chateau Larose-Trintaudon (1 and 3), Haut-Medoc (4), Bordeaux (5), France (6), 2000 (7) (Note that when it comes to Chateau-named wines from Bordeaux, **the name of the product (the wine) and the name of the producer (the chateau) are one and the same**, as there is only one Chateau Larose-Trintaudon or Chateau Blah Blah Blah, n'est ce pas?)

On the tasting mat, or better yet (and especially if you are tasting more than four or five wines) on separate sheets of paper, allow each taster to make notes on each wine based on these criteria: color, nose, flavor, body, length of finish on the palate. You might ask "Did you like it?" and/or "What would be a good dish to pair with this wine?"

WINE	COLOR	NOSE	BODY
Name of the wine, producer, any special attributes, any subregions and/or regions, state (U.S.), or country (foreign), vintage (if any)	Your perception of depth, hue, and clarity	What the wine smells like to you: aroma and/or bouquet	Your impression of the wine on the palate: light, medium, or full
1.			
2.			
3.			
4.			
5.			
6.			
7.			
8.			

At-home tasting sheet.

- Maps of the wine regions represented at your tasting are a nice plus for your guests. Use the maps in this book, or utilize the interactive maps available at www.kobrandwine.com/maps/map_list.php. You might want to print these out, but if you've got a large computer monitor, it might be more fun to play with these maps online, highlighting specific areas (for example, the *premier cru* vineyard sites of the Chablis district in Burgundy). Looking at maps gives people a sense of place for the wines.

The tasting can be done indoors or outdoors—the more light, the better to see the true color of the

TASTE	FINISH	FOOD MATCH
Flavor components that you experience on your palate	Duration of flavors after tasting (short, medium, or long); any new flavors?	What would you like to eat with this wine? Why?
1.		
2.		
3.		
4.		
5.		
6.		
7.		
8.		

wine—as a prelude to dinner, or as its own little party. You should pour between 1 and 2 ounces (30 and 60 milliliters) per person per wine; 1½ ounces (45 milliliters) is ideal. It's very important to make sure your guests stay for at least a couple of hours after the tasting, and never let a friend drive drunk. If everybody is on the same page with the concept of the tasting, this should not be an issue.

As to what wines to serve, think thematically: New World reds under $15, white wines from the Loire Valley, sparkling wines of the world, American wines not from California, zigging and zagging with Zinfandel. Of course, if money is no object, then feel free to host a tasting of Opus One: 1995 to 2005; the *premier grand crus* of the Haut-Medoc: 1995 to 2005; Barolo versus Barbaresco: the 1998 vintage; and so on. At home, we prefer tasting accessible, affordable wines that our friends can appreciate, enjoy, and can have some fun with, followed by a simple dinner, picnic, or cookout at home with the "partials," the leftover wines. For an exotic and unexpected twist, have a tasting followed by a dinner at home of good Chinese takeout, the best pizza in town, or some new dishes from that new Lebanese restaurant. You get the picture.

As for us, we'll be busy planning our next blind tasting at home: "$6.99 Chardonnays: World-Class, Kick-Ass, or We'll Pass." See you there.

Life is short: Drink (and share) that special bottle!

WHEN IT COMES TO the subject of rare and expensive wines that you have been saving for those special occasions, our advice is simple, direct, and concise: drink up!

So many wine lovers are the stewards of rare and wonderful wines that they are saving for a special occasion. In a world where every day we are increasingly reminded how fleeting life can be, we might want to reexamine the concept and definition of "special occasion" to make it more inclusive, more elastic, more fun. Get those bottles out of the dusty cellar,

stand them up in the light of day, and bring them to your table to enjoy. Opening and sharing a rare and wonderful wine makes the food taste better, the conversation more sophisticated (or at least the same old stories more bearable), your dining companions seem more attractive. Even close friends and family realize, perhaps for the first time, that you and your home exude a glowing warmth and generosity.

Yes, we call wine lovers who cellar treasured and rare wines "stewards," not "owners." Unless you get inordinate pleasure from looking at or stroking bottles with labels, you "own" very little until that bottle is opened and that wine is drunk. If you collect wine to resell it, you merely steward that wine from the previous cellar to your cellar to the buyer's cellar, and the only pleasure is profit; you might as well invest in pork bellies or any other commodity. As anyone who has ever tasted truly great wine can attest, it is a magical elixir that provides pleasure so far beyond dollars, pounds, or euros that the *sale* of fine wines and the *enjoyment* of fine wines do not even inhabit the same pleasure universe.

We often wonder if even the most wine-stained among us realize how truly rare is the opportunity to taste great wine. No more than one-tenth of 1% of the wine produced in the world is destined to be among the treasured classics. Fortunately, the equivalent of about 15 billion bottles of wine are produced every year, so about 1.5 million bottles from each worldwide vintage might be keepers. This collection is diminished even more by the relative quality of the vintage; the reputation of the producer; the wine futures market, especially in Bordeaux; the auction block; the finest restaurants, who get first dibs on treasured wines; and the generally rich and powerful, who, if they want to, can always get there first.

We the many, who are neither so rich nor so powerful, can afford very few of life's large luxuries. Occasionally, we purchase or perhaps receive as a gift a little luxury: a fine bottle of wine, a wine to be shared with special people at a special time. *Now* is that time, a moment that will never come again, so don't wait for that "special dinner." Make tonight's dinner special: special for the one you love more than any other, special for your kids home from college, special for the friends whose support you rely on and who rely on you, special for the folks who don't always feel so special but you know they are. Sharing your finest wines creates a very special atmosphere, as the table becomes a place not only for celebration but also for meditation.

With our first look, our first smell, our first sip, we are transported to a place where riches and power run a distant second to pure pleasure, and for that brief shining moment we are as rich as the richest person, as happy as the happiest, and power just doesn't matter.

Warm weather wines: Sparklers for summer

GEEZERS THAT WE ARE, the other day we were indulging our fondness for old British Invasion rock, listening to the Kinks play "Sunny Afternoon." It didn't seem at all difficult for Ray Davies to sing with his tongue in his cheek. His comedic lament:

Taxman comin' to take my yacht,
He's taking everything I've got;
All I've got's this sunny afternoon.
And just now I'm sitting here,
Sipping on my ice-cold beer.
All I've got's this sunny afternoon.

Rocker Davies had the right idea: when all else in life seems to be going to rack and ruin, just sit back, enjoy the sunshine, and have a cold one. Except there's one kink in the Kinks' message: the song serves the needs of beer hounds, but how do wine lovers relax on a sunny afternoon, putting all the cares of the world behind them? Allow us to suggest:

And just now we're looking cute,
Sipping on our ice-cold brut,
All we've got's this sunny afternoon.

We're Bubbleheads. Love those bubbles. And what better time to enjoy refreshing, thirst-quenching sparkling wines than the summer in multiseason environs or anyplace that's warm year-round? Please

don't expect us to wait for the holiday season (when more than 40% of all sparklers are consumed) or for a birthday, anniversary, or some other holiday. No, we want our bubbles now!

Why should we relegate Champagne and other wonderful sparklers to the rarefied dustbin of special occasion wines? Are we secretly so pleasure-negative that we feel we deserve to feel the sexy exhilaration that bubbles provide only once in a while, and then only on socially acceptable rites and festivals? When did carbonated pleasure become a commodity to be doled out to us at holidays for being good little boys and girls? Enough!

There is just no good excuse for not enjoying sparkling wines year-round, but especially in warm weather, when the exciting combination of acidity and carbonation both satisfies our thirst and cleanses our palate. Just the image of a champagne bottle in a silver or glass ice bucket quickens the pulse, as does the exquisite *perlage* of small bubbles rising in a straight line from a single point of departure in a beautiful flute or tulip glass. If ever form followed function, it does so in a crystal flute of bubbly.

The first taste of the wine! So refreshing, so heady, so romantic. The bubbles, sustained as if by magic, dance on your tongue well after the initial sip. By the second glass, we truly sing the body electric, and all is right with the world.

And please don't consign good sparkling wines to the realm of aperitifs and hors d'oeuvres. You can have great fun planning an all-bubbly dinner: a light blanc de blancs with poached fish in lemongrass broth, followed by a medium-bodied brut with a mushroom risotto and a full-bodied rosé reserved for a perfectly roasted chicken or grilled filet mignon served with roasted new potatoes and ratatouille. A toast to the host with a blanc de noirs sparkler is followed by a delightful dessert of coconut, mango, and blackberry sorbets served on a banana waffle with a softly sweet *demi-sec* sparkler.

Now what's stopping you from indulging in the beauty of the bubbles, the sensuality of the sparkle? Expense? Pish-tosh. What century are you living in? Sparkling wines are real bargains. The best estate-bottled sparklers made in the United States, Iron Horse

(Sonoma/Green Valley) and Roederer Estate (Mendocino/Anderson Valley), are bargains at under $25. Fine wines from Domaine Carneros (Napa Valley/Carneros), Argyle (Oregon/Willamette Valley), and the very exciting Gruet (New Mexico), and Chateau Frank (Finger Lakes, New York) are even less. And don't forget the *petillant* pride of the South, Biltmore Estate Brut from the Vanderbilts' humble abode in North Carolina (available at the estate or at the Biltmore Web site for about $25 to $30).

Champagne taste with a six-pack budget? Remember just one word…Cava! These *methode champenoise* sparklers from outside of Barcelona, Spain, are charming, sexy, and satisfying, and most are available for less than $10. A current favorite is Cristalino (look for the brut and the rosé) as well as Juve y Camps, Sumarocca, Paul Cheneau, and the ubiquitous Freixenet and Cordoniu. For a very special vintage wine at about $20, the Llopart "Leopardi" Brut Nature (aged forty-six to fifty-two months) is an amazing bargain in prestige bubbly.

And please don't forget Prosecco. This light, frothy, fruity sparkler is a crowd- and budget-pleaser, terrific on a hot day and with spicy foods. Look for Prosecco from Mionetto, Zardetto, Valdo, and many other producers.

True Champagne, the real deal from that eponymous region of France, while more expensive than other sparklers, can be surprisingly affordable. We love sparkling wines from all over the world, but the one wine that is truly *terroir*-driven is Champagne. Chalk soil (formed by ancient receding oceans) and low temperatures (it is the coldest wine region in France) give Champagne the earthy/yeasty aroma and complex flavor with subtly searing acidity that is unique in the world of sparkling wines.

Expensive vintage-dated and *cuvee de prestige* Champagnes are easy to find, but look a little deeper and you will find some real bargains. Look for Phillipponnat, Nicolas Feuillatte, Jacquart, Gosset, Charbaut, Pol Roger, Montaudon, Vranken, Alfred Gratien, Lanson, Jacquesson, Ayala, Charles Heidsieck, and Deutz, all of which retail in the $25 to $40 range.

France produces some very fine sparklers outside of the Champagne region in the $10 to $20 range.

Look for Cremant d'Alsace (Willm, Lucien Albrecht) or Cremant de Loire (Monmousseau, Gratien et Meyer).

We think we've made the case for sparkling wines to be an important part of your wine regimen, never again to be cast aside until the "right occasion." The truth is this: if we were told that we could drink only one category of wine for the rest of our lives, our choice would be sparkling wine. Why? Because it's sexy and it's fun, and in a world where we're only allowed one kind of wine to drink, we think we'll need all the sexy fun we can get.

Warm weather wines: Whites for summer

IN 1935, George and Ira Gershwin wrote "Summertime," the most memorable song featured in the American opera classic *Porgy and Bess*. The lyrics begin: "Summertime and the livin' is easy…." This timeless lullaby perfectly describes our approach to eating and drinking during the hot months of summer: slow down, take it easy, bask in the warm sunshine, and enjoy lighter meals with lighter wines. And the wines don't have to lighten your wallet, either.

Summer should be a season for rest, relaxation, and recuperation. We still may work 9 to 5 but it's light when we get up, and it's still daylight when we drive home; that alone should put us in a sunny mood. And most of us can manage to get away or just goof off for at least a couple of long, lazy weekends, while the lucky ones sneak a week or two. Ah, summer! That cherished time of year that means life in the great outdoors of fun, friends, family, and food.

We are summer-lovers, and so are most of our friends. We live in the beautiful Hudson Valley in shorts and T-shirts whenever we can, and we cook and dine al fresco every chance we get. We love to fire up the grill and then jump in the water to meditate on the menu, which is inevitably based on what's fresh from the garden and what looked good at the fish market or butcher. And, of course, there's the wine….

So many light wines are a pleasure to imbibe in the summertime. Good Pinot Grigio is a great match with rotisserie chicken. New World Sauvignon Blanc—especially those from California and Chile, and "fruit salad in a glass" from New Zealand and South Africa—is terrific with grilled salmon served with spicy fruit salsas. Dry and semidry Rieslings are magnificent foils for many spicy Cajun, Thai, or Indian dishes. Vinho Verde from Portugal is a low-alcohol, spritzy wine that is a fabulous match with ceviche and also a wonderful aperitif. A simple summer meal of mussels in saffron broth was made to go with Muscadet from the Loire Valley. White Zinfandel or a dry-to-semidry rosé is terrific with North Carolina–style barbecue of pulled-pork sandwiches. And don't forget lighter reds—Beaujolais-Villages or Valpolicella Classico, among others, served with a bit of a chill, for those burgers and steaks hot off the grill.

Summer wines should be full of fruit, cool and refreshing, and as informal and inexpensive as the summer-lovers' dress code. When you're relaxing and talking, playing killer croquet or bad-ass badminton, hard-hearted horseshoes, or simply silently swimming, you don't want to ruminate over ponderous, serious wines full of complexity and depth. When the sun is shining, you want the alcohol to be low, so that you don't become groggy, and you're able to have safe and responsible fun fun fun so that Daddy won't take the T-bird away. Save those big reds and oaky whites for sitting by the fireplace in late autumn, winter, and early spring, dining on lamb stews, hearty soups, and scripted meals. Just as food is seasonal—greens, tomatoes, and corn are the cornerstones of the true summer-lover's diet—so is wine. So bring on the wines of summer: light, crisp whites, thirst-quenching dry rosés, and fruity, luscious reds!

Vinho Verde

In the mood for a salad of fresh greens studded with boiled, steamed, or grilled lobster and drizzled with a dreamy dressing of coarsely puréed watermelon, onion, and ripe peaches? What could be better with this light and simple dish than a Vinho Verde from Portugal, an elegant, dry white wine that is redolent of grapefruit, with just a bit of spritz for a refreshing cleansing of the palate.

Vinho Verde is the ultimate summer-lover's wine: about 8% to 9% alcohol, and it's not afraid of an ice cube or two, or even a little sparkling water for a magnificent wine spritzer. Vinho Verde is the reigning monarch of the land of ABC (anything but Chardonnay), and she is a ruler who favors almost unbelievably progressive taxation. Basic Vinho Verde sells for about $6 to $10 per bottle, a truly great wine value, so buy a case or two for the summer. You want to drink this charming wine as young as possible, so look for the most current vintage or bottling date (in very small print on the back label).

Entre-Deux-Mers

One of the delights of writing about wine is turning *WineWise* readers on to a wonderful wine that they may never have tried or maybe never even thought about trying. When the wine is also a great value, the enjoyment we take in our job doubles.

This particular summer white carries a passport from the European Union. No matter: it is at home in the backyards, on the decks, by the seashore or by the pool, and in the hills and mountains of the United States. If you welcome this wine once during the summer, you will beg a case or two to stay as a guest for the entire season.

The wine is Entre-Deux-Mers, a dry white wine from Bordeaux in France. For the record, Entre-Deux-Mers is comprised of a blend of mostly Sauvignon Blanc and Semillon grapes. It is meant for early drinking, is light-to-medium-bodied with crisp and refreshing acidity, and is a perfect summer wine.

Entre-Deux-Mers produces a wine with a minimum alcohol content of 10%, but most in the American market are 11% to 12%. The moderate alcohol makes these wines very attractive mates for light and simple foods, especially fish, seafood, and white meats. Salsas trump sauces with this wine, and there is just nothing better with *caprese,* a tomato and fresh mozzarella salad with fresh basil, good olive oil, and a touch of balsamic vinegar.

Unfortunately, Entre-Deux-Mers can be difficult (but by no means impossible) to find, and here's the reason:

1. Raise your hand if prior to reading *WineWise* you were familiar with a wine labeled "Entre-Deux-Mers."
2. Now raise your hand if prior to reading *WineWise* you were familiar with a wine labeled "Bordeaux."

We're willing to bet that 90% of readers raised their hand only once, and it wasn't for choice No. 1. The winemakers in Entre-Deux-Mers realize this problem, and so very often they will label their wine simply as "Bordeaux" because it is easier to sell with the less specific but legally allowed label. This is a fact of life in our increasingly vanilla world, but it is still wrong. "Bordeaux Blanc" usually sells for more money than Entre-Deux-Mers; the reverse should be true.

But what is bad news for the reputation of Entre-Deux-Mers is good news for the consumer. Thirty-five years ago Entre-Deux-Mers sold at retail for $4 per bottle. Today, you can still buy estate-bottled—*mise en bouteilles au chateau*—Entre-Deux-Mers for about $10. In thirty-five-year-old dollars, when you figure the annual rate of inflation, the wine now costs less than nothing. It's like the *vignerons* of Entre-Deux-Mers are paying you to drink their wine!

And there are stellar producers of this lovely summer-perfect wine, including our personal favorite, Chateau Bonnet, which now sports a consumer-friendly screw cap. Other very fine Entre-Deux-Mers producers include Chateau Fondarzac, Chateau Moulin de Launay, Chateau Roquefort, Chateau Thieuley, and Chateau Turcaud.

Back to the Gershwin brothers and their song that brought us to the party. Entre-Deux-Mers is a perfect accompaniment to "Summertime." It is such an enjoyable warm-weather wine that it is sure to confirm that "yo' daddy's rich, an' yo' ma is good-lookin'." You can't ask more from any wine.

The bounty of the Loire Valley

As we mentioned in our chapter on French wines (see pages 140–179), the wines of the Loire are intrinsically linked with summer sun and fun, elegantly simple and coolly refreshing. From the numerous appellations along the Loire Valley comes an almost limitless array of bright whites, dry rosés, and lollipop reds that make any backyard bash so much more enjoyable. If you were so inclined, you could spend the full three months of summer metaphorically cruising up and down the Loire, sampling all of its wine wares, and never having to repeat one. Add that to your list of "must do before I'm fifty" (or sixty, or…).

Start at the western end of the valley and sample all of Muscadet's simple pleasures, from straightforward, razor-sharp Muscadet *tout court* to the greater complexities of the *sur lie* style with noticeable yeasty, brioche-like aromas and flavors. These wines are terrific relaxation beverages, the best timing mechanism ever invented for making sure that the corn, still in its husk, cooks gently on top of the grill: just reach out every now and then and give the corn a quarter turn. Since we are all concerned about enjoying and appreciating every drop of wine we consume, we also want to be sure that we don't simply load up on alcohol. Take advantage of Muscadet's simplicity to create your very own spritzer, with lime or lemon wedges and club soda. So simple and so perfect. Whether your Muscadet is spritzed or not, you may become convinced that you will never again face a dish of steamed clams and mussels or raw oysters without Muscadet to wash it all down as a decadent lead-in to a summer feast.

Move inland down the Loire Valley toward the center, tie up at some virtual mooring, and you could spend the next month exploring all that this area has to offer, with dry to semidry Chenin Blancs and ripe, juicy, light Cabernet Francs. The villages of Saumur and Vouvray produce incomparable Chenin-based white wines, and we have spent many an enjoyable summer evening musing over our next course with the sensual promise provided in a glass of still Vouvray or Saumur—especially sparkling Saumur, one of the great undiscovered wonders of the world of sparkling wine. And don't keep those reds from Chinon or Saumur Champigny locked in the closet or sitting in the sun; dunk them in the ice bucket or let them doze undisturbed in the fridge for a while until they get the lightest chill that will make their Cabernet Franc red berry flavors sing rather than just wilt in the heat.

Put out a sumptuous spread of smoked trout, grilled salmon, egg rolls, prosciutto and melon, baby lamb chops, grilled pork tenderloin, potato salad—and the wines of the central Loire Valley will show you just how well they are suited to summer backyard living.

Of course, like many an errant sailor, you may decide that the central Loire Valley is where you will permanently drop anchor, but if the urge to move on grabs you, you don't have far to go upstream before Sancerre and Pouilly-Fumé call to you as the sirens they are, beguiling you to stop and try the wonders of these Sauvignon Blancs (and don't forget to try Sancerre *rouge* and *rosé*, each made from Pinot Noir). This is where the grilled tuna, seafood sausage, and asparagus come in. And for those who have really paced themselves well, a fresh goat cheese with a white Sancerre will send us all to sleep happy and sated.

Warm weather wines: Riveting rosés of summer

HERE IS A WARM-WEATHER MANTRA for you to channel your inner sunshine: "Summer-lovers love rosé." During the cool months of the year, rosé wines get little notice and less respect. Rosé is all but forgotten or ignored by wine geeks, but for wine and food lovers who adore fresh, cool flavors of orange and strawberries, dry rosé is a revelation.

Paired with a chilled dry rosé, grilled salmon served medium-rare with "creamers" (tiny roasted red potatoes) and roasted summer garlic alongside a salad of garden greens dressed with extra-virgin olive oil and fresh herbs is nothing short of perfection. A wine that will enhance your food as well as slake your thirst, rosé is to summer as falling leaves are to autumn, an undeniable part of the landscape. Try rosé wines from

California or Italy, but especially from Spain or from Provence, France, many under $15.

If we had to choose but one summer wine to accompany a variety of lighter grilled foods, we know what we'd choose in a heartbeat. While we're happy that we don't have to make such a dramatic choice, we honestly believe that we could be happy chilling out and grilling out with a glass of cold rosé.

Rosé, the often-overlooked, much-maligned, misunderstood vacuous *vin*? Rosé, the pathetic, penurious plonk, the quintessential quaff? Rosé, the classless clinker of know-nothing nattering nabobs? Yes, rosé gets almost no respect from wine snobs, but it is the perfect drink for the hot, the thirsty, and the hungry.

Like virtually all important and mysterious enigmas, the perfection of rosé lies in those same qualities long identified, often erroneously, as faults in the wine. To wit: rosé has no real character; it's neither white nor red; it's not really sweet, but you can't call it dry; it's so simple to drink; it's a pizza wine; it's a picnic wine; it's a wine for the beach; it's an inexpensive, unsophisticated wine; it's so unhip to drink rosé. Sounds perfect to us.

Rosé is the near-perfect wine to drink with elegant yet simple food: grilled salmon, lamb and veggie kabobs, a beautiful burger, a succulent steak, grilled sausages, a salad of grill-roasted sweet corn with grilled tomatoes and ripe peaches. Rosé is a wine that does not dull the senses; it refreshes and reinvigorates them.

A dry to semidry rosé is the ultimate wine to serenade a Mediterranean-influenced barbecue, to create fireworks at an all-American cookout on the Fourth of July, to dive in with a Floribbean nut-encrusted grilled grouper, or to meditate on the essence of spa-inspired vegetarian fare.

Fresh, crisp rosé will transport you to the world of cool, refreshing, very dry white wines, but with more than a little of the fruitiness and depth of a light red. Even among the driest rosés, a vein of strawberry or citrus fruits will appear out of nowhere. Rosé at its best is a simple, flexible, and affordable accompaniment to all the food we love to cook and eat in the fresh air.

When we're feeling warm and a little groggy from too much sun, we like our rosé as cold as a lager beer, and have shocked our hipper-than-thou friends by adding an ice cube or three to our glasses. We also like to make refreshing rosé spritzers by adding some sparkling water. The ice and water dilute the alcohol—most rosé wines are 12% to 13% alcohol, so a few ice cubes or bubbles in the glass can knock that down a few percentage points, making the simplest foods sing out and allowing you and your guests to go back to swimming, volleyball, bocce, or that most competitive of outdoor sports, horseshoes, later in the day.

Especially during warm weather, when enjoying grilled fish, shellfish, and mollusks as well as sandwiches, pizzas, and grilled vegetables, rosé wines deserve a prominent place on your table. Try dry and semidry rosé wines and you may find that, because of their affinity with your food as well as their friendly price points, rosé will bring a welcome chill to the grill.

Warm weather wines: Fruity reds of summer

THE PERFECTLY GRILLED BURGER, cooked and served outdoors, is as much a part of summer's iconography as fireworks on the Fourth of July. Serve it with fresh tomatoes, lettuce, onion, salted cucumbers picked that day, a sauce of ketchup, mustard, and mayo, with just a touch of Tabasco, all piled on hearth-baked bread, with homemade potato salad on the side, and just ask yourself as you taste this American delicacy, "Does it gets any better than this?"

Yes, it does. Pair that burger with a light, fruity, but dry red, such as Barbera from California's Amador County, Beaujolais-Villages from France, a young red Rioja from Spain, Alentejo from Portugal, or perhaps best of all some fruity reds from Italy—a Valpolicella Classico from Veneto, a simple Chianti from Tuscany, or a Dolcetto from Piedmont (each of these wines can be found easily for under $15). Now, take a sip and taste a second sauce, a true "secret sauce" for that burger, revealed only to your palate. These wines smell and taste of red summer berries. The fruit of the wine harmonizes with the earthy, sweet flavors of the burger, creating a simultaneous counterpoint and complement for the sensual nexus of flavors going on in this dish.

When it comes to wine and the image of its pompous poobahs, what's more fun than a little harmless sacrilege? We will surely be cast out of Snobovia, but we say chill these reds. That's right—serve 'em cool, serve 'em cold. Why? Putting a chill on these simple reds will bring out their fresh flavors and pump up the refreshing acidity that we crave on a hot day to refresh our palates. If you taste these wines warm (made even warmer in the glass by your hand and by the sun), they might taste flat and flabby and lose some of their many charms. So treat these reds like whites or rosés when you enjoy them in the summer sunshine.

The pleasures of summer are many, but fleeting. But for those precious few languorous months of intense warmth and sunshine, let's celebrate the glorious summer season with glorious summer wines.

Winter warmers: Reds for winter

AS AUTUMN TURNS TO WINTER, we begin to eat heartier foods and drink heartier wines. For us, this means enjoying full-bodied wines—especially big reds—with the aromatic and comforting stews, slow-cooked meats, brawny pasta dishes, and roasted vegetables that help to offset the chill of cold weather. When it's cold outside you can warm up inside with a hearty dish and a hearty wine.

"To everything there is a season," and that's true for seasonal foods served with seasonal wines. In the summertime, you might enjoy cold stone crabs in a lemongrass broth with a glass or two of chilled Sauvignon Blanc, but in the winter you are more likely to gravitate to a lamb stew served with garlic-roasted potatoes and a few glasses of Cabernet Sauvignon or Syrah to take away your physical and psychic chill.

These days, winter warmers can be found from all over the wine world and at all different price points. These wines are red, full-bodied, and complex. Think about some of these wines with a plate of Hungarian goulash, a rib-eye steak with creamy mashed potatoes, pasta with sausages, a classic cassoulet of beans, pork, and duck, or its Portuguese and Brazilian cousin, *feijoada*. Slow-roasted root vegetables sprinkled liberally with Parmigiano Reggiano cheese is a robust dish without meat that can support a winter warmer, too.

So what are some of our favorite winter warmers? From the New World—the United States, South America, Australia, New Zealand, and South Africa—look for wines made from Cabernet Sauvignon, Cabernet Franc, and Cab-based blends, as well as Syrah/Shiraz (sometimes blended with Grenache and Mourvedre, the GSM blend). We especially like earthy, stick-to-your-ribs Zinfandels during the winter months.

When we think of robust winter-friendly wines from Europe, the first place we think about is the Rhone Valley of France, where the reds are powerful, earthy, and so satisfying. From the southern Rhone consider the quintessential winter warmer, Chateauneuf-du-Pape, as well as a few of its neighbors, Gigondas and Vacqueyras, where you should find excellent value. From the northern Rhone you'll find pricier but delicious full-bodied Syrah-based wines to warm you up: Hermitage, Cote Rotie, Cornas, St-Joseph. The value wine to look for here is Crozes-Hermitage.

Italy: where to start, when to stop? We're sure we'll miss more than a few Italian winter warmers, but here are some of our regional favorites:

Piedmont: Barolo, Barbaresco, Gattinara, and Ghemme, all based on the Nebbiolo grape. The value wines here are Nebbiolo d'Alba, or Langhe Nebbiolo.

Tuscany: All driven by the Sangiovese grape, we love Brunello di Montalcino, Chianti Classico Riserva, Vino Nobile di Montepulciano, and Carmignano. The true value here is Rosso di Montalcino. Also, there are literally more than 1,000 red "Super Tuscans," based on Sangiovese, Cabernet Sauvignon, and Syrah: many blends, some single varietals, mostly expensive, and all quite powerful.

Southern Italy and islands: Taurasi, an incredibly full-bodied, black-ink wine from Campania; Salice Salentino Riserva from Puglia; Cannonau di Sardegna from Sardinia; Nero d'Avola from Sicily. Values include Aglianico del Vulture from Basilicata and Primitivo (psst . . . it's Zinfandel!) from Puglia.

From Spain, look for Rioja Reserva and Gran Reserva; Ribero del Duero Reserva; red wines from Priorat and Montsant; Cabernet Sauvignon and blends from Penedes. From Portugal, the red wines of Bairrada are real powerhouses, based on the Baga grape, and utilizing Cabernet Sauvignon to *lighten* the blend! Also, the red wines of the Douro Valley are perfect winter wines. Of course, after dinner the chill of the season will be practically erased by fortified Port or Madeira—a cozy fireplace in a glass. Values here include 5 Year-Old Malmsey Madeira, as well as Late-Bottled Vintage and Tawny Ports.

Best winter choices from Greece include the reds Naoussa and Nemea, as well as single varietals and blends made from Cabernet Sauvignon and Syrah. Also, try Lebanon's classic powerful red, Chateau Musar. From Israel, look for single-vineyard Cabernet Sauvignon and Shiraz.

Kosher wines: Not just for Passover anymore

THE IMAGE OF KOSHER WINES in the United States, at least until recently, has been pretty much abysmal. There is little doubt that the traditional, ceremonial, virtually undrinkable kosher jug made from Concord grapes will always be available for those who, by either habit or desire, choose to drink the stuff on high holy days or with their Friday night Sabbath dinner. We are happy to report, however, that kosher wines do not have to be the product of God in His or Her wrathful phase. The "new" kosher wines can only be described as great wines that just happen to be kosher, and for that all of us, Jewish or not, can only sing out, "Amen!"

Not too long ago we had the pleasure of tasting a few dozen kosher wines from all over the world—the United States, Italy, Spain, France, Australia, Chile, and of course Israel. The differences between these wines and the stereotypical Concord jugs are palpable and pleasurable. We no longer feel as though we might be atoning for what must be some pretty serious sins when we taste kosher wines. Instead, these blessed bottles allow wine lovers of all religious persuasions and permutations—including those who worship only Bacchus—to enjoy, indulge, and luxuriate, without suffering, without guilt (a big step forward for those of us who were raised in a traditional Jewish home, where guilt is a dish best served either hot or cold, but repeatedly).

So what makes a wine kosher? This question is not as easy to answer as it might seem. For example, a majority of Conservative and Reformed Jews, many of whom do not eat and drink only kosher food and wine on a daily basis, believe that all wines—like all fruits—are kosher and do not need any further elaboration. This secular interpretation flies in the face of Orthodox Jewish law and custom. Essentially, the Orthodox approach to kosher wine includes the following rules:

- The wine must be made under the general supervision of a rabbi, who must be certified or licensed to perform such duties.
- All equipment and machinery used to make the wine must be used to produce only kosher wines. If a wine is certified as "kosher for Passover," equipment and machinery must undergo a special cleaning and sanitizing procedure and can be used only for that purpose.
- Any yeasts, filtering agents, or clarifying agents must be certified as kosher. No milk or gelatin can be used for clarification.
- No artificial coloring or preservatives can be used.
- Only Sabbath-observant Jews can be involved in the growing of the grapes, the winemaking process, the service of the wine, and the consumption of the wine, unless the wine has gone through a pasteurization process known as *mevushal*.

In the modern kosher wine industry, both non-*mevushal* wines, and *mevushal* wines, are available. *Mevushal*, which in Hebrew means "boiled," is actually a flash heating and cooling process that is perhaps as much ritual as it is science, and harks back to the origins of Judaism itself. The most revered rabbis insisted that all wine must be boiled so that the wines would not taste good enough to enjoy for pleasure—just barely good enough to drink to observe the sacraments of faith (again with the guilt!).

White and rosé wines that undergo *mevushal* are flash-pasteurized before the juice is fermented; reds immediately following alcoholic fermentation. The pasteurization process occurs as either the juice or the wine is heated to 185°F/85°C for a few moments and then cooled very quickly. According to researchers at the University of California at Davis, *mevushal* wines do not even come close to the time and temperature threshold at which a wine drinker can perceive any difference in color, nose, or taste of the wine.

Good kosher wines—both *mevushal* and non-*mevushal*—are increasingly available to the general public in wine shops and restaurants and via the Internet. These wines are worth tasting by all those who enjoy good wine, and also make a thoughtful gift if you're having dinner at the home of a friend who keeps kosher.

The next sections list, by region, some of the exciting kosher wines that we've tasted recently. (Unless indicated otherwise, all wines are *mevushal* and kosher for Passover.) Kosher wines are a fast-growing consumer category, and all we can do here is just scratch the surface. Retailers and restaurateurs are bound to have some of the wines; the Internet is a good place to start exploring what is available. Go to www.kosher-wine.com for a good selection and www.machers.com for a basic introduction to kosher wines in general.

California

Herzog is the major California line of wines produced by the Royal Wine Company, the largest producer of kosher wines in the world. We have tasted many Herzog wines over the years and have found a steady and impressive improvement in both grape sourcing and winemaking. Today, some of the wines are amongst the best kosher wines available from California. We particularly like the Lodi Old Vine Zinfandel, sourced from sixty-five-year-old vines grown in the Richard Watts vineyard (under $20) and the Chalk Hill Warnecke Vineyard Cabernet Sauvignon (non-*mevushal*; about $50.)

At Four Gates Winery, Benyamin Cantz produces estate-bottled wines produced from 3.5 acres/1.4 hectares of certified organic grapes on dry-farmed vineyards situated on a south-facing slope of California's Santa Cruz Mountains. At a total production of about 4,800 bottles (400 cases), Four Gates is perhaps the smallest kosher winery in the United States. Both the Chardonnay and the Pinot Noir are two of the purest, most balanced, *terroir*-driven wines we've tasted from California in quite some time. Showing beautifully now, both of these wines will improve with a bit of age, especially the Pinot Noir. Four Gates also produces estate-bottled organic Cabernet Franc and Merlot. All of the wines sell for about $20 to $35 each. These are true artisan wines made by a dedicated *mensch*. To find out more about Four Gates, or to purchase wines, do yourself a *mitzvah* and contact Benyamin Cantz at www.fourgateswine.com or call 831-457-2673.

Chile

Alfasi is the major kosher producer here, with Cabernet Sauvignon, Merlot, and Malbec/Syrah bottlings all selling for about $10. The wines are well made and true to their varietal types; good values.

Australia

Teal Lake is the kosher category leader here, with solid wines at about $10 to $15 from the Southeastern Australia mega-appellation. We enjoyed the Teal Lake Shiraz quite a bit. Estate-bottled kosher wines are made by Beckett's Flat in the Margaret River region of Western Australia. Reds include Shiraz and Shiraz/Cabernet, whites Chardonnay and Sauvignon Blanc/Semillon. The wines range from about $20 to $25 each.

Israel

We really enjoyed the Carmel Emerald Riesling/Chenin Blanc from the Shomron region (about $8): a perfect hot-weather fruity off-dry sipper, great for spicy foods, lighter fish dishes, and salads. The Binyamina Chardonnay, also from Shomron (about $15) is well made, with luscious fruit and toasty oak. We also tasted good non-*mevushal* 2002 Cabernet Sauvignon and Merlot from Israel, made by Galil from fruit grown in the highly regarded region of Upper Galilee (each under $15).

Note that Israel produces both kosher and non-kosher wines; check the label if you are looking for kosher wines only.

France

Several Champagne producers, including Perrier-Jouet and Nicolas Feuillatte, produce kosher versions of their wines, as do about twenty Bordeaux chateaux (including Smith Haut-Lafitte, Giscours, Leoville Poyferre, and Fonbadet), as well as inexpensive Bordeaux, such as Mouton-Cadet. Fortant makes kosher versions of their *vin de pays* varietals. Roberto Cohen is a major kosher producer in Burgundy, making everything from inexpensive Beaujolais to moderately expensive Chablis to painfully expensive *grand cru* Burgundy. Kosher wines are available from Alsace (look for Abarbanel), the Loire Valley, and the Rhone Valley as well.

Spain

Tio Pepe, the Sherry that even rival Sherry producers bring as a gift, makes a lovely kosher Fino Sherry (about $16). We also very much enjoyed the lively Rioja Cosecha from Ramon Cardova, made from 100% Tempranillo grapes picked from old vines in Haro (about $15). Tierra Salvaje in the Yecla region produces a variety of still wines and a kosher brut *reserva* Cava sparkler (all under $20, some under $10). In the small but burgeoning Montsant region, the Capcanes cooperative produces the award-winning red, Pereaj Ha'abib Flor de Primavera in the $40 to $50 range.

Italy

Italy, too, produces some good kosher wines, with Bartenura importing wines from Piedmont and Veneto. Rashi makes a good Barolo (under $40), while Borgo Reale focuses on reds from the province of Puglia in the south (under $20).

Living with screw caps, glass stoppers, and boxes: Twist and pour!

FOR SEVERAL YEARS NOW, we have been supporting the move toward screw cap closures for wines, and we applaud the work and commitment of those producers who have taken this route. If wine truly is a noble beverage, it makes no sense to stopper it with a piece of tree bark that is susceptible to all kinds of mold and bacteria. Add to this the fact that wine with a cork stopper is the only beverage that requires a special tool to get at your favorite vino and you have a recipe for limiting consumption via intimidation ("What if I break the cork?") and encouraging snobbism. It is a terrible thing to be on the right beach with the right sunset, the right person, the right wine, and—shock! horror! squealing embarrassment!—no corkscrew.

So, for all those who have embraced screw caps, we say right on! But why stop there? Why not make wine truly accessible by packaging it the way that many other beverages are marketed—boxes, cartons, cans? The naysayers here will argue that screw caps and boxes take away from the "romance" of wine. Leaving aside the question of what is romantic about a grungy, moldy piece of tree bark, while we would certainly argue that there are some special occasions when we do enjoy the ritual of presentation and pouring, for the most part we want our wine to be practical and accessible so that we can enjoy it with a minimum of fuss. Recent statistics show that for wine consumption at home, Australians purchase 50% of their wine in boxes, and the Scandinavian nations are not far behind. Our guess is that more and more Americans will slowly but surely follow suit (we're now at about 30%).

The most important thing to understand is that screw caps and boxes do *not* mean low-quality wine—quite the opposite. As closure and container, both the screw cap and the box are safer and better than corks and bottles. The cork can deteriorate and become infected by mold, and the bottle, after opening, will inevitably allow air to oxidize the wine. But the screw cap is inert and guarantees that the wine will remain in good condition, and the boxes on the market are designed with a pouch inside that collapses as the wine is poured, ensuring almost no contact with air and no oxidation. As a recent experiment, we tried a selection of boxed wines to vet them for style and quality. We kept one of the boxes that we had poured from, and three weeks later tried the wine again. It was still fresh and bright, fruity and delicious, with no signs of oxidation or deterioration.

From our sampling of boxed wines, we came away with the general conclusion that most of them are not only acceptable but good. We were particularly impressed with Hardys "Stamp of Australia" Southeastern Australia Shiraz, Banrock Station Southeastern Australia Chardonnay, the Vendange California Pinot Grigio and Three Thieves California Pinot Grigio (both in small Tetrapaks), and the Black Box Napa Valley Chardonnay and Paso Robles Cabernet Sauvignon. Most impressive is the price, which ranged from the equivalent of $3.75 a bottle to $6.50 a bottle. You can't beat that for value when the wine is good.

We're also happy with the increasingly popular Vino-Seal (in Europe, Vino-Lok) glass wine closure, which is very pretty and 100% recyclable. The closure looks very much like the decorative stoppers in wine decanters and utilizes a sterile and inert O-ring, protecting the wine from oxidation or bacterial spoilage. These closures are gaining in popularity, and we expect to see more of these corkscrew-free stoppers in more and more bottles of good wine.

Screw caps, glass stoppers, and boxes make sense to us, especially in our modern world where convenience and accessibility have become so important. Your boxed white wine can sit in the fridge; all you have to do is take your glass to it, open the spigot, and pour. It's just like having an ice water dispenser as part of your fridge, though (so far) for the wine you will have to open the door. At the very least, all of this convenience will make us appreciate it even more when somebody presents us with that very special bottle and proceeds to dazzle us with their nimble use of that ancient and curious implement, the corkscrew.

chapter 16

Loving the list
wine in restaurants

When it comes to restaurant wine lists, wine lovers have little to complain about these days, because it is easy to find excellent formal restaurants with superb wine lists, along with simpler roadhouses, bistros, and trattorias—informal restaurants and wine bars of all kinds—with exciting wine choices. Thanks to the Internet and forward-thinking restaurateurs, we can even peruse many restaurant wine lists and menus online and make some decisions before we arrive at our "wine destination" restaurant.

It takes hard work and passion to maintain, enhance, and improve a restaurant wine list, and kudos to the restaurateurs and wine professionals who do so. Many restaurants have ideal wine programs, some do a very good job, some are just okay, and some definitely need improvement. To build a terrific wine list takes time, energy, money, talent, and attitude, and so most good wine lists are in a constant state of becoming. If a restaurant rests on its laurels (or in this case its vines), that establishment risks losing customers, because we may perceive the wine list as stale and ho-hum, and in the restaurant business customer perception is reality.

Here are some of the things to look for—and discover—in a great restaurant wine list.

The wine list should be customer-friendly

FIRST, the list should be clean, graphically appealing, and easy to read. We know that restaurants often have subdued, soft lighting, but we shouldn't have to resort to using one of those tiny flashlights to read the list.

Second, the list should be arranged in some logical order: grape varietal, geographical designation, body of the wine, and food pairings are just some of the ways to do it. If the list is organized by varietal, you might want to skip past the Chardonnay and Cabernet in search of something new and different. We love lists that place Chardonnay and Cabernet last instead of first. You'll always find those two grape types no matter where they are on the list, but you might miss an interesting Gewurztraminer, Riesling, Sauvignon Blanc, or even a Torrontes from Argentina among the whites, or a delicious Syrah, Grenache, Tempranillo, or Xynomavro from Greece, especially if they get buried between the vanilla (Chardonnay) and chocolate (Cabernet). If you live in a wine-growing region—and in the United States that means most every state in the Union—it's always nice to have a highlighted section of well-chosen local and regional wines; we love to eat and drink local.

If the list is organized geographically—by country and wine regions—we like to see an easy-to-follow, consistent format. For a small list arranged this way, it's probably best to highlight a country (e.g., Italy) and then include the name of the region in each listing (Chianti Classico Riserva, Badia a Coltibuono, Tuscany 2003). If the list is large, with many wines from many regions, or if the list is dedicated to the wines of just one country (in this case, Italy), then major regions should probably get their own subheads on the list (e.g., Tuscany), and the wine listed above would read Chianti Classico Riserva, Badia a Coltibuono 2003. Above all, we like to see customer-friendly geographical lists, with a wide variety of choices and price points.

Arranging a wine list by the body of the wine (light, light-to-medium, medium, medium-to-full, full, *really* full, etc.) can be a tricky business because it can often be highly subjective. One woman's medium-bodied wine is another's medium-to-full bodied wine. One man's *really* full-bodied wine is another's "just full-bodied" wine. We think that these types of wine lists provide a general road map for the restaurant's approach to wine and wine styles and should be taken with a grain of salt. These "body" lists also assume a degree of familiarity with wine and food pairing that not everybody has (after all, not everyone has read *WineWise* . . . yet), and we think that may be why you don't see too many successful wine lists arranged this way. Likewise, if the list is arranged by food pairings (wines for veggies, wines for fish, wines for meat), we use it as a thumbnail sketch to match the restaurant menu. There can be a world of difference between the wine you choose for salmon poached in lemongrass broth and the one you pick to pair with grilled salmon served with rice and black beans. A wine that foots the bill for a filet mignon may seem a bit light for a well-marbled porterhouse steak.

The computer age is surely a mixed blessing, but it's all good for wine lists. The reason we say this is that computers allow restaurateurs to keep their wine lists current and complete. There is almost no reason why a wine on a computerized list should be suddenly unavailable or would have mysteriously undergone a vintage change. Customers don't want to go to the effort of choosing one wine from many, after choosing one dish from many, and then be told that they can't have that wine, or that the vintage is different. If this happens, most of us will feel rushed to make a second choice and generally uncomfortable, even if we have no idea—*especially* if we have no idea—if the available wine or vintage is better or worse than the one listed and originally chosen. It is a fact of modern life that to stay on top of a wine list, the restaurateur, sommelier, or whoever is in charge may have to tweak the info on the list—updating vintages or prices, adding new wines, removing ones that are sold out—several times per week. A bit of a drag for the restaurant, perhaps, but so easy thanks to fast computers and printers. And so customer-friendly.

The wine list should relate to the menu

CALL US TRADITIONAL, but we still think that it's important that there's an understandable relationship between the restaurant's food and wine. A steakhouse is likely to feature lots of blockbuster red wines and a smaller number of carefully chosen whites. A restaurant known for its fish might do the exact opposite, but with a bit more emphasis on "crossover" reds (Pinot Noir being a near-perfect example of a wine that works with many fish dishes). A vegetarian restaurant? Some of the most exciting vegetarian restaurants have exciting wine lists, often featuring wines made from organically grown or biodynamically grown grapes. Asian restaurants and pan-American restaurants where the food may be pretty spicy often feature small or large lists of fruit- and spice-driven whites (Riesling, Gewurztraminer, Pinot Grigio, and Southern Hemisphere Sauvignon Blanc are just some examples) and light, fruity reds (Beaujolais, Valpolicella, and lighter examples of Cote du Rhone, Pinot Noir, and Zinfandel come to mind), as well as dry rosés and a nice selection of sparklers. Those bubbles do wonders in putting out the fire of curries and chilies.

If a *trattoria* or *ristorante* wine list is, say, all Italian, a good selection of affordable wines from many of the twenty wine regions of Italy should be available. Likewise, a Spanish-inspired *tapas* bar that specializes in the delicious "small plates" of Spain may offer Spanish wines only, including a variety of Sherries, to help create the authentic *tapas* experience. A Greek restaurant might have a harder time selling the public on a totally Greek list, but Greek wines should be featured (they are great—try 'em!). You get the picture.

Go off the beaten path

IF YOU'VE BEEN READING *WineWise* closely, by now you must realize that we love wines whose origins are off the beaten path. After all, just how much California Cab, Aussie Shiraz, or throw-a-dart-at-the-map Chardonnay can you drink before you want to explore the rest of the world? Bring on the "new" wines of Spain—especially from the lesser known *denominaciones,* such as Rueda, Jumilla, and Toro—Portugal, Greece, Canada, and the forty-nine American states other than California (fact: all fifty states produce wine, even Alaska). Let's explore the glories of southern Italy as well as the sunny wines of southern France. Skip Chile and fly to Argentina (or even to Uruguay to try a red Tannat). Don't forget the wonderful whites of Alsace and Austria and the redolent reds of Israel and Lebanon.

We don't advise you to go off the beaten path just to be different; we truly enjoy these wines with food and think you will too. As an added WineWise bonus, these lesser-known, often underappreciated wines are great values and can form the most affordable part of an adventurous wine list. If you don't see wines from some of these places in your favorite restaurants (or retail shops), ask for them. An engaging wine list is often based on two aspects of the same self-fulfilling prophecy: if you request and drink these wines, more of them will appear on the list, but if you don't request and drink them, a restaurant has little or no incentive to offer them. We can hear James Earl Jones now: "If you drink it, they will come." Truly, a creative wine list can be an affordable field of dreams.

The service staff should know the wine list

HOWEVER THE LIST IS ARRANGED, and whatever wines are featured, in the end it is just a list of wines. But we believe that wine is often a hand-sold item that takes a bit of discussion, a bit of chatting back and forth between the customer and the server. That server might be a waiter, a sommelier, a manager, an owner, or anyone working in the restaurant, as long as he or she can speak intelligently, enthusiastically, and honestly about the wine list. If the server loves a wine that he or she thinks will work well with the foods ordered by the guests, and if it is reasonably priced, we usually welcome that recommendation. We hate it when a server recommends a wine that he or she, or someone whose opinion the server respects, has never tasted, as the customer can see through that BS. If a question arises that a server can't answer due to lack of experience with a particular wine, he or she should quickly fetch someone in the restaurant who can answer the question.

Customers often blame service staff for poor food and wine service, but we know from years of hard experience that most service staff want to please the customer, even if some have not been trained properly to provide professional wine service before "hitting the floor." If the restaurant does not take the time for training, wine service can dissolve into a *Saturday Night Live* or *Fawlty Towers* moment, but without the laughs.

We're also not big fans of wine-speak. We like easy-to-decipher words such as *delicious, medium-to-full-bodied,* or *refreshing.* The server should always assume the customer is the expert (sometimes that's true) and should never try to intimidate the guest with a bunch of puffed-up but in the end superficial jargon that makes the customer feel small.

The wine on the list should be the wine in the bottle

IF THE LIST is inconsistent or incorrect, the customer can become confused, and this confusion can bite the restaurant in the glass. Here's an example of inconsistency that comes to mind. Last year, we ordered the following featured wine in what appeared to be a "wine destination" restaurant: a Cabernet Sauvignon, Hess Collection, Napa Valley, California 2002 for $47, which seemed like a very fair price for this wine—an astounding bargain, in fact. This wine sold for about $36 at retail.

The wine that was brought to our table was Cabernet Sauvignon, Hess Select, California 2002 for $47, which seemed like a complete rip-off. This wine sold for about $16 at retail.

When we quietly pointed out that we specifically ordered the estate-bottled Napa Valley bottling

of the Hess wine—a wine made solely from grapes harvested atop Napa's glorious Mount Veeder, not the anywhere-in-California bottling—we received the following answer, complete with tons of attitude: "Well, the Napa Valley is in California, you know." Anyway, we did not accept the wine, and ordered something else. And what do we remember about the entire dining experience? Nothing, except what we perceived to be a wine rip-off (although it might have just been wine ignorance, but we doubt it), and thinking about how many people had ordered that featured wine, paid for it, never knew the difference, and thought the wine was just okay but definitely overpriced. So the moral of the story is that to ensure a good customer experience, the restaurant should make sure the wine list is consistent, clear, and correct.

Wines by the glass, "quatrinos," wine flights, and half bottles

A LIST OF WINES by the glass and/or by the "quatrino" [a small decanter or flask that is usually about 9 or 10 ounces (270 or 300 milliliters) of wine—roughly a glass and a half], a selection of wine "flights" (three or four glasses, 2-to-3-ounce (60-to-90 milliliter) pours in each glass, of wines that are somehow thematically linked), and a list of half bottles [12.7 ounces (375 milliliters), a little more than two glasses] have become increasingly popular with the American wine drinker. Making wines available in these ways customizes the dining experience for guests, allowing them to sample several wines and still stay within their budget (the price budget, but also the alcohol budget; especially if you drive to and from restaurants, a seriously low alcohol budget is necessary for a happy, healthy, and safe dining experience). Sometimes all we want is a glass of Sauvignon Blanc, but a flight of four 2-ounce (60-milliliter) glasses of Sauvignon Blanc—one from France, one from California, one from New Zealand, one from Chile—is hard to resist. Three Zinfandels—one from Mendocino, one from Sonoma, one from Paso Robles—iz a zinful pleazure. Likewise, a party of four may want a white for two people and a red for two people but desire little more than a glass per person. Half bottles, "quatrinos," and/or a good selection of wines by the glass at different price points is the answer.

The standard "pour" for a single wine by the glass is usually between 5 and 6 ounces (150 and 180 milliliters). You should expect to pay somewhere between 20% and 25% of the price of a bottle for a glass of wine. In other words, a wine that appears on the wine list for $44 per bottle [25.4 ounces (750 milliliters)] should be in the $10 to $12 range per 6 ounce (180-milliliter) glass. Five ounces (150 milliliters) should be closer to $8 to $10 per glass. Often, wines by the glass don't appear on the by-the-bottle list, but if you simply want a good glass of wine, we suggest you don't spend too much time doing the math; just enjoy your glass of wine with your meal as one of life's affordable pleasures (and drive safely).

BYOB?/What's the corkage fee?

BYOB is short for "bring your own bottle," and you'd be surprised how many BYOB restaurants there are in both large cities and small towns. Some states limit the amount of wine and liquor licenses available or charge license fees that are prohibitive for small restaurant owners. There are cities where BYOB has become a way of life (Philadelphia and Montreal come to mind), and restaurant customers enjoy bringing their own wines to dinner. Dinner becomes more affordable, and in a simple twist of fate, BYOB restaurants make the customer match the food to the wine, not vice versa. If you don't know the menu of the BYOB place you want to go to, check its Web site to see if the menu is online, or call ahead to ask about the menu. That should give you some ideas for the wines you want to bring along to the restaurant.

Playing the numbers game

Although they are sometimes wildly popular, we are not big fans of wine lists that feature the "scores" granted to wines by wine journalists and critics. Sources for these scores, based on a 100-point scale, are most often Robert Parker, who publishes

The Wine Advocate, or the writers and editors at *The Wine Spectator*.

Maybe it's great for the wine producer if his or her wine gets a score of 94 from Parker or a 96 from the *Spectator*, but what does it really mean to the wine consumer, the restaurant customer? Featuring these scores on wine lists speaks volumes about a kind of insecurity surrounding our own taste, both on the part of the restaurant and the customer. We really believe that when it comes to wine, you should trust your own palate and not follow the pack who

think that if they are drinking a wine with a score of 95 they are drinking ambrosia, but if they are drinking a wine scored a mere 81 they should not let themselves get too excited.

Remember also that the price and/or value of the wine is rarely a factor in the scoring of wines. It will come as no surprise that the highest-scoring wines on a wine list are also often the most expensive. To us, this smacks of subtle intimidation: if you want to sample the best, pay the most. We don't like this, because we believe that

good wines should be available to everyone, and we know for a fact that those wines don't have to be expensive to be good.

We'll never forget sitting in a restaurant whose wine list was organized by scores and overhearing a fellow at the next table ordering "the '95 Cabernet Sauvignon." We soon learned that he was ordering not a 1995 Cab but a wine from the 1998 vintage that was listed with a score of 95! We could only shake our old-fashioned heads. Trust your own palate, people!

Corkage is a great word that describes the fee a restaurant charges to open and serve wines that customers bring with them to the restaurant. Policies vary widely—some restaurants discourage it or completely forbid customers to bring their own wines, while some welcome those same wine-toting folks with open arms. If you're planning on bringing some of your own wines to the restaurant, call ahead to find out what that restaurant's corkage policy is and how much they charge. You may be surprised to learn that some restaurants charge less than $10 per bottle while others charge more than $25. Some restaurants only allow you to bring wines that do not appear on their list, while others will not charge a corkage fee for your own bottle if you also order a wine from their list. Corkage policies and fees are all over the place, so make sure you check with the restaurant before you bring in a bottle of your own wine. Also, remember that in the United States most servers survive on tips. If you bring in a bottle or two of wine and pay a reasonable corkage fee, don't forget to tip your server generously to at least partially make up for the lost income generated by your choice to bring your own wine.

Reasonable wine pricing, please!

RESTAURANT CUSTOMERS want to have a good time when they dine out, and most are not interested in pinching pennies, but neither do they want to feel ripped off when they order a bottle of wine. The perception of value on a wine list is an important consideration for most diners. If they pay $14 in a retail wine shop for one of their favorite wines and they see it on a wine list for $35, they are not going to be happy. Long ago, after more arguments than we care to count, we decided that there is no standard restaurant markup on any bottle of wine. The restaurateur and his or her wine staff must make those decisions, but we still do believe in a useful rule of thumb: the wine should never cost double its retail price on the wine list. In other words, we doubt there would be much consumer resistance to paying $25 (instead of $35) for that same $14 bottle, and it may

lead to ordering a second bottle of the same or different wine. A reasonable consumer perception is that $10 or $11 above retail is a fair profit (even though many restaurants, depending on the state in which they're located, can buy wines at wholesale prices, and so the profit on that $25 bottle might actually be as much as $15 or $16). Obviously, on rare and truly hard-to-find bottles of singular pedigree, all bets are off, and the restaurant can charge whatever it wants.

A final word about wine list pricing (a very touchy subject these days, for both consumers and restaurateurs): there is nothing wrong with featuring some expensive wines on the list, as long as there is a good selection of wines at all price points. There is no reason why any restaurant can't offer white or red wines, even sparkling wines (Cava or Prosecco, for example) for less than $25 per bottle. That doesn't mean that all the bottles have to be $25 or less—although there is a place for such lists, and they can be wildly popular—but it does mean that almost any restaurant customer, including those of modest means and/or inclinations, can enjoy a bottle or two of wine with friends and family. The very same restaurant that offers some good wine bargains can also offer wines at any other reasonable price points, well into the hundreds of dollars, as long as each price point is well represented. Intimidating customers with the price of a wine list is a sure way to lose those customers and many of those former customers' friends (potential future customers).

Finding the "sweet spot": How to find good value on the wine list

JUST ABOUT EVERYONE loves to dine out for special occasions—celebrating birthdays, anniversaries, job promotions, a juicy book contract, whatever—and on these occasions we might be in the mood to splurge. We choose a fine and expensive restaurant and expect to blow a small fortune on dinner. For these rare and expensive nights, it's kind of exciting to throw caution to the winds and order that rare and expensive wine: a beautiful Burgundy, a killer Cab, a cool *cuvee de prestige* Champagne, a sexy Syrah. Enough alliteration; you know what we mean—a night of exotic fun, at least until the credit card statement arrives.

Yup, special-occasion dining, complete with special (and expensive) wines, is a rare and (we hope) memorable treat. But don't you also like to go out to get a bite to eat with friends and/or family at a favorite restaurant, not to celebrate anything special, but simply to reaffirm friendship, to catch up on the latest news (or gossip), or just to hang out and let someone else do the cooking and do the dishes? On days or nights like these, you're looking to relax, and you're certainly not interested in blowing a wad on wine. So how do you drink good wine without spending a lot of money? How can you be WineWise in a restaurant? It's easy.

First, don't pick a fancy, expensive restaurant. Meet your friends at a place where the food and wine are good, the service is bright and friendly, and the price is reasonable. Ask to see the wine list as soon as you sit down, to give you some time to peruse the list. Don't hesitate to ask for a couple of copies of the list if more than one person at the table is interested in choosing wine. (We really like informal restaurants where the wine list is appended to the menu, so that everybody gets a chance to look at the list. Why shouldn't they?)

Don't be afraid to settle on a per-bottle price range for the wines you plan to order. Choosing wine is not an exercise in impressing people with how much money you spend (or think you have to spend). It's about ordering an enjoyable wine to accompany an enjoyable meal. If the wine list seems out of whack—too expensive for the place, or just plain too expensive for you—make a note of this, and carefully consider if you want to come back next time. The solution to this problem: order your wine by the glass and stay within your budget.

We're thankful that the above scenario happens less and less these days, as restaurateurs know that their customers want to enjoy a bottle of wine with dinner, and if the customer is unhappy, he or she doesn't come back. Most good restaurants have good

wine lists: a choice of enjoyable wines at various price points. There are low-priced wines, moderately priced wines, expensive wines, and ultra-expensive wines to choose from, but what really constitutes good value in a bottle of wine?

Value is a relative term—relative to how much money you have to spend on a bottle of wine. Ironically, if money is no object, the most expensive wine on the list might be the best value, because that 1990 Brunello di Montalcino is selling for just about the same price as in a good wine shop, with almost a 0% markup. Unfortunately, the price is $325. So if you have the money, this is a great value. But let's stop dreaming and get back to reality.

Most of the time value wine is represented by a moderately priced wine that delivers great pleasure. It underpromises (price) and overdelivers (pleasure). The good news is that there are lots of value wines appearing on wine lists if you just know where to look.

Just as it's unlikely that you are going to choose that $325 Brunello as your value wine, we also would warn you away from choosing the least expensive wines on the list, especially if they are from well-known New World regions, such as California, Chile, and Australia. There is absolutely nothing wrong with these wines, but they might not represent great value. We have seen Chardonnay from California, Cabs from Chile, and Shiraz wines from Australia that retail in supermarkets and shops for less than $10 selling for more than $30 on many restaurant wine lists. Although $30 is usually a reasonable price to pay for a bottle of wine in a restaurant, the markup on these wines can sometimes be as high as 500%(!), based on the wholesale price of the wine. If the restaurant buys the wine for the wholesale price of $6 and charges $30 for the wine, there's your 500% markup. This does not represent good—or even mediocre—value. Plus, wines in these categories can usually be found easily in supermarkets and wine shops, where at $10 to $12 retail they are good values. So we suggest you drink these wines at home, not in restaurants.

We've already mentioned that one place to look for good value is off the beaten path (see page 325): wines that aren't as well known as they should be from regions that are just beginning to gain renown for the quality of their wines. Again, we encourage you to take a serious look at these wines, since they often represent good value, and certainly deliver the goods: the pleasure of a good wine at a good price.

If you're looking at a wine list that is not that creative, a boilerplate list that features well-known producers and "brands," chances are the bottom end of the list is not where you're going to find true value. Likewise, at the top end of the list, the percentage of markup on the wine may be less, but you pay for wine in dollars, not in percentages, and these wines may be just plain unaffordable. You need to find the sweet spot in the wine list: the place where the wine is simultaneously affordable and good, where pleasure is paramount. But how to find the sweet spot? *WineWise* readers should have little trouble finding it if they explore the list just a little.

WineWise wine list of value wines

Over time, we've found that certain wines deliver excellent value on most wine lists, and we'd like to share those wines with you. While not all of these may be represented on every restaurant's list, some of them will be.

This list is not complete by any means, because by the time you read it we're sure that other value-driven but delicious wines will pop up on lists all over the country. But for now, here are some consistently outstanding WineWise values.

Sparkling wines

Cava from Spain

Prosecco from Italy

Cremant d'Alsace and sparklers from the Loire Valley of France

American *methode champenoise* bubbly from California, Washington State, Oregon, New York State, and New Mexico

White wines

United States

California: Sauvignon Blanc, Viognier, Gewurztraminer, Pinot Gris

Oregon: Pinot Gris, Chardonnay

Washington State: Riesling, Gewurztraminer, Chardonnay

New York State: Riesling, Chardonnay

Canada: Riesling, Pinot Gris, Chardonnay

Chile: Sauvignon Blanc

Argentina: Torrontes

Australia: Riesling, Sauvignon Blanc, "Rhone" varietals and blends (Viognier, Marsanne, Rousanne), Verdelho

New Zealand: Sauvignon Blanc, Chardonnay

South Africa: Sauvignon Blanc, Chardonnay, Chenin Blanc

France

Alsace: Gewurztraminer, Riesling, Pinot Gris, Muscat, Pinot Blanc

Bordeaux: Entre-Deux-Mers and Graves

Burgundy: Bourgogne, Chablis, Macon-Villages, Rully, Montagny

Loire Valley: Saumur, Vouvray, Savennieres, Quincy, Menetou-Salon

Rhone Valley: Cotes du Rhone

Spain: whites from Rueda, Penedes, and Rioja; Albarino from Rias Baixas; Godello from Ribeiro

Italy

Piedmont: Gavi, Arneis

Tuscany: Vernaccia di San Gimignano

Umbria: Orvieto Classico

Veneto: Soave Classico, Pinot Grigio

Friuli and Alto Adige: Pinot Grigio, Pinot Bianco, Sauvignon Blanc, Chardonnay, Riesling, Gewurztraminer, varietal blends

Trentino: Pinot Grigio

Marche: Verdicchio dei Castelli di Jesi Classico

Campania: Falanghina, Fiano di Avellino, Greco di Tufo

Sardinia: Vermentino di Gallura

Portugal: Vinho Verde from Minho, dry Muscat from Terras do Sado and wines from Bucelas

Greece: Charming whites made from Moschofilero, Malagousia, Robola, and Assyrtiko grapes, as well as blends with international varietals (Sauvignon Blanc, etc.)

Germany: Riesling from the Rhine and Mosel river valleys

Austria: Gruner Veltliner and Riesling

Red and rosé wines

United States

California: Zinfandel, Syrah, Rhone blends (Syrah,

Let's say you're looking at a wine list whose least expensive wine is $23 and whose most expensive wine is $450. Ignore these wines for now, but take an informal survey of where *most* of the wines are priced. And now let's say after a little bit of detective work you notice that the overwhelming majority of the wines are priced between $29 and $55. Take the average of these wines—$42—and there's your sweet spot. This doesn't mean that you can't spend $36 or $51, but chances are good if you stick close to $42, you'll get a good wine at a good price. Test: find a wine that you've bought in the supermarket or retail shop, a wine that you paid about $20 for and enjoyed. If that wine is under $40 on the wine list, go for it. If the wine is much more than $40, pass it by, because you know that it is not a good value. If this test yields consistent negative results, you can assume you are looking at an overpriced wine list, but if the results are consistently positive, you've found a value-driven, consumer-friendly list.

Grenache, Mourvedre), Sonoma and Mendocino Cabernet Sauvignon

Oregon: a small selection of value-driven Pinot Noir

Washington State: Syrah, Merlot, Cabernet Sauvignon, Lemberger

New York State: Long Island Merlot, Cabernet Sauvignon, Cabernet Franc (and blends of these)

Canada: Cabernet Franc, Pinot Noir, and Gamay

Chile: single-vineyard Cabernet Sauvignon and Merlot

Argentina: Malbec, Bonarda

Australia: Barossa Shiraz and McLaren Vale Grenache

New Zealand: Cabernet Sauvignon, Merlot, and blends

South Africa: Cabernet Sauvignon and blends, Shiraz

France

Alsace: Pinot Noir

Bordeaux: second labels of the famous chateaux, St-Emilion, Lalande de Pomerol, Fronsac, and the satellite appellations of Cotes de Blaye and Cotes de Bourg

Burgundy: Bourgogne, Cote de Nuits-Villages, Cote de Beaune-Villages, Pernand-Vergelesses, Savigny-les-Beaunes, Mercurey, Rully, Givry

Beaujolais: Moulin-a-Vent, Morgon, Brouilly, Fleurie

Loire Valley: Chinon, Bourgueil, Saumur-Champigny, Sancerre

Rhone Valley: Cotes du Rhone, Rasteau, St-Joseph, Crozes-Hermitage, Vacqueyras, Gigondas reds, and Tavel dry rosé

Midi and Provence: dry rosés and hearty reds such as Minervois, Fitou, Faugeres, Corbieres, Aix-en-Provence, Cotes du Roussillon

Spain

Cosecha, crianza, and *reserva* wines from Rioja and Ribera del Duero

Reds from Montsant, Bierzo, Cigales, Toro, Jumilla, Campo de Borja

Rosés (*rosados*) from Navarra

Italy

Piedmont Nebbiolo d'Alba, Dolcetto, Barbera, Grignolino, Ruché

Tuscany: Chianti Classico, Rosso di Montalcino, Morellino di Scansano

Umbria: Lungarotti's "Rubesco" and Rosso di Montefalco

Veneto: Valpolicella Classico Superiore, Valpolicella Classico "Ripasso," Bardolino Classico Superiore, Merlot, and proprietary blends

Friuli and Alto Adige: Merlot, Cabernet Sauvignon, Pinot Noir, Lagrein, Teroldego Rotliano, proprietary blends

Puglia: Salice Salentino and blends based on the Negroamaro grape, Primitivo (Zinfandel)

Basilicata: Aglianico del Vulture

Sardinia: Cannonau di Sardegna and Cannonau (Grenache) blends

Sicily: Nero d'Avola and red blends

Portugal: crisp, dry rosés and excellent reds from the Douro Valley, Bairrada, Beiras, Alentejo, Ribatejo, and Dao regions

Greece: excellent reds made from Xynomaro, such as Naoussa, and Agiorgitiko grapes, such as Nemea, as well as Syrah, Cabernet Sauvignon, and blends; very tasty dry rosés, too

Austria: Blauer Zweigelt and Blaufrankisch

Dessert wines/sweet wines (often served by the glass)

United States: Sweet white Muscat wines, such as "Electra" by Quady in California, sweet Rieslings from New York State and the Pacific Northwest

Italy: white semisparkling Moscato d'Asti and sparkling Asti, and the red sparkler Brachetto d'Acqui

Greece: Muscat of Samos (white), Mavrodaphne (red)

Cyprus: fortified Commandaria St. John

Spain: fortified Pedro Ximenez and Sweet Amontillado Sherry

Portugal: fortified 5 Year-Old Malmsey Madeira, Late-Bottled Vintage Porto

Proper wine temperature

SPARKLING, WHITE, AND ROSÉ WINES should be served cold, and an ice bucket should be brought to your table. Some restaurants opt to have "ice bucket stations," which is okay, but only if your wine is always visible to you and proper service by your waiter, wine steward, or sommelier is maintained.

Sparkling wines, simple whites, and rosé wines are normally kept in the ice bucket to maintain their cool temperature, which helps to balance the wine's acids and alcohol on your palate; if the wine gets warm, it starts to taste "hot." But when it comes to complex white wines, such as a fine white Burgundy or full-bodied rich California Chardonnay, some of us like the wine to come closer to room temperature. The reason is that if a complex white is served too cold, you may miss the nuances of aroma and flavor; they'll be numbed by the cold. The ice bucket should always be handy for these wines, but don't hesitate to ask your server to take the wine out of the bucket after you taste it, and later ask him or her to place it back in the bucket if the wine starts to get too warm for your liking.

The decanting option

WHEN SHOULD you ask your server to decant your wine? Most of the time decanting is not necessary, especially if you're drinking a wine that is meant to be drunk young and does not exhibit a lot of complexity. There's certainly no reason to decant sparkling wines (it will ruin the bubbles) or rosé wines. We think that there really is no good reason to decant white wines, but we've noticed that some sommeliers are offering to decant complex whites that can age a bit, in order to aerate them and emphasize their volatile elements. There's nothing wrong with this extra touch of service, but we think you'll achieve the same result by pouring the wine in a good wine glass, swirling, smelling, and tasting.

As for decanting red wines, there are two good reasons to do so. The first and best-known reason for decanting a wine is to separate the sediment from the wine, usually an older wine. The proper way to decant an older red is to pour the wine from the bottle into the decanter while illuminating the neck of the bottle with a light source; a candle is the classic tool. When sediment begins to appear in the neck of the bottle, your server will stop pouring. About a half hour later, repeat the decanting procedure; you'll probably get another glass or so out of the bottle once the sediment settles again.

Not everyone believes that older red wines, especially delicate older reds, should be decanted. The reason for this thinking is that when the wine is decanted it takes a big hit of oxygen, and the delicate wine might not be able to handle such dramatic exposure to air all at once. We have witnessed wines that fall apart shortly after decanting, so there is something to this idea. Decanting an older wine, whether at home or in a restaurant, is a personal choice that you should make.

The second good reason to decant a red wine may surprise you, and we actually think it may be more important than decanting old reds as described above. You might want to decant a young red wine that has the potential to age in order to aerate the wine, allowing it to "open up" and demonstrate its potential. We like decanting younger reds because the air really allows the wine to "breathe," providing another layer of complexity, another layer of enjoyment. A similar outcome can be achieved if you are drinking out of elegant wineglasses with large bowls and you aerate the wine by swirling. And again, decanting is a personal choice.

Good glassware, please!

WE THINK servers should make sure that the proper glassware is set in advance of the actual wine service. Great wines deserve great glasses, but at the very least the glasses should be aesthetically pleasing, not too thick or heavy, and totally clear (and clean). When held up to the light, the glass should almost disappear, allowing the wine to "float" in midair. If the theme of the restaurant is ultra-informal, the glasses may not be elegant, merely serviceable, but the wines shouldn't be too expensive, either.

Some restaurateurs believe that certain wines deserve better stemware than others, based on the price and pedigree of the wine. We understand that argument, but we also understand the plight of the diner who orders a simple but tasty Chianti served in a modified jelly glass and then looks over to the next table to see a couple drinking an expensive Napa Cabernet out of elegant crystal stemware. Customers should never feel like chopped liver, but treating one customer better than another based on their check totals accomplishes exactly that negative outcome. We say: good glasses for everyone!

chapter 17

Got cash?
our bargain choices

Well, we've reached the final chapter of *Wine-Wise*, but by no means the final word on wine. If you've been reading along faithfully (or at least showing intermittent bursts of enthusiasm and interest), you've probably picked up on the fact that all three of the authors have something in common: when it comes to wine: we love a bargain.

How to define a "bargain"? It's not always the least expensive wine, though price is certainly an issue. We've found that there are many bargain wines available to savvy wine consumers, some priced incredibly low, some moderately priced. What bargain wines have in common, though, is one basic trait: they provide good value for money and often exceed expectations.

In the following pages each of us is going to present you with his own list of bargain wines: hundreds of bargain wines from all over the world at varying price points, starting at about $5 and stepping up to under $30. Most of these wines can be found easily, a few you'll have to search for, but we know from experience that all of these wines will be enjoyable. At the very least, you'll find some exciting choices to accompany your next lunch or dinner, or some interesting components for a home wine tasting. Not all these wines will curl your toes but quite a few will.

Let the bargains begin . . . .

Steven's laundry list: Best bargain wines

FOR WINE LOVERS ON A BUDGET, there has never been a better time to buy and enjoy wines. Most of these wines are just plain good and provide tasty foils for your dinner at home. Some of them are truly extraordinary, especially when you figure in how little you pay for them. Some of these wines are likely to be found in supermarkets, big-box stores, and large wine shops, but just as many will show up in specialty stores.

The beauty of these wines is that they are not too hard to find, and if you can't find one, you can find another. Feel free to experiment, and I guarantee you'll find several wines that you return to time and again for the pleasure (and value) they give. I can also guarantee, because taste is subjective, that there will be a few wines on my list that you'll taste once and forget, or maybe not like at all. But isn't it better to find that out by paying about $10 for that bottle rather than $40?

I've tried to create a list of good, accessible wines with a weekly wine budget in mind. Once you start using this list and enjoying these wines, you'll find that you, your friends, and your family can enjoy a different wine every night while spending between $50 and $75 per week. This makes wine fun, not fancy, and makes you WineWise.

In putting together my list, I've decided to use a two-tier system: best bargain wines under $12 and best bargain wines under $20. Most of the under-$12 selections will actually sell for under $10 (in fact, these prices start at below $5), but I'm giving myself a cushion for inflation, the strength or weakness of the dollar for imports, different markups by retailers, state taxes, and so on. In this category you're likely to find established brands, names of producers you're already familiar with, along with some new surprises.

In the best bargain wines under $20 section, you may find some wines you've already tried, but I hope you'll find some new wines to enjoy. By the way, I consider spending $15 to $20 for a bottle of wine a bit of a splurge that falls into the "affordable luxury" column of my household budget. You might want to consult the under-$20 section for when you're having friends over for dinner, for romantic occasions, and even for visits from the in-laws. These wines are special: they deliver great, even memorable quality at a reasonable price.

Note on the character of the wines and vintages

Most of the white wines are dry to semidry, medium-bodied, and quite food-flexible. A few are light-bodied (such as Vinho Verde from Portugal). The rosé wines are mostly dry to semidry, with the exception of the "blush" wines (White Zinfandel, White Merlot, etc.), which are semisweet. The reds tend to follow the body of their varietal composition, with most of them in the medium-to-full-bodied range. As usual, Pinot Noir and Merlot will probably be lighter than Cabernet Sauvignon and Syrah/Shiraz, and so forth. The European reds with geographical names are mostly in the medium-to-full-bodied category. All of the sparklers are dry to off-dry, except for Asti and Brachetto d'Acqui, which will be lightly sweet. Fortified sweet wines (Port, Madeira, sweet Sherries, etc.) will be pretty full-bodied, while the still sweeties will be light-to-medium-bodied.

I've decided not to include vintage years in this list, as these wines are made to a consistent standard year after year. Some vintages will be better, some worse, but these wines are consistently good, consistently enjoyable.

How I've arranged my best bargains

Both the under-$12 and under-$20 best bargain lists feature these categories: sparkling wines, white wines, rosé wines, red wines, and sweet/fortified wines. You'll notice that within these categories the wines are listed alphabetically by the name of the producer (Columbia Crest Merlot from Washington State will come way before Xplorador Malbec from Argentina). This speaks to the versatility of the list and the overall quality of the wines, and I want to encourage you to mix and match—a French white one night, a Spanish red the next; a California Sauvignon Blanc on Tuesday, an Argentine Syrah on Thursday. The idea is to enjoy great wines at a great price, to learn a bit about the wines as you go, but more important, to learn more about your own taste.

I've chosen more than 250 wines—all good to great, and all at affordable prices. Happily, based on their price-to-quality ratio, these value-driven wines underpromise and overdeliver. In other words, they're true WineWise wines.

Enjoy!

Steven Kolpan

Steven Kolpan's best bargain wines under $12

SPARKLING WINE

Bouvet Brut, France

Cavas Hill Cava, Spain

Cristalino Cava, Spain

Domaine Ste. Michelle, Washington State

Freixenet Brut Nature Vintage Cava, Spain

Paul Chenau Cava, Spain

Segura Viudas Cava, Spain

Valdo Prosecco, Italy

Zardetto Prosecco, Italy

WHITE WINE

Alamos Chardonnay, Argentina

Aldial "Naia" Rueda, Spain

Antinori Orvieto Classico, Italy

Aveleda Vinho Verde, Portugal

Banfi Le Rime, Italy

Bert Simon Estate Riesling, Germany

Brancott Sauvignon Blanc, New Zealand

Cape Indaba Sauvignon Blanc, South Africa

Carmen Reserve Sauvignon Blanc, Chile

Casa Lapostolle Sauvignon Blanc or Chardonnay, Chile

Casillero del Diablo Sauvignon Blanc, Riesling, Gewurztraminer, or Chardonnay, Chile

Caves Plaimont Colombelle, France

Cecchi Orvieto Classico, Italy

Chateau Bonnet Entre-Deux-Mers, France

Chateau de Chesnaie Muscadet Sevre-et-Maine Sur Lie, France

Coppola "Bianco" Pinot Grigio, California

Cousino Macul Chardonnay or "Dona Isadora" Riesling, Chile

Covey Run Riesling or Gewurztraminer, Washington State

Deinhard Riesling, Germany

Domaine Wachau Riesling, Austria

Dr. Loosen "Dr. L" Riesling, Germany

Famega Vinho Verde, Portugal

Familia Zuccardi Santa Julia Torrontes, Argentina

Fetzer Valley Oaks Chardonnay, Riesling, or Gewurztraminer, California

Frey Gewurztraminer or Sauvignon Blanc, California

Frontera Sauvignon Blanc or Chardonnay, Chile

Hardys "Nottage Hill" Sauvignon Blanc, Australia

Hogue Riesling, Gewurztraminer, Fumé Blanc, or Pinot Grigio, Washington State

Jekel Riesling, California

Kendall-Jackson Vintner's Reserve Sauvignon Blanc

La Vieille Ferme, France

Lindemans Semillon-Chardonnay, "Bin 75" Riesling, or "Bin 65" Chardonnay, Australia

Marques de Caceres Rioja, Spain

Marques de Riscal Rueda, Spain

Matua Valley Sauvignon Blanc, Riesling, or Chardonnay, New Zealand

McWilliams Riesling, Australia

Mirassou Chardonnay or Sauvignon Blanc, California

MontGras Reserve Sauvignon Blanc or Chardonnay, Chile

Ocone Falanghina del Taburno, Italy

Pepperwood Grove Chardonnay, Viognier, or Pinot Grigio, California

Placido Pinot Grigio or Chardonnay, Italy

Rosemount Chardonnay, Riesling, or Traminer-Riesling, Australia

Rudolf Muller "Bishop of Riesling," Germany

Screw Kappa Napa Sauvignon Blanc or Chardonnay, California

Sella & Mosca Vermentino di Sardegna, "La Cala," Italy

Smoking Loon Sauvignon Blanc, Chardonnay, Pinot Grigio, or Viognier, California

Stonehaven "Winemaker's Selection" Riesling or Chardonnay, Australia

Valdesil Godello, Spain

Veramonte Sauvignon Blanc, Chile

Villa Maria Sauvignon Blanc, New Zealand

Xplorador Chardonnay, Chile

Yalumba Riesling "Y," Australia

ROSÉ WINE

Beringer White Zinfandel, California

Caves Plaimont "Retrouvees Rosé," France

Centine, Banfi, Italy

Chivite "Gran Fuedo," Spain

Condesa de Leganza, Spain

Guigal Cotes du Rhone, France

Jean-Luc Colombo "Cote Bleue," France

La Vieille Ferme, France

Marques de Caceres, Spain

Muga, Spain

Mulderbosch, South Africa

Perrin, France

Premius, France

Rene Barbier, Spain

RED WINE

Alamo Malbec, Argentina

Aliança Reserva Dao, Portugal

Banfi Chianti or Chianti Classico, Italy

Bava "Libera" Barbera d'Asti, Italy

Bogle Merlot, Petite Sirah, or Zinfandel, California

Brampton Shiraz, South Africa

Casillero del Diablo Cabernet Sauvignon, Merlot, Carmenere, Shiraz, or Malbec, Chile

Cecchi Chianti Classico, Italy

Chateau de la Chaize Brouilly, France

Colombo Cotes du-Rhone "Les Abeilles," France

Concha y Toro Cabernet Sauvignon/Merlot, Chile

Conde de Valdemar Rioja Crianza, Spain

Coppola Rosso, California

Cousino Macul Cabernet Sauvignon, Chile

Fra Guerau, Montsant, Spain

Georges Duboeuf Beaujolais-Villages, France

Hardys "Nottage Hill" Shiraz, Australia

Hogue Cabernet Sauvignon, Merlot, or Syrah, Washington State

Jaboulet "Parallele 45," Cotes du-Rhone, France

Jadot Beaujolais-Villages, France

Lindemans Reserve or "Bin 45" Cabernet Sauvignon, Australia

Marietta Old Vines Red, California

Melini Chianti Classico, Italy

Mirassou Pinot Noir, Cabernet Sauvignon, or Merlot, California

Norton "Oak Cask" Malbec, Argentina

Pepperwood Grove Pinot Noir, Cabernet Sauvignon, Syrah, Merlot, or Zinfandel, California

Rosemount Shiraz or Grenache-Shiraz, Australia

Ruffino "Aziano" Chianti Classico, Italy

Screw Kappa Napa Cabernet Sauvignon, Merlot, or Zinfandel, California

Smoking Loon Syrah, Pinot Noir, Merlot, or Cabernet Sauvignon, California

Stonehaven "Winemaker's Selection" Shiraz, Merlot, or Shiraz/Cabernet, Australia

Torres "Coronas" or "Sangre de Toro," Spain

Xplorador Carmenere, Cabernet Sauvignon, or Merlot (Chile), or Malbec (Argentina)

Yalumba "Oxford Landing" Shiraz, or "Bush Vine" Grenache, Australia

Zaccagnini Montepulciano d'Abruzzo, Italy

SWEET WINE/FORTIFIED WINE

D'oro, Riunite, Italy

Leonard Kreusch Late Harvest Riesling, Germany

Quady Electra (white) or Elysium (red), California

Robert Pecota Moscato d'Andrea (half bottle), California

Royal Oporto LBV, Portugal
Sandeman's Ruby or Tawny Port, Portugal
Tishbi Emerald Riesling, Israel

Steven Kolpan's best bargain wines under $20

SPARKLING WINE

Banfi Brut or "Rosa Regale" Brachetto d'Acqui, Italy
Bellenda Vintage Prosecco, Italy
Domaine Carneros, California
Gloria Ferrer, California
Gruet Brut or Blanc de Noirs, New Mexico
Juve y Camps Cava, Spain
Leopardi Cava, Spain
Mionetto Prosecco, Italy
Roederer Estate, California
Willm Cremant d'Alsace, France

WHITE WINE

Albarei Albarino, Spain
Artesa Chardonnay, California
Au Bon Climat Pinot Gris/Pinot Blanc, California
Benziger Family Fumé Blanc or Chardonnay, California
Biblia Chora Estate, Greece
Bonterra Viognier or Chardonnay, California
Boutari Moschofilero, Greece
Buitenverwachting Sauvignon Blanc, South Africa
Castello Banfi "San Angelo" Pinot Grigio or "Serena" Sauvignon Blanc, Italy
Chiarlo Gavi, Italy
Columbia Crest "Grand Estates" Chardonnay, Washington State
Concha y Toro "Marques de Casa Concha" Chardonnay or "Terrunyo" Sauvignon Blanc, Chile
Coppola Diamond Series Chardonnay, California
Crios de Susana Balbo Torrontes, Argentina
Domaine Gerovassiliou Malagousia, Greece
Domaine Triennes "Ste-Fleur" Viognier, France

Ferarri-Carano Fumé Blanc, California
Feudi di San Gregorio Falanghina, Italy
Godeval Godello, Spain
Goulaine Vouvray, France
Hans Lang Dry Riesling or Charta Riesling, Germany
Hells Canyon "Bird Dog White," Idaho
Hermann Wiemer Dry Riesling, New York State
Hogue "Genesis" Riesling, Chardonnay, or Viognier, Washington State
Honig Sauvignon Blanc, California
Hugel Gewurztraminer, Riesling, Pinot Gris, or Pinot Blanc, France
Husch Sauvignon Blanc, California
Joseph Drouhin Macon-Villages or St-Veran, France
King Estate Pinot Gris, Oregon
Konstantin Frank Dry Riesling, Semi-Dry Riesling, or Chardonnay, New York State
Kumeu River Chardonnay, New Zealand
Leyda Sauvignon Blanc, Chile
Loimer Riesling, Austria
Lolonis Ladybug White, Fumé Blanc, or Chardonnay, California
Louis Jadot Bourgogne Chardonnay or Macon-Villages, France
Millbrook Estate Tocai Friulano or Chardonnay, New York State
Montes "Alpha" Chardonnay, Chile
Morgadio Albarino, Spain
Movia Pinot Grigio or Sauvignon Blanc, Slovenia
Mulderbosch Sauvignon Blanc or Chardonnay, South Africa
Olivier Leflaive Bourgogne Blanc "Les Setilles," France
Pellegrini Chardonnay, New York State
Planeta "La Segreta," Italy
Ponzi Pinot Gris, Oregon
Quivira Sauvignon Blanc, California
Sauvignon Republic Sauvignon Blanc, California
Selbach-Oster Riesling Spatlese, Germany
Shaw & Smith Sauvignon Blanc, Australia
Sokol Blosser Pinot Gris, Oregon
Stonehaven "Winemaker's Selection" Riesling or Chardonnay, Australia

St. Supery Sauvignon Blanc, California

The Crossings Sauvignon Blanc, New Zealand

Trimbach Gewurztraminer, Riesling, Pinot
Gris, or Muscat, France

Von Kesselstatt Estate Riesling, Germany

Zaca Mesa Viognier, California

Zind-Humbrecht Gewurztraminer or Riesling,
France

ROSÉ WINE

Benessere, California

Chateau d'Aqueria Tavel, France

Crios de Susana Balbo Rosé of Malbec,
Argentina

Iron Horse, California

Mas de Gourgonnier, France

Regaleali, Italy

Turkey Flat, Australia

RED WINE

A to Z Pinot Noir, Oregon

Alexander Valley Vineyards Cabernet
Sauvignon, California

Argiolas "Costera" or "Perdera," Italy

Badia a Coltibuono Chianti Classico, Italy

Banfi "Centine," or Chianti Classico Riserva,
Italy

Baron Herzog Cabernet Sauvignon, Zinfandel,
or Syrah, California

Barone Ricasoli "Brolio" Chianti Classico, Italy

Benziger Family Cabernet Sauvignon, Merlot,
Zinfandel, or Syrah, California

Boutari Naoussa, Greece

Cambria "Tepusquet" Syrah, California

Carmen Reserve Cabernet Sauvignon, Merlot,
or Syrah, Chile

Chapoutier Cotes du Rhone "Belleruche," France

Chateau Greysac, Medoc, France

Chateau Larose-Trintaudon, Haut-Medoc,
France

Concha y Toro "Marques de Casa Concha"
Cabernet Sauvignon or Merlot, Chile

Conde de Valdemar Rioja Reserva, Spain

Columbia Crest "Grand Estates" Merlot,
Cabernet Sauvignon, or Shiraz, Washington
State

Coppola "Diamond" Claret, Merlot, Cabernet
Sauvignon, Pinot Noir, or Syrah, California

Coudolet de Beaucastel Cotes du Rhone, France

Cousino Macul "Antiguas" Cabernet Sauvignon
or "Finis Terrae," Chile

Crios de Susana Balbo Malbec, Cabernet
Sauvignon, or Syrah/Bonarda, Argentina

d'Arenberg Shiraz, Grenache, or Shiraz/
Grenache, Australia

Edmunds St. John "Rocks and Gravel" or Syrah,
California

Frey Zinfandel, Syrah, Petite Sirah, or Cabernet
Sauvignon, California

Gabbiano Chianti Classico or Chianti Classico
Riserva, Italy

Georges Duboeuf Julienas, Morgon, Brouilly,
Moulin-a-Vent, Chenas, or St-Amour, France

Guigal Cotes du Rhone, France

Hells Canyon "Retriever Red" or "Seven Devils,"
Idaho

Hogue "Genesis" Cabernet Sauvignon, Merlot,
or Syrah, Washington State

Jaboulet "Les Jalets" Crozes-Hermitage, France

Joel Gott Zinfandel or Syrah, California

Joguet "Cuvee Terroir," Chinon, France

Lenz Estate Merlot, New York State

Leyda "Las Brisas" Pinot Noir, or Carmenere
Reserve, Chile

Lolonis Ladybug Red, Zinfandel, Merlot, or
Cabernet Sauvignon, California

Louis M. Martini Cabernet Sauvignon,
California

Luciano Sandrone Dolcetto d'Alba, Italy

Masi Valpolicella Classico or "Campofiorin,"
Italy

Millbrook Estate Hudson Valley Pinot Noir or
Cabernet Franc, New York State

Montecillo Rioja Reserva, Spain

Montes "Alpha" Syrah, Cabernet Sauvignon, or
Merlot, Chile

Montevina "Terra d'Oro" Zinfandel,
Sangiovese, Syrah, or Barbera, California

Penfolds Bin 128 Shiraz, Australia

Perrin Vacqueyras, France

Pio Cesare Dolcetto d'Alba or Barbera d'Alba,
Italy

Planeta "La Segreta," Italy

Produttori del Barbaresco Langhe Nebbiolo, Italy

Quivira Zinfandel, California

Qupe Syrah, California

Ramos Pinto "Duas Quintas," Portugal

Renato Ratti Dolcetto d'Alba or Nebbiolo d'Alba, Italy

Schneider Cabernet Franc or "Potato Barn," New York State

Seghesio Zinfandel, California

Stonehaven Limestone Coast Shiraz, Australia

Taurino "Notarpanaro" Rosso del Salento, Italy

Veramonte "Primus," Chile

Wynn's Shiraz, Australia

SWEET WINE/FORTIFIED WINE

All Sherry from Spain, especially Hidalgo, Lustau, Osborne, "Tio Pepe," and Domecq

Alois Lageder Moscato Giallo, Italy

Blandys 5 Year Sercial, 5 Year Malmsey, or "Rainwater" Madeira, Portugal

Cascina Castlet Moscato d'Asti, Italy

Ceretto "Santo Stefano," Moscato d'Asti, Italy

Chiarlo Moscato d'Asti "Nivole" (half bottle), Italy

Cockburn's Special Reserve or "Anno" LBV Port, Portugal

Croft Fine Ruby Port or "Distinction" Ruby Port, Portugal

Dow Fine Ruby, "Trademark," or LBV Port, Portugal

Fonseca Bin No. 27 Port, Portugal

Grahams Fine Tawny, "Six Grapes," or LBV Port, Portugal

Osborne Ruby, Tawny, or LBV Port, Portugal

Paolo Saracco Moscato d'Asti, Italy

Quinta do Crasto LBV Port, Portugal

Quinta do Infantado Ruby, or Tawny Port, Portugal

Ramos Pinto "Fine Ruby" Port, Portugal

Sandeman's Founders Reserve Port, Portugal

Smith-Woodhouse "Rich Ruby" Port, Portugal

Taylor Fladgate First Estate Port, Portugal

Warre's Warrior Port, Portugal

Brian's best bargains

OKAY, I'll come clean from the get-go. I was born in London, England, entered the London wine trade, and was trained by English wine merchants in what is good, and why. My palate is unabashedly European, and I tend to avoid the big openness of many modern New World wines. Even so, you will find on my list wines from around the world. However, you will not find many Cabernet Sauvignons or Chardonnays. Most of my Chardonnay choices are from the southern reaches of Burgundy in France, a lighter, crisper style that I really enjoy.

For many years now I have prided myself on spending relatively little on wines to enjoy every day. I simply cannot bring myself to spend more than $12 on a regular basis. More often than not, my "house" wine is $6.99 or $7.99. We are blessed to be living at a time when there is so much good wine available, with so much of it at reasonable prices.

So I am pleased to include a category of under-$10 wines. Many of these are $5.99, and some are listed in my local stores at $9.99. Of course, with tax and with regional variation, some of these wines will go over $10 at the checkout, but not by much.

I have also included an under-$20 category and an under-$30 category. In fact, it is very rare for me to spend more than $15 for any wine, and many of the under-$20 wines in my list are less than $15. But occasionally I want something special, and for that I am happy to go up to $20. Sometimes I even want something very special, and $30 becomes the limit.

From my opening remarks, you should conclude that my choices in each list will usually be less than full-bodied—Shiraz and the odd Cabernet Sauvignon are the obvious exceptions. Most of the whites are light-to-medium-bodied, and most of the reds are medium-bodied. The order of each listing is: producer name, wine name (grape, brand, or place), region, U.S. state, or foreign nation. Take note of the nuanced differences between some listings from the same producer, such as Cline Syrah, California, versus Cline Syrah, Sonoma County, California. The first is sourced from all over the state of California and comes in at under $10; the second is sourced only from Sonoma County and costs considerably more (though it is under $20). The same is true for several other listings that look similar but are very different.

I have used varietal and regional headings within the broader categories of sparkling, white, rosé, and red. Under the varietal headings I have clustered the wines by geographic grouping. I have also included a heading called "Yours to Discover"; there's got to be some element of surprise and mystery!

I am confident that any wine listed by any one of us is worth trying. It may not knock your socks off, but it will at least be an honest, well-made wine, true to its type. If two of us list the same wine, that wine just might be the cat's meow. And if all three of us have selected the same wine, then you've got the full Monty!

So make your choice, get the glasses ready, and off to the store we go! Santé!

Brian Smith

Brian Smith's bargain bottles under $10

SPARKLING WINE
Cristalino Brut, Cava, Spain

WHITE WINE
Chardonnay
Lindemans Bin 65 Chardonnay, Southeastern Australia

Cave de Lugny Macon Lugny "Les Charmes," Burgundy, France

Chenin Blanc
Chateau Benoit Chenin Blanc, Willamette Valley, Oregon

Snoqualmie Chenin Blanc, Columbia Valley, Washington

Pinot Grigio
Lurton Pinot Grigio, Mendoza, Argentina

Vignabaldo Pinot Grigio, Umbria, Italy

Riesling
Leasingham Riesling, Clare Valley, Australia

Lindemans "Bin 75" Riesling, Southeastern Australia

Pauly Bergweiler "Noble House" Riesling, Mosel, Germany

Saint M Riesling, Pfalz, Germany

St. Urbans-Hof Riesling Qualitatswein, Mosel, Germany

S. A. Prum "Essence" Riesling Qualitatswein, Mosel, Germany

Jekel Riesling, Monterey, California

Chateau Benoit Riesling, Willamette Valley, Oregon

Covey Run Riesling, Columbia Valley, Washington

Hogue Riesling, Columbia Valley, Washington

Sauvignon Blanc
Veramonte Sauvignon Blanc, Casablanca Valley, Chile

Viu Manent Sauvignon Blanc, Colchagua Valley, Chile

Chateau Bonnet, Entre-Deux-Mers, Bordeaux, France

Brancott Sauvignon Blanc, Marlborough, New Zealand

Southern Right Sauvignon Blanc, Walker Bay, South Africa

Oracle Sauvignon Blanc, Western Cape, South Africa

Brampton Sauvignon Blanc, Western Cape, South Africa

Yours to Discover
Chateau de la Ragotiere Muscadet Sevre et Maine, Loire Valley, France

Chapelle de la Bastide Picpoul de Pinet, Coteaux du Languedoc, France

Domaine de la Haute Fevre Muscadet Sevre et Maine, Loire Valley, France

Alianca Vinho Verde, Portugal

Las Brisas, Rueda, Spain

ROSÉ WINE
Mas des Bressades, Costieres de Nimes, France

Cortijo III Rioja Rosé, Spain

Les Vignes Retrouvees Cotes de St-Mont,
France
Marques de Caceres Rioja Rosé, Spain
Marques de Caza, La Mancha, Spain

RED WINE
Barbera
Marchesi di Barolo Barbera Monferrato
Maraia, Piedmont, Italy

Cabernet Sauvignon
Hardys Cabernet Sauvignon, Southeastern
Australia
Columbia Crest "Two Vines" Cabernet
Sauvignon, Columbia Valley, Washington

Merlot
Red Diamond Merlot, Western Australia
Montes Merlot Reserva, Colchagua Valley, Chile
Errazuriz Merlot, Central Valley, Chile

Rhone Region and Rhone Influenced
Colombo "Les Abeilles" Cotes du Rhone,
France
J. Vidal Fleury Cotes du Rhone, France
Paul Jaboulet Aine "Paralelle 45" Cotes du
Rhone, France
Goats Do Roam, Western Cape, South Africa

Sangiovese
Rocca delle Macie Sangiovese di Toscana, Italy
Cecchi Chianti, Toscana, Italy
Gabbiano Chianti, Toscana, Italy
Villa Sopita, Sangiovese, Umbria, Italy
Vignabaldo Sangiovese, Umbria, Italy

Syrah/Shiraz
McWilliams Hanwood Estate Shiraz,
Southeastern Australia
Cline Syrah, California
Red Diamond Shiraz, Western Australia
Hardys Shiraz, Southeastern Australia

Tempranillo
Torres Coronas, Penedes, Spain
Riscal Tempranillo, Castilla y Leon, Spain

Zinfandel
Cline Zinfandel, California
Ravenswood Zinfandel, California

Yours to Discover
Frescobaldi Remole, Toscana, Italy
Terre Arnolfe, Colli Amerini, Italy
Las Rocos de San Alejandro Garnacha,
Calatayud, Spain

Brian Smith's bargain wines under $20

SPARKLING WINE
Lucien Albrecht Blanc de Blancs Cremant
d'Alsace, France
De Vallois Saumur Grande Cuvee, France
Rotari Brut, Trento, Italy
Rotari Brut Rosé, Trento, Italy
Nino Franco Rustico Prosecco, Italy
Segura Viudas Heredad Cava, Spain
Gloria Ferrer Brut, Sonoma County, California
Gruet Brut Rosé, New Mexico
Gruet Brut, New Mexico

WHITE WINE
Chardonnay
McGuigan Chardonnay, Hunter Valley,
Australia
Houghton Chardonnay, Western Australia
Latour Macon Lugny "Les Genievres,"
Burgundy, France
Thibert-Parisse Macon Prisse, Burgundy,
France
Domaine des Vercheres Macon Villages,
Burgundy, France
Domaine Thomas St-Veran, Burgundy, France
Graham Beck Chardonnay, Robertson, South
Africa
Chalone Chardonnay, Monterey County,
California
Acacia Chardonnay, California
Mount K Chardonnay, Santa Barbara,
California

La Crema Chardonnay, Sonoma Coast, California

La Crema Chardonnay, Russian River Valley, California

Domaine Chandon Chardonnay, Carneros, California

Hartford Chardonnay, Sonoma Coast, California

Hawk Crest Chardonnay, California

Argyle Chardonnay, Willamette Valley, Oregon

Chenin Blanc

Chateau Moncontour Vouvray, Loire Valley, France

Gewurztraminer

Adler Fels Gewurztraminer, Russian River Valley, California

Pinot Blanc

Trimbach Pinot Blanc, Alsace, France

Pinot Gris/Pinot Grigio

Schlumberger Pinot Gris "Les Princes Abbes," Alsace, France

Tiefenbrunner Pinot Grigio delle Venezie, Italy

Kris Pinot Grigio delle Venezie, Italy

Lungarotti Pinot Grigio, Umbria, Italy

Estancia Pinot Grigio, California

Firesteed Pinot Gris, Oregon

Riesling

Annie's Lane Riesling, Clare Valley, Australia

Schlumberger Riesling "Les Princes Abbes," Alsace, France

Dr. L Riesling Qualitatswein, Mosel, Germany

Monchhof Urziger Wurzgarten Riesling Qualitatswein, Mosel, Germany

Monchhof Estate Riesling Qualitatswein, Mosel, Germany

Sauvignon Blanc

Groom Sauvignon Blanc, Adelaide Hills, Australia

Philippe Portier, Quincy, Loire Valley, France

Domaine des Berthiers Pouilly-Fumé, Loire Valley, France

Domaine du Bouchot Pouilly-Fumé, Loire Valley, France

Domaine des Buissonnes Sancerre, Loire Valley, France

Kim Crawford Sauvignon Blanc, Marlborough, New Zealand

Villa Maria Sauvignon Blanc, Marlborough, New Zealand

Neil Ellis Sauvignon Blanc, Stellenbosch, South Africa

Joel Gott Sauvignon Blanc, California

Yours to Discover

La Yunta Torrontes, La Rioja, Argentina

Loan Semillon, Barossa Valley, Australia

Mas de Bressades Roussanne Viognier Vin de Pays du Gard, France

Hugel Gentil, Alsace, France

Chateau du Caillou, Graves, Bordeaux, France

Chateau Barthe, Graves, Bordeaux, France

Vina Godeval, Valdeorras, Spain

Martin Codax Albarino, Rias Baixas, Spain

Can Feixes, Penedes, Spain

RED WINE

Barbera

Michele Chiarlo Barbera d'Asti, Piemonte, Italy

La Ghersa Barbera d'Asti, Piemonte, Italy

Beaujolais Region

Chateau de la Chaize Brouilly, Beaujolais, France

Domaine Mont Chavy Morgon, Beaujolais, France

Bordeaux Region

Chateau Puygueraud, Cotes des Francs, Bordeaux, France

Chateau Larose Trintaudon, Haut Medoc, Bordeaux, France

Chateau Bel Air, Haut Medoc, Bordeaux, France

Cabernet Sauvignon

Catena Cabernet Sauvignon, Mendoza, Argentina

Wynn's Coonawarra Estate Cabernet Sauvignon, Coonawarra, Australia

Leasingham Cabernet Sauvignon, Clare Valley, Australia

Avalon Cabernet Sauvignon, Napa, California

Chateau Ste. Michelle Indian Wells Cabernet Sauvignon, Columbia Valley, Washington

Malbec

Altos Las Hormigas Malbec, Mendoza, Argentina

Norton Malbec Reserve, Mendoza, Argentina

Pinot Noir

Kim Crawford Pinot Noir, Marlborough, New Zealand

Chalone Pinot Noir, Monterey County, California

Ramsay Pinot Noir, North Coast, California

La Crema Pinot Noir, Sonoma Coast, California

Acacia Pinot Noir, California

Laurier Pinot Noir, Carneros, California

Rhone Region

Santa Duc Cotes du Rhone, France

Perrin Reserve Cotes du Rhone, France

Santa Duc Cairanne Cotes du Rhone Villages, France

Guigal Cotes du Rhone, France

Sangiovese

Monte Antico, Toscana, Italy

Conte Contini Capezzana Barco Reale di Carmignano, Toscana, Italy

Gabbiano Chianti Classico, Toscana, Italy

Ruffino Aziano Chianti Classico, Toscana, Italy

Coltibuono Cetamura Chianti, Toscana, Italy

Syrah/Shiraz

McGuigan Shiraz, Limestone Coast, Australia

Green Point Shiraz, Victoria, Australia

Lengs & Cooter Shiraz, South Australia

3 Rings Shiraz, Barossa Valley, Australia

Norman's Old Vine Shiraz, South Australia

Piping Shrike Shiraz, Barossa Valley, Australia

Tintara Shiraz, McLaren Vale, Australia

Graham Beck Shiraz, Coastal Region, South Africa

Cline Syrah, Sonoma County, California

Tempranillo

Herencia Remondo La Montesa Rioja, Spain

Montecillo Crianza Rioja, Spain

Marques de Riscal Reserva Rioja, Spain

Conde de Valdemar Crianza Rioja, Spain

Conde de Valdemar Reserva Rioja, Spain

Zinfandel

Dry Creek Heritage Zinfandel, Sonoma County, California

Gnarly Head Zinfandel, Lodi, California

Ravenswood Zinfandel, Lodi, California

Yours to Discover

d'Arenberg Stump Jump GSM, South Australia

Marc Bredif Chinon, Loire Valley, France

Domaine des Pensees Sauvages Corbieres, France

Masi Campofiorin Ripasso, Veneto, Italy

Argiolas Costera, Sardinia, Italy

Altos de la Hoya Monastrell, Jumilla, Spain

SWEET WINE/FORTIFIED WINE

Lustau Papirusa Manzanilla, Jerez, Spain

Cockburns Late Bottled Vintage Port, Portugal

San Felice Vin Santo di Chianti Classico, Toscana, Italy

Brian Smith's bargain wines under $30

WHITE WINE
Chenin Blanc

Rusden Christian Chenin Blanc, Barossa Valley, Australia

Chardonnay

Simi Chardonnay Reserve, Russian River Valley, California

Chalone Chardonnay, Chalone, California

Acacia Chardonnay, Carneros, California

Sauvignon Blanc

Domaine Thomas Sancerre La Crele, Loire Valley, France

RED WINE
Bordeaux Region

Clos Floridene, Graves, Bordeaux, France

Chateau Clarke, Listrac, Bordeaux, France

Chateau Greysac, Medoc, France

Chateau Potensac, Medoc, France

Pinot Noir

Acacia Pinot Noir, Carneros, California

Chalone Pinot Noir, Chalone, California

Wild Horse Pinot Noir, Central Coast, California

Rex Hill Pinot Noir, Oregon

Willakenzie Estate Pinot Noir, Oregon

Rhone Region

J.-L. Chave St-Joseph, Rhone, France

Rochecourbe St-Joseph, Rhone, France

Sangiovese

Gabbiano Chianti Classico Riserva, Toscana, Italy

Yours to Discover

Le Volte, Toscana, Italy

SWEET WINE/FORTIFIED WINE

Dow's Ten-Year-Old Tawny Port, Portugal

Michael's bargains and great values

I LIVE IN THE HUDSON VALLEY, and I feel fortunate to have access to fabulous wines from around the world. Some of my best-value wines can easily be found throughout the United States, while others are off the beaten path but worth the effort to track down. As in the previous chapters of this book, wines referred to as inexpensive are under $15, and moderately priced wines are under $30. (Retail prices of the wines listed below may vary by a couple of dollars depending on where they are purchased).

My wife, Jenny, and I drink wine almost every night, and a lot of it costs under $12 a bottle. When we splurge on something sumptuous, we want either some oomph, pizzazz, and razzmatazz, or silky-smooth elegance for that $30-plus a bottle.

Of course, not all moderately to expensively priced wines are worth the money, nor are all $12 wines great values. If my $25 wine can compete with a wine costing $75, I consider that to be a great value wine. Here is an example. One of my favorite reds is Brunello di Montalcino from Tuscany, Italy. Today, prices for this wine start at $50 and escalate to $150 for some single-vineyard and riserva versions. On the other hand, Rosso di Montalcino (also known as "baby Brunello") is made from the same grapes and hails from the same region as its big brother, yet only costs about $23. What's the catch? Rosso di Montalcino is bottled younger and may be sourced from younger vines. In this case, young is good for the value seeker, especially if you plan to drink the wine in the near future as opposed to cellaring it.

Because I want to encourage you to peruse the entire list of wine choices, I've organized my list of wines by country, with the American wines first and the French last. Remember that whenever you take a chance on lesser-known grape varieties or off-the-beaten-path regions, you will get more bang for your buck than if you had played it safe. Another point I want to stress is that many of the wines I suggest are from family-owned wineries that have a sense of integrity not always found in corporations. The best wineries, family-owned or corporate, will put their name only on the bottles they are proud of and will sell you the best wine they can make at a fair price.

All of these wines really come alive when paired with food, and I hope you will experiment with some of the suggestions we offer in *WineWise* as well as come up with your own combinations. To get the best value—and most enjoyment—out of these wines, please drink them in good health and in good company.

Cheers!

Michael Weiss

Sparkling wines: Dry and semidry under $15

Domaine Ste. Michelle, Blanc de Blancs, Washington State

Luis Pato, Baga, Beiras, Portugal

Juve Y Camps, Brut and Rosé, Cava, Penedes, Spain

Pares Balta, Brut, Cava, Penedes, Spain

Cristalino, Brut and Rosé, Cava, Penedes, Spain

Zardetto, Prosecco, Veneto, Italy

Monmousseau, Vouvray Mousseux, Loire, France

Willm, Cremant d'Alsace, Alsace, France

Sparkling wines: Dry and semidry under $30

Iron Horse, Brut, "Wedding Cuvee," and "Russian Cuvee," California

Handley, Rosé, California

Roederer Estate, Brut, California

Domaine Carneros, Brut, California

Hagafen, Brut, California

Chateau Frank, Blanc de Blancs (dry) and "Celebre" (semidry), New York State

Gruet, Brut and Blanc de Noirs, New Mexico

Argyle, Brut, Oregon

Cave Spring, Brut, Ontario, Canada

Yarden, Brut and Blanc de Blancs, Israel

Tselopos, "Amalia," Peloponnese, Greece

Spiropolous, "Ode Panos," Peloponnese, Greece

Banfi, Brut, Piedmont, Italy

White wines: Semidry, fruity, and floral under $15

Dr. Konstantin Frank, Riesling, "dry " and semidry," New York State

Hogue, Riesling, Washington State

Cave Spring, Riesling, "Estate," Ontario, Canada

Inniskillin, Riesling, Ontario, Canada

Handley, Gewurztraminer, California

Lenz, Gewurztraminer, New York State

Columbia Crest, Gewurztraminer, Washington State

Jacob's Creek, Riesling, South Australia

Trapiche, Torrontes, "Astica," Mendoza, Argentina

Torres, "Vina Esmeralda," Penedes, Spain

Boutari, Moschofilero, Mantinia, Greece

Trimbach, Muscat, Alsace, France

White wines: Semidry, fruity, and floral under $30

Smith Madrone, Riesling, California

Navarro, Gewurztraminer, California

Chateau Ste. Michelle/Dr. Loosen, Riesling, "Eroica," Washington State

Hillebrand, Riesling, "Trius dry," Ontario, Canada

Petaluma, Riesling, Clare Valley, Australia

Dr. Loosen, Riesling, Erdener Treppfchen, Kabinett, Mosel, Germany

J. J. Prum, Riesling, Wehlener Sonnenuhr, Kabinett, Mosel, Germany

Lucien Albrecht, Riesling, Alsace, France

Josmeyer, Gewurztraminer, Alsace, France

White wines: Dry under $15

Lolonis, Fumé Blanc and "Ladybug," California

Barefoot, Sauvignon Blanc, California

Gustavo-Thrace, "Third Bottle," California

Benziger, Fumé Blanc and Chardonnay, California

Millbrook, Chardonnay, New York State

Red Rooster, Pinot Gris, British Columbia, Canada

Dona Paula, Sauvignon Blanc, "Los Cardos," Mendoza, Argentina

Giesen, Sauvignon Blanc, Marlborough, New Zealand

Esporao, "Monte Velho," Alentejo, Portugal

Adega de Moncao, Muralhos de Moncao, Vinho Verde, Minho, Portugal

Quinta da Aveleda, Vinho Verde and Alvarinho, Minho, Portugal

Quinta do Ameal, Vinho Verde, Minho, Portugal

Muros Antigos, Alvarinho, Minho, Portugal

Quinta da Romeira, Bucelas, Portugal

Campante," Reboreda," Ribeiro, Spain

Naia, "Aldial," Rueda, Spain

Can Feixes, Penedes, Spain

Pares Balta, "Blanc de Pacs," Penedes, Spain

Mercouri, "Foloi," Peloponnese, Greece

Emery, Athiri, Rhodes, Greece

Bava, Chardonnay, "Thou," Piedmont, Italy

Vietti, Arneis, Piedmont, Italy

Feudi di San Gregorio, Falanghina, Campania, Italy

Pieropan, Soave Classico, Veneto, Italy

Jean-Luc Colombo, Cotes du Rhone, "Figuieres," Rhone, France

Hugel, Pinot Blanc, "Cuvee Les Amours," Alsace, France

Marquis de Goulaine, Muscadet Sevre et Maine, Loire, France

Chateau Bonnet, Bordeaux, France

White wines: Dry under $30

Cakebread, Sauvignon Blanc, California

Rochioli, Sauvignon Blanc, California

Clos Pegase, Sauvignon Blanc, California

Iron Horse, Chardonnay, "Unoaked Estate" and "Estate," California

Logan, Chardonnay, California

Qupe, Marsanne, California

Malivoire, Chardonnay, "Estate," Ontario, Canada

Cave Spring, Chardonnay, "CSV," Ontario, Canada

Mitchelton, Marsanne, Victoria, Australia

Kumeu River, Sauvignon Blanc, Auckland, New Zealand

Mulderbosch, Sauvignon Blanc, Stellenbosch, South Africa

"Tiara," Niepoort, Douro, Portugal

Morgadio, Albarino, Galicia, Spain

Itsas Mendi, Txacoli, Basque, Spain

Antinori, Vermentino, Tuscany, Italy

Gentilini, Robola, Cephalonia, Greece

Sigalas, Santorini, Greece

Nicolas Joly, Savennieres, Loire, France

Olivier Leflaive, Rully Premier Cru, Burgundy, France

Pascal Jolivet, Sancerre, Loire, France

Rosé wines: Dry under $15

Iron Horse, Pinot Noir, California

Bonny Doon, "Vin Gris de Cigare," California

Quinta de Covela, Portugal

Gonzalez Lara "Fuente del Conde," Cigales, Spain

Marques de Caceres, Rioja, Spain

Muga, Rioja, Spain

Julian Chivite, "Gran Feudo," Navarra, Spain

Kir Yanni, "Akakies," Amyndeon, Greece

Jean-Luc Colombo, "Cote Bleue," Provence, France

Mas de la Dame, "Cuvee Gourmande," Provence, France

Red wines: Dry under $15

Benziger, Syrah, and Cabernet Sauvignon, California

Calera, Pinot Noir, California

Kenwood, Pinot Noir, California

Lolonis, "Ladybug" Red, California

Bedell, Merlot, New York

Alexander Valley Vineyards, Cabernet Sauvignon, California

Trentadue, "Old Patch Red," California

Jackson Triggs, Cabernet Sauvignon, British Columbia, Canada

Hundred Acres, Shiraz, "Layer Cake," Barossa, Australia

Kinakinoon, Shiraz, "The Lackey," South Australia

St. Hallet, Grenache, South Australia

Sincerity, Cabernet Sauvignon/Merlot, Colchagua, Chile

Concha y Toro, Malbec, "Xplorador," Mendoza, Argentina

Symington, "Altano," Douro, Portugal

Alianca, "Particular," Dao, Portugal

Quinta de Saes, Dao, Portugal

Jose Maria de Fonseca, "Periquita," Terras do Sado, Portugal

Joao Portugal Ramos, Trincadeira, Alentejo, Portugal

Esporao, Reserva and "Monte Velho," Alentejo, Portugal

Campo de Borja, "Borsao," and "Tres Picos," Campo de Borja, Spain

Agatipo Rico, "Carchelo," Jumilla, Spain

Rejadorada,Toro, Spain

Conde de Valdemar, Crianza, Rioja, Spain

Torres, "Coronas," Penedes, Spain

Dominio Tares, "Baltos," Bierzo, Spain

Luna Beribede, Mencia, Bierzo, Spain

San Alejandro, Garnacha, "Los Rocas," Calatayud, Spain

Castano, Monastrell, Yecla, Spain

Tsepelos, Agiorgitiko, Nemea, Greece

Gerovassiliou, Syrah, Epanomi, Greece

Cabernet Sauvignon, Recanati, Israel

Bava, "Libera," Barbera d'Asti, Piedmont, Italy

Renato Ratti, Nebbiolo, "Ochetti," Piedmont, Italy

Banfi, "Centine" and "Col di Sasso," Tuscany, Italy

Argiolas, "Costera," Sardinia, Italy

Walden, Cotes du Roussillon, France

Chateau Revelette, Aix-en-Provence, France

Joguet, Chinon, "Les Petites Roches," Loire, France

Chateau La Cote de Mons, Premiere Cotes de Bordeaux, France

Red wines: Dry under $30

Ridge, Zinfandel, California

Gustavo-Thrace, Zinfandel, California

Jade Mountain, "La Provencala," California

Lolonis, Petite Sirah, "Orpheus," and Cabernet Sauvignon, California

Preston, Syrah-Sirah and Zinfandel, California

Justin, Syrah, California

Foppiano, Petite Sirah, California

Pindar, "Mythology," New York State

Sumac Ridge, Cabernet Sauvignon, "Black Sage Vineyard," British Columbia, Canada

Pirramimma, Grenache, Mc Laren Vale, Australia

D'Arenberg, Grenache, "The Custodian," McLaren Vale, Australia

Susana Balbo, Malbec, Mendoza, Argentina

Chateau Musar, Lebanon

Luis Pato, Vinhas Velhas and Baga-Touriga Nacional, Beiras, Portugal

Quinta do Crasto, Reserva, Douro, Portugal

Adriano Ramos Pinto, Duas Quintas Reserva, Douro, Portugal

Alves de Sousa, Quinta do Vale da Raposa, Grande Escolha, Douro, Portugal

Quinta dos Roques, Reserva, Dao, Portugal

Quinta da Bageiras, Garrafeira, Bairrada, Portugal

Campolargo, 'Termao," Bairrada, Portugal

Casa Santos Lima, "Touriz," Estremadura, Portugal

La Rioja Alta, "Vina Alberdi" Reserva, Rioja, Spain

Alejandro Fernandez, "Dehesa La Granja" and "Pesquera," Spain

Alvaro Palacios, "Petalos," Bierzo, Spain

Papantonis, "Meden Agan," Peloponnese, Greece

Tsantali, Rapsani, Reserve, Thessaly, Greece

Produttori Barbaresco, Nebbiolo del Langhe, Piedmont, Italy

Elio Grasso, Barbera d'Alba, Piedmont, Italy

San Luigi, "Aprelis," Tuscany, Italy

Badia a Coltibuono, Chianti Classico Riserva, Tuscany, Italy

Banfi, Rosso di Montalcino, Tuscany, Italy

Biondi-Santi, Rosso di Montalcino, Tuscany, Italy

Capezzana, Carmignano, Reserva, Tuscany,
    Italy
D'Angelo, Aglianico del Vulture, Basilicata, Italy
Domaine Combier, Crozes-Hermitage, Rhone,
    France
Louis Cheze, St. Joseph, Rhone, France
Jean-Luc Colombo, Cotes du Rhone, Rhone,
    and "Cote Bleue," Provence, France
Louis Jadot, Moulin-a-Vent, "Chateau St-
    Jacques," Burgundy, France
Faiveley, Mercurey, "Clos des Myglands,"
    Burgundy, France
Les Clos de Paulilles, Collioure, Roussillon,
    France

Fortified wines: Dry under $15

Gonzalez Byass, Fino, "Tio Pepe," Sherry, Spain
Hidalgo, Manzanilla, "La Gitana," Sherry, Spain
Lustau, Fino " Jarana" and Amontillado, "Los
    Arcos," Sherry, Spain

Fortified wines: Dry under $30

Leacocks, Ten-Year Sercial, Madeira, Portgual
Justino, Five-Year Sercial, Madeira, Portugal
Sandeman, Amontillado, "Royal Esmeralda,"
    Sherry, Spain
Williams and Humbert, Fifteen-Year Oloroso,
    "Dry Sack," Sherry, Spain

Fortified wines: Sweet under $15

J. M. Fonseca, Moscatel de Setubal, "Alambre,"
    Portugal
K.E.O. Commandaria, "St. John," Cyprus

Fortified wines: Sweet under $30

Fonseca, "Bin 27," Porto, Portugal
Graham's, "Six Grapes," Porto, Portugal
Quinta do Crasto, Late-Bottled Vintage Porto,
    Portugal
Adriano Ramos Pinto Late-Bottled Vintage
    Porto and Ten-Year Tawny Porto, Portugal
Taylor Fladgate, Ten-Year Tawny Porto,
    Portugal
Dow's, Ten-Year Tawny Porto, Portugal
Cossart-Gordon, Five-Year Bual, Madeira,
    Portugal
Leacock, Five-Year Malmsey, Madeira, Portugal
Lustau, Pedro Ximenez, "San Emilio," Sherry,
    Spain

Index

for summer, 312
values in, 330
Spatburgunder (grape), 49
Spatlese, 253, 258
Spicy foods, pairing wine with, 256, 290–291
Spinach, pairing wine with, 291–292
Spitting, 307
Spring Mountain District AVA (California), 78–79
Squid ink, pairing wine with, 293
Stags Leap District AVA (California), 75–77
Stainless-steel tanks, fermentation in, 7, 9
Stanton & Killeen, 127
Starches, pairing wine with, 287
Steadman, Ralph, 113
Steiermark region (Austria), 31, 263
Steinfeder, 262
Stellenbosch region (South Africa), 43, 136
Sterea Ellada (Greece), 275
Stewart, Potter, 47
"Stickies," 126, 127
Still wines, 2
Styles, wine, 2
Sugar(s):
    and alcohol level, 2
    in sweet wines, 8–9
    and taste, 16–17
"Summertime" (Gershwin), 312
Summer wines, 170, 311–316
"Sunny Afternoon" (the Kinks), 311
Superior (Portugal), 236
Superiore (Italy), 203, 204, 206
Super Tuscans (Italy), 39, 40, 45, 186, 189, 194–195
Supply and demand, 10
Sur lie, 8
Swedish dishes, pairing wine with, 298
Sweet foods, pairing wine with, 290
Sweetness, 16–17
Sweet wines, 2, 8–9, 331, 338–339, 341, 346, 350
Switzerland, 41, 45, 52
Syrah/Shiraz (grape), 13, 50–53
    aromas, 15
    Australian wines, 53, 120, 122–124, 126–128
    Austrian wines, 263
    bargains, 343, 345
    British Columbia wines, 270
    and Cabernet Sauvignon, 42
    California wines, 52–53
    Chilean wines, 113
    French wines, 51
    Greek wines, 275
    Italian wines, 52
    Long Island wines, 107
    New Zealand wines, 130
    pairing, with food, 282, 289, 290, 292, 294, 296–300, 302
    Rhone Valley, 175–176
    Rhone Valley wines, 122
    South African wines, 133, 136
    Swiss wines, 52
    Washington State wines, 53, 95, 98–99
Syrian dishes, pairing wine with, 299

T

Table wines, sweet, 301–302
Tamarind, pairing wine with, 292
Tannin, 8, 16
Tasmania (Australia), 128
Tasting wine, 14–17, 306–310
Taurasi DOCG (Italy), 208
Tawny Porto (Portugal), 242–244
Te Mata, 131
Temperature, wine, 294–295, 332
Tempranillo (grape), 234
    bargains, 343, 345
    in Cabernet blends, 39, 41
    Spanish wines, 215, 218, 225
Teroldego Rotaliano DOC (Italy), 206–207
Terras do Sado VR (Portugal), 235, 236, 245
Terroir (*terroir* wines), 6, 11, 63
Texas, 35
Texture, 17
Thai food, pairing wine with, 295
Thessaly (Greece), 275
Ticino region (Switzerland), 45
Tinta de Toro (grape), 224
Tinta Negra Mole (grape), 246
Tinta Roriz (grape), 234, 240
Tinto del Pais (grape), 224
Tinto Fino (grape), 224
Tocai Friulano (grape), 184, 207
Tongue, 16
Torgiano Rosso Riserva DOCG (Italy), 195
Toro DO (Spain), 224
Torres family, 221
Torrontes (grape), 117
Touraine, France, 172
Touriga Nacional (grape), 234, 240, 244
Tourism, 62
Tower of Power, 283–285
Trader Joe's, 306
Trajadura (grape), 235
Tramin, (Italy), 31
Trebbiano (grape), 184
Treixadura (grape), 227
Trentino-Alto Adige region (Italy), 206–207
Trentino DOC (Italy), 206–207
Trento DOC (Italy), 206–207
Trincadeira (grape), 235
Trocken, 252, 253, 261
Trockenbeerenauslese, 253
Tsantali, 275
Tuscany (Italy), 189, 191–195, 192*m*
    best wine producers, 192–193
    Brunello di Montalcino, 191–192
    Cabernet Sauvignon, 39, 40
    Carmignano, 191
    Chianti, 189
    Merlot, 45
    Morellino di Scansano, 192
    Super Tuscans, 194–195
    Vernaccia di San Gimignano, 192
    Vino Nobile di Montepulciano, 189, 191
    winter warmers from, 317
Tygerberg region (South Africa), 136–137

U

Umbria (Italy), 193, 195
Umpqua Valley AVA (Oregon), 103
Unfiltered (label term), 66
United States. *See also specific states and regions, e.g.:* California
    Cabernet Sauvignon grape in, 41–42
    Chardonnay grape in, 22–23
    Gewurztraminer grape in, 31–32
    labels, 63–67
    Merlot grape in, 45–46
    Pinot Grigio grape in, 33–34
    Pinot Noir grape in, 49
    Riesling grape in, 28–29
    Sauvignon Blanc grape in, 24–25
    Syrah/Shiraz grape in, 50
    value wines from, 330–331
    Viognier grape in, 35
    wine culture in, 60–63
    Zinfandel grape in, 53–56
University of California at Davis, 56

V

Valais region (Switzerland), 52
Valdadige DOC (Italy), 206
Valdeorras DO (Spain), 227
Valle Central (Chile), 112
Valpolicella Classico DOC (Italy), 206
Valpolicella DOC (Italy), 204, 206
Valtellina Superiore DOCG (Italy), 203
Value wines, finding, 328–331
Vanillin, 8
Varietal labels, 64
Veal, pairing wine with, 286
Vega-Sicilia, 225
Vegetables, pairing wine with, 287–288
Vendange tardive, 28, 31, 148
Veneto region (Italy), 41, 204, 206
Verdejo (grape), 216, 225
Verdelho (grape), 126, 128
Verdelho Madeira (Portugal), 246
Verdicchio (grape), 184, 196
Verdicchio dei Castelli di Jesi DOC (Italy), 196
Verdicchio di Matelica DOC (Italy), 196
Vermentino (grape), 184
Vermentino di Gallura DOCG (Italy), 210
Vernaccia (grape), 184
Vernaccia di San Gimignano DOCG (Italy), 192, 193
Vertical pairings, 289–290
Very old reserve Sherry/VORS (Spain), 230–231
Very old Sherry/VOS (Spain), 230–231
Victoria (Australia), 50, 126–128
Vidal (grape), 104, 269
Vietnamese food, pairing wine with, 295
Vilana (grape), 273
Village AOCs:
    Burgundy, 160, 164
    Cote de Beaune, 166
    German wines, 251
    Rhone Valley, 174–177
Vinas del Montsant, 223
Vin de Pays d'Oc (France), 40, 51
Vines, density of, 5–6
Vineyards, 5–6